Caliban and the Witch

Caliban
and the
Witch

Silvia
Federici

Autonomedia

Acknowledgements

To the many witches I have met in the Women's Movement, and to the other witches whose stories have accompanied me for more than twenty-five years, nevertheless leaving an inexhaustible desire to tell, to let people know, to make sure that they will not be forgotten.

To our brother Jonathan Cohen whose love, courage and uncompromising resistance to injustice have helped me not lose faith in the possibility of changing the world and in men's ability to make the struggle for women's liberation their own.

To the people who have helped me to produce this volume. I thank George Caffentzis with whom I have discussed every aspect of this book; Mitchel Cohen for his excellent comments, his editing of parts of the manuscript, and his enthusiastic support for this project; Ousseina Alidou and Maria Sari for introducing me to the work of Maryse Condé; Ferruccio Gambino for making me aware of the existence of slavery in 16th- and 17th-century Italy; David Goldstein for the materials he has given me on the witches' "pharmakopeia"; Conrad Herold, for contributing to my research on witch hunting in Peru; Massimo de Angelis, for giving me his writings on primitive accumulation and for the important debate on this topic which he organized in *The Commoner;* Willy Mutunga for the materials he has given me on the legal aspects of witchcraft in East Africa. I thank Michaela Brennan and Veena Viswanatha for reading the manuscript and giving me advice and support. I also thank Mariarosa Dalla Costa, Nicholas Faraclas, Leopolda Fortunati, Everet Green, Peter Linebaugh, Bene Madunagu, Maria Mies, Ariel Salleh, Hakim Bey. Their works have been a reference point for the perspective that shapes *Caliban and the Witch,* though they may not agree with all that I have written here.

Special thanks to Jim Fleming, Sue Ann Harkey, Ben Meyers and Erika Biddle, who have given many hours of their time to this book and, with their patience and assistance, have given me the possibility of finishing it, despite my endless procrastination. — New York, April 2004

Autonomedia
POB 568 Williamsburgh Station, Brooklyn, NY 11211-0568 USA
www.autonomedia.org   info@autonomedia.org

Designed by Sue Ann Harkey

First edition, 2004. Second, revised edition, 2014.
ISBN 1-57027-059-7

Printed in the United States of America

Table of Contents

Woodcut of witches conjuring a shower of rain. In Ulrich Molitor, DE LAMIIES ET PYTHONICIS MULIERIBUS (On Female Sorcerers and Soothsayers) (1489).

Preface

Caliban and the Witch presents the main themes of a research project on women in the "transition" from feudalism to capitalism that I began in the mid-1970s, in collaboration with an Italian feminist, Leopoldina Fortunati. Its first results appeared in a book that we published in Italy in 1984: *Il Grande Calibano. Storial del corpo social ribelle nella prima fase del capitale* (Milano: Franco Angeli) [*The Great Caliban. History of the Rebel Body in the First Phase of Capitalism*].

My interest in this research was originally motivated by the debates that accompanied the development of the Feminist Movement in the United States concerning the roots of women's "oppression," and the political strategies which the movement should adopt in the struggle for women's liberation. At the time, the leading theoretical and political perspectives from which the reality of sexual discrimination was analyzed were those proposed by the two main branches of the women's movement: the Radical Feminists and the Socialist Feminists. In my view, however, neither provided a satisfactory explanation of the roots of the social and economic exploitation of women. I objected to the Radical Feminists because of their tendency to account for sexual discrimination and patriarchal rule on the basis of transhistorical cultural structures, presumably operating independently of relations of production and class. Socialist Feminists, by contrast, recognized that the history of women cannot be separated from the history of specific systems of exploitation and, in their analyses, gave priority to women as workers in capitalist society. But the limit of their position, in my understanding of it at the time, was that it failed to acknowledge the sphere of reproduction as a source of value-creation and exploitation, and thus traced the roots of the power differential between women and men to women's exclusion from capitalist development — a stand which again compelled us to rely on cultural schemes to account for the survival of sexism within the universe of capitalist relations.

It was in this context that the idea of tracing the history of women in the transition from feudalism to capitalism took form. The thesis which inspired this research was first articulated by Mariarosa Dalla Costa and Selma James, as well as other activists in the Wages For Housework Movement, in a set of documents that in the 1970s were very controversial, but eventually reshaped the discourse on women, reproduction, and capitalism. The most influential among them were Mariarosa Dalla Costa's *Women and the Subversion of the Community* (1971), and Selma James' *Sex, Race and Class* (1975).

Against the Marxist orthodoxy, which explained women's "oppression" and subordination to men as a residuum of feudal relations, Dalla Costa and James argued that the exploitation of women has played a central function in the process of capitalist accumulation, insofar as women have been the producers and reproducers of the most essential capitalist commodity: labor-power. As Dalla Costa put it, women's unpaid labor in the home has been the pillar upon which the exploitation of the waged workers, "wage slavery," has been built, and the secret of its productivity (1972:31). Thus, the power differential between women and men in capitalist societry cannot be attributed to the irrelevance of housework for capitalist accumulation — an irrelevance belied by the strict rules that have governed women's lives — nor to the survival of timeless cultural schemes. Rather, it should be interpreted as the effect of a social system of production that does not recognize the production and reproduction of the worker as a social-economic activity, and a source of capital accumulation, but mystifies it instead as a natural resource or a personal service, while profiting from the wageless condition of the labor involved.

By rooting the exploitation of women in capitalist society in the sexual division of labor and women's unpaid work, Dalla Costa and James showed the possibility of transcending the dichotomy between patriarchy and class, and gave patriarchy a specific historical content. They also opened the way for a reinterpretation of the history of capitalism and class struggle from a feminist viewpoint.

It was in this spirit that Leopoldina Fortunati and I began to study what can only be euphemistically described as the "transition to capitalism," and began to search for a history that we had not been taught in school, but proved to be decisive for our education. This history not only offered a theoretical understanding of the genesis of housework in its main structural components: the separation of production from reproduction, the specifically capitalist use of the wage to command the labor of the unwaged, and the devaluation of women's social position with the advent of capitalism. It also provided a genealogy of the modern concepts of femininity and masculinity that challenged the postmodern assumption of an almost ontological predisposition in "Western Culture" to capture gender through binary oppositions. Sexual hierarchies, we found, are always at the service of a project of domination that can sustain itself only by dividing, on a continuously renewed basis, those it intends to rule.

The book that resulted from this research, *Il Grande Calibano: storia del corpo sociale ribelle nella prima fase del capitale* (1984), was an attempt to rethink Marx's analysis of primitive accumulation from a feminist viewpoint. But in this process, the received Marxian categories proved inadequate. Among the casualties was the Marxian identification of capitalism with the advent of wage labor and the "free" laborer, which contributes to hide and naturalize the sphere of reproduction. *Il Grande Calibano* was also critical of Michel Foucault's theory of the body; as we argued, Foucault's analysis of the power techniques and disciplines to which the body has been subjected has ignored the process of reproduction, has collapsed female and male histories into an undifferentiated whole, and has been so disinterested in the "disciplining" of women that it never mentions one of the most monstruous attacks on the body perpetrated in the modern era: the witch-hunt.

The main thesis in *Il Grande Calibano* was that in order to understand the history of women in the transition from feudalism to capitalism, we must analyze the changes that capitalism has introduced in the process of social reproduction and, especially, the reproduction of labor-power. Thus, the book examined the reorganization of housework, family life, child-raising, sexuality, male-female relations, and the relation between production and reproduction in 16th and 17th-century Europe. This analysis is reproduced in *Caliban and the Witch*; however, the scope of the present volume differs from that of *Il Grande Calibano,* as it responds to a different social context and to our growing knowledge of women's history.

Shortly after the publication of *Il Grande Calibano,* I left the United States and took a teaching position in Nigeria, where I remained for nearly three years. Before leaving, I had buried my papers in a cellar, not expecting that I should need them for some time. But the circumstances of my stay in Nigeria did not allow me to forget this work. The years between 1984 and 1986 were a turning point for Nigeria, as for most African countries. These were the years when, in response to the debt crisis, the Nigerian government engaged in negotiations with the International Monetary Fund and the World Bank, which eventually resulted in the adoption of a Structural Adjustment Program, the World Bank's universal recipe for economic recovery across the planet.

The declared purpose of the program was to make Nigeria competitive on the international market. But it was soon apparent that this involved a new round of primitive accumulation, and a rationalization of social reproduction aimed at destroying the last vestiges of communal property and community relations, and thereby impose more intense forms of labor exploitation. Thus, I saw unfolding under my eyes processes very similar to those that I had studied in preparation for *Il Grande Calibano*. Among them were the attack on communal lands, and a decisive intervention by the State (instigated by World Bank) in the reproduction of the work-force: to regulate procreation rates, and, in this case, reduce the size of a population that was deemed too demanding and indisciplined from the viewpoint of its prospected insertion in the global economy. Along with these policies, aptly named the "War Against Indiscipline," I also witnessed the fueling of a misogynous campaign denouncing women's vanity and excessive demands, and the development of a heated debate similar, in many respects, to the 17th century *querelles des femmes,* touching on every aspect of the reproduction of labor-power: the family (polygamous vs. monogamous, nuclear vs. extended), child-raising, women's work, male and female identity and relations.

In this context, my work on the transition took on a new meaning. In Nigeria I realized that the struggle against structural adjustment is part of a long struggle against land privatization and the "enclosure" not only of communal lands but also of social relations that stretches back to the origin of capitalism in 16th-century Europe and America. I also realized how limited is the victory that the capitalist work-discipline has won on this planet, and how many people still see their lives in ways radically antagonistic to the requirements of capitalist production. For the developers, the multinational agencies and foreign investors, this was and remains the problem with places like Nigeria. But for me it was a source of great strength, as it proved that, worldwide, formidable forces still contrast the imposition of a way of life conceived only in capitalist terms. The strength I gained was also due to my encounter with Women in Nigeria (WIN), the country's first feminist organization, which enabled me to better understand the struggles that Nigerian women have been making to defend their resources and to refuse the new model of patriarchy imposed on them, now promoted by the World Bank.

By the end of 1986, the debt crisis reached the academic institutions and, no longer able to support myself, I left Nigeria, in body if not in spirit. But the thought of the attacks launched on the Nigerian people never left me. Thus, the desire to restudy "the transition to capitalism" has been with me since my return. I had read the Nigerian events through the prism of 16th-century Europe. In the United States, it was the Nigerian proletariat that brought me back to the struggles over the commons and the capitalist disciplining of women, in and out of Europe. Upon my return, I also began to teach in an interdisciplinary program for undergraduates where I confronted a different type of "enclosure": the enclosure of knowledge, that is, the increasing loss, among the new generations, of the historical sense of our common past. This is why in *Caliban and the Witch* I reconstruct the anti-feudal struggles of the Middle Ages and the struggles by which the European proletariat resisted the advent of capitalism. My goal in doing so is not only to make available to non-specialists the evidence on which my analysis relies, but to revive among younger generations the memory of a long history of resistance that today is in danger of being erased. Saving this historical memory is crucial if we are to find an alternative to capitalism. For this possibility will depend on our capacity to hear the voices of those who have walked similar paths.

Introduction

Since Marx, studying the genesis of capitalism has been an obligatory step for activists and scholars convinced that the first task on humanity's agenda is the construction of an alternative to capitalist society. Not surprisingly, every new revolutionary movement has returned to the "transition to capitalism," bringing to it the perspectives of new social subjects and uncovering new grounds of exploitation and resistance.[1] This volume is conceived within this tradition, but two considerations in particular have motivated this work.

First, there has been the desire to rethink the development of capitalism from a feminist viewpoint, while, at the same time, avoiding the limits of a "women's history" separated from that of the male part of the working class. The title, *Caliban and the Witch,* inspired by Shakespeare's *The Tempest,* reflects this effort. In my interpretation, however, Caliban represents not only the anti-colonial rebel whose struggle still resonates in contemporary Caribbean literature, but is a symbol for the world proletariat and, more specifically, for the proletarian body as a terrain and instrument of resistance to the logic of capitalism. Most important, the figure of the witch, who in *The Tempest* is confined to a remote background, in this volume is placed at the center-stage, as the embodiment of a world of female subjects that capitalism had to destroy: the heretic, the healer, the disobedient wife, the woman who dared to live alone, the obeha woman who poisoned the master's food and inspired the slaves to revolt.

The second motivation behind this volume has been the worldwide return, with the new global expansion of capitalist relations, of a set of phenomena usually associated with the genesis of capitalism. Among them are a new round of "enclosures" that have expropriated millions of agricultural producers from their land, and the mass pauperization and criminalization of workers, through a policy of mass incarceration recalling the "Great Confinement" described by Michel Foucault in his study of history of madness. We have also witnessed the worldwide development of new diasporic movements accompanied by the persecution of migrant workers, again reminiscent of the "Bloody Laws" that were introduced in 16th and 17th-century Europe to make "vagabonds" available for local exploitation. Most important for this book has been the intensification of violence against women, including, in some countries (e.g., South Africa and Brazil), the return of witch-hunting.

Why, after 500 years of capital's rule, at the beginning of the third millennium, are workers on a mass scale still defined as paupers, witches, and outlaws? How are land expropriation and mass pauperization related to the continuing attack on women? And what do we learn about capitalist development, past and present, once we examine it through the vantage-point of a feminist perspective?

It is with these questions in mind that in this work I have revisited the "transition" from feudalism to capitalism from the viewpoint of women, the body, and primitive accumulation. Each of these concepts refers to a conceptual framework that is a reference point for this work: the Feminist, the Marxist, and the Foucauldian. Thus, I will begin my introduction with some observations on the relation of my analysis to these different perspectives.

"Primitive accumulation" is the term that Marx uses, in *Capital* Vol. 1, to characterize the historical process upon which the development of capitalist relations was premised. It is a useful term, for it provides a common denominator through which we can conceptualize the changes that the advent of capitalism produced in economic and social relations. But its importance lies, above all, in the fact that "primitive accumulation" is treated by Marx as a foundational process, revealing the structural conditions for the existence of capitalist society. This enables us to read the past as something which survives into the present, a consideration which is essential to my usage of the term in this work.

However, my analysis departs from Marx's in two ways. Whereas Marx examines primitive accumulation from the viewpoint of the waged male proletariat and the development of commodity production, I examine it from the viewpoint of the changes it introduced in the social position of women and the production of labor-power.[2] Thus, my description of primitive accumulation includes a set of historical phenomena that are absent in Marx, and yet have been extremely important for capitalist accumulation. They include (i) the development of a new sexual division of labor subjugating women's labor and women's reproductive function to the reproduction of the work-force; (ii) the construction of a new patriarchal order, based upon the exclusion of women from waged-work and their subordination to men; (iii) the mechanization of the proletarian body and its transformation, in the case of women, into a machine for the production of new workers. Most important, I have placed at the center of my analysis of primitive accumulation the witch-hunts of the 16th and 17th centuries, arguing that the persecution of the witches, in Europe as in the New World, was as important as colonization and the expropriation of the European peasantry from its land were for the development of capitalism.

My analysis also departs from Marx's in its evaluation of the legacy and function of primitive accumulation. Though Marx was acutely aware of the murderous character of capitalist development — its history, he declared, "is written in the annals of humanity in characters of fire and blood" — there can be no doubt that he viewed it as a necessary step in the process of human liberation. He believed that it disposed of small-scale property, and that it increased (to a degree unmatched by any other economic system) the productive capacity of labor, thus creating the material conditions for the liberation of humanity from scarcity and necessity. He also assumed that the violence that had presided over the earliest phases of capitalist expansion would recede with the maturing of capitalist relations, when the exploitation and disciplining of labor would be accomplished mostly through the workings of economic laws (Marx 1909 Vol. 1). In this, he was deeply mistaken. A return of the most violent aspects of primitive accumulation has accompanied every phase of capitalist globalization, including the present one, demonstrating that the continuous expulsion of farmers from the land, war and plunder on a world scale, and the degradation of women are necessary conditions for the existence of capitalism in all times.

I should add that Marx could never have presumed that capitalism paves the way to human liberation had he looked at its history from the viewpoint of women. For this history shows that, even when men achieved a certain degree of formal freedom, women were always treated as socially inferior beings and were exploited in ways similar to slavery. "Women," then, in the context of this volume, signifies not just a hidden history that needs to be made visible; but a particular form of exploitation and, therefore, a unique perspective from which to reconsider the history of capitalist relations.

This project is not new. From the beginning of the Feminist Movement women have revisited the "transition to capitalism" even though they have not always recognized it. For a while, the main framework that shaped women's history was a chronological one. The most common designation feminist historians have used to describe the transition period has been "early modern Europe," which, depending on the author, could designate the 13th or the 17th century.

In the 1980s, however, a number of works appeared that took a more critical approach. Among them were Joan Kelly's essays on the Renaissance and the *Querelles des femmes*, Carolyn Merchant's *The Death of Nature* (1980), Leopoldina Fortunati's *L'Arcano della Riproduzione* (1981) (now available in English, Fortunati 1995), Merry Wiesner's *Working Women in Renaissance Germany* (1986), and Maria Mies' *Patriarchy and Accumulation on a World Scale* (1986). To these works we must add the many monographs that over the last two decades have reconstructed women's presence in the rural and urban economies of medieval and early modern Europe, and the vast literature and documentary work that has been produced on the witch-hunt and the lives of women in pre-colonial America and the Caribbean islands. Among the latter, I want to remember in particular Irene Silverblatt's *The Moon, the Sun, and the Witches* (1987), the first account on the witch-hunt in colonial Peru; and Hilary Beckles' *Natural Rebels. A Social History of Barbados* (1995) which, together with Barbara Bush's *Slave Women in Caribbean Society:1650–1838* (1990), is one of the major texts on the history of enslaved women in the Caribbean plantations.

What this scholarly production has confirmed is that to reconstruct the history of women or to look at history from a feminist viewpoint means to redefine in fundamental ways the accepted historical categories and to make visible hidden structures of domination and exploitation. Thus, Kelly's essay, "Did Women have a Renaissance?" (1977) undermined the classical historical periodization that celebrates the Renaissance as an outstanding example of cultural achievement. Carolyn Merchant's *The Death of Nature* (1980) challenged the belief in the socially progressive character of the scientific revolution, arguing that the advent of scientific rationalism produced a cultural shift from an organic to a mechanical paradigm that legitimized the exploitation of women and nature.

Especially important has been Maria Mies' *Patriarchy and Accumulation on a World Scale* (1986), now a classic work, that re-examines capitalist accumulation from a non-Eurocentric viewpoint, connecting the destiny of women in Europe to that of Europe's colonial subjects, and providing for a new understanding of women's place in capitalism and the globalization process.

Caliban and the Witch builds upon these works, as on the studies contained within *Il Grande Calibano* (a work I discuss in the Preface). However, its historical scope is broader, as the book connects the development of capitalism, on one side, to the social struggles and the reproduction crisis of the late feudal period and, on the other, to what Marx defines as the "formation of the proletariat." In this process, the book addresses a number of historical and methodological questions that have been at the center of the debate on women's history and feminist theory.

The most important historical question addressed by the book is how to account for the execution of hundreds of thousands of "witches" at the beginning of the modern era, and how to explain why the rise of capitalism was coeval with a war against women. Feminist scholars have developed a framework that throws much light on this question. It is generally agreed that the witch-hunt aimed at destroying the control that women had exercised over their reproductive function and served to pave the way for the development of a more oppressive patriarchal regime. It is also argued that the witch-hunt was rooted in the social transformations that accompanied the rise of capitalism. But the specific historical circumstances under which the persecution of witches was unleashed, and the reasons why the rise of capitalism demanded a genocidal attack on women have not been investigated. This is the task I take on in *Caliban and the Witch*, as I begin to analyze the witch-hunt in the context of the demographic and economic crisis of the 16th and 17th centuries, and the land and labor policies of the mercantilist era. My work here is only a sketch of the research that would be necessary to clarify the connections I have mentioned, and especially the relation between the witch-hunt and the contemporary development of a new sexual division of labor, confining women to reproductive work. It is sufficient, however, to demonstrate that the persecution of witches (like the slave trade and the enclosures) was a central aspect of the accumulation and formation of the modern proletariat, in Europe as well as in the "New World."

There are other ways in which *Caliban and the Witch* speaks to "women's history" and feminist theory. First, it confirms that "the transition to capitalism" is a test case for feminist theory, as the redefinition of productive and reproductive tasks and male-female relations that we find in this period, both realized with the maximum of violence and state intervention, leave no doubt concerning the constructed character of sexual roles in capitalist society. The analysis I propose also allows us to transcend the dichotomy between "gender" and "class." If it is true that in capitalist society sexual identity became the carrier of specific work-functions, then gender should not be considered a purely cultural reality, but should be treated as a specification of class relations. From this viewpoint, the debates that have taken place among postmodern feminists concerning the need to dispose of "women" as a category of analysis, and define feminism purely in oppositional terms, have been misguided. To rephrase the point I already made: if "femininity" has been constituted in capitalist society as a work-function masking the production of the work-force under the cover of a biological destiny, then "women's history" is "class history," and the question that has to be asked is whether the sexual division of labor that has produced that particular concept has been transcended. If the answer is a negative one (as it must be when we consider the present organization of reproductive labor), then "women" is a legitimate category of analysis, and the activities associated with "reproduction" remain a crucial ground of struggle for women, as they were for the feminist movement of the 1970s which, on this basis, connected itself with the history of the witches.

A further question addressed by *Caliban and the Witch* is raised by the contrasting perspectives offered by the feminist and Foucauldian analyses of the body in their applications to an understanding of the history of capitalist development. From the beginning of the Women's Movement, feminist activists and theorists have seen the concept of the "body" as key to an understanding of the roots of male dominance and the construction of female social identity. Across ideological differences, the feminists have realized that a hierarchical ranking of human faculties and the identification of women with a degraded conception of corporeal reality has been instrumental, historically, to the consolidation of patriarchal power and the male exploitation of female labor. Thus, analyses of sexuality, procreation, and mothering have been at the center of feminist theory and women's history. In particular, feminists have uncovered and denounced the strategies and the violence by means of which male-centered systems of exploitation have attempted to discipline and appropriate the female body, demonstrating that women's bodies have been the main targets, the privileged sites, for the deployment of power-techniques and power-relations. Indeed, the many feminist studies which have been produced since the early 1970s on the policing of women's reproductive function, the effects on women of rape, battering, and the imposition upon them of beauty as a condition for social acceptability, are a monumental contribution to the discourse on the body in our times, falsifying the perception common among academics which attributes its discovery to Michel Foucault.

Starting from an analysis of "body-politics," feminists have not only revolutionized the contemporary philosophical and political discourse, but they have also begun to revalorize the body. This has been a necessary step both to counter the negativity attached to the identification of femininity with corporeality, and to create a more holistic vision of what it means to be a human being.[3] This valorization has taken various forms, ranging from the quest for non-dualistic forms of knowledge, to the attempt (with feminists who view sexual "difference" as a positive value) to develop a new type of language and "[rethink] the corporeal roots of human intelligence."[4] As Rosi Braidotti has pointed out, the body that is reclaimed is never to be understood as a biological given. Nevertheless, such slogans as "repossessing the body" or "speaking the body"[5] have been criticized by post-structuralist, Foucauldian theorists, who reject as illusory any call for instinctual liberation. In turn, feminists have accused Foucault's discourse on sexuality of being oblivious to sexual differentiation, while at the same time appropriating many of the insights developed by the Feminist Movement. This criticism is quite appropriate. Moreover, Foucault is so intrigued with the "productive" character of the power-techniques by which the body has been invested, that his analysis practically rules out any critique of power-relations. The nearly apologetic quality of Foucault's theory of the body is accentuated by the fact that it views the body as constituted by purely discursive practices, and is more interested in describing how power is deployed than in identifying its source. Thus, the Power by which the body is produced appears as a self-subsistent, metaphysical entity, ubiquitous, disconnected from social and economic relations, and as mysterious in its permutations as a godly Prime Mover.

Can an analysis of the transition to capitalism and primitive accumulation help us to go beyond these alternatives? I believe it can. With regard to the feminist approach, our first step should be to document the social and historic conditions under which the body has become a central element and the defining sphere of activity for the constitution of femininity. Along these lines, *Caliban and the Witch* shows that the body has been for women in capitalist society what the factory has been for male waged workers: the primary ground of their exploitation and resistance, as the female body has been appropriated by the state and men and forced to function as a means for the reproduction and accumulation of labor. Thus, the importance which the body in all its aspects — maternity, childbirth, sexuality — has acquired in feminist theory and women's history has not been misplaced. *Caliban and the Witch* also confirms the feminist insight which refuses to identify the body with the sphere of the private and, in this vein, speaks of "body politics." Further, it explains how the body can be for women both a source of identity and at the same time a prison, and why it is so important for feminists and, at the same time, so problematic to valorize it.

As for Foucault's theory, the history of primitive accumulation offers many counter-examples to it, proving that it can be defended only at the price of outstanding historical omissions. The most obvious is the omission of the witch-hunt and the discourse of demonology in his analysis of the disciplining of the body. Undoubtedly, they would have inspired different conclusions had they been included. For both demonstrate the repressive character of the power that was unleashed against women, and the implausibility of the complicity and role-reversal that Foucault imagines to exist between victims and their persecutors in his description of the dynamic of micro-powers.

A study of the witch-hunt also challenges Foucault's theory concerning the development of "bio-power," stripping it of the mystery by which Foucault surrounds the emergence of this regime. Foucault registers the shift — presumably in 18th-century Europe — from a type of power built on the right to kill, to a different one exercised through the administration and promotion of life-forces, such as population growth; but he offers no clues as to its motivations. Yet, if we place this shift in the context of the rise of capitalism the puzzle vanishes, for the promotion of life-forces turns out to be nothing more than the result of a new concern with the accumulation and reproduction of labor-power. We can also see that the promotion of population growth by the state can go hand in hand with a massive destruction of life; for in many historical circumstances — witness the history of the slave trade — one is a condition for the other. Indeed, in a system where life is subordinated to the production of profit, the accumulation of labor-power can only be achieved with the maximum of violence so that, in Maria Mies' words, violence itself becomes the most productive force.

In conclusion, what Foucault would have learned had he studied the witch-hunt, rather than focusing on the pastoral confession, in his *History of Sexuality* (1978), is that such history cannot be written from the viewpoint of a universal, abstract, asexual subject. Further, he would have recognized that torture and death can be placed at the service of "life" or, better, at the service of the production of labor-power, since the goal of capitalist society is to transform life into the capacity to work and "dead labor."

From this viewpoint, primitive accumulation has been a universal process in every phase of capitalist development. Not accidentally, its original historical exemplar has sedimented strategies that, in different ways, have been re-launched in the face of every major capitalist crisis, serving to cheapen the cost of labor and to hide the exploitation of women and colonial subjects.

This is what occurred in the 19th century, when the responses to the rise of socialism, the Paris Commune, and the accumulation crisis of 1873 were the "Scramble for Africa" and the simultaneous creation in Europe of the nuclear family, centered on the economic dependence of women to men — following the expulsion of women from the waged work-place. This is also what is happening today, as a new global expansion of the labor-market is attempting to set back the clock with respect to the anti-colonial struggle, and the struggles of other rebel subjects — students, feminists, blue collar workers — who, in the 1960s and 1970s, undermined the sexual and international division of labor.

It is not surprising, then, if large-scale violence and enslavement have been on the agenda, as they were in the period of the "transition," with the difference that today the conquistadors are the officers of the World Bank and the International Monetary Fund, who are still preaching the worth of a penny to the same populations which the dominant world powers have for centuries robbed and pauperized. Once again, much of the violence unleashed is directed against women, for in the age of the computer, the conquest of the female body is still a precondition for the accumulation of labor and wealth, as demonstrated by the institutional investment in the development of new reproductive technologies that, more than ever, reduce women to wombs.

Also the "feminization of poverty" that has accompanied the spread of globalization acquires a new significance when we recall that this was the first effect of the development of capitalism on the lives of women.

Indeed, the political lesson that we can learn from *Caliban and the Witch* is that capitalism, as a social-economic system, is necessarily committed to racism and sexism. For capitalism must justify and mystify the contradictions built into its social relations — the promise of freedom vs. the reality of widespread coercion, and the promise of prosperity vs. the reality of widespread penury — by denigrating the "nature" of those it exploits: women, colonial subjects, the descendants of African slaves, the immigrants displaced by globalization.

At the core of capitalism there is not only the symbiotic relation between waged-contractual labor and enslavement but, together with it, the dialectics of accumulation and destruction of labor-power, for which women have paid the highest cost, with their bodies, their work, their lives.

It is impossible therefore to associate capitalism with any form of liberation or attribute the longevity of the system to its capacity to satisfy human needs. If capitalism has been able to reproduce itself it is only because of the web of inequalities that it has built into the body of the world proletariat, and because of its capacity to globalize exploitation. This process is still unfolding under our eyes, as it has for the last 500 years.

The difference is that today the resistance to it has also achieved a global dimension.

Endnotes

1. The study of the transition to capitalism has a long history, which not accidentally coincides with that of the main political movements of this century. Marxist historians such as Maurice Dobb, Rodney Hilton, Christopher Hill revisited the "transition" in the 1940s and 1950s, in the wake of the debates generated by the consolidation of the Soviet Union, the rise of new socialist states in Europe and Asia, and what at the time appeared as an impending capitalist crisis. The "transition" was again revisited in the 1960s by Third Worldist theorists (Samir Amin, André Gunder Frank), in the context of the contemporary debates over neo-colonialism, "underdevelopment," and the "unequal exchange" between the "First" and the "Third World."

2. These two realities, in my analysis, are closely connected, since in capitalism reproducing workers on a generational basis and regenerating daily their capacity to work has become "women's labor," though mystified, because of its un-waged condition, as a personal service and even a natural resource.

3. Not surprisingly, a valorization of the body has been present in nearly all the literature of "second wave" 20th-century feminism, as it has characterized the literature produced by the anti-colonial revolt and by the descendants of the enslaved Africans. On this ground, across great geographic and cultural boundaries, Virginia Woolf's *A Room of One's Own* (1929) anticipates Aimé Cesaire's *Return to the Native Land* (1938), when she mockingly scolds her female audience and, behind it, a broader female world, for not having managed to produce anything but children.

   "Young women, I would say ... [y]ou have never made a discovery of any sort of importance. You have never shaken an empire or lead an army into battle. The plays of Shakespeare are not by you.... What is your excuse? It is all very well for you to say, pointing to the streets and squares and forests of the globe swarming with black and white and coffee-colored inhabitants... we have had other work on our hands. Without our doing, those seas would be unsailed and those fertile lands a desert. We have borne and bred and washed and taught, perhaps to the age of six or seven years, the one thousand six hundred and twenty-three million human beings who are, according to statistics, at present in existence, and that, allowing that some had help, takes time." (Woolf, 1929: 112)

   This capacity to subvert the degraded image of femininity, which has been constructed through the identification of women with nature, matter, and corporeality, is the power of the feminist "discourse on the body," that tries to unbury what male control of our corporeal reality has suffocated. It is an illusion, however, to conceive of women's liberation as a "return to the body." If the female body — as I argue in this work — is a signifier for a field of reproductive activities that have been appropriated by men and the state, and turned into an instrument for the production of labor-power (with all that this entails in terms of sexual rules and regulations, aesthetic canons, and punishments), then the body is the site of a fundamental alienation that can be overcome only with the end of the work-discipline which defines it.

This thesis holds true for men as well. Marx's portrait of the worker who feels at home only in his bodily functions already intuited this fact. Marx, however, never conveyed the magnitude of the attack to which the male body was subjected with the advent of capitalism. Ironically, like Michel Foucault, Marx too stressed the productivity of the power to which workers are subordinated — a productivity that becomes for him the condition for the workers' future mastery of society. Marx did not see that the development of workers' industrial powers was at the cost of the underdevelopment of their powers as social individuals, although he recognized that workers in capitalist society become so alienated from their labor, from their relations with others, and the products of their work as to become dominated by them as if by an alien force.

4. Braidotti (1991) 219. For a discussion of feminist thought on the body, see Ariel Salleh's *EcoFeminism as Politics* (1997), especially Chapters 3 through 5; and Rosi Braidotti's *Patterns of Dissonance* (1991) especially the section entitled "Repossessing the Body: A Timely Project" (pp. 219-224).

5. I am referring here to the project of *ècriture feminine,* a literary theory and movement that developed in France in the 1970s, among feminist students of Lacanian psychoanalysis, who were seeking to create a language expressing the specificity of the female body and female subjectivity (Braidotti, op. cit.).

Woman carrying a basket of spinach. Women in the Middle Ages often kept gardens, where they grew medical herbs. Their knowledge of the properties of herbs is one of the secrets they handed down from generation to generation. Italian, c. 1385.

All the World Needs a Jolt
Social Movements and Political Crisis in Medieval Europe

All the world must suffer a big jolt. There will be such a game that the
ungodly will be thrown off their seats, and the downtrodden will rise.
—Thomas Müntzer,
*Open Denial of the False Belief of the Godless World
on the Testimony of the Gospel of Luke, Presented to Miserable and
Pitiful Christendom in Memory of its Error,* 1524

There is no denying that, after centuries of struggle, exploitation
does continue to exist. Only its form has changed. The surplus labor
extracted here and there by the masters of today's world is not smaller
in proportion to the total amount of labor than the surplus extracted
long ago. But the change in the conditions of exploitation is not in
my view negligible.... What is important is the history, the striving
for liberation....
—Pierre Dockes, *Medieval Slavery and Liberation,* 1982

Introduction

A history of women and reproduction in the "transition to capitalism" must begin with the
struggles that the European medieval proletariat — small peasants, artisans, day laborers —
waged against feudal power in all its forms. Only if we evoke these struggles, with their rich
cargo of demands, social and political aspirations, and antagonistic practices, can we understand
the role that women had in the crisis of feudalism, and why their power had to be destroyed
for capitalism to develop, as it was by the three-century-long persecution of the witches. From
the vantage point of this struggle, we can also see that capitalism was not the product of an
evolutionary development bringing forth economic forces that were maturing in the womb
of the old order. Capitalism was the response of the feudal lords, the patrician merchants, the
bishops and popes, to a centuries-long social conflict that, in the end, shook their power, and
truly gave "all the world a big jolt." Capitalism was the counter-revolution that destroyed the
possibilities that had emerged from the anti-feudal struggle — possibilities which, if realized,

might have spared us the immense destruction of lives and the natural environment that has marked the advance of capitalist relations worldwide. This much must be stressed, for the belief that capitalism "evolved" from feudalism and represents a higher form of social life has not yet been dispelled.

How the history of women intersects with that of capitalist development cannot be grasped, however, if we concern ourselves only with the classic terrains of class struggle — labor services, wage rates, rents and tithes — and ignore the new visions of social life and the transformation of gender relations which these conflicts produced. These were not negligible. It is in the course of the anti-feudal struggle that we find the first evidence in European history of a grassroots women's movement opposed to the established order and contributing to the construction of alternative models of communal life. The struggle against feudal power also produced the first organized attempts to challenge the dominant sexual norms and establish more egalitarian relations between women and men. Combined with the refusal of bonded labor and commercial relations, these conscious forms of social transgression constructed a powerful alternative not only to feudalism but to the capitalist order by which feudalism was replaced, demonstrating that another world was possible, and urging us to question why it was not realized. This chapter searches for some answers to this question, while examining how the relations between women and men and the reproduction of labor-power were redefined in oppositon to feudal rule.

The social struggles of the Middle Ages must also be remembered because they wrote a new chapter in the history of liberation. At their best, they called for an egalitarian social order based upon the sharing of wealth and the refusal of hierarchies and authoritarian rule. These were to remain utopias. Instead of the heavenly kingdom, whose advent was prophesied in the preaching of the heretics and millenarian movements, what issued from the demise of feudalism were disease, war, famine, and death — the four horsemen of the Apocalypse, as represented in Albrecht Dürer's famous print — true harbingers of the new capitalist era. Nevertheless, the attempts that the medieval proletariat made to "turn the world upside down" must be reckoned with; for despite their defeat, they put the feudal system into crisis and, in their time, they were "genuinely revolutionary," as they could not have succeeded without "a radical reshaping of the social order" (Hilton, 1973: 223-4). Reading the "transition" from the viewpoint of the anti-feudal struggle of the Middle Ages also helps us to reconstruct the social dynamics that lay in the background of the English Enclosures and the conquest of the Americas, and above all unearth some of the reasons why in the 16th and 17th centuries the extermination of the "witches," and the extension of state control over every aspect of reproduction, became the cornerstones of primitive accumulation.

Serfdom as a Class Relation

While the anti-feudal struggles of the Middle Ages cast some light on the development of capitalist relations, their own political significance will remain hidden unless we frame them in the broader context of the history of serfdom, which was the dominant class relation in feudal society and, until the 14th century, the focus of anti-feudal struggle.

Farmers preparing the soil for sowing. Access to land was the foundation of the power of the serfs. English miniature, ca. 1340.

Serfdom developed in Europe, between the 5th and 7th centuries A.D., in response to the breakdown of the slave system, on which the economy of imperial Rome had been built. It was the result of two related phenomena. By the 4th century, in the Roman territories and the new Germanic states, the landlords had to grant the slaves the right to have a plot of land and a family of their own, in order to stem their revolts, and prevent their flight to the "bush" where maroon communities were forming at the margins of the empire.[1] At the same time, the landlords began to subjugate the free peasants, who, ruined by the expansion of slave-labor and later the Germanic invasions, turned to the lords for protection, although at the cost of their independence. Thus, while slavery was never completely abolished, a new class relation developed that homogenized the conditions of former slaves and free agricultural workers (Dockes 1982: 151), placing all the peasantry in a subordinate condition, so that for three centuries (from the 9th to the 11th), "peasant" *(rusticus, villanus)* would be synonymous with "serf" *(servus)* (Pirenne, 1956: 63).

As a work relation and a juridical status, serfdom was an enormous burden. The serfs were bonded to the landlords; their persons and possessions were their masters' property and their lives were ruled in every respect by the law of the manor. Nevertheless, serfdom redefined the class relation in terms more favorable to the workers. Serfdom marked the end of gang-labor, of life in the *ergastula*,[2] and a lessening of the atrocious punishments (the iron collars, the burnings, the crucifixions) on which slavery had relied. On the feudal estates, the serfs were subjected to the law of the lord, but their transgressions were judged on the basis of "customary" agreements and, in time, even of a peer-based jury system.

The most important aspect of serfdom, from the viewpoint of the changes it introduced in the master-servant relation, is that it gave the serfs direct access to the means of their reproduction. In exchange for the work which they were bound to do on the lords' land (the *demesne*), the serfs received a plot of land (*mansus* or *hide*) which they could use to support themselves, and pass down to their children "like a real inheritance, by simply paying a succession due" (Boissonnade 1927:134).As Pierre Dockes points out in *Medieval Slavery and Liberation* (1982), this arrangement increased the serfs' autonomy and improved their living conditions, as they could now dedicate more time to their reproduction and negotiate the extent of their obligations, instead of being treated like chattel subject to an unconditional rule. Most important, having the effective use and possession of a plot of land meant that the serfs could always support themselves and, even at the peak of their confrontations with the lords, they could not easily be forced to bend because of the fear of starvation. True, the lord could throw recalcitrant serfs off the land, but this was rarely done, given the difficulty of recruiting new laborers in a fairly closed economy and the collective nature of peasant struggles. This is why — as Marx noted — on the feudal manor, the exploitation of labor always depended on the direct use of force.[3]

The experience of self-reliance which the peasants gained from having access to land also had a political and ideological potential. In time, the serfs began to look at the land they occupied as their own, and to view as intolerable the restrictions that the aristocracy imposed on their freedom. "Land to the tillers" — the demand that has echoed through the 20th century, from the Mexican and Russian revolutions to the contemporary struggles against land privatization — is a battle cry which the medieval serfs would have certainly recognized as their own. But the strength of the "villeins" stemmed from the fact that access to land was a reality for them.

With the use of land also came the use of the "commons" — meadows, forests, lakes, wild pastures — that provided crucial resources for the peasant economy (wood for fuel, timber for building, fishponds, grazing grounds for animals) and fostered community cohesion and cooperation (Birrell 1987:23). In Northern Italy, control over these resources even provided the basis for the development of communal self-administrations (Hilton 1973: 76). So important were the "commons" in the political economy and struggles of the medieval rural population that their memory still excites our imagination, projecting the vision of a world where goods can be shared and solidarity, rather than desire for self-aggrandizement, can be the substance of social relations.[4]

The medieval servile community fell short of these goals, and should not be idealized as an example of communalism. In fact, its example reminds us that neither "communalism" nor "localism" can be a guarantee of egalitarian relations unless the community controls its means of subsistence and all its members have equal access to them. This was not the case with the serfs on the feudal manors. Despite the prevalence of collective forms of work and collective "contracts" with the landlords, and despite the local character of the peasant economy, the medieval village was not a community of equals. As established by a vast documentation coming from every country of Western Europe, there were many social differences within the peasantry that separated free peasants and those of servile status, rich and poor peasants, peasants with secure land tenure and landless laborers working for a wage on the lord's demesne, and women and men.[5]

Land was usually given to men and transmitted through the male lineage, though there were many cases of women who inherited it and managed it in their name.[6] Women were also excluded from the offices to which the better-off male peasants were appointed, and, to all effects, they had a second-class status (Bennett 1988:18–29; Shahar

1983). This perhaps is why their names are rarely mentioned in the manorial registers, except for those of the courts in which the serfs' transgressions were recorded. Nevertheless, female serfs were less dependent on their male kin, less differentiated from them physically, socially, and psychologically, and were less subservient to men's needs than "free" women were to be later in capitalist society.

Women's dependence on men within the servile community was limited by the fact that over the authority of their husbands and fathers prevailed that of the lords, who claimed possession of the serfs' persons and property, and tried to control every aspect of their lives, from work to marriage and sexual behavior.

It was the lord who commanded women's work and social relations, deciding, for instance, whether a widow should remarry and who should be her spouse, in some areas even claiming the *ius primae noctis* — the right to sleep with a serf's wife on her wedding night. The authority of male serfs over their female relatives was further limited by the fact that the land was generally given to the family unit, and women not only worked on it but could dispose of the products of their labor, and did not have to depend on their husbands for support. The partnership of the wife in land possession was so well understood in England that "[w]hen a villein couple married it was common for the man to come and turn the land back to the lord, taking it again in both his name and that of his wife" (Hanawalt 1986b: 155).[7] Furthermore, since work on the servile farm was organized on a subsistence basis, the sexual division of labor in it was less pronounced and less discriminating than in a capitalist farm. In the feudal village no social separation existed between the production of goods and the reproduction of the work-force; all work contributed to the family's sustenance. Women worked in the fields, in addition to raising children, cooking, washing, spinning, and keeping an herb garden; their domestic activities were not devalued and did not involve different social relations from those of men, as they would later, in a money-economy, when housework would cease to be viewed as real work.

If we also take into account that in medieval society collective relations prevailed over familial ones, and most of the tasks that female serfs performed (washing, spinning, harvesting, and tending to animals on the commons) were done in cooperation with other women, we then realize that the sexual divison of labor, far from being a source of isolation, was a source of power and protection for women. It was the basis for an intense female sociality and solidarity that enabled women to stand up to men, despite the fact that the Church preached women's submission to men, and Canonic Law sanctified the husband's right to beat his wife.

The position of women on the feudal manor cannot be treated, however, as if it were a static reality.[8] For the power of women and their relations with men were, at all times, determined by the struggles which their communities fought against the landlords, and the changes that these struggles produced in the master-servant relation.

The Struggle on the Commons

By the end of the 14th century, the revolt of the peasantry against the landlords had become endemic, massified, and frequently armed. However, the organizational strength that the peasants demonstrated in this period was the outcome of a long conflict that, more or less openly, ran through the Middle Ages.

Contrary to the schoolbook portrait of feudal society as a static world, in which each estate accepted its designated place in the social order, the picture that emerges from a study of the feudal manor is rather that of relentless class struggle.

As the records of the English manorial courts indicate, the medieval village was the theater of daily warfare (Hilton 1966: 154; Hilton, 1985: 158–59). At times, this reached moments of great tension, when the villagers killed the bailiff or attacked their lord's castle. Most frequently, however, it consisted of an endless litigation, by which the serfs tried to limit the abuses of the lords, fix their "burdens," and reduce the many tributes which they owed them in exchange for the use of the land (Bennett, 1967; Coulton, 1955: 35–91; Hanawalt 1986a: 32–35).

The main objective of the serfs was to keep hold of their surplus-labor and products and broaden the sphere of their economic and juridical rights. These two aspects of servile struggle were closely connected, as many obligations issued from the serfs' legal status. Thus, in 13th-century England, both on the lay and ecclesiastical estates, male peasants were frequently fined for claiming that they were not serfs but free men, a challenge that could result in a bitter litigation, pursued even by appeal to the royal court (Hanawalt 1986a: 31). Peasants were also fined for refusing to bake their bread at the oven of the lords, or grind their grain, or olives at their mills, which allowed them to avoid the onerous taxes that the lords imposed for the use of these facilities (Bennett 1967: 130–31; Dockes 1982: 176–79). However, the most important terrain of servile struggle was the work that, on certain days of the week, the serfs had to carry out on the land of the lords. These "labor services" were the burdens that most immediately affected the serfs' lives and, through the 13th century, they were the central issue in the servile struggle for freedom.[9]

The serfs' attitude towards the *corveé*, as labor services were also called, transpires through the entries in the books of the manorial courts, where the penalties imposed on the tenants were recorded. By the mid 13th century, the evidence speaks for a "massive withdrawal" of labor (Hilton 1985: 130–31). The tenants would neither go nor send their children to work on the land of the lords when summoned at harvest time,[10] or they would go to the fields too late, so that the crops would spoil, or they worked sloppily, taking long breaks and generally maintaining an insubordinate attitude. Hence the lords' need for constant and close supervision and vigilance, as evinced by this recommendation:

> Let the bailiff and the messor, be all the time with the ploughmen, to
> see that they do their work well and thoroughly, and at the end of the
> day see how much they have done.... And because customary servants
> neglect their work it is necessary to guard against their fraud; further
> it is necessary that they are overseen often; and beside the bailiff must
> oversee all, that they work well and if they do not do well, let them
> be reproved (Bennett 1967: 113).

A similar situation is portrayed in *Piers Plowman* (c. 1362–70), William Langland's allegorical poem, where in one scene the laborers, who had been busy in the morning, passed the afternoon sitting and singing and, in another one, idle people flocked in at harvest time seeking "no deed to do, but to drink and to sleep" (Coulton 1955: 87).

Also the obligation to provide military services at wartime was strongly resisted. As H. S. Bennett reports, force was always needed to recruit in the English villages, and a medieval commander rarely managed to keep his men at war, for those who enlisted deserted at the first opportunity, after pocketing their pay. Exemplary are the pay-rolls of the Scottish campaign of the year 1300, which indicate that while 16,000 recruits had been ordered to enlist in June, by mid July only 7,600 could be mustered and this "was the crest of the wave... by August little more than 3,000 remained." As a result, increasingly the king had to rely on pardoned criminals and outlaws to bolster his army (Bennett 1967: 123–25).

Another source of conflict was the use of non-cultivated lands, including woods, lakes, hills, which the serfs considered a collective property. "[W]e can go to the woods..." — the serfs declared in a mid 12th-century English chronicle — "and take what we want, take fish from the fish pond, and game from the forests; we'll have our will in the woods, the waters and the meadows" (Hilton, 1973: 71).

Still, the most bitter struggles were those against the taxes and burdens that issued from the jurisdictional power of the nobility. These included the *manomorta* (a tax which the lord levied when a serf died), the *mercheta* (a tax on marriage that increased when a serf married someone from another manor), the *heriot* (an inheritance tax paid by the heir of a deceased serf for the right to gain entry to his holding, usually consisting of the best beast of the deceased), and, worst of all, the *tallage*, a sum of money arbitrarily decided, that the lords could exact at will. Last but not least was the *tithe,* a tenth of the peasant income, that was exacted by the clergy, but usually collected by the lords in the clergy's name.

Together with the labor service, these taxes "against nature and freedom" were the most resented among the feudal dues, for not being compensated by any allotments of land or other benefits, they revealed all the arbitrariness of feudal power. Thus, they were strenuously resisted. Typical was the attitude of the serfs of the monks of Dunstable who, in 1299, declared that "they would rather go down to hell than be beaten in this matter of tallage," and, "after much controversy," they bought their freedom from it (Bennett, 1967: 139). Similarly, in 1280, the serfs of Hedon, a village of Yorkshire, let it be understood that, if the tallage was not abolished, they would rather go to live in the nearby towns of Revensered and Hull "which have good harbours growing daily, and no tallage" (*ibid.*: 141). These were no idle threats. The flight to the city or town[11] was a constant component of servile struggle, so that, again and again, on some English manors, "men are reported to be fugitives, and dwelling in the neighboring towns; and although order is given that they be brought back, the town continues to shelter them...." (*ibid.*: 295–96).

To these forms of open confrontation we must add the manifold, invisible forms of resistance, for which subjugated peasants have been famous in all times and places: "foot dragging, dissimulation, false compliance, feigned ignorance, desertion, pilfering, smuggling, poaching...." (Scott 1989: 5) These "everyday forms of resistance," stubbornly carried on over the years, without which no adequate account of class relations is possible, were rife in the medieval village.

This may explain the meticulousness with which the servile burdens were specified in the manorial records:

> For instance, [the manorial records] often do not say simply that a man
> must plow, sow and harrow one acre of the lord's land. They say he
> must plow it with so many oxen as he has in his plow, harrow it with
> his own horse and sack.... Services (too) were remembered in minute
> detail....We must remember the cotmen of Elton who admitted that
> they were bound to stack the lord's hay in his meadow and again in
> his barnyard, but maintained that they were not bound in custom to
> load it into carts to be carried from the first place to the second
> (Homans 1960: 272).

In some areas of Germany, where the dues included yearly donations of eggs and
poultry, tests of fitness were devised, in order to prevent the serfs from handing down to
the lords the worst among their chickens:

> The hen (then) is placed in front of a fence or a gate; if frightened she
> has the strength to fly or scramble over, the bailiff must accept her, she
> is fit. A gosling, again, must be accepted if it is mature enough to pluck
> grass without loosing its balance and sitting down ignominiously
> (Coulton 1955: 74–75).

Such minute regulations testify to the difficulty of enforcing the medieval "social
contract," and the variety of battlefields available to a combative tenant or village. Servile
duties and rights were regulated by "customs," but their interpretation too was an object
of much dispute. The "invention of traditions" was a common practice in the confrontation between landlords and peasants, as both would try to redefine them or forget them,
until a time came, towards the middle of the 13th century, when the lords put them down
in writing.

Liberty and Social Division

Politically, the first outcome of the servile struggles was the concession to many villages
(particularly in Northern Italy and France) of "privileges" and "charters" that fixed the
burdens and granted "an element of autonomy in the running of the village
community"providing, at times, for true forms of local self-government. These charters
stipulated the fines that were to be meted out by the manorial courts, and established
rules for juridical proceedings, thus eliminating or reducing the possibility of arbitrary
arrests and other abuses (Hilton 1973: 75). They also lightened the serfs' duty to enlist as
soldiers and abolished or fixed the tallage; often they granted the "liberty" to "hold stal-
lage," that is to sell goods at the local market and, more rarely, the right to alienate land.
Between 1177 and 1350, in Loraine alone, 280 charters were conceded (*ibid.*: 83).
    However, the most important resolution of the master-serf conflict was the *com-
mutation* of labor services with money payments (money rents, money taxes) that placed
the feudal relation on a more contractual basis. With this momentous development, serf-

dom practically ended, but, like many workers' "victories" which only in part satisfy the original demands, commutation too co-opted the goals of the struggle, functioning as a means of social division and contributing to the disintegration of the feudal village.

To the well-to-do peasants who, possessing large tracts of land, could earn enough money to "buy their blood" and employ other laborers, commutation must have appeared as a great step on the road to economic and personal independence; for the lords lessened their control over their tenants when they no longer depended directly on their work. But the majority of poorer peasants — who possessed only a few acres of land barely sufficient for their survival — lost even the little they had. Compelled to pay their dues in money, they went into chronic debt, borrowing against future harvests, a process that eventually caused many to lose their land. As a result, by the 13th century, when commutations spread throughout Western Europe, social divisions in the rural areas deepened, and part of the peasantry underwent a process of proletarianization. As Bronislaw Geremek writes:

> Thirteenth-century documents contain increasing amounts of information about "landless" peasants who manage to eke out a living on the margins of village life by tending to flocks.... One finds increasing numbers of "gardeners," landless or almost landless peasants who earned their living by hiring out their services.... In Southern France the *"brassiers"* lived entirely by "selling" the strength of their arms (*bras*) and hiring themselves out to richer peasants or landed gentry. From the beginning of the fourteenth century the tax registers show a marked increase in the number of impoverished peasants, who appear in these documents as "indigents," "poor men" or even "beggards" (Geremek 1994: 56).[12]

The commutation to money-rent had two other negative consequences. First, it made it more difficult for the producers to measure their exploitation, because as soon as the labor-services were commuted into money payments, the peasants could no longer differentiate between the work that they did for themselves and that which they did for the landlords. Commutation also made it possible for the now-free tenants to employ and exploit other workers, so that, "in a further development," it promoted "the growth of independent peasant property," turning "the old self-employing possessors of the land" into a capitalist tenant (Marx 1909: Vol. III, 924 ff).

The monetization of economic life, then, did not benefit all people, contrary to what is claimed by supporters of the market economy, who welcome it as the creation of a new "common" replacing land-bondage and introducing in social life the criteria of objectivity, rationality, and even personal freedom (Simmel 1900). With the spread of monetary relations, values certainly changed, even among the clergy, who began to reconsider the Aristotelian doctrine of the "sterility of money" (Kaye 1998) and, not coincidentally, to revise its views concerning the redeeming quality of charity to the poor. But their effects were destructive and divisive. Money and the market began to split the peasantry by transforming income differences into class differences, and by producing a mass of poor people who could survive only on the basis of periodic donations (Geremek 1994: 56–62). To the growing influence of money we must also attribute the systematic attack to which Jews were subjected, starting in the 12th century, and the steady deterioration of their legal and social status in the same period. There is, in fact, a revealing correlation between the displacement of the Jews by Christian competitors, as moneylenders to Kings, popes and the higher clergy, and the new discriminatory rules (e.g., the wearing of distinctive clothing) that were adopted by the clergy against them, as well as their expulsion from England and France. Degraded by the Church, further separated by the Christian population, and forced to confine their moneylending (one of the few occupations available to them) to the village level, the Jews became an easy target for indebted peasants, who often vented on them their anger against the rich (Barber 1992: 76).

Women, too, in all classes, were most negatively affected by the increasing commercialization of life, for their access to property and income was further reduced by it. In the Italian commercial towns, women lost their right to inherit a third of their husbands' property (the *tertia*). In the rural areas, they were further excluded from land possession, especially when single or widowed. As a result, by the 13th century, they were leading the movement away from the country, being the most numerous among the rural immigrants to the towns (Hilton 1985: 212), and by the 15th century, women formed a large percentage of the population of the cities. Here, most of them lived in poor conditions, holding low-paid jobs as maids, hucksters, retail traders (often fined for lack of a license), spinsters, members of the lower guilds, and prostitutes.[13] However, living in the urban centers, among the most combative part of the medieval population, gave them a new social autonomy. City laws did not free women; few could afford to buy the "city

Women building the city walls, from Christine de Pizan, THE CITY OF WOMEN, *1405.*

freedom," as the privileges connected with city life were called. But in the city, women's subordination to male tutelage was reduced, as they could now live alone, or with their children as heads of families, or could form new communities, often sharing their dwellings with other women. While usually the poorest members of urban society, in time women gained access to many occupations that later would be considered male jobs. In the medieval towns, women worked as smiths, butchers, bakers, candlestick makers, hat-makers, ale-brewers, wool-carders, and retailers (Shahar 1983: 189–200; King 1991:64–67)."In Frankfurt, there were approximately 200 occupations in which women participated between 1300 and 1500" (Williams and Echols 2000: 53). In England, seventy-two out of eighty-five guilds included women among their members. Some guilds, including silk-making, were dominated by them; in others, female employment was as high as that of men.[14] By the 14th century, women were also becoming schoolteachers as well as doctors and surgeons, and were beginning to compete with university-trained men, gaining at times a high reputation. Sixteen female doctors — among them several Jewish women specialized in surgery or eye therapy — were hired in the 14th century by the municipality of Frankfurt which, like other city administrations, offered its population a system of public health-care. Female doctors, as well as midwives or *sage femmes,* were dominant in obstetrics, either in the pay of city governments or supporting themselves with the compensation they received from their patients. After the Caesarian cut was introduced in the 13th century, female obstetrics were the only ones who practiced it (Opitz 1996: 370–71).

As women gained more autonomy, their presence in social life began to be recorded more frequently: in the sermons of the priests who scolded their indiscipline (Casagrande 1978); in the records of the tribunals where they went to denounce those who abused them (S. Cohn 1981); in the city ordinances regulating prostitution (Henriques 1966); among the thousands of non-combatants who followed the armies (Hacker 1981); and above all, in the new popular movements, especially that of the heretics.

We will see later the role that women played in the heretic movements. Here suffice it to say that, in response to the new female independence, we see the beginning of a misogynous backlash most evident in the satires of the *fabliaux,* where we find the first traces of what historians have defined as "the struggle for the breeches."

The Millenarian and the Heretic Movements

It was the growing landless proletariat which emerged in the wake of commutation that was the protagonist (in the 12th and 13th centuries) of the millenarian movements, in which we find, beside impoverished peasants, all the wretched of feudal society: prostitutes, defrocked priests, urban and rural day laborers (N.Cohn 1970). The traces of the millenarians' brief apparition on the historical scene are scanty, and they tell us a story of short-lived revolts, and of a peasantry brutalized by poverty and by the clergy's inflammatory preaching that accompanied the launching of the Crusades. The significance of their rebellion, however, is that it inaugurated a new type of struggle, already projected beyond the confines of the manor and stimulated by aspirations to total change. Not surprisingly, the rise of millenarianism was accompanied by the spread of prophecies and apocalyptic visions announcing the end of the world and the imminence of the Last Judgment, "not as visions of a more or less distant future to be awaited, but as impending events in which many now living could take active part" (Hilton 1973: 223).

A typical example of millenarianism was the movement sparked by the appearance of the Pseudo Baldwin in Flanders in 1224–25. The man, a hermit, had claimed to be the popular Baldwin IX who had been killed in Constantinople in 1204. This could not be proven, but his promise of a new world provoked a civil war in which the Flemish textile workers became his most ardent supporters (Nicholas 1992: 155). These poor people (weavers, fullers) closed ranks around him, presumably convinced that he was going to give them silver and gold and full social reform (Volpe 1922: 298-9). Similar to this movement were those of the Pastoreaux (shepherds) — peasants and urban workers who swept through Northern France around 1251, burning and pillaging the houses of the rich, demanding a betterment of their condition[15] — and the movement of the Flagellants that, starting from Umbria (Italy), spread in several countries in 1260, the date when, according to the prophecy of the abbot Joachim da Flora, the world was supposed to end (Russell 1972a: 137).

It was not the millenarian movement, however, but popular heresy that best expressed the search by the medieval proletariat for a concrete alternative to feudal relations and its resistance to the growing money-economy.

Heresy and millenarianism are often treated as one subject, but while a precise distinction cannot be drawn, there are significant differences between the two movements.

The millenarian movements were spontaneous, without an organizational structure or program. Usually a specific event or a charismatic individual spurred them on,

A procession of flagellants during the Black Death.

but as soon as they were met by force they collapsed. By contrast, the heretic movement was a conscious attempt to create a new society. The main heretical sects had a social program that also reinterpreted the religious tradition, and they were well-organized from the viewpoint of their reproduction, the dissemination of their ideas, and even their self-defense. Not surprisingly, they had a long duration, despite the extreme persecution to which they were subjected, and they played a crucial role in the anti-feudal struggle.

Today, little is known about the many heretic sects (Cathars, Waldenses, The Poor of Lyon, Spirituals, Apostolics) that for more than three centuries flourished among the "lower classes" in Italy, France, the Flanders, and Germany, in what undoubtedly was the most important opposition movement of the Middle Ages (Werner 1974; Lambert 1977). This is largely due to the ferocity with which they were persecuted by the Church, which spared no effort to erase every trace of their doctrines. Crusades — like the one moved against the Albigensians[16] — were called against the heretics, as they were called to liberate the Holy Land from the "infidels." By the thousands, heretics were burned at the stake, and to eradicate their presence the Pope created one of the most perverse institutions ever recorded in the history of state repression: the Holy Inquisition (Vauchez 1990: 162–70).[17]

Nevertheless, as Charles H. Lea (among others) has shown, in his monumental history of the persecution of heresy, even on the basis of the limited records available to us, we can form an impressive picture of their activities and creeds and the role of heretical resistance in the anti-feudal struggle (Lea 1888).

Although influenced by Eastern religions brought to Europe by merchants and crusaders, popular heresy was less a deviation from the orthodox doctrine than a protest movement, aspiring to a radical democratization of social life.[18] Heresy was the equivalent of "liberation theology" for the medieval proletariat. It gave a frame to peoples' demands for spiritual renewal and social justice, challenging both the Church and secular authority by appeal to a higher truth. It denounced social hierarchies, private property and the accumulation of wealth, and it disseminated among the people a new, revolutionary conception of society that, for the first time in the Middle Ages, redefined every aspect of daily life (work, property, sexual reproduction, and the position of women), posing the question of emancipation in truly universal terms.

The heretic movement also provided an alternative community structure that had an international dimension, enabling the members of the sects to lead a more autonomous life, and to benefit from a wide support network made of contacts, schools, and safe-houses upon which they could rely for help and inspiration in times of need. Indeed, it is no exaggeration to say that the heretic movement was the first "proletarian international"— such was the reach of the sects (particularly the Cathars and Waldenses) and the links they established among themselves with the help of commercial fairs, pilgrimages, and the constant border-crossing of refugees generated by the persecution.

At the root of popular heresy was the belief that god no longer spoke through the clergy, because of its greed, corruption and scandalous behavior. Thus the two major sects presented themselves as the "true churches." However, the heretics' challenge was primarily a political one, since to challenge the Church was to confront at once the ideological pillar of feudal power, the biggest landowner in Europe, and one of the institutions most responsible for the daily exploitation of the peasantry. By the 11th century, the Church had become a despotic power that used its alleged divine investiture to govern with an iron fist and fill its coffers by endless means of extortion. Selling absolutions, indulgences and religious offices, calling the faithful to church only to preach to them the sanctity of the tithes, and making of all sacraments a market, were common practices from the pope to the village priest, so much so that the corruption of the clergy became proverbial throughout Christianity. Things degenerated to the point that the clergy would not bury the dead, baptize or grant absolution from sin unless it received some compensation. Even the communion became an occasion for a bargain, and "[i]f an unjust demand was resisted the recalcitrant was excommunicated, and then had to pay for reconciliation in addition to the original sum" (Lea 1961:11).

In this context, the propagation of the heretical doctrines not only channeled the contempt that people felt for the clergy; it gave them confidence in their views and instigated their resistance to clerical exploitation. Taking the lead from the New Testament, the heretics taught that Christ had no property, and that if the Church wanted to regain its spiritual power it should divest itself from all its possessions. They also taught that the sacraments were not valid when administered by sinful priests, that the exterior forms of worship — buildings, images, symbols — should be discarded because only inner belief mattered. They also exhorted people not to pay the tithes, and denied the existence of Purgatory, whose invention had been for the clergy a source of lucre through paid masses and the sales of indulgences.

In turn, the Church used the charge of heresy to attack every form of social and political insubordination. In 1377, when the cloth workers in Ypres (Flanders) took arms against their employers, they were not only hanged as rebels but were burned by the Inquisition as heretics (N. Cohn 1970: 105). There are also records of female weavers being threatened with excommunication for not having delivered promptly the product of their work to the merchants or not having properly done their work (Volpe, 1971: 31). In 1234, to punish his peasant tenants who refused to pay the tithes, the Bishop of Bremen called a crusade against them "as though they were heretics" (Lambert 1992: 98). But heretics were persecuted also by the secular authorities, from the Emperor to the urban patricians, who realized that the heretic appeal to the "true religion" had subversive implications and questioned the foundations of their power.

Heresy was as much a critique of social hierarchies and economic exploitation as it was a denunciation of clerical corruption. As Gioacchino Volpe points out, the rejection of all forms of authority and a strong anti-commercial sentiment were common elements among the sects. Many heretics shared the ideal of apostolic poverty[19] and the desire to return to the simple communal life that had characterized the primitive church. Some, like the Poor of Lyon and the Brethren of the Free Spirit, lived on donated alms. Others supported themselves by manual labor.[20] Still others experimented with "communism," like the early Taborites in Bohemia, for whom the establishment of equality and communal ownership were as important as religious reform.[21] Of the Waldenses too an Inquisitor reported that "they avoid all forms of commerce to avoid lies, frauds and oaths," and he described them as walking barefoot, clad in woolen garments, owning nothing and, like apostles, holding all things in common (Lambert 1992: 64). The social content of heresy, however, is best expressed in the words of John Ball, the intellectual leader of

Peasants hang a monk who has sold indulgences. Niklaus Manuel Deutsch, 1525.

the English Peasant Rising of 1381, who denounced that "we are made in the image of God, but we are treated like beasts," and added, "Nothing will go well in England... as long as there will be gentlemen and villeins" (Dobson 1983: 371).[22]

The most influential among the heretical sects, the Cathars, also stand out as unique in the history of European social movements because of their abhorrence for war (including the Crusades), their condemnation of capital punishment (which provoked the Church's first explicit pronouncement in support of the death penalty)[23] and their tolerance for other religions. Southern France, their stronghold before the crusade against the Albigensians, "was a safe haven for Jews when anti-semitism in Europe was mounting; [here] a fusion of Cathar and Jewish thought produced the Cabbala, the tradition of Jewish mysticism" (Spencer 1995b: 171). The Cathars also rejected marriage and procreation and were strict vegetarians, both because they refused to kill animals and because they wished to avoid any food, like eggs and meats, resulting from sexual generation.

This negative attitude towards natality has been attributed to the influence exerted on the Cathars by Eastern dualist sects like the Paulicians — a sect of iconoclasts who rejected procreation as the act by which the soul is entrapped in the material world (Erbstosser 1984:13–14) — and, above all, the Bogomils, who proselytized in the 10th century among the peasantry of the Balkans. A popular movement "born amidst peasants whose physical misery made conscious of the wickedness of things" (Spencer 1995b: 15), the Bogomils preached that the visible world is the work of the devil (for in the world of God the good would be the first), and they refused to have children not to bring new slaves into this "land of tribulations," as life on earth was called in one of their tracts (Wakefield and Evans 1991: 457).

The influence of the Bogomils on the Cathars is well-established, [24] and it is likely that the Cathars' avoidance of marriage and procreation stemmed from a similar refusal of a life "degraded to mere survival" (Vaneigem 1998: 72), rather than from a "death-wish" or from contempt for life. This is suggested by the fact that the Cathars' anti-natalism was not associated with a degraded conception of women and sexuality, as it is often the case with philosophies that despise life and the body. Women had an important place in the sects. As for the Cathars' attitude toward sexuality, it seems that while the "perfected" abstained from intercourse, the other members were not expected to practice sexual abstinence, and some scorned the importance which the Church assigned to chastity, arguing that it implied an overvaluation of the body. Some heretics attributed a mystical value to the sexual act, even treating it like a sacrament (*Christeria*), and preached that practicing sex, rather than abstaining from it, was the best means to achieve a state of innocence. Thus, ironically, heretics were persecuted both as extreme ascetics and as libertines.

The sexual creeds of the Cathars were obviously a sophisticated elaboration of themes developed through the encounter with Eastern heretical religions, but the popularity they enjoyed and the influence they exercised on other heresies also speak of a wider experiential reality rooted in the conditions of marriage and reproduction in the Middle Ages.

We know that in medieval society, due to the limited availability of land and the protectionist restrictions which the guilds placed on entrance into the crafts, neither for the peasants nor for the artisans was it possible or desirable to have many children, and, indeed, efforts were made by peasant and artisan communities to control the number of children born among them. The most common method used to achieve this goal was the postponement of marriage, an event that, even among Orthodox Christians, came at a late age (if at all), the rule being "no land, no marriage" (Homans 1960: 37–39). A large number of young people, therefore, had to practice sexual abstinence or defy the Church's ban on sex outside of wedlock, and we can imagine that the heretical rejection of procreation must have found some resonance among them. In other words, it is conceivable that in the sexual and reproductive codes of the heretics we may actually see the traces of a medieval attempt at birth control. This would explain why, when population growth became a major social concern, at a time of severe demographic crisis and labor shortage in the late 14th century, heresy became associated with reproductive crimes, especially "sodomy," infanticide, and abortion. This is not to suggest that the heretics' reproductive doctrines had a decisive demographic impact; but rather, that for at least two centuries, a political climate was created in Italy, France, and Germany, whereby any form of contraception (including "sodomy," i.e. anal sex) came to be associated with heresy. The threat which the sexual doctrines of the heretics posed for the orthodoxy must also be viewed in the context of the efforts which the Church made to establish its control over marriage and sexuality, which enabled it to place everyone — from the Emperor to the poorest peasant — under its scrutiny and disciplinary rule.

The Politicization of Sexuality

As Mary Condren has pointed out in *The Serpent and the Goddess* (1989), a study of the penetration of Christianity into Celtic Ireland, the Church's attempt to regulate sexual behavior had a long history in Europe. From a very early period (after Christianity became a state religion in the 4th century), the clergy recognized the power that sexual desire gave women over men, and persistently tried to exorcise it by identifying holiness with avoidance of women and sex. Expelling women from any moment of the liturgy and from the administration of the sacraments; trying to usurp women's life-giving, magical powers by adopting a feminine dress; and making sexuality an object of shame — all these were the means by which a patriarchal caste tried to break the power of women and erotic attraction. In this process, "sexuality was invested with a new significance.... [It] became a subject for confession, where the minutest details of one's most intimate bodily functions became a topic for discussion" and where "the different aspects of sex were split apart into thought, word, intention, involuntary urges, and actual deeds of sex to form a science of sexuality" (Condren 1989: 86–87). A privileged site for the reconstruction of the Church's sexual canons are the Penitentials, the handbooks that, starting from the 7th century, were issued as practical guides for the confessors. In the first volume of his *History of Sexuality* (1978), Foucault stresses the role that these handbooks played in the production of sex as discourse and of a more polymorphous conception of sexuality in the 17th century. But the Penitentials were already instrumental to the production of a new sexual discourse

Punishment for adultery. The lovers are guided through the street tied to each other. From a 1296 manuscript from Toulouse, France.

in the Middle Ages. These works demonstrate that the Church attempted to impose a true sexual catechism, minutely prescribing the positions permitted during intercourse (actually only one was allowed), the days on which sex could be practiced, with whom it was permissible, and with whom forbidden.

This sexual supervision escalated in the 12th century when the Lateran Councils of 1123 and 1139 launched a new crusade against the common practice of clerical marriage and concubinage,[25] and declared marriage a *sacrament*, whose vows no power on earth could dissolve. At this time, the limitations imposed by the Penitentials on the sexual act were also reiterated.[26] Then, forty years later, with the III Lateran Council of 1179, the Church intensified its attack on "sodomy," targeting at once gay people and non-procreative sex (Boswell 1981: 277–86), and for the first time it condemned homosexuality ("the incontinence which is against nature") (Spencer 1995a: 114).

With the adoption of this repressive legislation sexuality was completely politicized. We do not have yet the morbid obsession with which the Catholic Church later approached sexual matters. But already by the 12th century we see the Church not only peeping into the bedroom of its flock, but making of sexuality a state matter. The unorthodox sexual choices of the heretics must also be seen, then, as an anti-authoritarian stand, an attempt the heretics made to wrench their bodies from the grip of the clergy. A clear example of this anti-clerical rebellion was the rise, in the 13th century, of new pantheist sects, like the Amalricians and the Brethren of the Free Spirit who, against the Church's effort to control sexual behavior, preached that God is in all of us and, consequently, that it is impossible for us to sin.

Women and Heresy

One of the most significant aspects of the heretic movement is the high status it assigned to women. As Gioacchino Volpe put it, in the Church women were nothing, but here they were considered equal; they had the same rights as men, and could enjoy a social life and mobility (wandering, preaching) that nowhere else was available to them in the Middle Ages (Volpe 1971: 20; Koch 1983: 247). In the heretical sects, above all among the Cathars and Waldenses, women had the right to administer the sacraments, preach, baptize and even acquire sacerdotal orders. It is reported that Waldes split from the orthodoxy because his bishop refused to allow women to preach, and it is said of the Cathars that they worshipped a female figure, the Lady of Thought, that influenced Dante's conception of Beatrice (Taylor 1954: 100). The heretics also allowed women and men to share the same dwellings, even if they were not married, since they did not fear that this would necessarily lead to promiscuous behavior. Heretical women and men often lived freely together, like brothers and sisters, as in the agapic communities of the early Church. Women also formed their own communities. A typical case was that of the Beguines, laywomen from the urban middle class who lived together (especially in Germany and Flanders), supporting themselves with their labor, outside of male control and without submitting to monastic rule (McDonnell 1954; Neel 1989).[27]

Not surprisingly, women are present in the history of heresy as in no other aspect of medieval life (Volpe 1971: 20). According to Gottfried Koch, already in the 10th century

Heretic woman condemned to be burned. Women had a large presence in the heretical movement in every country.

they formed a large part of the Bogomils. In the 11th century, it was again women who gave life to the heretical movements in France and Italy. At this time female heretics came from the most humble ranks of the serfs, and they constituted a true women's movement developing within the frame of the different heretic groups (Koch 1983: 246–47). Female heretics are also present in the records of the Inquisition; of some we know that they were burned, of others that they were "walled in" for the rest of their lives.

Can we say that this large female presence in the heretic sects was responsible for the heretics' "sexual revolution"? Or should we assume that the call for "free love" was a male ploy designed to gain easy access to women's sexual favors? These questions are not easily answered. We know, however, that women did try to control their reproductive function, as references to abortion and the use of contraceptives by women are numerous in the Penitentials. Significantly — in view of the future criminalization of such practices during the witch-hunt — contraceptives were referred to as "sterility potions" or *maleficia* (Noonan 1965: 155–61), and it was assumed that women were the ones who used them.

In the early Middle Ages, the Church still looked upon these practices with a certain indulgence, prompted by the recognition that women may wish to limit their births because of economic reasons. Thus, in the *Decretum*, written by Burchard, Bishop of Worms (circa 1010), after the ritual question —

> Have you done what some women are accustomed to do when they fornicate and wish to kill their offspring, act with their *maleficia*, and their herbs so that they kill or cut the embryo, or, if they have not yet conceived, contrive that they do not conceive? (Noonan 1965: 160)

— it was stipulated that the guilty ones should do penance for ten years; but it was also observed that "it makes a big difference whether she is a poor little woman and acted on account of the difficulty of feeding, or whether she acted to conceal a crime of fornication" (*ibid.*).

Things changed drastically, however, as soon as womens' control over reproduction seemed to pose a threat to economic and social stability, as it did in the aftermath of the demographic catastrophe produced by the "Black Death," the apocalyptic plague that, between 1347 and 1352, destroyed more than one third of the European population (Ziegler 1969: 230).

We will see later what role this demographic disaster played in the "labor crisis" of the late Middle Ages. Here we can notice that, after the spread of the plague, the sexual aspects of heresy became more prominent in its persecution, grotesquely distorted in ways that anticipate the later representations of the witches' Sabbat. By the mid-14th century the Inquisitors' reports were no longer content with accusing the heretics of sodomy and sexual license. Now heretics were accused of animal worship, including the infamous *bacium sub cauda* (the kiss under the tail), and of indulging in orgiastic rituals, night flights and child sacrifices (Russell 1972). The Inquisitors also reported the existence of a sect of devil-worshippers called Luciferans. Corresponding to this process, which marked the transition from the persecution of heresy to witch-hunting, the figure of the heretic increasingly became that of a woman, so that, by the beginning of the 15th century, the main target of the persecution against heretics became the witch.

This was not the end of the heretic movement, however. Its final consummation came in 1533, with the attempt by the Anabaptists to set up a City of God in the German town of Münster. This was crushed with a blood bath, followed by a wave of merciless reprisals that affected proletarian struggles all over Europe (Po-chia Hsia 1988a: 51–69).

Until then, neither the fierce persecution nor the demonization of heresy could prevent the dissemination of heretic beliefs. As Antonino De Stefano writes, excommunication, the confiscation of property, torture, death at the stake, the unleashing of crusades against heretics — none of these measures could undermine the "immense vitality and popularity" of the *haeretica pravitatis* (heretic evil) (De Stefano 1950: 769). "There is not one commune," wrote James de Vitry at the beginning of the 13th century, "in which heresy does not have its supporters, its defenders and believers." Even after the 1215 crusade against the Albigensians, that destroyed the Cathars' strongholds, heresy (together with Islam) remained the main enemy and threat the Church had to face. Its recruits came from all walks of life: the peasantry, the lower ranks of the clergy (who identified with the poor and brought to their struggles the language of the Gospel), the town burghers, and even the lesser nobility. But popular heresy was primarily a lower-class phenomenon. The environment in which it flourished was the rural and urban proletariat: peasants, cobblers, and cloth workers "to whom it preached equality, fomenting their spirit of revolt with prophetic and apocalyptic predictions" (*ibid.*: 776).

We get a glimpse of the popularity of the heretics from the trials which the Inquisition was still conducting in the 1330s, in the Trento region (Northern Italy), against those who had given hospitality to the Apostolics, when their leader, Fra Dolcino, had passed through the area thirty years before (Orioli 1993: 217–37). At the time of his coming, many doors had opened to give Dolcino and his followers shelter.

Again, in 1304, when announcing the coming of a holy reign of poverty and love, Fra Dolcino set up a community among the mountains of the Vercellese (Piedmont), the local peasants, already in revolt against the Bishop of Vercelli, gave him their support (Mornese and Buratti 2000). For three years the Dolcinians resisted the crusades and the blockade the Bishop mounted against them — with women in male attire fighting side by side with men. In the end, they were defeated only by hunger and by the over-whelming superiority of the forces the Church mobilized against them (Lea 1961: 615–20; Hilton 1973: 108). On the day when the troops amassed by the Bishop of Vercelli finally prevailed upon them, "more than a thousand heretics perished in the flames, or in the river, or by the sword, in the cruelest of deaths." Dolcino's companion, Margherita, was slowly burned to death before his eyes because she refused to abjure. Dolcino himself was slowly driven among the mountain roads and gradually torn to pieces, to provide a salutary example to the local population (Lea, 1961: 620).

Urban Struggles

Not only women and men but peasants and urban workers found in the heretic movement a common cause. This commonality of interests among people who could otherwise be assumed to have different concerns and aspirations can be accounted for on several grounds. First, in the Middle Ages, a tight relation existed between city and country. Many burghers were ex-serfs who had moved or fled to the city in the hope of a better life, and, while exercising their arts, continued to work the land, particularly at harvest time. Their thoughts and desires were still profoundly shaped by life in the village and by their con-tinuing relationship to the land. Peasants and urban workers were also brought together by the fact that they were subjected to the same political rulers, since by the 13th century (especially in Northern and Central Italy), the landed nobility and the urban patrician merchants were becoming assimilated, functioning as one power structure. This situation promoted among workers mutual concerns and solidarity. Thus, whenever the peasants rebelled they found beside themselves the artisans and day laborers, as well as the growing mass of the urban poor. This was the case during the peasant revolt in maritime Flanders, which began in 1323 and ended in June 1328, after the King of France and the Flemish nobility defeated the rebels at Cassel in 1327. As David Nicholas writes, "[t]he rebels' ability to continue the conflict for five years is conceivable only in the light of the city's involv-ment" (Nicholas 1992: 213–14). He adds that, by the end of 1324, the peasants in revolt had been joined by the craftsmen at Ypres and Bruges:

> Bruges, by now under the control of a weaver and fuller party, took direction of the revolt from the peasants.... A war of propaganda began, as monks and preachers told the masses that a new era had come and that they were the equals of the aristocrats (*ibid.*: 213–14).

Another peasant-urban worker alliance was that of the Tuchins, a movement of "bandits" operating in the mountains of Central France, in which artisans joined an organization that was typical of the rural populations (Hilton 1973: 128).

What united peasants and artisans was a common aspiration to the levelling of social differences. As Norman Cohn writes, this is evidenced in documents of various kinds:

> From the proverbs of the poor that lament that, "The poor man works always, worries and labours and weeps, never laughing from his heart, while the rich man laughs and sings..."
>
> From the miracle plays where it is stated that "...each man ought to have as much property as every other, and we have nothing we can call our own. The great lords have all the property and poor folk have nothing but suffering and adversity..."
>
> From the most widely read satires which denounced that, "Magistrates, provosts, beadles, mayors — nearly all live by robbery. They all batten on the poor, they all want to despoil them....The strong robs the weaker...." Or again: "Good working men make wheaten bread but they will never chew it; no, all they get is the siftings from the corn, and from good wine they get nothing but the dregs and from good cloth nothing but the chaff. Everything that is tasty and good goes to the nobles and the clergy...." (N. Cohn 1970: 99–100).

These complaints show how deep was the popular resentment against the inequalities that existed between the "big birds" and the "small birds," the "fat people" and the "lean people," as rich and poor were referred to in the Florentine political idiom of the 14th century. "Nothing will be well in England until we are of the same condition," John Ball proclaimed during his drive to organize the 1381 English Peasant Rising (*ibid.*: 199).

As we have seen, the main expressions of this aspiration to a more egalitarian society were the exaltation of poverty and the communism of goods. But the affirmation of an egalitarian perspective was also reflected in a new attitude towards work, most evident among the heretic sects. On one side, we have a "refusal of work" strategy, such as that adopted by the French Waldenses (the Poor of Lyon), and the members of some conventual orders (Franciscans, Spirituals), who, wishing to be free from mundane cares, relied on begging and community support for their survival. On the other, we have a new valorization of work, particularly manual labor, that achieved its most conscious formulations in the propaganda of the English Lollards, who reminded their followers that "The nobles have beautiful houses, we have only work and hardships, but it is from our work that everything comes" (*ibid.*; Christie-Murray 1976: 114–15).

Undoubtedly, the appeal to the "value of work" — a novelty in a society dominated by a military class — functioned primarily as a reminder of the arbitrariness of feudal power. But this new awareness also demonstrates the emergence of new social forces that played a crucial role in the downfall of the feudal system.

This valorization of work reflects the formation of an urban proletariat, made up in part of journeymen and apprentices — working under artisan masters, producing for the local market — but mostly by waged day-laborers, employed by rich merchants in industries producing for export. By the turn of the 14th century, in Florence, Siena, and Flanders, concentrations of up to 4,000 of such day-laborers (weavers, fullers, dyers) could be found in the textile industry. For them, life in the city was just a new type of serfdom, this time under the rule of the cloth merchants, who exercised the strictest control over their activities and the most despotic class rule. Urban wage-workers could not form any associations and were even forbidden to meet in any place and for any reason; they could not carry arms or even the tools of their trade; and they could not strike on pain of death (Pirenne 1956: 132). In Florence, they had no civil rights; unlike the journeymen, they were not part of any craft or guild, and they were exposed to the cruelest abuses at the hands of the merchants who, in addition to controlling the town government, ran their private tribunal and, with impunity, spied on them, arrested them, tortured them, and hanged them at the least sign of trouble (Rodolico 1971).

It is among these workers that we find the most extreme forms of social protest and the greatest acceptance of heretic ideas (*ibid.*: 56–59). Throughout the 14th century, particularly in the Flanders, cloth workers were engaged in constant rebellions against the bishop, the nobility, the merchants, and even the major crafts. At Bruges, when the main crafts gained power in 1348, wool workers continued to rebel against them. At Ghent, in 1335, a revolt by the local bourgeoisie was overtaken by a rebellion of weavers, who tried to establish a "workers' democracy" based on the suppression of all authorities, except those living by manual labor (Boissonnade 1927: 310–11). Defeated by an impressive coalition of forces (including the prince, the nobility, the clergy, the bourgeoisie), the weavers tried again in 1378, when they succeeded in establishing what (with some exaggeration, perhaps) has been called the first "dictatorship of the proletariat" known in history. Their goal, according to Prosper Boissonnade, was "to raise journeymen against masters, wage earners against great entrepreneurs, peasants against lords and clergy. It was said that they had contemplated the extermination of the whole bourgeois class, with the exception of children of six and the same for the nobles" (*ibid.*: 311). They were defeated only by a battle in the open field, at Roosebecque in 1382, where 26,000 of them lost their lives (*ibid.*).

The events at Bruges and Ghent were not isolated cases. In Germany and Italy as well, the artisans and laborers rebelled at every possible occasion, forcing the local bourgeoisie to live in a constant state of fear. In Florence, the workers seized power in 1379, led by the *Ciompi*, the day-laborers in the Florentine textile industry.[28] They too established a workers' government, but it lasted only a few months before being completely defeated by 1382 (Rodolico 1971). The workers at Liege, in the Low Countries, were more successful. In 1384, the nobility and the rich ("the great," as they were called), incapable of continuing a resistance which had lasted for more than a century, capitulated. From then on, "the crafts completely dominated the town," becoming the arbiter of the municipal government (Pirenne 1937: 201). The craftsmen had also given support to the peasants in revolt, in maritime Flanders, in a struggle that lasted from 1323 to 1328, which Pirenne describes as "a genuine attempt at a social revolution" (*ibid.*: 195). Here — according to a Flemish contemporary whose class allegiance is apparent — "the plague of insurrection was such that men became disgusted with life" (*ibid.*: 196). Thus, from 1320 to 1332, the "good people" of Ypres implored the king not to allow the town's inner bastions, within which they lived, to be demolished because they protected them from the "common people" (*ibid.*: 202–03).

Jaquerie. Peasants took arms in Flanders in 1323, in France in 1358, in England in 1381, in Florence, Ghent and Paris in 1370 and 1380.

The Black Death and the Labor Crisis

A turning point in the course of the medieval struggles was the Black Death, which killed, on an average, between 30% and 40% of the European population (Ziegler 1969: 230). Coming in the wake of the Great Famine of 1315–22, that weakened people's resistance to disease (Jordan 1996), this unprecedented demographic collapse profoundly changed Europe's social and political life, practically inaugurating a new era. Social hierarchies were turned upside down because of the levelling effects of the widespread morbidity. Familiarity with death also undermined social discipline. Confronted with the possibility of sudden death, people no longer cared to work or to abide by social and sexual regulations, but tried to have the best of times, feasting for as long as they could without thought of the future.

However, the most important consequence of the plague was the intensification of the labor crisis generated by the class conflict; for the decimation of the work-force made labor extremely scarce, critically increased its cost, and stiffened people's determination to break the shackles of feudal rule.

As Christopher Dyer points out, the scarcity of labor which the epidemic caused shifted the power relation to the advantage of the lower classes. When land had been scarce, the peasants could be controlled by the threat of expulsion. But after the population was decimated and land became abundant, the threats of the lords ceased to have any serious effect, as the peasants could now freely move and find new land to cultivate (Dyer 1968: 26). Thus, while the crops were rotting and livestock wandered in the fields, peasants and artisans suddenly became masters of the situation. A symptom of this new development was the growth of rent strikes, bolstered by threats of a mass exodus to other lands or to the city. As the manorial records laconically registered, the peasants "refused to pay" (*negant solvere*). They also declared that they "will not follow the customs any longer" (*negant consuetudines*), and ignored the orders of the lords to repair their houses, clean ditches, or chase escaped serfs (*ibid.*: 24).

By the end of the 14th century the refusal of rent and services had become a collective phenomenon. Entire villages jointly organized to stop paying fines, taxes and tallage, and no longer recognized the commuted services, or the injunctions of the manorial courts, which were the main instrument of feudal power. In this context, the quantity of rent and services withheld became less important than the fact that the class relation, on which the feudal order was based, was subverted. This is how an early 16th-century writer, whose words reflect the viewpoint of the nobility, summed up the situation:

> The peasants are too rich... and do not know what obedience means;
> they don't take law into any account, they wish there were no nobles...
> and they would like to decide what rent we should get for our lands
> (*ibid.*: 33).

In response to the increased cost of labor and the collapse of the feudal rent, various attempts were made to increase the exploitation of work, either through the restoration of labor services or, in some cases, the revival of slavery. In Florence, the importation of slaves was authorized in 1366.[29] But such measures only sharpened the class conflict. In England, it was an attempt by the nobility to contain the cost of labor, by means of a Labor Statute limiting the maximum wage, that caused the Peasant Rising of 1381. This spread from region to region and ended with thousands of peasants marching from Kent to London "to talk to the king" (Hilton 1973; Dobson 1983). Also in France, between 1379 and 1382, there was a "whirlwind of revolution" (Boissonnade 1927: 314). Proletarian insurrections exploded at Bezier, where forty weavers and cord-wainers were hanged. In Montpellier the workers in revolt proclaimed that "by Christmas we will sell Christian flesh at six pence a pound." Revolts broke out in Carcassone, Orleans, Amiens, Tournai, Rouen and finally in Paris, where in 1413 a "workers' democracy" came into power.[30] In Italy the most important revolt was that of the Ciompi. It began in July of 1382, when cloth-workers in Florence for a time forced the bourgeoisie to give them a share of government and declare a moratorium on all debts incurred by wage earners; they then proclaimed what, in essence, was a dictatorship of the proletariat ("God's people"), though one soon crushed by the combined forces of the nobility and the bourgeoisie (Rodolico 1971).

"Now is the time" — the sentence that recurs in the letters of John Ball — well illustrates the spirit of the European proletariat at the close of the 14th century, a time when, in Florence, the wheel of fortune was beginning to appear on the walls of taverns and work-shops, to symbolize the imminent change of lot.

In the course of this process, the political horizon and the organizational dimensions of the peasant and artisan struggle broadened. Entire regions revolted, forming assemblies and recruiting armies. At times, the peasants organized in bands, attacking the castles of the lords, and destroying the archives where the written marks of their servitude were kept. By the 15th century the confrontation between the peasants and the nobility turned into true wars, like that of the *remensas* in Spain, that lasted from 1462 to 1486.[31] In Germany a cycle of "peasant wars" began in 1476 with the conspiracy led by Hans

The Black Death destroyed one-third of the population of Europe. It was a turning point in European history, socially and politically.

the Piper. This escalated into four bloody rebellions led by Bundschuch ("Peasant Union") between 1493 and 1517, and culminating in a full-fledged war that lasted from 1522 to 1525, spreading over four countries (Engels 1977; Blickle 1977).

In all these cases, the rebels did not content themselves with demanding some restrictions to feudal rule, nor did they only bargain for better living conditions. Their aim was to put an end to the power of the lords. As the English peasants declared during the Peasant Rising of 1381, "the old law must be abolished." Indeed, by the beginning of the 15th century, in England at least, serfdom or villeinage had almost completely disappeared, though the revolt had been politically and militarily defeated and its leaders brutally executed (Titow 1969: 58).

What followed has been described as the "golden age of the European proletariat" (Marx 1909, Vol. I; Braudel 1967: 128ff.), a far cry from the canonic representation of the 15th century, which has been iconographically immortalized as a world under the spell of the dance of death and *memento mori*.

Thorold Rogers has painted a utopian image of this period in his famous study of wages and living conditions in medieval England. "At no time," Rogers wrote, "were wages [in England] so high and food so cheap" (Rogers 1894: 326ff). Workers sometimes were paid for every day of the year, although on Sunday and the main holidays they did not work. They were also fed by their employers, and were paid a *viaticum* for coming and going from home to work, at so much per mile of distance. In addition, they demanded to be paid in money, and wanted to work only five days a week.

As we shall see, there are reasons to be skeptical about the extent of this cornucopia. However, for a broad section of the western European peasantry, and for urban workers, the 15th century was a period of unprecedented power. Not only did the scarcity of labor give them the upper hand, but the spectacle of employers competing for their services strengthened their sense of self-value, and erased centuries of degradation and sub-servience. The 'scandal' of the high wages the workers demanded was only matched, in the eyes of the employers, by the new arrogance they displayed — their refusal to work, or to continue to work after having satisfied their needs (which they now could do more quickly because of their higher wages); their stubborn determination to hire themselves out only for limited tasks, rather than for prolonged periods of time; their demands for other perks beside their wages; and their ostentatious clothing which, according to the complaints of contemporary social critics, made them indistinguishable from the lords. "Servants are now masters and masters are servants," complained John Gower in *Mirour de l'omme* (1378), "the peasant pretends to imitate the ways of the freeman, and gives himself the appearance of him in his clothes" (Hatcher 1994: 17).

The condition of the landless also improved after the Black Death (Hatcher 1994). This was not just an English phenomenon. In 1348 the canons of Normandy complained that they could not find anyone to cultivate their lands who did not ask for more than what six servants had earned at the beginning of the century. Wages doubled and trebled in Italy, France and Germany (Boissonnade 1927: 316–20). In the lands of the Rhine and Danube, the daily agricultural wage became equivalent in purchasing power to the price of a pig or sheep, and these wage rates applied to women as well, for the differential between female and male earnings was drastically reduced in the wake of the Black Death.

What this meant for the European proletariat was not only the achievement of a standard of living that remained unparalleled until the 19th century, but the demise of serfdom. By the end of the 14th century land bondage had practically disappeared (Marx 1909, Vol. I: 788). Everywhere serfs were replaced by free farmers — copy holders or lease holders — who would accept work only for a substantial reward.

Sexual Politics, the Rise of the State and Counter-Revolution

However, by the end of the 15th century, a counter-revolution was already under way at every level of social and political life. First, efforts were made by the political authorities to co-opt the youngest and most rebellious male workers, by means of a vicious sexual politics that gave them access to free sex, and turned class antagonism into an antagonism against proletarian women. As Jacques Rossiaud has shown in *Medieval Prostitution* (1988), in France, the municipal authorities practically *decriminalized rape*, provided the victims were women of the lower class. In 14th-century Venice, the rape of an unmarried prole-tarian woman rarely called for more than a slap on the wrist, even in the frequent case in which it involved a group assault (Ruggiero 1989: 91–108). The same was true in most French cities. Here, the gang-rape of proletarian women became a common practice which the perpetrators would carry out openly and loudly at night, in groups of two to fifteen, breaking into their victims' homes, or dragging their victims through the streets, without any attempt to hide or disguise themselves. Those who engaged in these "sports" were young journeymen or domestic servants, and the penniless sons of well-to-do families, while the women targeted were poor girls, working as maids or washerwomen, of whom it was rumored that they were "kept" by their masters (Rossiaud 1988: 22). On average, half of the town male youth, at some point, engaged in these assaults, which Rossiaud describes as a form of class protest, a means for proletarian men — who were forced to postpone marriage for many years because of their economic conditions — to get back "their own," and take revenge against the rich. But the results were destructive for all workers, as the state-backed raping of poor women undermined the class solidarity that had been achieved in the anti-feudal struggle. Not surprisingly, the authorities viewed the disturbances caused by such policy (the brawls, the presence of youth gangs roaming the streets at night in search of adventure and disturbing the public quiet) as a small price to pay in exchange for a lessening of social tensions, obsessed as they were with the fear of urban insurrections, and the belief that if the poor gained the upper hand they would take their wives and hold them in common (*ibid.*: 13).

For proletarian women, so cavalierly sacrificed by masters and servants alike, the price to be paid was inestimable. Once raped, they could not easily regain their place in society. Their reputation being destroyed, they would have to leave town or turn to prostitution (*ibid.*; Ruggiero 1989: 99). But they were not the only ones to suffer. The legalization of rape created a climate of intense misogyny that degraded all women regardless of class. It also desensitized the population to the perpetration of violence against women,

Brothel, from a 15th-century German woodcut. Brothels were seen as a remedy for social protest, heresy, and homosexuality.

preparing the ground for the witch-hunt which began in this same period. It was at the end of the 14th century that the first witch-trials took place, and for the first time the Inquisition recorded the existence of an all-female heresy and sect of devil-worshippers.

Another aspect of the divisive sexual politics that the princes and municipal authorities pursued to diffuse workers' protest was the institutionalization of prostitution, implemented through the opening of municipal brothels soon proliferating throughout Europe. Enabled by the contemporary high-wage regime, state-managed prostitution was seen as a useful remedy for the turbulence of proletarian youth, who in *"la Grand Maison"* — as the state-brothel was called in France — could enjoy a privilege previously reserved for older men (Rossiaud 1988). The municipal brothel was also considered a remedy against homosexuality (Otis 1985), which in several European towns (e.g., Padua and Florence) was widely and publicly practiced, but in the aftermath of the Black Death was beginning to be feared as a cause of depopulation.[32]

Thus, between 1350–1450, publicly managed, tax-financed brothels were opened in every town and village in Italy and France, in numbers far superior to those reached in the 19th century. Amiens alone had 53 brothels in 1453. In addition, all the restrictions and penalties against prostitution were eliminated. Prostitutes could now solicit their clients in every part of town, even in front of the church during Mass. They were no longer bound to any particular dress codes or the wearing of distinguishing marks, because prostitution was officially recognized as a public service (*ibid.*: 9–10).

Even the Church came to see prostitution as a legitimate activity. The state-managed brothel was believed to provide an antidote to the orgiastic sexual practices of the heretic sects, and to be a remedy for sodomy, as well as a means to protect family life.

It is difficult retrospectively to tell how far playing the "sex card" helped the state to discipline and divide the medieval proletariat. What is certain is that this sexual "new deal" was part of a broader process which, in response to the intensification of social conflict, led to the centralization of the state, as the only agent capable of confronting the generalization of the struggle and safeguarding the class relation.

In this process, as we will see later in this work, the state became the ultimate manager of class relations, and the supervisor of the reproduction of labor-power — a function it has continued to perform to this day. In this capacity, state officers passed laws in many countries that set limits to the cost of labor (by fixing the maximum wage), forbid vagrancy (now harshly punished) (Geremek 1985: 61ff), and encouraged workers to reproduce.

Ultimately, the mounting class conflict brought about a new alliance between the bourgeoisie and the nobility, without which proletarian revolts may not have been defeated. It is difficult, in fact, to accept the claim, often made by historians, according to which these struggles had no chance of success due to the narrowness of their political horizons and the "confused nature of their demands." In reality, the objectives of the peasants and artisans were quite transparent. They demanded that "every man should have as much as another" (Pirenne 1937: 202) and, in order to achieve this goal, they joined with all those "who had nothing to lose," acting in concert, in different regions, not afraid to confront the well-trained armies of the nobility, despite their lack of military skills.

If they were defeated, it was because all the forces of feudal power — the nobility, the Church, and the bourgeoisie — moved against them united, despite their traditional divisions, by their fear of proletarian rebellion. Indeed, the image, that has been handed down to us, of a bourgeoisie perennially at war with the nobility, and carrying on its banners the call for equality and democracy, is a distortion. By the late Middle Ages, wherever we turn, from Tuscany to England and the Low Countries, we find the bourgeoisie already allied with the nobility in the suppression of the lower classes.[33] For in the peasants and the democratic weavers and cobblers of its cities, the bourgeoisie recognized an enemy far more dangerous than the nobility — one that made it worthwhile for the burghers even to sacrifice their cherished political autonomy. Thus, it was the urban bourgeoisie, after two centuries of struggles waged in order to gain full sovereignty within the walls of its communes, who reinstituted the power of the nobility, by voluntarily submitting to the rule of the Prince, the first step on the road to the absolute state.

Endnotes

1. The best example of a maroon society was the Bacaude who took over Gaul around the year 300 A.D. (Dockes 1982: 87). Their story is worth remembering. These were free peasants and slaves, who, exasperated by the hardships they suffered due to the skirmishes between the contenders to Rome's imperial throne, wandered off, armed with farm implements and stolen horses, in roving bands (hence their name: "band of fighters") (Randers–Pehrson 1983: 26). Townspeople joined them and they formed self-governing communities, where they struck coins, with "Hope" written on their face, elected leaders, and administered justice. Defeated in the open field by Maximilian, the colleague of the emperor Diocletian, they turned to "guerrilla" warfare, to resurface, in full force in the 5th century, when they became the target of repeated military actions. In 407 A.D., they were the protagonists of a "ferocious insurrection." The emperor Constantine defeated them in battle in Armorica (Brittany) (*ibid.*: 124). Here "rebellious slaves and peasants [had] created an autonomous 'state' organization, expelling the Roman officials, expropriating the landowners, reducing the slave holders to slavery, and [organizing] a judicial system and an army" (Dockes 1982: 87). Despite the many attempts made to repress them, the Bacaude were never completely defeated. The Roman emperors had to engage tribes of 'barbarian' invaders to subdue them. Constantine recalled the Visigoths from Spain and gave them generous donations of land in Gaul, hoping they would bring the Bacaude under control. Even the Huns were recruited to hunt them down (Renders–Pehrson 1983: 189). But we find the Bacaude again fighting with the Visigoths and Alans against the advancing Attila.

2. The *ergastula* were the dwelling of the slaves in the Roman villas. They were "subterranean prisons" in which the slaves slept in chains; they had windows so high (in the description of a contemporary landowner) that the slaves could not reach them (Dockes 1982: 69). They "were... found almost everywhere," in the regions the Romans conquered "where the slaves far outnumbered the free men" (*ibid.*: 208). The name *ergastolo* is still used in the Italian criminal justice vocabulary; it means "life sentence."

3. This is what Marx writes in *Capital,* Vol. III, in comparing the serf economy with the slave and the capitalist economies. "To what extent the laborer, the self-sustaining

serf, can here secure for himself a surplus above his indispensable necessities of life... depends, other circumstances remaining unchanged, upon the proportion in which his labor time is divided into labor time for himself and forced labor time for his feudal lord.... Under such conditions the surplus labor cannot be filched from [the serfs] by any economic measures, but must be forced from them by other measures, whatever may be the form assumed by them" (Marx 1909, Vol. III: 917–18).

4. For a discussion of the importance of the commons and common rights in England, see Joan Thirsk (1964), Jean Birrell (1987), and J.M. Neeson (1993). The ecological and eco-feminist movements have given the commons a new political significance. For an eco-feminist perspective on the importance of the commons in the economy of women's lives, see Vandana Shiva (1989).

5. For a discussion of social stratification among the European peasantry see R. Hilton (1985: 116–17, 141–51) and J.Z. Titow (1969: 56–59). Of special importance is the distinction between *personal* freedom and *tenurial* freedom. The former meant that a peasant was not a serf, though s/he may still be bound to provide labor services. The latter meant that a peasant held land that was not "burdened" by servile obligations. In practice, the two tended to coincide, but this began to change after the commutation when free peasants, to expand their holdings, began to acquire lands that carried servile burdens. Thus, "We do find peasants of free personal status (*liberi*) holding villein land and we do find villeins (*villani, nativi*) holding freehold land, though both these occurrences are rare and both were frowned upon" (Titow 1969: 56–57).

6. Barbara Hanawalt's examination of the wills from Kibworth (England) in the 15th century, shows that "men favored mature sons in 41 percent of their wills, while they left to the wife alone or the wife with a son the estate in 29 percent of the cases" (Hanawalt 1986b: 155).

7. Hanawalt sees the medieval marital relationship among peasants as a "partnership." "Land transactions in manorial courts indicate a strong practice of mutual responsibility and decision making.... Husband and wife also appear in purchasing or leasing pieces of land either for themselves or for their children" (Hanawalt 1986b: 16). For women's contribution to agricultural labor and control over their surplus produce also see Shahar (1983: 239–42). For women's extralegal contributions to their households, see B. Hanawalt (1986b:12). In England, "illegal gleaning was the most common way for a woman to get extra grain for her family" (*ibid.*).

8. This is the limit of some of the otherwise excellent studies produced, in recent years, on women in the Middle Ages, by a new generation of feminist historians. Understandably, the difficulty in presenting a synthetic view of a field whose empirical contours are still being reconstructed has led to a preference for descriptive analyses focussing on the main classifications of women's social life: "the mother," "the worker," "women in the rural areas," "women in the cities," often treated as if abstracted from social and economic change and social struggle.

9. As J. Z. Titow writes in the case of the English bonded peasants: "It is not difficult to see why the personal aspect of villeinage would be overshadowed by the problem of labour services in the minds of the peasants.... Disabilities arising out of unfree status would come into operation only sporadically.... Not so with the labour services, particularly week-work, which obliged a man to work for his landlord so many days a

week, every week, in addition to rendering other occasional services" (Titow 1969: 59).

10. "[T]ake the first few pages of the Abbots Langley rolls: men were fined for not coming to the harvest, or for not producing a sufficient number of men; they came late and when they did come performed the work badly or in an idle fashion. Sometimes not one but a whole group failed to appear and so left the lord's crop ungarnered. Others even when they came made themselves very unpleasant" (Bennett 1967: 112).

11. The distinction between "town" and "city" is not always clear. For our purposes the city is a population center with a royal charter, an episcopal see and a market, whereas a town is a population center (usually smaller than a city) with a regular market.

12. The following is a statistical picture of rural poverty in 13th-century Picardy: indigents and beggars, 13%; owners of small parcels of land, so unstable economically that a bad harvest is a threat to their survival, 33%; peasants with more land but without draught animals, 36%; wealthy farmers 19% (Geremek 1994: 57). In England, in 1280, peasants with less than three acres of land — not enough to feed a family — represented 46% of the peasantry (*ibid.*).

13. A silk spinners' song gives a graphic picture of the poverty in which female unskilled laborers lived in the towns:

> Always spinning sheets of silk
> We shall never be better dressed
> But always naked and poor,
> And always suffering hunger and thirst (Geremeck 1994: 65).

In French municipal archives, spinners and other female wage workers were associated with prostitutes, possibly because they lived alone and had no family structure behind them. In the towns, women suffered not only poverty but loss of kin, which left them vulnerable to abuse (Hughes 1975: 21; Geremek 1994: 65–66; Otis 1985: 18–20; Hilton 1985: 212–13).

14. For an analysis of women in the medieval guilds, see Maryanne Kowaleski and Judith M. Bennett (1989); David Herlihy (1995); and Williams and Echols (2000).

15. (Russell 1972: 136; Lea 1961: 126–27). Also the movement of the Pastoureaux was provoked by events in the East, this time the capture of King Louis IX of France by the Moslems, in Egypt, in 1249 (Hilton 1973: 100–02). A movement made of "humble and simple" people was organized to free him, but it quickly took on an anticlerical character. The Pastoreaux reappeared in Southern France in the spring and summer of 1320, still "directly influenced by the crusading atmosphere.... [They] had no chance of crusading in the east; instead, they spent their energies on attacking the Jewish communities of south-west France, Navarre and Aragon, often with the complicity of local consulates, before being wiped out or dispersed by royal officials" (Barber 1992: 135–36).

16. The Crusade against the Albigensians (Cathars from the town of Albi, in southern France) was the first large-scale attack against the heretics, and the first Crusade against Europeans. Pope Innocent III launched it in the regions of Toulouse and Montpellier after 1209. In its wake, the persecution of heretics dramatically intensified. In 1215, on the occasion of the fourth Lateran Council, Innocent III inserted in the council's canons a set of measures that condemned heretics to exile, to the confiscation of their properties, and excluded them from civil life. Later, in 1224,

the emperor Frederick II joined the persecution with the constitution *Cum ad conservandum* that defined heresy a crime of *lesa maiestatis*, to be punished with death by fire. In 1229, the Council of Toulouse established that heretics should be identified and punished. Proven heretics and their protectors were to burned at the stake. The house where a heretic was discovered was to be destroyed, and the land upon which it was built confiscated. Those who reneged their beliefs were to be immured, while those who relapsed were to suffer the supplice of fire. Then, in 1231-1233, Gregorio IX instituted a special tribunal with the specific function of eradicating heresy: the Inquisition. In 1252, Pope Innocent IV, with the consensus of the main theologians of the time, authorized the use of torture against heretics (Vauchez 1990: 163, 164, 165).

17. André Vauchez attributes the "success" of the Inquisition to its procedure. The arrest of suspects was prepared with utmost secrecy. At first, the persecution consisted of raids against heretics' meetings, organized in collaboration with public authorities. Later, when Waldenses and Cathars had already been forced to go underground, suspects were called in front of a tribunal without being told the reasons for their convocation. The same secrecy characterized the investigative process. The defendants were not told the charges moved against them, and those who denounced them were allowed to maintain their anonymity. Suspects were released, if they informed against their accomplices and promised to keep silent about their confessions. Thus, when heretics were arrested they could never know if anyone from their congregation had spoken against them (Vauchez 1990: 167–68). As Italo Mereu points out, the work of the Roman Inquisition left deep scars in the history of European culture, creating a climate of intolerance and institutional suspicion that continues to corrupt the legal system to this day. The legacy of the Inquisition is a culture of suspicion that relies on anonymous charges and preventive detention, and treats suspects as if already proven guilty (Mereu 1979).

18. Let us recall here Friedrich Engels' distinction between the heretical beliefs of peasants and artisans, associated with their opposition to feudal authority, and those of the town burghers, that were primarily a protest against the clergy (Engels 1977: 43).

19. The politicization of poverty, together with the rise of a money-economy, brought about a decisive change in the attitude of the Church towards the poor. Until the 13th century, the Church exalted poverty as a holy state and engaged in distributions of alms, trying to convince the rustics to accept their situation and not envy the rich. In Sunday sermons, priests were prodigal with tales like that of the poor Lazarus sitting in heaven at the side of Jesus, and watching his rich but stingy neighbor burning in flames. The exaltation of *sancta paupertas* ("holy poverty") also served to impress on the rich the need for charity as a means for salvation. This tactic procured the Church substantial donations of land, buildings and money, presumably to be used for distribution among the needy, and it enabled it to become one of the richest institutions in Europe. But when the poor grew in numbers and the heretics started to challenge the Church's greed and corruption, the clergy dismissed its homilies about poverty and introduced many "distinguo." Starting in the 13th century, it affirmed that only voluntary poverty has merit in the eyes of God, as a sign of humility and contempt for material goods; this meant, in practice, that help would now

be given only to the "deserving poor," that is, to the impoverished members of the nobility, and not to those begging in the streets or at city gates. The latter were increasingly looked upon with suspicion as guilty of laziness or fraud.

20. Much controversy took place among the Waldenses on the correct ways of supporting oneself. It was resolved, at the Bergamo Meeting of 1218, with a major split between the two main branches of the movement. The French Waldenses (Poor of Lyon) opted for a life supported by alms, while those of Lombardy decided that one must live out of his/her own labor and proceeded to form workers' collectives or cooperatives (*congregationes laborantium*)(di Stefano 1950: 775). The Lombard Waldenses continued to maintain private possessions — houses and other forms of property — and they accepted marriage and the family (Little 1978: 125).

21. George Arthur Holmes 1975: 202; N. Cohn 1970: 215–17; Hilton 1973: 124. As described by Engels, the Taborites were the revolutionary, democratic wing of the Hussite national liberation movement against the German nobility in Bohemia. Of them, Engels tells us only that "[T]heir demands reflected the desire of the peasantry and the urban lower classes to end all feudal oppression" (Engels 1977: 44n). But their remarkable story is more fully narrated in H. C. Lea's *The Inquisition of the Middle Ages* (Lea 1961: 523–40), in which we read that they were peasants and poorfolk, who wanted no nobles or gentlemen in their ranks and had republican tendencies. They were called Taborites because in 1419, when the Hussites in Prague first came under attack, they moved on to Mount Tabor. There they founded a new town, that became a center of both resistance against the German nobility, and experimentation with communism. The story has it that, on arrival from Prague, they put out large open chests in which each was asked to place his/her possessions, so that all things could be held in common. Presumably, this collective arrangement was shortlived, but its spirit lived on longer after its demise (Demetz 1997:152-157).

The Taborites distinguished themselves from the more moderate Calixtins because they included among their objectives the independence of Bohemia, and the retention of the property which they had confiscated (Lea 1961: 530). They did agree, however, on the four articles of faith that united the Hussite movement in front of its foreign enemies:

I. Free preaching of the Word of God;

II. Communion in [both wine and bread];

III. The abolition of the clergy's dominion over temporal possessions and its return to the evangelical life of Christ and the apostles;

IV. The punishment of all offenses against divine law without exception of person or condition.

Unity was much needed. To stamp out the revolt of the Hussites, the Church, in 1421, sent against Taborites and Calixtins an army of 150,000. "Five times," Lea writes, "during 1421, the crusaders invaded Bohemia, and five times they were beaten back." Two years later, at the Council of Siena, the Church decided that, if the Bohemian heretics could not be defeated militarily, they should be isolated and starved out through a blockade. But that too failed and Hussite ideas continued to spread into Germany, Hungary, and the Slavic territories to the South. Another army

John Hus being martyred at Gottlieben on the Rhine in 1413. After his death, his ashes were thrown into the river.

of 100,000 was once more launched against them, in 1431, again to no avail. This time the crusaders fled the battlefield even before the battle started, on "hearing the battle hymn of the dreaded Hussite troops"(*ibid.*).

What, in the end, destroyed the Taborites were the negotiations that took place between the Church and the moderate wing of the Hussites. Cleverly, the ecclesiastic diplomats deepened the split between the Calixtins and the Taborites. Thus, when another crusade was launched against the Hussites, the Calixtins joined the Catholic barons in the pay of the Vatican, and exterminated their brothers at the Battle of Lipan, on May 30, 1434. On that day, more than 13,000 Taborites were left dead on the battlefield.

Women were very active in the Taborite movement as in all heretic movements. Many fought in the battle for Prague in 1420 when 1500 Taborite women dug a long trench which they defended with stones and pitchforks (Demetz 1997).

22. These words — "the most moving plea for social equality in the history of the English language," according to the historian R. B. Dobson — were actually put into John Ball's mouth to incriminate him and make him appear like a fool, by a contemporary French chronicler, Jean Froissart, a stern opponent of the English Peasants' Revolt. The first sentence of the sermon, which John Ball was said to have given many times, (in Lord Berners' 16th-century translation) is as follows: "Ah, ye good people, matters goeth not well to pass in England, nor shall do till

everyting be common, and that there be no villains nor gentlemen, but that we may be all united together, and that the lords be no greater masters than we be" (Dobson 1983: 371).

23. By 1210 the Church had labeled the demand for the abolition of the death penalty an heretical "error," which it attributed to the Waldenses and the Cathars. So strong was the presumption that the opponents of the Church were abolitionists that every heretic who wanted to submit to the Church had to affirm that "the secular power can, without mortal sin, exercise judgement of blood, provided that it punishes with justice, not out of hatred, with prudence, not precipitation" (Mergivern 1997: 101). As J. J. Mergiven points out, the heretical movement took the moral high ground on this question, and "forced the 'orthodox,' ironically, to take up the defense of a very questionable practice" (*ibid.*: 103).

24. Among the evidence proving the Bogomils' influence on the Cathars there are two works that "the Cathars of Western Europe took over from the Bogomils." They are: *The Vision of Isaiah* and *The Secret Supper*, cited in Wakefield and Evans's review of Catharist literature (1969: 447–465).

    The Bogomils were for the Eastern Church what the Cathars were for the Western. Aside from their Manicheanism and anti-natalism, the Byzantine authorities were most alarmed by the Bogomils'"radical anarchism," civil disobedience, and class hatred. As Presbyter Cosmas wrote, in his sermons against them: "They teach their own people not to obey their masters, they revile the wealthy, hate the king, ridicule the elders, condemn the boyars, regard as vile in the eyes of God those who serve the king, and forbid every serf to work for his lord." The heresy had a tremendous and long-term influence on the peasantry of the Balkans. "The Bogomils preached in the language of the people, and their message was understood by the people... their loose organisation, their attractive solution of the problem of evil, and their commitment to social protest made their movement virtually indestructible" (Browning 1975: 164-166). The influence of the Bogomils on heresy is traceable in the use, common by the 13th century, of "buggery," to connote first heresy and then homosexuality (Bullough 1976a: 76ff.).

25. The ban which the Church imposed upon clerical marriages and concubinage was motivated, more than by any need to restore its reputation, by the desire to defend its property, which was threatened by too many subdivisions, and by the fear that the wives of the priests might unduly interfere in clerical affairs (McNamara and Wemple 1988: 93-95). The ruling of the Second Lateran Council strenghtened a resolution that had already been adopted in the previous century, but had not been observed in the midst of an open revolt against this innovation. The protest had climaxed in 1061 with an "organized rebellion" leading to the election of the Bishop of Parma as Antipope, under the title of Honorious II, and his subsequent, failed attempt to capture Rome (Taylor 1954: 35). The Lateran Council of 1123 not only banned clerical marriages, but declared those existent invalid, throwing the priests' families, above all their wives and children, into a state of terror and destitution. (Brundage 1987: 214, 216–17).

26. The reforming canons of the 12th century ordered married couples to avoid sex during the three Lenten seasons associated with Easter, Pentacost and Christmas, on every

Sunday of the year, on feast days prior to receiving communion, on their wedding nights, during their wife's menstrual periods, during pregnancy, during lactation, and while doing penance (Brundage 1987: 198–99). These restrictions were not new. They were reaffirmations of the ecclesiastic wisdom embodied in dozens of Penitentials. What was novel was that they now became incorporated within the body of Canon Law "which was transformed into an effective instrument for Church government and discipline in the twelfth century." Both the Church and the laity recognized that a legal requirement with explicit penalties would have a different status than a penance suggested by one's confessor. In this period, the most intimate relations between people became a matter for lawyers and penologists (Brundage 1987: 578).

27. The relation between the Beguines and heresy is uncertain. While some of their contemporaries, like James de Vitry — described by Carol Neel as "an important ecclesiastical administrator" — supported their initiative as an alternative to heresy, "they were finally condemned on suspicion of heresy by the Council of Vienne of 1312, likely because of the clergy's intolerance of women who escaped male control. The Beguines subsequently disappeared, "forced out of existence by ecclesiastical reprobation" (Neel 1989: 324–27, 329, 333, 339).

28. The Ciompi were those who washed, combed, and greased the wool so that it could be worked. They were considered unskilled workers and had the lowest social status. "*Ciompo*" is a derogatory term, meaning dirty and poorly dressed, probably due to the fact that the "ciompi" worked half-naked and were always greasy and stained with dyes. Their revolt began in July 1382, sparked by the news that one of them, Simoncino, had been arrested and tortured. Apparently, under torture he had been made to reveal that the *ciompi* had held a secret meeting during which, kissing each other on the mouth, they had promised to defend each other from the abuses of their employers. Upon hearing of Simoncino's arrest, workers rushed to the guild hall of the wool industry (*Palazzo dell' Arte*), demanding that their comrade be released. Then, after securing his release, they occupied the guild hall, put patrols on Ponte Vecchio, and hung the insignia of the "minor guilds" (*arti minori*) from the windows of the guild hall. They also occupied the city hall where they claimed to have found a room full of nooses which, they believed, were meant for them. Seemingly in control of the situation, the *ciompi* presented a petition demanding that they become part of the government, that they no longer be punished by the cutting of a hand for non-payment of debts, that the rich pay more taxes, and that corporal punishment be replaced by monetary fines. In the first week of August, they formed a militia and set up three new crafts, while preparations were made for an election in which, for the first time, members of the *ciompi* would participate. Their new power, however, lasted no more than a month, as the wool magnates organized a lock-out that reduced them to hunger. After their defeat, many were arrested, hung and decapitated; many more had to leave the city in an exodus that marked the beginning of the decline of the wool industry in Florence (Rodolico 1971: passim).

29. In the aftermath of the Black Death, every European country began to condemn idleness, and to persecute vagabondage, begging, and refusal of work. England took the initiative with the Statute of 1349 that condemned high wages and idleness, establishing that those who did not work, and did not have any means of survival,

had to accept work. Similar ordinances were issued in France in 1351, when it was recommended that people should not give food or hostel to healthy beggars and vagabonds. A further ordinance in 1354 established that those who remained idle, passing their time in taverns, playing dice or begging, had to accept work or face the consequences; first offenders would be put in prison on bread and water, while second offenders would be put in the stocks, and third offenders would be branded on the forehead. In the French legislation a new element appeared that became part of the modern struggle against vagabonds: forced labor. In Castile, an ordinance introduced in 1387 allowed private people to arrest vagabonds and employ them for one month without wages (Geremek 1985: 53–65).

30. The concept of "workers' democracy" may seem preposterous when applied to these forms of government. But we should consider that in the U.S., which is often viewed as a democratic country, not one industrial worker has yet become President, and the highest governmental organs are all composed of representatives from an economic aristocracy.

31. The *remensas* was a redemption tax that the servile peasants in Catalonia had to pay to leave their holdings. After the Black Death, peasants subject to the *remensas* were also subjected to a new taxation known as the "five evil customs" (*los malos usos*) that, in earlier times, had been applied in a less generalized way (Hilton 1973: 117–18). These new taxes, and the conflicts revolving around the use of abandoned holdings were the source of a protracted, regional war, in the course of which the Catalonian peasants recruited one man from every three households. They also strengthened their ties by means of sworn associations, took decisions at peasant assemblies and, to intimidate the landowners, put up crosses and other threatening signs all over the fields. In the last phase of the war, they demanded the end of rent and the establishment of peasant property rights (*ibid.*: 120–21; 133).

32. Thus, the proliferation of public brothels was accompanied by a campaign against homosexuals that spread even to Florence, where homosexuality was an important part of the social fabric "attracting males of all ages, matrimonial conditions and social rank." So popular was homosexuality in Florence that prostitutes used to wear male clothes to attract their customers. Signs of a change in Florence were two initiatives which the authorities introduced in 1403, when the city banned "sodomites" from public office, and set up a watchdog commission devoted to the extirpation of homosexuality: the Office of Decency. But significantly, the main step which the office took was to make preparations for the opening of new public brothels, so that, by 1418, the authorities were still looking for means to eradicate sodomy "from the city and from the county" (Rocke 1997: 30–32, 35). On the Florentine government's promotion of publicly funded prostitution as a remedy against population decline and "sodomy," see also Richard C. Trexler (1993):

> Like other Italian cities of the fifteenth century, Florence
> believed that officially sponsored prostitution combatted two
> other evils of incomparably greater moral and social import:
> male homosexuality — whose practice was thought to obscure
> the difference between the sexes and thus all difference and

decorum — and the decline in the legitimate population which
resulted from an insufficient number of marriages (p.32).

Trexler points out that the same correlation between the spread of homosexuality, population decline, and the sponsorship of public prostitution can be found in late fourteenth-century, early fifteenth-century Lucca, Venice and Siena, and that the growth in the number and social power of prostitutes eventually led to a backlash, so that whereas

> [i]n the early fifteenth century preachers and statesmen [in Florence] had deeply believed that no city could long endure in which females and males seemed the same ... [a] century later [they] wondered if it could survive when [upper] class women could not be distinguished from brothel prostitutes (ibid.: 65).

33. In Tuscany, where the democratization of political life had proceeded further than in any other European region, by the second half of the 15th century, there was an inversion of this tendency and a restoration of the power of the nobility, promoted by the mercantile bourgeoisie to block the rise of the lower classes. By this time, an organic fusion had occurred between the families of the merchants and those of the nobility, achieved by means of marriages and the sharing of prerogatives. This put an end to that social mobility that had been the major achievement of urban society and communal life in medieval Tuscany (Luzzati 1981: 187, 206).

Albrecht Dürer, THE FALL OF MAN (1510).
This powerful scene, on the expulsion of Adam and Eve from the
Garden of Eden, evokes the expulsion of the peasantry from its common
lands, which was starting to occur across western Europe at the very time
when Dürer was producing this work.

The Accumulation of Labor and the Degradation of Women:
Constructing "Difference" in the "Transition to Capitalism"

> I demand whether all wars, bloodshed and misery came not upon the creation when one man endeavoured to be a lord over another?... And whether this misery shall not remove... when all the branches of mankind shall look upon the earth as one common treasury to all.
> —Gerrard Winstanley, *The New Law of Righteousness,* 1649

> To him she was a fragmented commodity whose feelings and choices were rarely considered: her head and her heart were separated from her back and her hands and divided from her womb and vagina. Her back and muscle were pressed into field labor... her hands were demanded to nurse and nurture the white man.... [H]er vagina, used for his sexual pleasure, was the gateway to the womb, which was his place of capital investment — the capital investment being the sex-act and the resulting child the accumulated surplus....
> —Barbara Omolade, "Heart of Darkness," 1983

Part One: Introduction

The development of capitalism was not the only possible response to the crisis of feudal power. Throughout Europe, vast communalistic social movements and rebellions against feudalism had offered the promise of a new egalitarian society built on social equality and cooperation. However, by 1525 their most powerful expression, the "Peasant War" in Germany or, as Peter Blickle called it, the "revolution of the common man," was crushed.[1] A hundred thousand rebels were massacred in retaliation. Then, in 1535, "New

Jerusalem," the attempt made by the Anabaptists in the town of Münster to bring the kingdom of God to earth, also ended in a bloodbath, first undermined presumably by the patriarchal turn taken by its leaders who, by imposing polygamy, caused women among their ranks to revolt.[2] With these defeats, compounded by the spreads of witch-hunts and the effects of colonial expansion, the revolutionary process in Europe came to an end. Military might was not sufficient, however, to avert the crisis of feudalism.

By the late Middle Ages the feudal economy was doomed, faced with an accumulation crisis that stretched for more than a century. We deduce its dimension from some basic estimates indicating that between 1350 and 1500 a major shift occurred in the power-relation between workers and masters. The real wage increased by 100%, prices declined by 33%, rents also declined, the length of the working-day decreased, and a tendency appeared toward local self-sufficiency.[3] Evidence of a chronic disaccumulation trend in this period is also found in the pessimism of the contemporary merchants and landowners, and the measures which the European states adopted to protect markets, suppress competition and force people to work at the conditions imposed. As the entries in the registers of the feudal manors recorded, "the work [was] not worth the breakfast" (Dobb 1963: 54). The feudal economy could not reproduce itself, nor could a capitalist society have "evolved" from it, for self-sufficiency and the new high-wage regime allowed for the "wealth of the people," but "excluded the possibility of capitalistic wealth" (Marx 1909, Vol.1: 789).

It was in response to this crisis that the European ruling class launched the global offensive that in the course of at least three centuries was to change the history of the planet, laying the foundations of a capitalist world-system, in the relentless attempt to appropriate new sources of wealth, expand its economic basis, and bring new workers under its command.

As we know, "conquest, enslavement, robbery, murder, in brief force" were the pillars of this process (*ibid.*: 785). Thus, the concept of a "transition to capitalism" is in many ways a fiction. British historians, in the 1940s and 1950s, used it to define a period — roughly from 1450 to 1650 — in which feudalism in Europe was breaking down while no new social-economic system was yet in place, though elements of a capitalist society were taking shape.[4] The concept of "transition," then, helps us to think of a prolonged process of change and of societies in which capitalist accumulation coexisted with political formations not yet predominantly capitalistic. The term, however, suggests a gradual, linear historical development, whereas the period it names was among the bloodiest and most discontinuous in world history — one that saw apocalyptic transformations and which historians can only describe in the harshest terms: the Iron Age (Kamen), the Age of Plunder (Hoskins), and the Age of the Whip (Stone). "Transition," then, cannot evoke the changes that paved the way to the advent of capitalism and the forces that shaped them. In this volume, therefore, I use the term primarily in a temporal sense, while I refer to the social processes that characterized the "feudal reaction" and the development of capitalist relations with the Marxian concept of "primitive accumulation," though I agree with its critics that we must rethink Marx's interpretation of it.[5]

Marx introduced the concept of "primitive accumulation" at the end of *Capital* Volume I to describe the social and economic restructuring that the European ruling class initiated in response to its accumulation crisis, and to establish (in polemics with Adam Smith)[6] that: (i) capitalism could not have developed without a prior concentration of capital and labor; and that (ii) the divorcing of the workers from the means of production, not the abstinence of the rich, is the source of capitalist wealth. Primitive accumulation, then, is a useful concept, for it connects the "feudal reaction" with the development of a capitalist economy, and it identifies the *historical* and *logical* conditions for the development of the capitalist system, "primitive" ("originary") indicating a precondition for the existence of capitalist relations as much as a specific event in time.[7]

Marx, however, analyzed primitive accumulation almost exclusively from the viewpoint of the waged industrial proletariat: the protagonist, in his view, of the revolutionary process of his time and the foundation for the future communist society. Thus, in his account, primitive accumulation consists essentially in the expropriation of the land from the European peasantry and the formation of the "free," independent worker, although he acknowledged that:

> The discovery of gold and silver in America, the extirpation, enslavement and entombment in mines of the aboriginal population, [of America], the beginning of the conquest and looting of the East Indies, the turning of Africa into a preserve for the commercial hunting of black skins, are... the chief moments of primitive accumulation... (Marx 1909, Vol. I: 823).

Marx also recognized that "[a] great deal of capital, which today appears in the United States without any certificate of birth, was yesterday in England the capitalised blood of children" (*ibid.*: 829–30). By contrast, we do not find in his work any mention of the profound transformations that capitalism introduced in the reproduction of labor-power and the social position of women. Nor does Marx's analysis of primitive accumulation mention the "Great Witch-Hunt" of the 16th and 17th centuries, although this state-sponsored terror campaign was central to the defeat of the European peasantry, facilitating its expulsion from the lands it once held in common.

In this chapter and those that follow, I discuss these developments, especially with reference to Europe, arguing that:

I.   The expropriation of European workers from their means of subsistence, and the enslavement of Native Americans and Africans to the mines and plantations of the "New World," were not the only means by which a world proletariat was formed and "accumulated."

II. This process required the transformation of the body into a work-machine, and the subjugation of women to the reproduction of the work-force. Most of all, it required the destruction of the power of women which, in Europe as in America, was achieved through the extermination of the "witches."

III. Primitive accumulation, then, was not simply an accumulation and concentration of exploitable workers and capital. It was *also an accumulation of differences and divisions within the working class*, whereby hier-

archies built upon gender, as well as "race" and age, became constitutive of class rule and the formation of the modern proletariat.

IV. We cannot, therefore, identify capitalist accumulation with the liberation of the worker, female or male, as many Marxists (among others)
have done, or see the advent of capitalism as a moment of historical
progress. On the contrary, capitalism has created more brutal and insid-
ious forms of enslavement, as it has planted into the body of the proletariat deep divisions that have served to intensify and conceal
exploitation. It is in great part because of these imposed divisions —
especially those between women and men — that capitalist accumulation continues to devastate life in every corner of the planet.

Capitalist Accumulation and the Accumulation of Labor in Europe

Capital, Marx wrote, comes on the face of the earth dripping blood and dirt from head
to toe (1909, Vol. 1: 834) and, indeed, when we look at the beginning of capitalist development, we have the impression of being in an immense concentration camp. In the
"New World" we have the subjugation of the aboriginal populations to the regimes of
the *mita* and *cuatelchil*[8] under which multitudes of people were consumed to bring silver
and mercury to the surface in the mines of Huancavelica and Potosi. In Eastern Europe,
we have a "second serfdom," tying to the land a population of farmers who had never
previously been enserfed.[9] In Western Europe, we have the Enclosures, the Witch-Hunt,
the branding, whipping, and incarceration of vagabonds and beggars in newly constructed work-houses and correction houses, models for the future prison system. On
the horizon, we have the rise of the slave trade, while on the seas, ships are already trans-
porting indentured servants and convicts from Europe to America.

What we deduce from this scenario is that force was the main lever, the main economic power in the process of primitive accumulation[10] because capitalist development
required an immense leap in the wealth appropriated by the European ruling class and
the number of workers brought under its command. In other words, primitive accumulation consisted in an immense accumulation of labor-power — "dead labor" in the form
of stolen goods, and "living labor" in the form of human beings made available for
exploitation — realized on a scale never before matched in the course of history.

Significantly, the tendency of the capitalist class, during the first three centuries of
its existence, was to impose slavery and other forms of coerced labor as the dominant
work relation, a tendency limited only by the workers' resistance and the danger of the
exhaustion of the work-force.

This was true not only in the American colonies, where, by the 16th century,
economies based on coerced labor were forming, but in Europe as well. Later, I examine
the importance of slave-labor and the plantation system in capitalist accumulation. Here
I want to stress that in Europe, too, in the 15th century, slavery, never completely abolished,
was revitalized.[11]

As reported by the Italian historian Salvatore Bono, to whom we owe the most extensive study of slavery in Italy, there were numerous slaves in the Mediterranean areas in the 16th and 17th centuries, and their numbers grew after the Battle of Lepanto (1571) that escalated the hostilities against the Muslim world. Bono calculates that more than 10,000 slaves lived in Naples and 25,000 in the Napolitan kingdom as a whole (one per cent of the population), and similar figures apply to other Italian towns and to southern France. In Italy, a system of public slavery developed whereby thousands of kidnapped foreigners — the ancestors of today's undocumented immigrant workers — were employed by city governments for public works, or were farmed out to private citizens who employed them in agriculture. Many were destined for the oars, an important source of such employment being the Vatican fleet (Bono 1999: 6–8).

Slavery is "that form [of exploitation] towards which the master always strives" (Dockes 1982: 2). Europe was no exception. This must be emphasized to dispel the assumption of a special connection between slavery and Africa.[12] But in Europe slavery remained a limited phenomenon, as the material conditions for it did not exist, although the employers' desires for it must have been quite strong if it took until the 18th century before slavery was outlawed in England. The attempt to bring back serfdom failed as well, except in the East, where population scarcity gave landlords the upper hand.[13] In the West its restoration was prevented by peasant resistance culminating in the "German Peasant War." A broad organizational effort spreading over three countries (Germany, Austria, Switzerland) and joining workers from every field (farmers, miners, artisans, including the best German and Austrian artists),[14] this "revolution of the common man" was a watershed in European history. Like the 1917 Bolshevik Revolution in Russia, it shook the powerful to the core, merging in their consciousness with the Anabaptists takeover of Münster, which confirmed their fears that an international conspiracy was underway to overthrow their power.[15] After its defeat, which occurred in the same year as the conquest of Peru, and which was commemorated by Albrecht Dürer with the "Monument to the Vanquished Peasants" (Thea 1998: 65; 134–35), the revenge was merciless. "Thousands of corpses laid on the ground from Thuringia to Alsace, in the fields, in the woods, in the ditches of a thousand dismantled, burned castles," "murdered, tortured, impaled, martyred" (*ibid.*: 153, 146). But the clock could not be turned back. In various parts of Germany and the other territories that had been at the center of the "war," customary rights and even forms of territorial government were preserved.[16]

This was an exception. Where workers' resistance to re-enserfment could not be broken, the response was the expropriation of the peasantry from its land and the introduction of forced wage-labor. Workers attempting to hire themselves out independently or leave their employers were punished with incarceration and even with death, in the case of recidivism. A "free" wage labor-market did not develop in Europe until the 18th century, and even then, contractual wage-work was obtained only at the price of an intense struggle and by a limited set of laborers, mostly male and adult. Nevertheless, the fact that slavery and serfdom could not be restored meant that the labor crisis that had characterized the late Middle Ages continued in Europe into the 17th century, aggravated by the fact that the drive to maximize the exploitation of labor put in jeopardy the reproduction of the work-force. This contradiction — which still characterizes capitalist development[17] — exploded most dramatically in the American colonies, where work, disease, and disci-

Peasant unfurling the banner of "Freedom."

plinary punishments destroyed two thirds of the native American population in the decades immediately after the Conquest.[18] It was also at the core of the slave trade and the exploitation of slave labor. Millions of Africans died because of the torturous living conditions to which they were subjected during the Middle Passage and on the plantations. Never in Europe did the exploitation of the work-force reach such genocidal proportions, except under the Nazi regime. Even so, there too, in the 16th and 17th centuries, land privatization and the commodification of social relations (the response of lords and merchants to their economic crisis) caused widespread poverty, mortality, and an intense resistance that threatened to shipwreck the emerging capitalist economy. This, I argue, is the historical context in which the history of women and reproduction in the transition from feudalism to capitalism must be placed; for the changes which the advent of capitalism introduced in the social position of women — especially at the proletarian level, whether in Europe or America — were primarily dictated by the search for new sources of labor as well as new forms of regimentation and division of the work-force.

Albrecht Dürer, Monument to the
Vanquished Peasants. *(1526). This picture, representing a peasant enthroned on a collection of objects from his daily life, is highly
ambiguous. It can suggest that the peasants were
betrayed or that they themselves should be
treated as traitors. Accordingly, it has been interpreted either as a satire of the rebel peasants or
as a homage to their moral strength. What we
know with certainty is that Dürer was profoundly perturbed by the events of 1525, and,
as a convinced Lutheran, must have followed
Luther in his condemnation of the revolt.*

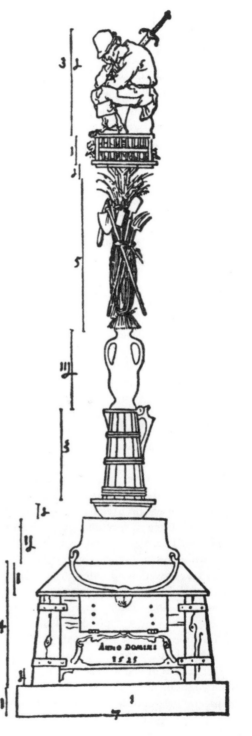

In support of this statement, I trace the main developments that shaped the advent of capitalism in Europe — land privatization and the Price Revolution — to argue that neither was sufficient to produce a self-sustaining process of proletarianization. I then examine in broad outlines the policies which the capitalist class introduced to discipline, reproduce, and expand the European proletariat, beginning with the attack it launched on women, resulting in the construction of a new patriarchal order, which I define as the "patriarchy of the wage." Lastly, I look at the production of racial and sexual hierarchies in the colonies, asking to what extent they could form a terrain of confrontation or solidarity between indigenous, African, and European women and between women and men.

Land Privatization in Europe, the Production of Scarcity, and the Separation of Production from Reproduction

From the beginning of capitalism, the immiseration of the working class began with war and land privatization. This was an international phenomenon. By the mid-16th century European merchants had expropriated much of the land of the Canary Islands and turned them into sugar plantations. The most massive process of land privatization and enclosure occurred in the Americas where, by the turn of the 17th century, one-third of the communal indigenous land had been appropriated by the Spaniards under the system of the *encomienda*. Loss of land was also one of the consequences of slave-raiding in Africa, which deprived many communities of the best among their youth.

In Europe land privatization began in the late-15th century, simultaneously with colonial expansion. It took different forms: the evictions of tenants, rent increases, and increased state taxation, leading to debt and the sale of land. I define all these forms as *land expropriation* because, even when force was not used, the loss of land occurred against the individual's or the community's will and undermined their capacity for subsistence. Two forms of land expropriation must be mentioned: war — whose character changed in this period, being used as a means to transform territorial and economic arrangements — and religious reform.

"[B]efore 1494 warfare in Europe had mainly consisted of minor wars characterized by brief and irregular campaigns" (Cunningham and Grell 2000: 95). These often took place in the summer to give the peasants, who formed the bulk of the armies, the time to sow their crops; armies confronted each other for long periods of time without much action. But by the 16th century wars became more frequent and a new type of warfare appeared, in part because of technological innovation but mostly because the European states began to turn to territorial conquest to resolve their economic crisis and wealthy financiers invested in it. Military campaigns became much longer. Armies grew tenfold, and they became permanent and professionalized.[19] Mercenaries were hired who had no attachment to the local population; and the goal of warfare became the elimination of the enemy, so that war left in its wake deserted villages, fields covered with corpses, famines, and epidemics, as in Albrecht Dürer's "The Four Horsemen of the Apocalypse" (1498).[20] This phenomenon, whose traumatic impact on the population is reflected in numerous artistic representations, changed the agricultural landscape of Europe.

Jaques Callot, THE HORRORS OF WAR *(1633). Engraving. The men hanged by military authorities were former soldiers turned robbers. Dismissed soldiers were a large part of the vagabonds and beggars that crowded the roads of 17th-century Europe.*

Many tenure contracts were also annulled when the Church's lands were confiscated in the course of the Protestant Reformation, which began with a massive land-grab by the upper class. In France, a common hunger for the Church's land at first united the lower and higher classes in the Protestant movement, but when the land was auctioned, starting in 1563, the artisans and day-laborers, who had demanded the expropriation of the Church "with a passion born of bitterness and hope," and had mobilized with the promise that they too would receive their share, were betrayed in their expectations (Le Roy Ladurie 1974: 173–76). Also the peasants, who had become Protestant to free themselves from the tithes, were deceived. When they stood by their rights, declaring that "the Gospel promises land freedom and enfranchisement," they were savagely attacked as fomenters of sedition (*ibid.*: 192).[21] In England as well, much land changed hands in the name of religious reform. W. G. Hoskin has described it as "the greatest transference of land in English history since the Norman Conquest" or, more succinctly, as "The Great Plunder."[22] In England, however, land privatization was mostly accomplished through the "Enclosures," a phenomenon that has become so associated with the expropriation of workers from their "common wealth" that, in our time, it is used by anti-capitalist activists as a signifier for every attack on social entitlements.[23]

In the 16th century, "enclosure" was a technical term, indicating a set of strategies the English lords and rich farmers used to eliminate communal land property and expand their holdings.[24] It mostly referred to the abolition of the open-field system, an arrangement by which villagers owned non-contiguous strips of land in a non-hedged field. Enclosing also included the fencing off of the commons and the pulling down of the shacks of poor cottagers who had no land but could survive because they had access to customary rights.[25] Large tracts of land were also enclosed to create deer parks, while entire villages were cast down, to be laid to pasture.

Though the Enclosures continued into the 18th century (Neeson 1993), even before the Reformation, more than two thousand rural communities were destroyed in this way (Fryde 1996: 185). So severe was the extinction of rural villages that in 1518 and again in 1548 the Crown called for an investigation. But despite the appointment of several royal commissions, little was done to stop the trend. What began, instead, was an intense struggle, climaxing in numerous uprisings, accompanied by a long debate on the merits and demerits of land privatization which is still continuing today, revitalized by the World Bank's assault on the last planetary commons.

Briefly put, the argument proposed by "modernizers," from all political perspectives, is that the enclosures boosted agricultural efficiency, and the dislocations they produced were well compensated by a significant increase in agricultural productivity. It is claimed that the land was depleted and, if it had remained in the hands of the poor, it would have ceased to produce (anticipating Garret Hardin's "tragedy of the commons"),[26] while its takeover by the rich allowed it to rest. Coupled with agricultural innovation, the argument goes, the enclosures made the land more productive, leading to the expansion of the food supply. From this viewpoint, any praise for communal land tenure is dismissed as "nostalgia for the past," the assumption being that agricultural communalism is backward and inefficient, and that those who defend it are guilty of an undue attachment to tradition.[27]

But these arguments do not hold. Land privatization and the commercialization of agriculture did not increase the food supply available to the common people, though more food was made available for the market and for export. For workers they inaugurated two centuries of starvation, in the same way as today, even in the most fertile areas of Africa, Asia, and Latin America, malnutrition is rampant due to the destruction of communal land-tenure and the "export or perish" policy imposed by the World Bank's structural adjustment programs. Nor did the introduction of new agricultural techniques in England compensate for this loss. On the contrary, the development of agrarian capitalism "worked hand in glove" with the impoverishment of the rural population (Lis and Soly 1979: 102). A testimony to the misery produced by land privatization is the fact that, barely a century after the emergence of agrarian capitalism, sixty European towns had instituted some form of social assistance or were moving in this direction, and vagabondage had become an international problem (*ibid.*: 87). Population growth may have been a contributing factor; but its importance has been overstated, and should be circumscribed in time. By the last part of the 16th century, almost everywhere in Europe, the population was stagnating or declining, but this time workers did not derive any benefit from the change.

There are also misconceptions about the effectiveness of the open-field system of agriculture. Neo-liberal historians have described it as wasteful, but even a supporter of land privatization like Jean De Vries recognizes that the communal use of agricultural fields had many advantages. It protected the peasants from harvest failure, due to the variety of strips to which a family had access; it also allowed for a manageable work-schedule (since each strip required attention at a different time); and it encouraged a democratic way of life, built on self-government and self-reliance, since all decisions — when to plant

Rural feast. All the festivals, games, and gatherings of the peasant community were held on the commons. 16th-century engraving by Daniel Hopfer.

or harvest, when to drain the fens, how many animals to allow on the commons — were taken by peasant assemblies.[28]

The same considerations apply to the "commons." Disparaged in 16th century literature as a source of laziness and disorder, the commons were essential to the reproduction of many small farmers or cottars who survived only because they had access to meadows in which to keep cows, or woods in which to gather timber, wild berries and herbs, or quarries, fish-ponds, and open spaces in which to meet. Beside encouraging collective decision-making and work cooperation, the commons were the material foundation upon which peasant solidarity and sociality could thrive. All the festivals, games, and gatherings of the peasant community were held on the commons.[29] The social function of the commons was especially important for women, who, having less title to land and less social power, were more dependent on them for their subsistence, autonomy, and sociality. Paraphrasing Alice Clark's statement about the importance of markets for women in pre-capitalist Europe, we can say that the commons too were for women the center of social life, the place where they convened, exchanged news, took advice, and where a women's viewpoint on communal events, autonomous from that of men, could form (Clark 1968: 51).

This web of cooperative relations, which R. D. Tawney has referred to as the "primitive communism" of the feudal village, crumbled when the open-field system was abolished and the communal lands were fenced off (Tawney 1967). Not only did cooperation in agricultural labor die when land was privatized and individual labor contracts replaced collective ones; economic differences among the rural population deepened, as the number of poor squatters increased who had nothing left but a cot and a cow, and no choice but to go with "bended knee and cap in hand" to beg for a job (Seccombe 1992). Social cohesion broke down;[30] families disintegrated, the youth left the village to join the increasing number of vagabonds or itinerant workers — soon to become the social problem of the age — while the elderly were left behind to fend for themselves. Particularly disadvantaged were older women who, no longer supported by their children, fell onto the poor rolls or survived by borrowing, petty theft, and delayed payments. The outcome was a peasantry polarized not only by the deepening economic inequalities, but by a web of hatred and resentments that is well-documented in the records of the witch-hunt, which show that quarrels relating to requests for help, the trespassing of animals, or unpaid rents were in the background of many accusations.[31]

The enclosures also undermined the economic situation of the artisans. In the same way in which multinational corporations take advantage of the peasants expropriated from their lands by the World Bank to construct "free export zones" where commodities are produced at the lowest cost, so, in the 16th and 17th centuries, merchant capitalists took advantage of the cheap labor-force that had been made available in the rural areas to break the power of the urban guilds and destroy the artisans' independence. This was especially the case in the textile industry that was reorganized as a rural cottage industry, and on the basis of the "putting out" system, the ancestor of today's "informal economy," also built on the labor of women and children.[32] But textile workers were not the only ones whose labor was cheapened. As soon as they lost access to land, all workers were plunged into a dependence unknown in medieval times, as their landless condition gave employers the power to cut their pay and lengthen the working-day. In Protestant areas this happened under the guise of religious reform, which doubled the work-year by eliminating the saints' days.

Not surprisingly, with land expropriation came a change in the workers' attitude towards the wage. While in the Middle Ages wages could be viewed as an instrument of freedom (in contrast to the compulsion of the labor services), as soon as access to land came to an end wages began to be viewed as instruments of enslavement (Hill 1975: 181ff).[33]

Such was the hatred that workers felt for waged labor that Gerrard Winstanley, the leader of the Diggers, declared that it that it did not make any difference whether one lived under the enemy or under one's brother, if one worked for a wage. This explains the growth, in the wake of the enclosures (using the term in a broad sense to include all forms of land privatization), of the number of "vagabonds" and "masterless" men, who preferred to take to the road and to risk enslavement or death — as prescribed by the "bloody" legislation passed against them —rather than to work for a wage.[34] It also explains the strenuous struggle which peasants made to defend their land from expropriation, no matter how meager its size.

In England, anti-enclosure struggles began in the late 15th century and continued throughout the 16th and 17th, when levelling the enclosing hedges became "the most common species of social protest" and the symbol of class conflict (Manning 1988: 311). Anti-enclosure riots often turned into mass uprisings. The most notorious was Kett's Rebellion, named after its leader, Robert Kett, that took place in Norfolk in 1549. This was no small nocturnal affair. At its peak, the rebels numbered 16,000, had an artillery, defeated a government army of 12,000, and even captured Norwich, at the time the second largest city in England.[35] They also drafted a program that, if realized, would have checked the advance of agrarian capitalism and eliminated all vestiges of feudal power in the country. It consisted of twenty-nine demands that Kett, a farmer and tanner, presented to the Lord Protector. The first was that "from henceforth no man shall enclose any more." Other articles demanded that rents should be reduced to the rates that had prevailed sixty-five years before, that "all freeholders and copy holders may take the profits of all commons," and that "all bond-men may be made free, for god made all free with his precious blood sheddying" (Fletcher 1973: 142–44). These demands were put into practice. Throughout Norfolk, enclosing hedges were uprooted, and only when another government army attacked them were the rebels stopped. Thirty-five hundred were slain in the massacre that followed. Hundreds more were wounded. Kett and his brother William were hanged outside Norwich's walls.

Anti-enclosure struggles continued, however, through the Jacobean period with a noticeable increase in the presence of women.[36] During the reign of James I, about ten percent of enclosure riots included women among the rebels. Some were all female protests. In 1607, for instance, thirty-seven women, led by a "Captain Dorothy," attacked coal miners working on what women claimed to be the village commons in Thorpe Moor (Yorkshire). Forty women went to "cast down the fences and hedges" of an enclosure in Waddingham (Lincolnshire) in 1608; and in 1609, on a manor of Dunchurch (Warwickshire) "fifteen women, including wives, widows, spinsters, unmarried daughters, and servants, took it upon themselves to assemble at night to dig up the hedges and level the ditches" (*ibid.*: 97). Again, at York in May 1624, women destroyed an enclosure and went to prison for it — they were said to have "enjoyed tobacco and ale after their feat" (Fraser 1984: 225–26). Then, in 1641, a crowd that broke into an enclosed fen at Buckden consisted mainly of women aided by boys (*ibid.*). And these were just a few instances of a confrontation in which women holding pitchforks and scythes resisted the fencing of the land or the draining of the fens when their livelihood was threatened.

This strong female presence has been attributed to the belief that women were above the law, being "covered" legally by their husbands. Even men, we are told, dressed like women to pull up the fences. But this explanation should not be taken too far. For the government soon eliminated this privilege, and started arresting and imprisoning women involved in anti-enclosure riots.[37] Moreover, we should not assume that women had no stake of their own in the resistance to land expropriation. The opposite was the case.

As with the commutation, women were those who suffered most when the land was lost and the village community fell apart. Part of the reason is that it was far more difficult for them to become vagabonds or migrant workers, for a nomadic life exposed them to male violence, especially at a time when misogyny was escalating. Women were also less mobile on account of pregnancies and the caring of children, a fact overlooked by scholars who consider the flight from servitude (through migration and other forms of nomadism) the paradigmatic forms of struggle. Nor could women become soldiers for pay, though some joined armies as cooks, washers, prostitutes, and wives;[38] but by the 17th century this option too vanished, as armies were further regimented and the crowds of women that used to follow them were expelled from the battlefields (Kriedte 1983: 55).

Women were also more negatively impacted by the enclosures because as soon as land was privatized and monetary relations began to dominate economic life, they found it more difficult than men to support themselves, being increasingly confined to reproductive labor at the very time when this work was being completely devalued. As we will see, this phenomenon, which has accompanied the shift from a subsistence to a money-economy, in every phase of capitalist development, can be attributed to several factors. It is clear, however, that the commercialization of economic life provided the material conditions for it.

With the demise of the subsistence economy that had prevailed in pre-capitalist Europe, the unity of production and reproduction which has been typical of all societies based on production-for-use came to an end, as these activities became the carriers of different social relations and were sexually differentiated. In the new monetary regime, only

Entitled "Women and Knaves," this picture by Hans Sebald Beham (c. 1530) shows the train of women that used to follow the armies even to the battlefield. The women, including wives and prostitutes, took care of the reproduction of the soldiers. Notice the woman wearing a muzzling device.

production-for-market was defined as a value-creating activity, whereas the reproduction of the worker began to be considered as valueless from an economic viewpoint and even ceased to be considered as work. Reproductive work continued to be paid — though at the lowest rates — when performed for the master class or outside the home. But the economic importance of the reproduction of labor-power carried out in the home, and its function in the accumulation of capital became invisible, being mystified as a natural vocation and labelled "women's labor." In addition, women were excluded from many waged occupations and, when they worked for a wage, they earned a pittance compared to the average male wage.

These historic changes — that peaked in the 19th century with the creation of the full-time housewife — redefined women's position in society and in relation to men. The sexual division of labor that emerged from it not only fixed women to reproductive work, but increased their dependence on men, enabling the state and employers to use the male wage as a means to command women's labor. In this way, the separation of commodity production from the reproduction of labor-power also made possible the development of a specifically capitalist use of the wage and of the markets as means for the accumulation of unpaid labor.

Most importantly, the separation of production from reproduction created a class of proletarian women who were as dispossessed as men but, unlike their male relatives, in a society that was becoming increasingly monetarized, had almost no access to wages, thus being forced into a condition of chronic poverty, economic dependence, and invisibility as workers.

As we will see, the devaluation and feminization of reproductive labor was a disaster also for male workers, for the devaluation of reproductive labor inevitably devalued its product: labor-power. But there is no doubt that in the "transition from feudalism to capitalism" women suffered a unique process of social degradation that was fundamental to the accumulation of capital and has remained so ever since.

Also in view of these developments, we cannot say, then, that the separation of the worker from the land and the advent of a money-economy realized the struggle which the medieval serfs had fought to free themselves from bondage. It was not the workers — male or female — who were liberated by land privatization. What was "liberated" was capital, as the land was now "free" to function as a means of accumulation and exploitation, rather than as a means of subsistence. Liberated were the landlords, who now could unload onto the workers most of the cost of their reproduction, giving them access to some means of subsistence only when directly employed. When work would not be available or would not be sufficiently profitable, as in times of commercial or agricultural crisis, workers, instead, could be laid off and left to starve.

The separation of workers from their means of subsistence and their new dependence on monetary relations also meant that the real wage could now be cut and women's labor could be further devalued with respect to men's through monetary manipulation. It is not a coincidence, then, that as soon as land began to be privatized, the prices of foodstuffs, which for two centuries had stagnated, began to rise.[39]

The Price Revolution and the Pauperization of the European Working Class

This "inflationary" phenomenon, which due to its devastating social consequences has been named the Price Revolution (Ramsey 1971), was attributed by contemporaries and later economists (e.g., Adam Smith) to the arrival of gold and silver from America, "pouring into Europe [through Spain] in a mammoth stream" (Hamilton 1965: vii). But it has been noted that prices had been rising before these metals started circulating through the European markets.[40] Moreover, in themselves, gold and silver are not capital, and could have been put to other uses, e.g., to make jewelry or golden cupolas or to embroider clothes. If they functioned as price-regulating devices, capable of turning even wheat into a precious commodity, this was because they were planted into a developing capitalist world, in which a growing percentage of the population — one-third in England (Laslett 1971: 53) — had no access to land and had to buy the food that they had once produced, and because the ruling class had learned to use the magical power of money to cut labor costs. In other words, prices rose because of the development of a national and international market-system encouraging the export-import of agricultural products, and because merchants hoarded goods to sell them later at a higher price. In September 1565, in Antwerp, "while the poor were literally starving in the streets," a warehouse collapsed under the weight of the grain packed in it (Hackett Fischer 1996: 88).

It was under these circumstances that the arrival of the American treasure triggered a massive redistribution of wealth and a new proletarianization process.[41] Rising prices ruined the small farmers, who had to give up their land to buy grain or bread when the harvests could not feed their families, and created a class of capitalist entrepreneurs, who accumulated fortunes by investing in agriculture and money-lending, at a time when having money was for many people a matter of life or death.[42]

The Price Revolution also triggered a historic collapse in the real wage comparable to that which has occurred in our time throughout Africa, Asia, and Latin America, in the countries "structurally adjusted" by the World Bank and the International Monetary Fund. By 1600, real wages in Spain had lost thirty percent of their purchasing power with respect to what they had been in 1511 (Hamilton 1965: 280), and the collapse was just as sharp in other countries. While the price of food went up eight times, wages increased only by three times (Hackett Fischer 1996: 74). This was not the work of the invisible hand of the market, but the product of a state policy that prevented laborers from organizing, while giving merchants the maximum freedom with regard to the pricing and movement of goods. Predictably, within a few decades, the real wage lost two-thirds of its purchasing power, as shown by the changes that intervened in the daily wages of an English carpenter, expressed in kilograms of grain, between the 14th and 18th century (Slicher Van Bath 1963: 327):

YEARS	KILOGRAMS OF GRAIN
1351–1400	121.8
1401–1450	155.1
1451–1500	143.5

1500–1550	122.4
1551–1600	83.0
1601–1650	48.3
1651–1700	74.1
1701–1750	94.6
1751–1800	79.6

It took centuries for wages in Europe to return to the level they had reached in the late Middle Ages. Things deteriorated to the point that, in England, by 1550, male artisans had to work forty weeks to earn the same income that, at the beginning of the century, they had been able to obtain in fifteen weeks. In Fran, [see graph, next page] wages dropped by sixty percent between 1470 and 1570 (Hackett Fischer 1996: 78).[43] The wage collapse was especially disastrous for women. In the 14th century, they had received half the pay of a man for the same task; but by the mid-16th century they were receiving only one-third of the reduced male wage, and could no longer support themselves by wage-work, neither in agriculture nor in manufacturing, a fact undoubtedly responsible for the massive spread of prostitution in this period.[44] What followed was the absolute impoverishment of the European working class, a phenomenon so widespread and general that, by 1550 and long after, workers in Europe were referred to as simply "the poor."

Evidence for this dramatic impoverishment is the change that occurred in the workers' diets. Meat disappeared from their tables, except for a few scraps of lard, and so did beer and wine, salt and olive oil (Braudel 1973: 127ff; Le Roy Ladurie 1974). From the 16th to the 18th centuries, the workers' diets consisted essentially of bread, the main expense in their budget. This was a historic setback (whatever we may think of dietary norms) compared to the abundance of meat that had typified the late Middle Ages. Peter Kriedte writes that at that time, the "annual meat consumption had reached the figure of 100 kilos per person, an incredible quantity even by today's standards. Up to the 19th century this figure declined to less than twenty kilos" (Kriedte 1983: 52). Braudel too speaks of the end of "carnivorous Europe," summoning as a witness the Swabian Heinrich Muller who, in 1550, commented that,

> ...in the past they ate differently at the peasant's house. Then, there was meat and food in profusion every day; tables at village fairs and feasts sank under their load. Today, everything has truly changed. For some years, in fact, what a calamitous time, what high prices! And the food of the most comfortably off peasants is almost worse than that of day-labourers and valets previously" (Braudel 1973: 130).

Not only did meat disappear, but food shortages became common, aggravated in times of harvest failure, when the scanty grain reserves sent the price of grain sky-high, condemning city dwellers to starvation (Braudel 1966, Vol. I: 328). This is what occurred in the famine years of the 1540s and 1550s, and again in the decades of the 1580s and 1590s, which were some of the worst in the history of the European proletariat, coinciding with widespread unrest and a record number of witch-trials. But malnutrition was ram-

Price Revolution and the Fall of the Real Wage, 1480–1640. The Price Revolution trig-gered a historic collapse in the real wage. Within a few decades, the real wage lost two-thirds of its purchasing power. The real wage did not return to the level it had reached in the 15th century until the 19th century (Phelps-Brown and Hopkins, 1981).

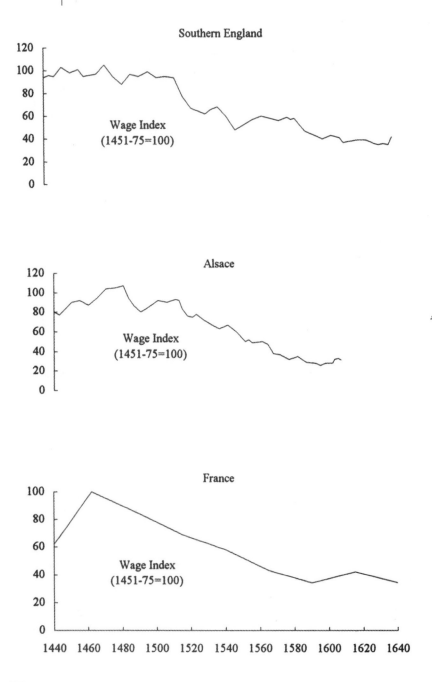

The social consequences of the Price Revolution are revealed by these charts, which indicate, respectively, the rise in the price of grain in England between 1490 and 1650, the concomitant rise in prices and property crimes in Essex (England) between 1566 and 1602, and the population decline measured in millions in Germany, Austria, Italy and Spain between 1500 and 1750 (Hackett Fischer, 1996).

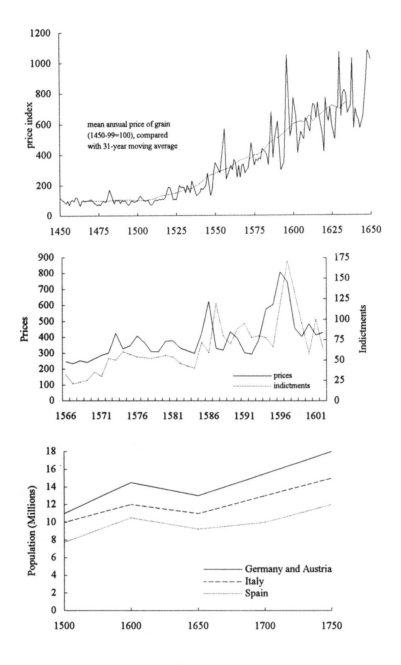

pant also in normal times, so that food acquired a high symbolic value as a marker of rank. The desire for it among the poor reached epic proportions, inspiring dreams of Pantagruelian orgies, like those described by Rabelais in his *Gargantua and Pantagruel (1552),* and causing nightmarish obsessions, such as the conviction (spread among northeastern Italian farmers) that witches roamed the countryside at night to feed upon their cattle (Mazzali 1988: 73).

Indeed, the Europe that was preparing to become a Promethean world-mover, presumably taking humankind to new technological and cultural heights, was a place where people never had enough to eat. Food became an object of such intense desire that it was believed that the poor sold their souls to the devil to get their hands on it. Europe was also a place where, in times of bad harvests, country-folk fed upon acorns, wild roots, or the barks of trees, and multitudes roved the countryside weeping and wailing, "so hungry that they would devour the beans in the fields" (Le Roy Ladurie 1974); or they invaded the cities to benefit from grain distributions or to attack the houses and granaries of the rich who, in turn, rushed to get arms and shut the city gates to keep the starving out (Heller 1986: 56-63).

That the transition to capitalism inaugurated a long period of starvation for workers in Europe — which plausibly ended because of the economic expansion produced by colonization — is also demonstrated by the fact that, while in the 14th and 15th centuries, the proletarian struggle had centered around the demand for "liberty" and less work, by the 16th and 17th, it was mostly spurred by hunger, taking the form of assaults on bakeries and granaries, and of riots against the export of local crops.[45] The authorities described those who participated in these attacks as "good for nothing" or "poor"and "humble people," but most were craftsmen, living, by this time, from hand to mouth.

It was the women who usually initiated and led the food revolts. Six of the thirty-one food riots in 17th-century France studied by Ives-Marie Bercé were made up exclusively of women. In the others the female presence was so conspicuous that Bercé calls them "women's riots."[46] Commenting on this phenomenon, with reference to 18th-century England, Sheila Rowbotham concluded that women were prominent in this type of protest because of their role as their families' caretakers. But women were also those most ruined by high prices for, having less access to money and employment than men, they were more dependent on cheap food for survival. This is why, despite their subordinate status, they took quickly to the streets when food prices went up, or when rumor spread that the grain supplies were being removed from town. This is what happened at the time of the Cordoba uprising of 1652, which started "early in the morning ... when a poor woman went weeping through the streets of the poor quarter, holding the body of her son who had died of hunger" (Kamen 1971: 364). The same occurred in Montpellier in 1645, when women took to the streets "to protect their children from starvation" (*ibid.*: 356). In France, women besieged the bakeries when they became convinced that grain was to be embezzled, or found out that the rich had bought the best bread and the remaining was lighter or more expensive. Crowds of poor women would then gather at the bakers' stalls, demanding bread and charging the bakers with hiding their supplies. Riots broke out also in the squares where grain markets were held, or along the routes taken by the carts with the corn to be exported, and "at the river banks where...boatmen could be seen loading the sacks." On these occasions the rioters ambushed the carts... with pitchforks and sticks... the men carrying away the sacks, the women gathering as much grain as they could in their skirts" (Bercé 1990: 171–73).

The struggle for food was fought also by other means, such as poaching, stealing from one's neighbors' fields or homes, and assaults on the houses of the rich. In Troyes in 1523, rumor had it that the poor had put the houses of the rich on fire, preparing to invade them (Heller 1986: 55–56). At Malines, in the Low Countries, the houses of speculators were marked by angry peasants with blood (Hackett Fischer 1996: 88). Not surprisingly, "food crimes" loom large in the disciplinary procedures of the 16th and 17th centuries. Exemplary is the recurrence of the theme of the "diabolical banquet" in the witch-trials, suggesting that feasting on roasted mutton, white bread, and wine was now considered a diabolic act in the case of the "common people." But the main weapons available to the poor in their struggle for survival were their own famished bodies, as in times of famine hordes of vagabonds and beggars surrounded the better off, half-dead of hunger and disease, grabbing their arms, exposing their wounds to them and, forcing them to live in a state of constant fear at the prospect of both contamination and revolt. "You cannot walk down a street or stop in a square — a Venetian man wrote in the mid-16th century — without multitudes surrounding you to beg for charity: you see hunger

Family of vagabonds. Engraving by Lucas van Leyden, 1520.

written on their faces, their eyes like gemless rings, the wretchedness of their bodies with skins shaped only by bones" (*ibid.*: 88). A century later, in Florence, the scene was about the same. "[I]t was impossible to hear Mass," one G. Balducci complained, in April 1650, "so much was one importuned during the service by wretched people naked and covered with sores" (Braudel 1966, Vol. II: 734–35).[47]

The State Intervention in the Reproduction of Labor: Poor Relief, and the Criminalization of the Working Class

The struggle for food was not the only front in the battle against the spread of capitalist relations. Everywhere masses of people resisted the destruction of their former ways of existence, fighting against land privatization, the abolition of customary rights, the imposition of new taxes, wage-dependence, and the continuous presence of armies in their neighborhoods, which was so hated that people rushed to close the gates of their towns to prevent soldiers from settling among them.

In France, one thousand "emotions" (uprisings) occurred between the 1530s and 1670s, many involving entire provinces and requiring the intervention of troops (Goubert 1986: 205). England, Italy, and Spain present a similar picture,[48] indicating that the pre-capitalist world of the village, which Marx dismissed under the rubric of "rural isolation," could produce as high a level of struggle as any the industrial proletariat has waged.

In the Middle Ages, migration, vagabondage, and the rise of "crimes against property" were part of the resistance to impoverishment and dispossession; these phenomena now took on massive proportions. Everywhere — if we give credit to the complaints of the contemporary authorities — vagabonds were swarming, changing cities, crossing borders, sleeping in the haystacks or crowding at the gates of towns — a vast humanity involved in a diaspora of its own, that for decades escaped the authorities' control. Six thousand vagabonds were reported in Venice alone in 1545. "In Spain vagrants cluttered the road, stopping at every town" (Braudel, Vol. II: 740).[49] Starting with England, always a pioneer in these matters, the state passed new, far harsher anti-vagabond laws prescribing enslavement and capital punishment in cases of recidivism. But repression was not effective and the roads of 16th and 17th-century Europe remained places of great (com)motion and encounters. Through them passed heretics escaping persecution, discharged soldiers, journeymen and other "humble folk" in search of employment, and then foreign artisans, evicted peasants, prostitutes, hucksters, petty thieves, professional beggars. Above all, through the roads of Europe passed the tales, stories, and experiences of a developing proletariat. Meanwhile, the crime rates also escalated, in such proportions that we can assume that a massive reclamation and reappropriation of the stolen communal wealth was underway.[50]

Today, these aspects of the transition to capitalism may seem (for Europe at least) things of the past or — as Marx put it in the *Grundrisse* (1973: 459) — "historical preconditions" of capitalist development, to be overcome by more mature forms of capitalism. But the essential similarity between these phenomena and the social consequences of the new phase of globalization that we are witnessing tells us otherwise. Pauperization, rebellion, and the escalation of "crime" are structural elements of capitalist accumulation as capitalism must strip the work-force from its means of reproduction to impose its own rule.

Vagrant being whipped through the streets.

That in the industrializing regions of Europe, by the 19th century, the most extreme forms of proletarian misery and rebellion had disappeared is not a proof against this claim. Proletarian misery and rebellions did not come to an end; they only lessened to the degree that the super-exploitation of workers had been exported, through the institutionalization of slavery, at first, and later through the continuing expansion of colonial domination.

As for the "transition" period, this remained in Europe a time of intense social conflict, providing the stage for a set of state initiatives that, judging from their effects, had three main objectives: (a) to create a more disciplined work-force; (b) to diffuse social protest; and (c) to fix workers to the jobs forced upon them. Let us look at them in turn.

In pursuit of social discipline, an attack was launched against all forms of collective sociality and sexuality including sports, games, dances, ale-wakes, festivals, and other group-rituals that had been a source of bonding and solidarity among workers. It was sanctioned by a deluge of bills: twenty-five, in England, just for the regulation of ale-houses, in the years between 1601 and 1606 (Underdown 1985: 47–48). Peter Burke (1978), in his work on the subject, has spoken of it as a campaign against "popular culture." But we can see that what was at stake was the desocialization or decollectivization of the reproduction of the work-force, as well as the attempt to impose a more productive use of leisure time. This process, in England, reached its climax with the coming to power of the Puritans in the aftermath of the Civil War (1642–49), when the fear of social indiscipline prompted the banning of all proletarian gatherings and merrymaking. But the "moral reformation" was equally intense in non-Protestant areas where, in the same period, religious processions were replacing the dancing and singing that had been held in and out of the churches. Even the individual's relation with God was privatized: in Protestant areas, with the institution of a direct relationship between the individual and the divinity; in the Catholic areas, with the introduction of individual confession. The church itself, as a community center, ceased to host any social activity other than those addressed to the cult. As a result, the physical enclosure operated by land privatization and the hedging of the commons was amplified by a process of social enclosure, the reproduction of workers shifting from the openfield to the home, from the community to the family, from the public space (the common, the church) to the private.[51]

Secondly, in the decades between 1530 and 1560, a system of public assistance was introduced in at least sixty European towns, both by initiative of the local municipalities and by direct intervention of the central state.[52] Its precise goals are still debated. While much of the literature on the topic sees the introduction of public assistance as a response to a humanitarian crisis that jeopardized social control, in his massive study of coerced labor, the French Marxist scholar Yann Moulier Boutang insists that its primary objective was "The Great Fixation" of the proletariat, that is, the attempt to prevent the flight of labor.[53]

In any event, the introduction of public assistance was a turning point in the state relation between workers and capital and the definition of the function of the state. It was the first recognition of the *unsustainability* of a capitalist system ruling exclusively by means of hunger and terror. It was also the first step in the reconstruction of the state as the guarantor of the class relation and as the chief supervisor of the reproduction and disciplining of the work-force.

Antecedents for this function can be found in the 14th century, when faced with the generalization of the anti-feudal struggle, the state had emerged as the only agency capable of confronting a working class that was regionally unified, armed, and no longer confined in its demands to the political economy of the manor. In 1351, with the passing of the Statute of Laborers in England, which fixed the maximum wage, the state had formally taken charge of the regulation and repression of labor, which the local lords were no longer capable of guaranteeing. But it was with the introduction of public assistance that the state began to claim "ownership" of the work-force, and a capitalist "division of labor" was instituted within the ruling class, enabling employers to relinquish any responsibility for the reproduction of workers, in the certainty that the state would intervene, either with the carrot or with the stick, to address the inevitable crises. With this innovation, a leap occurred also in the management of social reproduction, resulting in the introduction of demographic recording (census-taking, the recording of mortality, natality, marriage rates) and the application of accounting to social relations. Exemplary is the work of the administrators of the Bureau de Pauvres in Lyon (France), who by the end of the 16th century had learned to calculate the number of the poor, assess the amount of food needed by each child or adult, and keep track of the deceased, to make sure that nobody could claim assistance in the name of a dead person (Zemon Davis 1968: 244–46).

Along with this new "social science," an international debate also developed on the administration of public assistance anticipating the contemporary debate on welfare. Should only those unable to work, described as the "deserving poor," be supported, or should "able-bodied" laborers unable to find a job also be given help? And how much or how little should they be given, so as not to be discouraged from looking for work? These questions were crucial from the viewpoint of social discipline, as a key objective of public aid was to tie workers to their jobs. But, on these matters a consensus could rarely be reached.

While humanist reformers like Juan Luis Vives[54] and spokesmen for the wealthy burghers recognized the economic and disciplinary benefits of a more liberal and central-ized dispensation of charity (not exceeding the distribution of bread, however), part of the clergy strenuously opposed the ban on individual donations. But, across differences of systems and opinions, assistance was administered with such stinginess that it generated as much conflict as appeasement. Those assisted resented the humiliating rituals imposed on them, like wearing the "mark of infamy" (previously reserved for lepers and Jews), or (in France) participating in the annual processions of the poor, in which they had to parade singing hymns and holding candles; and they vehemently protested when the alms were not promptly given or were inadequate to their needs. In response, in some French towns, gibbets were erected at the time of food distributions or when the poor were asked to work in exchange for the food they received (Zemon Davis, 1968: 249). In England, as the 16th century progressed, receipt of public aid — also for children and the elderly — was made conditional on the incarceration of the recipients in "work-houses," where they became the experimental subjects for a variety of work-schemes.[55] Consequently, the attack on workers, that had begun with the enclosures and the Price Revolution, in the space of a century, led to the *criminalization of the working class,* that is, the formation of a vast proletariat either incarcerated in the newly constructed work-houses and correction-houses, or seeking its survival outside the law and living in open antagonism to the state — always one step away from the whip and the noose.

From the viewpoint of the formation of a laborious work-force, this was a deci-sive failure, and the constant preoccupation with the question of social discipline in 16th and 17th-century political circles indicates that the contemporary statesmen and entrepreneurs were keenly aware of it. Moreover, the social crisis that this general state of rebelliousness provoked was aggravated in the second half of the 16th century by a new economic contraction, in great part caused by the dramatic population decline that occurred in Spanish America after the Conquest, and the shrinking of the colonial economies.

Population Decline, Economic Crisis, and the Disciplining of Women

Within less than a century from the landing of Columbus on the American continent, the colonizers' dream of an infinite supply of labor (echoing the explorers' estimate of an "infinite number of trees" in the forests of the Americas) was dashed.

Europeans had brought death to America. Estimates of the population collapse which affected the region in the wake of the colonial invasion vary. But scholars almost unanimously liken its effects to an "American Holocaust." According to David Stannard (1992), in the century after the Conquest, the population declined by 75 million across

South America, representing 95% of its inhabitants (1992: 268–305). This is also the estimate of André Gunder Frank who writes that "within little more than a century, the Indian population declined by ninety percent and even ninety-five percent in Mexico, Peru, and some other regions" (1978: 43). In Mexico, the population fell "from 11 million in 1519 to 6.5 million in 1565 to about 2.5 million in 1600" (Wallerstein 1974: 89n). By 1580 "disease... assisted by Spanish brutality, had killed off or driven away most of the people of the Antilles and the lowlands of New Spain, Peru and the Caribbean littoral" (Crosby:1972:38), and it would soon wipe out many more in Brazil. The clergy rationalized this "holocaust" as God's punishment for the Indians' "bestial" behavior (Williams 1986: 138); but its economic consequences were not ignored. In addition, by the 1580s, population began to decline also in western Europe, and continued to do so into the 17th century, reaching a peak in Germany where one third of the population was lost.[56]

With the exception of the Black Death (1345–1348), this was a population crisis without precedents, and statistics, as awful as they are, tell only a part of the story. Death struck at "the poor." It was not the rich, for the most part, who perished when the plague or the smallpox swept the towns, but craftsmen, day-laborers and vagabonds (Kamen 1972: 32–33). They died in such numbers that their bodies paved the streets, and the authorities denounced the existence of a conspiracy, instigating the population to hunt for the malefactors. But the population decline was also blamed on low natality rates and the reluctance of the poor to reproduce themselves. To what extent this charge was justified is difficult to tell, since demographic recording, before the 17th century, was rather uneven. But we know that by the end of the 16th century the age of marriage was increasing in all social classes, and that, in the same period, the number of abandoned children — a new phenomenon — started to grow. We also have the complaints of ministers who from the pulpit charged that the youth did not marry and procreate, in order not to bring more mouths into the world than they could feed.

The peak of the demographic and economic crisis were the decades of the 1620s and 1630s. In Europe, as in the colonies, markets shrank, trade stopped, unemployment became widespread, and for a while there was the possibility that the developing capitalist economy might crash. For the integration between the colonial and European economies had reached a point where the reciprocal impact of the crisis rapidly accelerated its course. This was the first international economic crisis. It was a "General Crisis," as historians have called it (Kamen 1972: 307ff.; Hackett Fischer 1996: 91).

It is in this context that the question of the relation between labor, population, and the accumulation of wealth came to the foreground of political debate and strategy to produce the first elements of a population policy and a "bio-power" regime.[57] The crudeness of the concepts applied, often confusing "populousness" with "population,"[58] and the brutality of the means by which the state began to punish any behavior obstructing population growth, should not deceive us in this respect. It is my contention that it was the population crisis of the 16th and 17th centuries, not the end of famine in Europe in the 18th (as Foucault has argued) that turned reproduction and population growth into state matters, as well as primary objects of intellectual discourse. I further argue that the intensification of the persecution of "witches," and the new disciplinary methods that the state adopted in this period to regulate procreation and break women's control over reproduction, are also to be traced to this crisis. The evidence for this argument is circumstantial, and it should be recognized that other factors contributed to increase the determination of the European power-structure to control more strictly women's reproductive function. Among them, we must include the increasing privatization of property and economic relations that (within the bourgeoisie) generated a new anxiety concerning the question of paternity and the conduct of women. Similarly, in the charge that witches sacrificed children to the devil — a key theme in the "great witch-hunt" of the 16th and 17th centuries — we can read not only a preoccupation with population decline, but also the fear of the propertied classes with regard to their subordinates, particularly low-class women who, as servants, beggars or healers, had many opportunities to enter their employers' houses and cause them harm. It cannot be a pure coincidence, however, that at the very moment when population was declining, and an ideology was forming that stressed the centrality of labor in economic life, severe penalties were introduced in the legal codes of Europe to punish women guilty of reproductive crimes.

The concomitant development of a population crisis, an expansionist population theory, and the introduction of policies promoting population growth is well-documented. By the mid-16th century the idea that the number of citizens determines a nation's wealth had become something of a social axiom. "In my view," wrote the French political thinker and demonologist Jean Bodin, "one should never be afraid of having too many subjects or too many citizens, for the strength of the commonwealth consists in men" (*Commonwealth,* Book II). The Italian economist Giovanni Botero (1533-1617) had a more sophisticated approach, recognising the need for a balance between the number of people and the means of subsistence. Still, he declared that "the greatness of a city" did not depend on its physical size or the circuit of its walls, but exclusively on the number of its residents. Henry IV's saying that "the strength and wealth of a king lie in the number and opulence of his citizens" sums up the demographic thought of the age.

Concern with population growth is detectable also in the program of the Protestant Reformation. Dismissing the traditional Christian exaltation of chastity, the Reformers valorized marriage, sexuality, and even women because of their reproductive capacity. Woman is "needed to bring about the increase of the human race," Luther conceded, reflecting that "whatever their weaknesses, women possess one virtue that cancels them all: they have a womb and they can give birth" (King 1991: 115).

Support for population growth climaxed with the rise of Mercantilism[59] which made the presence of a large population the key to the prosperity and power of a nation. Mercantilism has often been dismissed by mainstream economists as a crude system of thought because of its assumption that the wealth of nations is proportional to the quantity of laborers and money available to them. The brutal means which the mercantilists applied in order to force people to work, in their hunger for labor, have contributed to their disrepute, as most economists wish to maintain the illusion that capitalism fosters freedom rather than coercion. It was a mercantilist class that invented the work-houses, hunted down vagabonds, "transported" criminals to the American colonies, and invested in the slave trade, all the while asserting the "utility of poverty" and declaring "idleness" a social plague. Thus, it has not been recognized that in the mercantilists' theory and practice we find the most direct expression of the requirements of primitive accumulation and the first capitalist policy explicitly addressing the problem of the reproduction of the work-force. This policy, as we have seen, had an "intensive" side consisting in the imposition of a totalitarian regime using every means to extract the maximum of work from every individual, regardless of age and condition. But it also had an "extensive one" consisting in the effort to expand the size of population, and thereby the size of the army and the work-force.

As Eli Hecksher noted, "an almost fanatical desire to increase population prevailed in all countries during the period when mercantilism was at its height, in the later part of the 17th century" (Heckscher 1966: 158). Along with it, a new concept of human beings also took hold, picturing them as just raw materials, workers and breeders for the state (Spengler 1965: 8). But even prior to the heyday of mercantile theory, in France and England the state adopted a set of pro-natalist measures that, combined with Public Relief, formed the embryo of a capitalist reproductive policy. Laws were passed that put a premium on marriage and penalized celibacy, modeled on those adopted by the late Roman Empire for this purpose. The family was given a new importance as the key institution providing for the transmission of property and the reproduction of the work-force. Simultaneously, we have the beginning of demographic recording and the intervention of the state in the supervision of sexuality, procreation, and family life.

But the main initiative that the state took to restore the desired population ratio was the launching of a true war against women clearly aimed at breaking the control they had exercised over their bodies and reproduction. As we will see later in this volume, this war was waged primarily through the witch-hunt that literally demonized any form of birth-control and non-procreative sexuality, while charging women with sacrificing children to the devil. But it also relied on the redefinition of what constitutes a reproductive crime. Thus, starting in the mid-16th century, while Portuguese ships were returning from Africa with their first human cargoes, all the European governments began to impose the severest penalties against contraception, abortion and infanticide.

This last practice had been treated with some leniency in the Middle Ages, at least in the case of poor women; but now it was turned into a capital crime, and punished more harshly than the majority of male crimes.

> In sixteenth century Nuremberg, the penalty for maternal infanticide was drowning; in 1580, the year in which the severed heads of three women convicted of maternal infanticide were nailed to the scaffold for public contemplation, the penalty was changed to beheading (King 1991: 10).[60]

New forms of surveillance were also adopted to ensure that pregnant women did not terminate their pregnancies. In France, a royal edict of 1556 required women to register every pregnancy, and sentenced to death those whose infants died before baptism after a concealed delivery, whether or not proven guilty of any wrongdoing. Similar statutes were passed in England and Scotland in 1624 and 1690. A system of spies was also created to surveil unwed mothers and deprive them of any support. Even hosting an unmarried pregnant woman was made illegal, for fear that she might escape the public scrutiny; while those who befriended her were exposed to public criticism (Wiesner 1993: 51–52; Ozment 1983: 43).

As a consequence women began to be prosecuted in large numbers, and more were executed for infanticide in 16th and 17th-century Europe than for any other crime, except for witchcraft, a charge that also centered on the killing of children and other violations of reproductive norms. Significantly, in the case of both infanticide and witchcraft, the statutes limiting women's legal responsibility were lifted. Thus, women walked, for the first time, into the courtrooms of Europe, in their own name as legal adults, under charge of being witches and child murderers. Also the suspicion under which midwives came in this period — leading to the entrance of the male doctor into the delivery room — stemmed more from the authorities' fears of infanticide than from any concern with the midwives' alleged medical incompetence.

With the marginalization of the midwife, the process began by which women lost the control they had exercised over procreation, and were reduced to a passive role in child delivery, while male doctors came to be seen as the true "givers of life" (as in the alchemical dreams of the Renaissance magicians). With this shift, a new medical practice also prevailed, one that in the case of a medical emergency prioritized the life of the fetus over that of the mother. This was in contrast to the customary birthing process which women had controlled; and indeed, for it to happen, the community of women that had gathered around the bed of the future mother had to be first expelled from the delivery room, and midwives had to be placed under the surveillance of the doctor, or had to be recruited to police women.

In France and Germany, midwives had to become spies for the state, if they wanted to continue their practice. They were expected to report all new births, discover the fathers of children born out of wedlock, and examine the women suspected of having secretly given birth. They also had to examine suspected local women for any sign of lactation when foundlings were discovered on the Church's steps (Wiesner 1933: 52). The same type of collaboration was demanded of relatives and neighbors. In Protestant countries and towns, neighbors were supposed to spy on women and report all relevant sexual details: if a woman received a man when her husband was away, or if she entered a house with a man and shut the door behind her (Ozment 1983: 42–44). In Germany, the pro-natalist crusade reached such a point that women were punished if they did not make enough of an effort during child-delivery or showed little enthusiasm for their offspring (Rublack 1996: 92).

The outcome of these policies that lasted for two centuries (women were still being executed in Europe for infanticide at the end of the 18th century) was the enslavement of women to procreation. While in the Middle Ages women had been able to use various forms of contraceptives, and had exercised an undisputed control over the birthing process, from now on their wombs became public territory, controlled by men and the state, and procreation was directly placed at the service of capitalist accumulation.

In this sense, the destiny of West European women, in the period of primitive accumulation, was similar to that of female slaves in the American colonial plantations who, especially after the end of the slave-trade in 1807, were forced by their masters to become breeders of new workers. The comparison has obviously serious limits. European women were not openly delivered to sexual assaults — though proletarian women could be raped with impunity and punished for it. Nor had they to suffer the agony of seeing their children taken away and sold on the auction block. The economic profit derived from the births imposed upon them was also far more concealed. In this sense, it is the condition of the enslaved woman that most explicitly reveals the truth

Albrecht Dürer, THE BIRTH OF THE VIRGIN (1502-1503). Child-birth was one of the main events in the life of a woman and an occasion in which female cooperation triumphed.

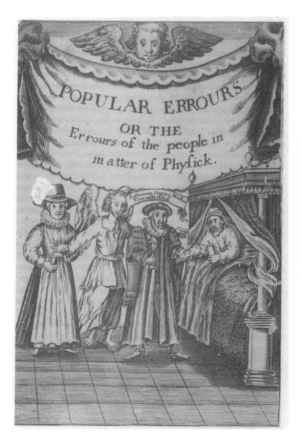

The masculinization of medical practice is portrayed in this English design picturing an angel pushing a female healer away from the bed of a sick man. The banner denounces her incompetence.

and the logic of capitalist accumulation. But despite the differences, in both cases, the female body was turned into an instrument for the reproduction of labor and the expansion of the work-force, treated as a natural breeding-machine, functioning according to rhythms outside of women's control.

This aspect of primitive accumulation is absent in Marx's analysis. Except for his remarks in the *Communist Manifesto* on the use of women within the bourgeois family — as producers of heirs guaranteeing the transmission of family property — Marx never acknowledged that procreation could become a terrain of exploitation and by the same token a terrain of resistance. He never imagined that women could refuse to reproduce, or that such a refusal could become part of class struggle. In the *Grundrisse* (1973: 100) he argued that capitalist development proceeds irrespective of population numbers because, by virtue of the increasing productivity of labor, the labor that capital exploits constantly diminishes in relation to "constant capital" (that is, the capital invested in machinery and other production assets), with the consequent determination of a "surplus population." But this dynamic, which Marx defines as the "law of population typical of the capitalist mode of production" (*Capital*,Vol. 1: 689ff.), could only prevail if procreation were a purely biological process, or an activity responding automatically to economic change, and if capital and the state did not need to worry about "women going on strike against child making." This, in fact, is what Marx assumed. He acknowledged that capitalist development has been accompanied by an increase in population, of which he occasionally discussed the causes. But, like Adam Smith, he saw this increase as a "natural effect" of economic development, and in *Capital,* Vol.1, he repeatedly contrasted the determination of a "surplus population" with the population's "natural increase." Why procreation should be "a fact of nature" rather than a social, historically determined activity, invested by diverse interests and power relations, is a question Marx did not ask. Nor did he imagine that men and women might have different interests with respect to child-making, an activity which he treated as a gender-neutral, undifferentiated process.

In reality, so far are procreation and population changes from being automatic or "natural" that, in all phases of capitalist development, the state has had to resort to regulation and coercion to expand or reduce the work-force. This was especially true at the time of the capitalist take-off, when the muscles and bones of workers were the primary means of production. But even later — down to the present — the state has spared no efforts in its attempt to wrench from women's hands the control over reproduction, and to determine which children should be born, where, when, or in what numbers. Consequently, women have often been forced to procreate against their will, and have experienced an alienation from their bodies, their "labor," and even their children, deeper than that experienced by any other workers (Martin 1987:19-21). No one can describe in fact the anguish and desperation suffered by a woman seeing her body turn against herself, as it must occur in the case of an unwanted pregnancy. This is particularly true in those situations in which out-of-wedlock pregnancies are penalized, and when having a child makes a woman vulnerable to social ostracism or even death.

The Devaluation of Women's Labor

The criminalization of women's control over procreation is a phenomenon whose importance cannot be overemphasized, both from the viewpoint of its effects on women and its consequences for the capitalist organization of work. As is well documented, through the Middle Ages women had possessed many means of contraception, mostly consisting of herbs which turned into potions and "pessaries" (suppositories) were used to quicken a woman's period, provoke an abortion, or create a condition of sterility. In *Eve's Herbs: A History of Contraception in the West* (1997), the American historian John Riddle has given us an extensive catalogue of the substances that were most used and the effects expected of them or most likely to occur.[61] The criminalization of contraception expropriated women from this knowledge that had been transmitted from generation to generation, giving them some autonomy with respect to child-birth. It appears that, in some cases, this knowledge was not lost but was only driven underground; yet when birth control again made its appearance on the social scene, contraceptive methods were no longer of the type that women could use, but were specifically created for use by men. What demographic consequences followed from this shift is a question that for the moment I will not pursue, though I refer to Riddle's work for a discussion of this matter. Here I only want to stress that by denying women control over their bodies, the state deprived them of the most fundamental condition for physical and psychological integrity and degraded maternity to the status of forced labor, in addition to confining women to reproductive work in a way unknown in previous societies. Nevertheless, forcing women to procreate against their will or (as a feminist song from the 1970s had it) forcing them to " produce children for the state,"[62] only in part defined women's function in the new sexual division of labor. A complementary aspect was the definition of women as non-workers, a process much studied by feminist historians, which by the end of the 17th century was nearly completed.

By this time women were losing ground even with respect to jobs that had been their prerogatives, such as ale-brewing and midwifery, where their employment was subjected to new restrictions. Proletarian women in particular found it difficult to obtain any job other than those carrying the lowest status: as domestic servants (the occupation of a third of the female work-force), farm-hands, spinners, knitters, embroiderers, hawkers, wet nurses. As Merry Wiesner (among others) tells us, the assumption was gaining ground (in the law, in the tax records, in the ordinances of the guilds) that women should not work outside the home, and should engage in "production" only in order to help their husbands. It was even argued that any work that women did at home was "non-work" and was worthless even when done for the market (Wiesner 1993: 83ff). Thus, if a woman sewed some clothes it was "domestic work" or "housekeeping," even if the clothes were not for the family, whereas when a man did the same task it was considered "productive." Such was the devaluation of women's labor that city governments told the guilds to overlook the production that women (especially widows) did in their homes, because it was not real work, and because the women needed it not to fall on public relief. Wiesner adds that women accepted this fiction and even apologized for asking to

The prostitute and the soldier. Often a camp follower, the prostitute performed the function of a wife for soldiers and other proletarians, washing and cooking for the men she served in addition to providing sexual services.

A prostitute inviting a client. The number of prostitutes increased immensely in the aftermath of land privatization and the commercialization of agriculture which expelled many peasant women from the land.

work, pleading for it on account of their need to support themselves (*ibid.*: 84–85). Soon all female work, if done in the home, was defined as "housekeeping," and even when done outside the home it was paid less than men's work, and never enough for women to be able to live by it. Marriage was now seen as a woman's true career, and women's inability to support themselves was taken so much for granted, that when a single woman tried to settle in a village, she was driven away even if she earned a wage.

Combined with land dispossession, this loss of power with regard to wage employment led to the massification of prostitution. As Le Roy Ladurie reports, the growth in the number of prostitutes in France was visible everywhere:

> From Avignon to Narbonne to Barcelona "sporting women" (*femmes de debauche*) stationed themselves at the gates of the cities, in streets of red-light districts... and on the bridges... [so that] by 1594 the "shameful traffic" was flourishing as never before (Le RoyLadurie 1974: 112–13).

The situation was similar in England and Spain, where, everyday, in the cities, poor women arriving from the countryside, and even the wives of craftsmen, rounded up the family income with this work. A proclamation issued by the political authorities in Madrid, in 1631, denounced the problem, complaining that many vagabond women were now wandering among the city's streets, alleys, and taverns, enticing men to sin with them (Vigil 1986: 114-5). But no sooner had prostitution become the main form of subsistence for a large female population than the institutional attitude towards it changed. Whereas in the late Middle Ages it had been officially accepted as a necessary evil, and prostitutes had benefited from the high wage regime, in the 16th century, the situation was reversed. In a climate of intense misogyny, characterized by the advance of the Protestant Reformation and witch-hunting, prostitution was first subjected to new restrictions and then criminalized. Everywhere, between 1530 and 1560, town brothels were closed and prostitutes, especially street-walkers, were subjected to severe penalties: banishment, flogging, and other cruel forms of chastisement. Among them was "the ducking stool" or *acabussade* — "a piece of grim theatre," as Nickie Roberts describes it — whereby the victims were tied up, sometimes they were forced into a cage, and then were repeatedly immersed in rivers or ponds, till they almost drowned (Roberts 1992: 115–16). Meanwhile, in 16th-century France, the raping of a prostitute ceased to be a crime.[63] In Madrid, as well, it was decided that female vagabonds and prostitutes should not be allowed to stay and sleep in the streets and under the porticos of the town, and if caught should be given a hundred lashes, and then should be banned from the city for six years in addition to having their heads and eyebrows shaved.

What can account for this drastic attack on female workers? And how does the exclusion of women from the sphere of socially recognized work and monetary relations relate to the impositon of forced maternity upon them, and the contemporary massification of the witch-hunt?

Looking at these phenomena from the vantage point of the present, after four centuries of capitalist disciplining of women, the answers may seem to impose themselves. Though women's waged work, housework, and (paid) sexual work are still studied all too often in isolation from each other, we are now in a better position to see that the discrimination that women have suffered in the waged work-force has been directly rooted in their function as unpaid laborers in the home. We can thus connect the banning of prostitution and the expulsion of women from the organized workplace with the creation of the housewife and the reconstruction of the family as the locus for the production of labor-power. However, from a theoretical and a political viewpoint, the fundamental question is under what conditions such degradation was possible, and what social forces promoted it or were complicitous with it.

The answer here is that an important factor in the devaluation of women's labor was the campaign that craft workers mounted, starting in the late 15th century, to exclude female workers from their work-shops, presumably to protect themselves from the assaults of the capitalist merchants who were employing women at cheaper rates. The craftsmen's efforts have left an abundant trail of evidence.[64] Whether in Italy,

A prostitute being subjected to the torture of the accabussade. "She will be submerged in the river several times and then imprisoned for life."

Like the "battle for the breeches," the image of the domineering wife challenging the sexual hierarchy and beating her husband was one of the favorite targets of 16th and 17th-century social literature.

France, or Germany, journeymen petitioned the authorities not to allow women to compete with them, banned them from their ranks, went on strike when the ban was not observed, and even refused to work with men who worked with women. It appears that the craftsmen were also interested in limiting women to domestic work because, given their economic difficulties, "the prudent household management on the part of a wife" was becoming for them an indispensable condition for avoiding bankruptcy and for keeping an independent shop. Sigrid Brauner (the author of the above citation) speaks of the importance accorded by the German artisans to this social rule (Brauner 1995: 96–97). Women tried to resist this onslaught, but — faced with the intimidating tactics male workers used against them — failed. Those who dared to work out of the home, in a public space and for the market, were portrayed as sexually aggressive shrews or even as "whores" and "witches" (Howell 1986: 182–83).[65] Indeed, there is evidence that the wave of misogyny that by the late 15th century was mounting in the European cities — reflected in the male obsession with the "battle for the breeches" and with the character of the disobedient wife, pictured in the popular literature in the act of beating her husband or riding on his back — emanated also from this (self-defeating) attempt to drive women from the workplace and from the market.

On the other hand, it is clear that this attempt would not have succeeded if the authorities had not cooperated with it. But they obviously saw that it was in their interest to do so. For, in addition to pacifying the rebellious journeymen, the displacement of women from the crafts provided the necessary basis for their fixation in reproductive labor and their utilization as low-waged workers in cottage industry.

Women: The New Commons and the Substitute for the Lost Land

It was from this alliance between the crafts and the urban authorities, along with the continuing privatization of land, that a new sexual division of labor or, better, a new "sexual contract,"[66] in Carol Pateman's words (1988), was forged, defining women in terms — mothers, wives, daughters, widows — that hid their status as workers, while giving men free access to women's bodies, their labor, and the bodies and labor of their children.

According to this new social-sexual contract, proletarian women became for male workers the substitute for the land lost to the enclosures, their most basic means of reproduction, and a communal good anyone could appropriate and use at will. Echoes of this "primitive appropriation" can be heard in the concept of the "common woman" (Karras 1989)[67] which in the 16th century qualified those who prostituted themselves. But in the new organization of work *every woman (other than those privatized by bourgeois men) became a communal good,* for once women's activities were defined as non-work, women's labor began to appear as a natural resource, available to all, no less than the air we breathe or the water we drink.

This was for women a historic defeat. With their expulsion from the crafts and the devaluation of reproductive labor poverty became feminized, and to enforce men's "primary appropriation" of women's labor, a new patriarchal order was constructed, reducing women to a double dependence: on employers and on men. The fact that unequal power relations between women and men existed even prior to the advent of capitalism, as did a discriminating sexual division of labor, does not detract from this assessment. For in pre-capitalist Europe women's subordination to men had been tempered by the fact that they had access to the commons and other communal assets, while in the new capitalist regime *women themselves became the commons,* as their work was defined as a natural resource, laying outside the sphere of market relations.

The Patriarchy of the Wage

Significant, in this context, are the changes that took place within the family which, in this period, began to separate from the public sphere and acquire its modern connotations as the main center for the reproduction of the work-force.

The counterpart of the market, the instrument for the privatization of social relations and, above all, for the propagation of capitalist discipline and patriarchal rule, the family emerges in the period of primitive accumulation also as the most important institution for the appropriation and concealment of women's labor.[68]

We see this in particular when we look at the working-class family. This is a subject that has been understudied. Previous discussions have privileged the family of propertied men, plausibly because, at the time to which we are referring, it was the dominant form and the model for parental and marital relations. There has also been more interest in the family as a political institution than as a place of work. What has been emphasized, then, is that in the new bourgeois family, the husband became the representative of the state, charged with disciplining and supervising the "subordinate classes," a category that for

16th and 17th-century political theorists (Jean Bodin, for example) included the man's wife and his children (Schochet 1975).Thus, the identification of the family as a micro-state or a micro-church, and the demand by the authorities that single workers live under the roof and rule of a master. It is also pointed out that within the bourgeois family the woman lost much of her power, being generally excluded from the family business and confined to the supervision of the household.

But what is missing in this picture is a recognition that, while in the upper class it was *property* that gave the husband power over his wife and children, a similar power was granted to working-class men over women by means of *women's exclusion from the wage*.

Exemplary of this trend was the family of the cottage workers in the putting-out system. Far from shunning marriage and family-making, male cottage workers depended on it, for a wife could "help" them with the work they would do for the merchants, while caring for their physical needs, and providing them with children, who from an early age could be employed at the loom or in some subsidiary occupation.Thus, even in times of population decline, cottage workers apparently continued to multiply; their families were so large that a contemporary 17th-century Austrian, looking at those living in his village, described them as packed in their homes like sparrows on a rafter. What stands out in this type of arrangement is that though the wife worked side-by-side with her husband, she too producing for the market, it was the husband who now received her wage.This was true also for other female workers once they married. In England "a married man… was legally entitled to his wife's earnings" even when the job she did was nursing or breast-feeding.Thus, when a parish employed women to do this kind of job, the records "frequently hid (their) presence as workers" registering the payment made in the men's names."Whether the payment was made to the husband or to the wife depended on the whim of the clerk" (Mendelson and Crawford 1998: 287).

This policy, making it impossible for women to have money of their own, created the material conditions for their subjection to men and the appropriation of their labor by male workers. It is in this sense that I speak of *the patriarchy of the wage*.[69] We must also rethink the concept of "wage slavery." If it is true that male workers became only formally free under the new wage-labor regime, the group of workers who, in the transition to capitalism, most approached the condition of slaves was working-class women.

At the same time — given the wretched conditions in which waged workers lived — the housework that women performed to reproduce their families was nec-essarily limited. Married or not, proletarian women needed to earn some money, which they did by holding multiple jobs. Housework, moreover, requires some repro-ductive capital: furniture, utensils, clothing, money for food. But waged workers lived poorly, "slaving away by day and night" (as an artisan from Nuremberg denounced in 1524), just to stave off hunger and feed their wives and children (Brauner 1995: 96). Most barely had a roof over their heads, living in huts where other families and animals also resided, and where hygiene (poorly observed even among the better off) was totally lacking; their clothes were rags, their diet at best consisted of bread, cheese and some vegetables. Thus, we do not find in this period, among the working class, the classic figure of the full-time housewife. It was only in the 19th century — in response to the first intense cycle of struggle against industrial work — that the "modern fam-ily" centered on the full-time housewife's unpaid reproductive labor was generalized in the working class, in England first and later in the United States.

Its development (following the passage of Factory Acts limiting the employment of women and children in the factories) reflected the first long-term investment the capitalist class made in the reproduction of the work-force beyond its numerical expansion. It was the result of a trade-off, forged under the threat of insurrection, between the granting of higher wages, capable of supporting a "non-working" wife, and a more intensive rate of exploitation. Marx spoke of it as a shift from "absolute" to "relative surplus," that is, a shift from a type of exploitation based upon the lengthening of the working day to a maximum and the reduction of the wage to a minimum, to a regime where higher wages and shorter hours would be compensated with an increase in the productivity of work and the pace of production. From the capitalist perspective, it was a social revolution, overriding a long-held commitment to low wages. It resulted from a new deal between workers and employers, again founded on the exclusion of women from the wage — putting an end to their recruitment in the early phases of the Industrial Revolution. It was also the mark of a new capitalist affluence, the product of two centuries of exploitation of slave labor, soon to be boosted by a new phase of colonial expansion.

In the 16th and 17th centuries, by contrast, despite an obsessive concern with the size of population and the number of "working poor," the actual investment in the reproduction of the work-force was extremely low. Consequently, the bulk of the reproductive labor done by proletarian women was not for their families, but for the families of their employers or for the market. One third of the female population, on average, in England, Spain, France, and Italy, worked as maids. Thus, in the proletariat, the tendency was towards the postponement of marriage and the disintegration of the family (16th-century English villages experienced a yearly turnover of fifty percent). Often the poor were even forbidden to marry, when it was feared that their children would fall on public relief, and when this actually happened, the children were taken away from them and farmed out to the parish to work. It is estimated that one third or more of the population of rural Europe remained single; in the towns the rates were even higher, especially among women; in Germany, forty percent were either "spinsters" or widows (Ozment 1983: 41–42).

Nevertheless — though the housework done by proletarian women was reduced to a minimum, and proletarian women had always to work for the market — within the working-class community of the transition period we already see the emergence of the sexual division of labor that was to become typical of the capitalist organization of work. At its center was an increasing differentiation between male and female labor, as the tasks performed by women and men became more diversified and, above all, became the carriers of different social relations.

Impoverished and disempowered as they may be, male waged workers could still benefit from their wives' labor and wages, or they could buy the services of prostitutes. Throughout this first phase of proletarianization, it was the prostitute who often performed for male workers the function of a wife, cooking and washing for them in addition to serving them sexually. Moreover, the criminalization of prostitution, which punished the woman but hardly touched her male customers, strengthened male power. Any man could now destroy a woman simply by declaring that she was a prostitute, or by publicizing that she had given in to his sexual desires. Women would have to plead with men "not to take away their honor" (the only property left to them) (Cavallo and Cerutti

1980: 346ff), the assumption being that their lives were now in the hands of men who (like feudal lords) could exercise over them a power of life and death.

The Taming of Women and the Redefinition of Femininity and Masculinity: Women the Savages of Europe

It is not surprising, then, in view of this devaluation of women's labor and social status, that the insubordination of women and the methods by which they could be "tamed" were among the main themes in the literature and social policy of the "transition" (Underdown 1985a: 116–36).[70] Women could not have been totally devalued as workers and deprived of autonomy with respect to men without being subjected to an intense process of social degradation; and indeed, throughout the 16th and 17th centuries, women lost ground in every area of social life.

A key area of change in this respect was the law, where in this period we can observe a steady erosion of women's rights.[71] One of the main rights that women lost was the right to conduct economic activities alone, as *femme soles*. In France, they lost the right to make contracts or to represent themselves in court, being declared legal "imbeciles." In Italy, they began to appear less frequently in the courts to denounce abuses perpetrated against them. In Germany, when a middle-class woman became a widow, it became customary to appoint a tutor to manage her affairs. German women were also forbidden to live alone or with other women and, in the case of the poor, even with their own families, since it was expected that they would not be properly controlled. In sum, together with economic and social devaluation, women experienced a process of legal infantilization.

Women's loss of social power was also expressed through a new sexual differentiation of space. In the Mediterranean countries women were expelled not only from many waged jobs but also from the streets, where an unaccompanied woman risked being subjected to ridicule or sexual assault (Davis 1998). In England, too, ("a women's paradise" in the eyes of some Italian visitors), the presence of women in public began to be frowned upon. English women were discouraged from sitting in front of their homes or staying near their windows; they were also instructed not to spend time with their female friends (in this period the term "gossip"— female friend — began to acquire a disparaging connotation). It was even recommended that women should not visit their parents too often after marriage.

How the new sexual division of labor reshaped male-female relations can be seen from the broad debate that was carried out in the learned and popular literature on the nature of female virtues and vices, one of the main avenues for the ideological redefinition of gender relations in the transition to capitalism. Known from an early phase as *"la querelle des femmes,"* what transpires from this debate is a new sense of curiosity for the subject, indicating that old norms were breaking down, and the public was becoming aware that the basic elements of sexual politics were being reconstructed. Two trends within this debate can be identified. On the one hand, new cultural canons were constructed maximizing the differences between women and men and creating more feminine and more masculine prototypes (Fortunati 1984). On the other hand, it was established that women were inher-

A scold is paraded through the community wearing the "bridle," an iron contraption used to punish women with a sharp tongue. Significantly, a similar device was used by European slavetraders in Africa to subdue their captives and carry them to their ships.

ently inferior to men — excessively emotional and lusty, unable to govern themselves — and had to be placed under male control. As with the condemnation of witchcraft, consensus on this matter cut across religious and intellectual lines. From the pulpit or the written page, humanists, Protestant reformers, counter-reformation Catholics, all cooperated in the vilification of women, constantly and obsessively.

Women were accused of being unreasonable, vain, wild, wasteful. Especially blamed was the female tongue, seen as an instrument of insubordination. But the main female villain was the disobedient wife, who, together with the "scold," the "witch," and the "whore" was the favorite target of dramatists, popular writers, and moralists. In this sense, Shakespeare's *The Taming of the Shrew* (1593) was the manifesto of the age. The punishment of female insubordination to patriarchal authority was called for and celebrated in countless misogynous plays and tracts. English literature of the Elizabethan and Jacobean period feasted on such themes. Typical of this genre is John Ford's *'Tis a Pity She's a Whore* (1633) which ends with the didactic assassination, execution and murder of three of the four female characters. Other classic works concerned with the disciplining of women are Joseph Swetnam's *The Arraignment of Lewed, Idle, Forward, Inconstant Women* (1615); and *The Parliament of Women* (1646), a satire primarily addressed against middle class women, which portrays them as busy making laws in order to gain supremacy over their husbands.[72] Meanwhile, new laws and new forms of torture were introduced to control women's behavior in and out of the home, confirming that the literary denigration of women expressed a precise political project aiming to strip them of any autonomy and social power. In the Europe of the Age of Reason, the women accused of being scolds were muzzled like dogs and paraded in the streets; prostitutes were whipped, or caged and subjected to fake drownings, while capital punishment was established for women convicted of adultery (Underdown 1985a: 117ff).

It is no exaggeration to say that women were treated with the same hostility and sense of estrangement accorded "Indian savages" in the literature that developed on this subject after the Conquest. The parallel is not casual. In both cases literary and cultural denigration was at the service of a project of expropriation. As we will see, the demonization of the American indigenous people served to justify their enslavement and the plunder of their resources. In Europe, the attack waged on women justified the appropriation of their labor by men and the criminalization of their control over reproduction. Always, the price of resistance was extermination. None of the tactics deployed against European women and colonial subjects would have succeeded, had they not been sustained by a campaign of terror. In the case of European women it was the witch-hunt that played the main role in the construction of their new social function, and the degradation of their social identity.

The definition of women as demonic beings, and the atrocious and humiliating practices to which so many of them were subjected left indelible marks in the collective female psyche and in women's sense of possibilities. From every viewpoint — socially, economically, culturally, politically — the witch-hunt was a turning point in women's lives; it was the equivalent of the historic defeat to which Engels alludes, in *The Origin of the Family, Private Property and the State* (1884), as the cause of the downfall of the

Frontispiece of THE PARLIAMENT OF WOMEN *(1646), a work typical of the anti-women satire that dominated English Literature in the period of the Civil War.*

matriarchal world. For the witch-hunt destroyed a whole world of female practices, collective relations, and systems of knowledge that had been the foundation of women's power in pre-capitalist Europe, and the condition for their resistance in the struggle against feudalism.

Out of this defeat a new model of femininity emerged: the ideal woman and wife — passive, obedient, thrifty, of few words, always busy at work, and chaste. This change began at the end of the 17th century, after women had been subjected for more than two centuries to state terrorism. Once women were defeated, the image of femininity constructed in the "transition" was discarded as an unnecessary tool, and a new, tamed one took its place. While at the time of the witch-hunt women had been portrayed as savage beings, mentally weak, unsatiably lusty, rebellious, insubordinate, incapable of self-control, by the 18th century the canon has been reversed. Women were now depicted as passive, asexual beings, more obedient, more moral than men, capable of exerting a positive moral influence on them. Even their irrationality could now be valorized, as the Dutch philosopher Pierre Bayle realized in his *Dictionnaire Historique et Critique* (1740), in which he praised the power of the female "maternal instinct," arguing that that it should be viewed as a truly providential device, ensuring that despite the disadvantages of childbirthing and childraising, women do continue to reproduce.

Colonization, Globalization, and Women

While the response to the population crisis in Europe was the subjugation of women to reproduction, in colonial America, where colonization destroyed ninety five percent of the aboriginal population, the response was the slave trade which delivered to the European ruling class an immense quantity of labor-power.

As early as the 16th century, approximately one million African slaves and indigenous workers were producing surplus-value for Spain in colonial America, at a rate of exploitation far higher than that of workers in Europe, and contributing to sectors of the European economy that were developing in a capitalist direction (Blaut 1992a: 45–46).[73] By 1600, Brazil alone exported twice the value in sugar of all the wool that England exported in the same year (*ibid.*: 42). The accumulation rate was so high in the Brazilian sugar plantations that every two years they doubled their capacity. Gold and silver too played a key role in the solution to the capitalist crisis. Gold imported from Brazil reactivated commerce and industry in Europe (DeVries 1976: 20). More than 17,000 tons were imported by 1640, giving the capitalist class there an exceptional advantage in access to workers, commodities, and land (Blaut 1992a: 38–40). But the true wealth was the labor accumulated through the slave trade, which made possible a mode of production that could not be imposed in Europe.

It is now established that the plantation system fueled the Industrial Revolution, as argued by Eric Williams, who noted that hardly a brick in Liverpool and Bristol was not cemented with African blood (1944: 61–63). But capitalism may not even have taken off without Europe's "annexation of America," and the "blood and sweat" that for two centuries flowed to Europe from the plantations. This must be stressed, as it helps us realize how essential slavery has been for the history of capitalism, and why, periodically, but systematically, whenever the capitalist system is threatened by a major economic crisis, the capitalist class has to launch a process of "primitive accumulation," that is, a process of large-scale colonization and enslavement, such as the one we are witnessing at present (Bales 1999).

The plantation system was crucial for capitalist development not only because of the immense amount of surplus labor that was accumulated from it, but because it set a model of labor management, export-oriented production, economic integration and international division of labor that have since become paradigmatic for capitalist class relations.

With its immense concentration of workers and its captive labor force uprooted from its homeland, unable to rely on local support, the plantation prefigured not only the factory but also the later use of immigration and globalization to cut the cost of labor. In particular, the plantation was a key step in the formation of an international division of labor that (through the production of "consumer goods") integrated the work of the slaves into the reproduction of the European work-force, while keeping enslaved and waged workers geographically and socially divided.

The colonial production of sugar, tea, tobacco, rum, and cotton — the most important commodities, together with bread, in the production of labor-power in Europe — did not take off on a large scale until after the 1650s, after slavery had been institutionalized and wages in Europe had begun to (modestly) rise (Rowling 1987: 51, 76, 85). It must be mentioned here, however, because, when it did take off, two mechanisms were introduced that significantly restructured the reproduction of labor internationally. On one side, a global assembly line was created that cut the cost of the commodities necessary to produce labor-power in Europe, and linked enslaved and waged workers in ways that pre-figured capitalism's present use of Asian, African, and Latin American workers as providers of "cheap" consumer goods (cheapened by death squads and military violence) for the "advanced" capitalist countries.

On the other side, the metropolitan wage became the vehicle by which the goods produced by enslaved workers went to the market, and the value of the products of enslaved-labor was realized. In this way, as with female domestic work, the integration of enslaved labor into the production and reproduction of the metropolitan work-force was further established, and the wage was further redefined as an instrument of accumulation, that is, as a lever for mobilizing not only the labor of the workers paid by it, but also for the labor of a multitude of workers hidden by it, because of the unwaged conditions of their work.

Did workers in Europe know that they were buying products resulting from slave labor and, if they did, did they object to it? This is a question we would like to ask them, but it is one which I cannot answer. What is certain is that the history of tea, sugar, rum, tobacco, and cotton is far more significant than we can deduce from the contribution which these commodities made, as raw materials or means of exchange in the slave trade, to the rise of the factory system. For what traveled with these "exports" was not only the blood of the slaves but the seeds of a new science of exploitation, and a new division of the working class by which waged-work, rather than providing an alternative to slavery, was made to depend on it for its existence, as a means (like female unpaid labor) for the expansion of the unpaid part of the waged working-day.

So closely integrated were the lives of the enslaved laborers in America and waged laborers in Europe that in the Caribbean islands, where slaves were given plots of land ("provision grounds") to cultivate for their own use, how much land was allotted to them, and how much time was given to them to cultivate it, varied in proportion to the price of sugar on the world-market (Morrissey 1989: 51–59) — plausibly determined by the dynamics of workers' wages and workers' struggle over reproduction.

It would be a mistake, however, to conclude that the integration of slave labor in the production of the European waged proletariat created a community of interests between European workers and the metropolitan capitalists, presumably cemented by their common desire for cheap imported goods.

In reality, like the Conquest, the slave trade was an epochal misfortune for European workers. As we have seen, slavery (like the witch-hunt) was a major ground of experimentation for methods of labor-control that were later imported into Europe. Slavery also affected the European workers' wages and legal status; for it cannot be a coincidence that only with the end of slavery did wages in Europe decisively increase and did European workers gain the right to organize.

It is also hard to imagine that workers in Europe profited from the Conquest of America, at least in its initial phase. Let us remember that it was the intensity of the anti-feudal struggle that instigated the lesser nobility and the merchants to seek colonial expansion, and that the conquistadors came from the ranks of the most-hated enemies of the European working class. It is also important to remember that the Conquest provided the European ruling class with the silver and gold used to pay the mercenary armies that defeated the urban and rural revolts; and that, in the same years when Arawaks, Aztecs, and Incas were being subjugated, workers in Europe were being driven from their homes, branded like animals, and burnt as witches.

We should not assume, then, that the European proletariat was always an accomplice to the plunder of the Americas, though individual proletarians undoubtedly were. The nobility expected so little cooperation from the "lower classes" that initially the Spaniards allowed only a few to embark. Only 8,000 Spaniards migrated legally to the Americas in the entire 16th century, the clergy making up 17% of the lot (Hamilton 1965: 299; Williams 1986: 38–40). Even later, people were forbidden from settling overseas independently, because it was feared that they might collaborate with the local population.

For most proletarians, in the 17th and 18th centuries, access to the New World was through indentured servitude and "transportation," the punishment which the authorities in England adopted to rid the country of convicts, political and religious dissidents, and the vast population of vagabonds and beggars that was produced by the enclosures. As Peter Linebaugh and Marcus Rediker point out in *The Many-Headed Hydra* (2000), the colonizers' fear of unrestricted migration was well-founded, given the wretched living conditions that prevailed in Europe, and the appeal exercised by the reports that circulated about the New World, which pictured it as a wonder land where people lived free from toil and tyranny, masters and greed, and where "myne" and "thyne" had no place, all things being held in common (Linebaugh and Rediker 2000; Brandon 1986: 6–7). So strong was the attraction exercised by the New World that the vision of a new society it provided apparently influenced the political thought of the Enlightenment, contributing to the emergence of a new concept of "liberty," taken to signify masterlessness, an idea previously unknown in European political theory (Brandon 1986: 23–28). Not surprisingly, some Europeans tried to "lose themselves" in this utopian world where, as Linebaugh and Rediker powerfully put it, they could reconstruct the lost experience of the commons (2000: 24). Some lived for years with Indian tribes despite the restrictions placed on those who settled in the American colonies and the heavy price to be paid if caught, since escapees were treated like traitors and put to death. This was the fate of some young English settlers in Virginia who, having run away to live with the Indians, on being caught were condemned by the colony's councilmen to be "burned, broken on the wheel... [and] hanged or shot to death" (Koning 1993: 61). "Terror created boundaries," Linebaugh and Rediker comment (2000: 34). Yet, as late as 1699, the English still had a great difficulty persuading the people whom the Indians had captivated to leave their Indian manner of living.

> No argument, no entreaties, no tears [a contemporary reported]... could persuade many of them to leave their Indian friends. On the other hand, Indian children have been carefully educated among the English, clothed and taught, yet there is not one instance that any of these would remain, but returned to their own nations (Koning 1993: 60).

As for the European proletarians who signed themselves away into indentured servitude or arrived in the New World in consequence of a penal sentence, their lot was not too different, at first, from that of the African slaves with whom they often worked side by side. Their hostility to their masters was equally intense, so that the planters viewed them as a dangerous lot and, by the second half of the 17th century, began to limit their use and introduced a legislation aimed at separating them from the Africans. But only at the end of the 18th century were racial boundaries irrevocably drawn (Moulier Boutang 1998). Until then, the possibility of alliances between whites, blacks, and aboriginal peoples, and the fear of such unity in the European ruling class' imagination, at home and on the plantations, was constantly present. Shakespeare gave voice to it in *The Tempest* (1612) where he pictured the conspiracy organized by Caliban, the native rebel, son of a witch, and by Trinculo and Stephano, the ocean-going European proletarians, suggesting the possibility of a fatal alliance among the oppressed, and providing a dramatic counterpoint to Prospero's magic healing of the discord among the rulers.

In *The Tempest* the conspiracy ends ignominiously, with the European proletarians demonstrating to be nothing better than petty thieves and drunkards, and with Caliban begging forgiveness from his colonial master. Thus, when the defeated rebels are brought in front of Prospero and his former enemies Sebastian and Antonio (now reconciled with him), they are met with derision and thoughts of ownership and division:

SEBASTIAN. What things are these, my lord Antonio?
Will money buy them?

ANTONIO. Very like; one of them is a plain fish, and, no doubt, marchetable.

PROSPERO. Mark but the badges of these men, my lords,
Then say if they be true. This mis-shapen knave,
His mother was a witch, and one so strong
That could control the moon, make flows and ebbs,
And deal in her command without her power.
These three have robbed me; and this demi-devil—
For he's a bastard one — had plotted with them
To take my life. Two of these fellows you
Must know and own. This thing of darkness I
Acknowledge mine. (Shakespeare, Act V, Scene 1, lines 265–276)

Offstage, however, the threat continued. "Both on Bermuda and Barbados white servants were discovered plotting with African slaves, as thousands of convicts were being shipped there in the 1650s from the British islands" (Rowling 1987: 57). In Virginia the peak in the alliance between black and white servants was Bacon's Rebellion of 1675–76, when African slaves and British indentured servants joined together to conspire against their masters.

It is for this reason that, starting in the 1640s, the accumulation of an enslaved proletariat in the Southern American colonies and the Caribbean was accompanied by the construction of racial hierarchies, thwarting the possibility of such combinations. Laws were passed depriving Africans of previously granted civic rights, such as citizenship, the right to bear arms, and the right to make depositions or seek redress in a tribunal for injuries suffered. The turning point was when slavery was made an hereditary condition, and the slave masters were given the right to beat and kill their slaves. In addition, marriages between "blacks" and "whites" were forbidden. Later, after the American War of Independence, white indentured servitude, deemed a vestige of British rule, was eliminated. As a result, by the late 18th century, colonial America had moved from "a society with slaves to a slave society" (Moulier Boutang 1998: 189), and the possibility of solidarity between Africans and whites had been severely undermined. "White," in the colonies, became not just a badge of social and economic privilege "serving to designate those who until 1650 had been called 'Christians' and afterwards 'English' or 'free men'" (*ibid.*:194), but a moral attribute, a means by which social hegemony was naturalized. "Black" or "African," by contrast, became synonymous with slave, so much so that free black people — still a sizeable presence in early 17th-century America — were later forced to prove that they were free.

Sex, Race and Class in the Colonies

Would Caliban's conspiracy have had a different outcome had its protagonists been women? Had the instigators been not Caliban but his mother, Sycorax, the powerful Algerian witch that Shakespeare hides in the play's background, and not Trinculo and Stephano but the sisters of the witches who, in the same years of the Conquest, were being burned in Europe at the stake?

This question is a rhetorical one, but it serves to question the nature of the sexual division of labor in the colonies, and of the bonds that could be established there between European, indigenous, and African women by virtue of a common experience of sexual discrimination.

In *I, Tituba, Black Witch of Salem* (1992), Maryse Condé gives us an insight into the kind of situation that could produce such bonding, by describing how Tituba and her new mistress, the Puritan Samuel Parris' young wife, gave each other support at first against his murderous contempt for women.

An even more outstanding example comes from the Caribbean, where low-class English women "transported" from Britain as convicts or indentured servants became a significant part of the labor-gangs on the sugar estates. "Considered unfit for marriage by propertied white males, and disqualified for domestic service," because of their insolence and riotous disposition, "landless white women were dismissed to manual labor in plantations, public construction works, and the urban service sector. In these worlds they socialized intimately with the slave community, and with enslaved black men." They established households and had children with them (Beckles 1995: 131–32). They also cooperated as well as competed with female slaves in the marketing of produce or stolen goods.

But with the institutionalization of slavery, which was accompanied by a lessening of the burden for white workers, and a decrease in the number of women arriving from Europe as wives for the planters, the situation changed drastically. Regardless of their social origin, white women were upgraded, or married off within the ranks of the white power structure, and whenever possible they became owners of slaves themselves, usually female ones, employed for domestic work (*ibid.*).[74]

This, however, was not an automatic process. Like sexism, racism had to be legislated and enforced. Among the most revealing prohibitions we must again count that marriage and sexual relations between blacks and whites were forbidden, white women who married black slaves were condemned, and the children resulting from such marriages were enslaved for life. Passed in Maryland and Virginia in the 1660s, these laws prove that a segregated, racist society was instituted from above, and that intimate relations between "blacks" and "whites" must have been very common, indeed, if life-enslavement was deemed necessary to terminate them.

As if following the script laid out by the witch-hunt, the new laws demonized the relation between white women and black men. When they were passed in the 1660s, the witch-hunt in Europe was coming to an end, but in America all the taboos surrounding the witch and the black devil were being revived, this time at the expense of black men.

"Divide and rule" also became official policy in the Spanish colonies, after a period when the numerical inferiority of the colonists recommended a more liberal attitude towards inter-ethnic relations and alliances with the local chiefs through marriage. But, in the 1540s, as the increase in the number of *mestizos* was undermining colonial privilege, "race" was established as a key factor in the transmission of property, and a racial hierarchy was put in place to separate indigenous, *mestizos*, and *mulattos* from each other and from the white population (Nash 1980).[75] Prohibitions relating to marriage and female sexuality served here, too, to enforce social exclusion. But in Spanish America, segregation along racial lines succeeded only in part, checked by migration, population

A female slave being branded. The branding of women by the devil had figured prominently in the European witch-trials, as a symbol of total subjugation. But in reality, the true devils were the white slave traders and plantation owners who (like the men in this picture) did not hesitate to treat the women they enslaved like cattle.

decline, indigenous revolt, and the formation of a white urban proletariat with no prospect of economic advancement, and therefore prone to identify with mestizos and mulattos more than with the white upper-class. Thus, while in the plantation societies of the Caribbean the differences between European and Africans increased with time, in the South American colonies a "re-composition" became possible, especially among low-class European, *mestiza*, and African women who, beside their precarious economic position, shared the disadvantages deriving from the double standard built into the law, which made them vulnerable to male abuse.

Signs of this "recomposition" can be found in the records which the Inquisition kept in 18th-century Mexico of the investigations it conducted to eradicate magical and heretic beliefs (Behar 1987: 34–51). The task was hopeless, and soon the Inquisition lost interest in the project, convinced that popular magic was no longer a threat to the political order. But the testimonies it collected reveal the existence of multiple exchanges among women in matters relating to magical cures and love remedies, creating in time a new cultural reality drawn from the encounter between the African, European and indigenous magical traditions. As Ruth Behar writes:

> Indian women gave hummingbirds to Spanish healers for use in sexual attraction, mulatta women told mestiza women how to tame their husbands, a loba sorceress introduced a coyota to the Devil. This "popular" system of belief ran parallel to the system of belief of the Church, and it spread as quickly as Christianity did in the New World, so that after a while it became impossible to distinguish in it what was "Indian" or "Spanish" or "African" (*ibid.*).[76]

Assimilated in the eyes of the Inquisition as people "without reason," this variegated female world which Ruth Behar describes is a telling example of the alliances that, across colonial and color lines, women could build, by virtue of their common experience, and their interest in sharing the traditional knowledges and practices available to them to control their reproduction and fight sexual discrimination.

Like discrimination on the basis of "race," this was more than a cultural baggage which the colonizers brought from Europe with their pikes and horses. No less than the destruction of communalism, it was a strategy dictated by specific economic interest and the need to create the preconditions for a capitalist economy, and as such always adjusted to the task at hand.

In Mexico and Peru, where population decline recommended that female domestic labor in the home be incentivized, a new sexual hierarchy was introduced by the Spanish authorities that stripped indigenous women of their autonomy, and gave their male kin more power over them. Under the new laws, married women became men's property, and were forced (against the traditional custom) to follow their husbands to their homes. A *compadrazgo* system was also created further limiting their rights, placing the authority over children in male hands. In addition, to ensure that indigenous women reproduced the workers recruited to do *mita* work in the mines, the Spanish authorities legislated that no one could separate husband from wife, which meant that women were forced to follow their husbands whether they wanted it or not, even to areas known to be death camps, due to the pollution created by the mining (Cook Noble 1981:205-6).[77]

The intervention of the French Jesuits in the disciplining and training of the Montagnais-Naskapi, in mid-17th century Canada, provides a revealing example of how gender differences were accumulated. The story is told by the late anthropologist Eleanor Leacock in her *Myths of Male Dominance* (1981), where she examines the diary of one of its protagonists. This was Father Paul Le Jeune, a Jesuit missionary who, in typical colonial fashion, had joined a French trading post to Christianize the Indians, and turn them into citizens of "New France." The Montagnais-Naskapi were a nomadic Indian nation that had lived in great harmony, hunting and fishing in the eastern Labrador Peninsula. But by the time of Le Jeune's arrival, their community was being undermined by the presence of Europeans and the spread of fur-trading, so that some men, eager to strike a commercial alliance with them, were amenable to letting the French dictate how they should govern themselves (Leacock 1981: 39ff).

As often happened when Europeans came in contact with native American populations, the French were impressed by Montagnais-Naskapi generosity, their sense of cooperation and indifference to status, but they were scandalized by their "lack of morals;" they saw that the Naskapi had no conception of private property, of authority, of male superiority, and they even refused to punish their children (Leacock 1981: 34–38). The Jesuits decided to change all that, setting out to teach the Indians the basic elements of civilization, convinced that this was necessary to turn them into reliable trade partners. In this spirit, they first taught them that "man is the master," that "in France women do not rule their husbands," and that courting at night, divorce at either partner's desire, and sexual freedom for both spouses, before or after marriage, had to be forbidden. Here is a telling exchange Le Jeune had, on this score, with a Naskapi man:

> "I told him it was not honorable for a woman to love anyone else except her husband, and that this evil being among them, he himself was not sure that his son, who was present, was his son. He replied, 'Thou has no sense. You French people love only your children; but we love all the children of our tribe.' I began to laugh seeing that he philosophized in horse and mule fashion" (*ibid*.: 50).

Backed by the Governor of New France, the Jesuits succeeded in convincing the Naskapi to provide themselves with some chiefs, and bring "their" women to order. Typically, one weapon they used was to insinuate that women who were too independent and did not obey their husbands were creatures of the devil. When, angered by the men's attempts to subdue them, the Naskapi women ran away, the Jesuits persuaded the men to chase after their spouses and threaten them with imprisonment:

> "Such acts of justice" — Le Jeune proudly commented in one particular case — "cause no surprise in France, because it is usual there to proceed in that manner. But among these people... where everyone considers himself from birth as free as the wild animals that roam in their great forests... it is a marvel, or rather a miracle, to see a peremptory command obeyed, or any act of severity or justice performed" (*ibid*.: 54).

The Jesuits' greatest victory, however, was persuading the Naskapi to beat their children, believing that the "savages'" excessive fondness for their offspring was the major obstacle to their Christianization. Le Jeune's diary records the first instance in which a girl was publicly beaten, while one of her relatives gave a chilling lecture to the bystanders on the historic significance of the event: "This is the first punishment by beating (he said) we inflict on anyone of our Nation..." (*ibid*.: 54–55).

The Montagnais-Naskapi men owed their training in male supremacy to the fact that the French wanted to instill in them the "instinct" for private property, to induce them to become reliable partners in the fur trade. Very different was the situation on the plantations, where the sexual division of labor was immediately dictated by the planters' requirements for labor-power, and by the price of commodities produced by the slaves on the international market.

Until the abolition of the slave trade, as Barbara Bush and Marietta Morrissey have documented, both women and men were subjected to the same degree of exploitation; the planters found it more profitable to work and "consume" slaves to death than to encourage their reproduction. Neither the sexual division of labor nor sexual hierarchies were thus pronounced. African men had no say concerning the destiny of their female companions and kin; as for women, far from being given special consideration, they were expected to work in the fields like men, especially when sugar and tobacco were in high demand, and they were subject to the same cruel punishments, even when pregnant (Bush 1990: 42–44).

Ironically then, it would seem that in slavery women "achieved" a rough equality with the men of their class (Momsen 1993). But their treatment was never the same. Women were given less to eat; unlike men, they were vulnerable to their masters' sexual assaults; and more cruel punishment were inflicted on them, for in addition to the physical agony women had to bear the sexual humiliation always attached to them and the damage done, when pregnant, to the fetuses they carried.

A new page, moreover, opened after 1807, when the slave trade was abolished and the Caribbean and American planters adopted a "slave breeding" policy. As Hilary Beckles points out, in relation to the island of Barbados, plantation owners had attempted to control the reproductive patterns of female slaves since the 17th century, "[encouraging] them to have fewer or more children in any given span of time," depending on how much field labor was needed. But only when the supply of African slaves diminished did the regulation of women's sexual relations and reproductive patterns become more systematic and intense (Beckles 1989: 92).

In Europe, forcing women to procreate had led to the imposition of capital punishment for contraception. In the plantations, where slaves were becoming a precious commodity, the shift to a breeding policy made women more vulnerable to sexual assault, though it led to some "ameliorations" of women's work conditions: a reduction of work-hours, the building of lying-in-houses, the provision of midwives assisting the delivery, an expansion of social rights (e.g., of travel and assembly)(Beckles: 1989: 99–100; Bush 1990: 135). But these changes could not reduce the damages inflicted on women by field-labor, nor the bitterness women experienced because of their lack of freedom. With the exception of Barbados, the planters' attempt to expand the work-force through "natural reproduction" failed, and the birth rates on the plantations remained "abnormally low" (Bush 136–37; Beckles 1989, *ibid.*). Whether this phenomenon was a result of outright resistance to the perpetuation of slavery, or a consequence of the physical debilitation produced by the harsh conditions to which enslaved women were subjected, is still a matter of debate (Bush 1990: 143ff). But, as Bush points out, there are good reasons to believe that the main cause of the failure was the refusal of women to procreate, for as soon as slavery was eradicated, even when their economic conditions in some respect deteriorated, the communities of freed slaves began to grow (Bush 1990).[78]

Women's refusals of victimization also reshaped the sexual division of labor, as occurred in Caribbean islands where enslaved women turned themselves into semi-free market vendors of the products they cultivated in the "provision grounds" (in Jamaica, "polinks"), given by the planters to the slaves so that they could to support themselves. The planters adopted this measure to save on the cost of reproducing labor. But access to the "provision grounds" turned out to be advantageous for the slaves as well; it gave them more mobility, and the possibility to use the time allotted for their cultivation for other activities. Being able to produce small crops that could be eaten or sold boosted their independence. Those most devoted to the success of the provision grounds were women, who marketed the crops, re-appropriating and reproducing within the plantation system what had been one of their main occupations in Africa. As a result, by the mid-18th century, enslaved women in the Caribbean had carved out for themselves a place in the plantation economy, contributing to the expansion, if not the creation, of the island's food market. They did so both as producers of much of the food consumed by the slaves and the white population, and also as hucksters and market vendors of the crops they cultivated, supplemented with goods taken from the master's shop, or exchanged with other slaves, or given to them for sale by their masters.

It was in this capacity that female slaves also came into contact with white proletarian women, often former indentured servants, even after the latter had been removed from gang-labor and emancipated. Their relationship at times could be hostile: proletarian European women, who also survived mostly through the growing and marketing of food crops, stole at times the products that slave women brought to the market, or attempted to impede their sales. But both groups of women also collaborated in building a vast network of buying and selling relations which evaded the laws passed by the colonial authorities, who periodically worried that these activities may place the slaves beyond their control.

Despite the legislation introduced to prevent them from selling or limiting the places in which they could do so, enslaved women continued to expand their marketing activities and the cultivation of their provision plots, which they came to view as their own so that, by the late 18th century, they were forming a proto-peasantry with practically a monopoly of island markets. Thus, according to some historians, even before emancipation, slavery in the Caribbean had practically ended. Female slaves — against all odds — were a key force in this process, the ones who, with their determination, shaped the development of the slave community and of the islands' economies, despite the authorities' many attempts to limit their power.

Enslaved Caribbean women had also a decisive impact on the culture of the white population, especially that of white women, through their activities as healers, seers, experts in magical practices, and their "domination" of the kitchens, and bedrooms, of their masters (Bush 1990).

Not surprisingly, they were seen as the heart of the slave community. Visitors were impressed by their singing, their head-kerchiefs and dresses, and their extravagant manner of speaking which are now understood as a means of satirizing their masters. African and Creole women influenced the customs of poor female whites, whom a contemporary portrayed as behaving like Africans, walking with their children strapped on their hips, while balancing trays with goods on their heads (Beckles 1989: 81). But their main achievement was the development of a politics of self-reliance, grounded in survival strategies and female networks. These practices and the values attached to them, which Rosalyn Terborg Penn has identified as the essential tenets of contemporary African feminism, redefined the African community of the diaspora (pp. 3–7). They created not only the foundations for a new female African identity, but also the foundations for a new society committed — against the capitalist attempt to impose scarcity and dependence

Above: A family of slaves (detail). Enslaved women struggled to continue the activities they had carried on in Africa, such as marketing the produce they grew, which enabled them to better support their families and achieve some autonomy. (From Barbara Bush, 1990.)

Below: A festive gathering on a West Indian plantation. Women were the heart of such gatherings as they were the heart of the enslaved community, and the staunchest defenders of the culture brought from Africa.

as structural conditions of life — to the re-appropriation and concentration in women's hands of the fundamental means of subsistence, starting from the land, the production of food, and the inter-generational transmission of knowledge and cooperation.

Capitalism and the Sexual Divison of Labor

As this brief history of women and primitive accumulation has shown, the construction of a new patriarchal order, making of women the servants of the male work-force, was a major aspect of capitalist development.

On its basis a new sexual division of labor could be enforced that differentiated not only the tasks that women and men should perform, but their experiences, their lives, their relation to capital and to other sectors of the working class. Thus, no less than the international division of labor, the sexual division of labor was above all a power-relation, a division within the work-force, while being an immense boost to capital accumulation.

This point must be emphasized, given the tendency to attribute the leap capitalism brought about in the productivity of labor only to the specialization of work-tasks. In reality, the advantages which the capitalist class derived from the differentiation between agricultural and industrial labor and within industrial labor itself — celebrated in Adam Smith's ode to pin-making — pale when compared to those it derived from the degradation of women's work and social position.

As I have argued, the power-difference between women and men and the concealment of women's unpaid-labor under the cover of natural inferiority, have enabled capitalism to immensely expand the "unpaid part of the working day," and use the (male) wage to accumulate women's labor; in many cases, they have also served to deflect class antagonism into an antagonism between men and women. Thus, primitive accumulation has been above all an accumulation of differences, inequalities, hierarchies, divisions, which have alienated workers from each other and even from themselves.

As we have seen, male workers have often been complicitous with this process, as they have tried to maintain their power with respect to capital by devaluing and disciplining women, children, and the populations the capitalist class has colonized. But the power that men have imposed on women by virtue of their access to wage-labor and their recognized contribution to capitalist accumulation has been paid at the price of self-alienation, and the "primitive disaccumulation" of their own individual and collective powers.

In the next chapters I further examine this disaccumulation process by discussing three key aspects of transition from feudalism to capitalism: the constitution of the proletarian body into a work-machine, the persecution of women as witches, and the creation of "savages" and "cannibals" both in Europe and the New World.

Endnotes

1. Peter Blickle objects to the concept of a "peasant war" because of the social composition of this revolution, which included many artisans, miners, and intellectuals among its ranks. The Peasant War combined ideological sophistication, expressed in the twelve "articles" which the rebels put forward, and a powerful military organization. The twelve "articles" included: the refusal of bondage, a reduction of the tithes, a repeal of the poaching laws, an affirmation of the rights to gather wood, a lessening of labor services, a reduction of rents, an affirmation of the rights to use the common, and an abolition of death taxes (Bickle 1985: 195-201). The exceptional military prowess demonstrated by the rebels depended in part on the participation of professional soldiers in the revolt, including the Landsknechte — the famous Swiss soldiers who, at the time, were the elite mercenary troops in Europe. The Landsknechte headed the peasant armies, putting their military expertise at their service and, in various occasions, refused to move against the rebels. In one case, they motivated their refusal by arguing that they too came from the peasantry and that they depended on the peasants for their sustenance in times of peace. When it was clear that they could not be trusted, the German princes mobilized the troops of the Swabian League, drawn from more remote regions, to break the peasant resistance. On the history of the Landsknechte and their participation in the Peasant War, see Reinhard Baumann, *I Lanzichenecchi* (1994: 237-256).

2. The Anabaptists, politically, represented a fusion of "the late medieval social movements and the new anti-clerical movement sparked off by the Reformation." Like the medieval heretics, they condemned economic individualism and greed and supported a form of Christian communalism. Their take-over of Munster occurred in the wake of the Peasant War, when unrest and urban insurrections spread from Frankfurt to Cologne and other towns of Northern Germany. In 1531, the crafts took control of the city of Munster, renamed it New Jerusalem, and under the influence of immigrant Dutch Anabaptists, installed in it a communal government based upon the sharing of goods. As Po-Chia Hsia writes, the records of New Jerusalem were destroyed and its story has been told only by its enemies. Thus, we should not presume that events unfolded as narrated. According to the available records, women had at first enjoyed a high degree of freedom in the town; for instance, "they could divorce their unbelieving husbands and enter into new marriages." Things changed with the decision by the reformed government to introduce polygamy in 1534, which provoked an "active resistance" among women, presumably repressed with imprisonment and even executions (Po-Chia Hsia 1988a: 58-59). Why this decision was taken is not clear. But the episode deserves more investigation, given the divisive role that the crafts played in the "transition" with regard to women. We know, in fact, that the craft campaigned in several countries to exclude women from the waged work-place, and nothing indicates that they opposed the persecution of the witches.

3. For the rise of the real wage and the fall of prices in England, see North and Thomas (1973: 74). For Florentine wages, see Carlo M. Cipolla (1994: 206). For

the fall in the value of output in England see R. H. Britnel (1993: 156-171). On the stagnation of agricultural production in a number of European countries, see B.H. Slicher Van Bath (1963: 160-170). Rodney Hilton argues that this period saw "a contraction of the rural and industrial economies...probably felt in the first place by the ruling class.... Seigneurial revenues and industrial and commercial profits began to fall.... Revolt in the towns disorganized industrial production and revolt in the countryside strengthened peasant resistance to the payment of rent. Rent and profits thus dropped even further" (Hilton 1985: 240-241).

4. On Maurice Dobb and the debate on the transition to capitalism, see Harvey J. Kaye, *The British Marxist Historians*. New York: St. Martin's Press, (1984), 23-69.

5. Critics of Marx's concept of "primitive accumulation" include: Samir Amin (1974) and Maria Mies (1986). While Samir Amin focusses on Marx's Eurocentrism, Mies stresses Marx's blindness to the exploitation of women. A different critique is found in Yann Moulier Boutang (1998) who faults Marx for generating the impression that the objective of the ruling class in Europe was to free itself from an unwanted work-force. Moulier Boutang underlines that the opposite was the case: land expropriation aimed to fix workers to their jobs, not to encourage mobility. Capitalism — as Moulier Boutang stresses — has always been primarily concerned with preventing the flight of labor (pp. 16–27).

6. As Michael Perelman points out, the term "primitive accumulation" was actually coined by Adam Smith and rejected by Marx, because of its ahistorical character in Smith's usage. "To underscore his distance from Smith, Marx prefixed the pejorative 'so-called' to the title of the final part of the first volume of *Capital*, which he devoted to the study of primitive accumulation. Marx, in essence, dismissed Smith's mythical 'previous' accumulation in order to call attention to the actual historical experience" (Perlman 1985: 25-26).

7. On the relation between the historical and the logical dimension of "primitive accumulation" and its implications for political movements today see: Massimo De Angelis, "Marx and Primitive Accumulation. The Continuous Character of Capital 'Enclosures'." In *The Commoner*: www.commoner.org.uk; Fredy Perlman, *The Continuing Appeal of Nationalism*. Detroit: Black and Red, 1985; and Mitchel Cohen, "Fredy Perlman: Out in Front of a Dozen Dead Oceans" (Unpublished manuscript, 1998).

8. For a description of the systems of the *encomienda, mita,* and *catequil* see (among others) André Gunder Frank (1978),45; Steve J. Stern (1982); and Inga Clendinnen (1987). As described by Gunder Frank, the *encomienda* was "a system under which rights to the labor of the Indian communities were granted to Spanish landowners." But in 1548, the Spaniards "began to replace the *encomienda de servicio* by the *repartimiento* (called *catequil* in Mexico and *mita* in Peru), which required the Indian community's chiefs to supply the Spanish *juez repartidor* (distributing judge) with a certain number of days of labor per month.... The Spanish official in turn distributed this supply of labor to qualified enterprising labor contractors who were supposed to pay the laborers a certain minimum wage"(1978: 45). On the efforts of the Spaniards to bind labor in Mexico and Peru in the course of the various

stages of colonization, and the impact on it of the catastrophic collapse of the indigenous population, see again Gunder Frank (*ibid*.: 43-49).

9. For a discussion of the "second serfdom" see Immanuel Wallerstein (1974) and Henry Kamen (1971). It is important here to stress that the newly enserfed peasants were now producing for the international grain market. In other words, despite the seeming backward character of the work-relation imposed upon them, under the new regime, they were an integral part of a developing capitalist economy and international capitalist division of labor.

10. I am echoing here Marx's statement in *Capital*, Vol. 1: "Force... is in itself an economic power" (1909: 824). Far less convincing is Marx's accompanying observation, according to which: "Force is the midwife of every old society pregnant with a new one" (*ibid*.). First, midwives bring life into the world, not destruction. This methaphor also suggests that capitalism "evolved" out of forces gestating in the bosom of the feudal world — an assumption which Marx himself refutes in his discussion of primitive accumulation. Comparing force to the generative powers of a midwife also casts a benign veil over the process of capital accumulation, suggesting necessity, inevitability, and ultimately, progress.

11. Slavery had never been abolished in Europe, surviving in pockets, mostly as female domestic slavery. But by the end of the 15th century slaves began to be imported again, by the Portuguese, from Africa. Attempts to impose slavery continued in England through the 16th century, resulting (after the introduction of public relief) in the construction of work-houses and correction houses, which England pioneered in Europe.

12. See, on this point, Samir Amin (1974). To stress the existence of European slavery in the 16th and 17th centuries (and after) is also important because this fact has been often "forgotten" by European historians. According to Salvatore Bono, this self-induced oblivion was a product of the "Scramble for Africa," which was justified as a mission aimed to terminate slavery on the African continent. Bono argues that Europe's elites could not admit to having employed slaves in Europe, the alleged cradle of democracy.

13. Immanuel Wallerstein (1974), 90-95; Peter Kriedte (1978), 69-70.

14. Paolo Thea (1998) has powerfully reconstructed the history of the German artists who sided with the peasants.

    "During the Protestant Reformation some among the best 16th-century German artists abandoned their laboratories to join the peasants in struggle.... They drafted documents inspired by the principles of evangelic poverty, the common sharing of goods, and the redistribution of wealth. Sometimes... they took arms in support of the cause. The endless list of those who, after the military defeats of May–June 1525, met the rigors of the penal code, mercilessly applied by the winners against the vanquished, includes famous names. Among them are [Jorg] Ratget quartered in Pforzheim (Stuttgart), [Philipp] Dietman beheaded, and [Tilman] Riemenschneider mutilated — both in Wurzburg — [Matthias] Grunewald chased from the court of Magonza where he worked. Holbein the Young was so troubled by the events that he fled from Basel, a city that was torn apart by religious conflict." [My translation]

Also in Switzerland, Austria, and the Tyrol artists participated in the Peasant War, including famous ones like Lucas Cranach (Cranach the old) as well as myriad lesser painters and engravers (*ibid.*: 7). Thea points out that the deeply felt participation of the artists to the cause of the peasants is also demonstrated by the revaluation of rural themes depicting peasant life — dancing peasants, animals, and flora — in contemporary 16th-century German art (*ibid.*: 12-15; 73, 79, 80). "The countryside had become animated... [it] had acquired in the uprising a personality worth of being represented" (*ibid.*: 155). [My translation].

15.   It was through the prism of the Peasant War and Anabaptism that the European governments, through the 16th and 17th centuries, interpreted and repressed every form of social protest. The echoes of the Anabaptist revolution were felt in Elizabethan England and in France, inspiring utmost vigilance and severity with regard to any challenge to the constituted authority. "Anabaptist" became a cursed word, a sign of opprobrium and criminal intent, as "communist" was in the United States in the 1950s, and "terrorist" is today.

Early 17th-century German engraving reviling the Anabaptists' belief in the communistic sharing of goods.

16.   Village authority and privileges were maintained in the hinterland of some city-states. In a number of territorial states, the peasants "continued to refuse dues, taxes, and labor services"; "they let me yell and give me nothing," complained the abbot of Schussenried, referring to those working on his land (Blickle 1985: 172). In Upper Swabia (southwest Germany), though serfdom was not abolished, some of

the main peasant grievances relating to inheritance and marriage rights were accepted with the Treaty of Memmingen of 1526. "On the Upper Rhine, too, some areas reached settlements that were positive for the peasants" (*ibid*.:172-174). In Switzerland, in Bern and Zurich, serfdom was abolished. Improvements in the lot of the "common man" were negotiated in Tyrol and Salzburg (*ibid*.: 176-179). But "the true child of the revolution" was the territorial assembly, instituted after 1525 in Upper Swabia, providing the foundation for a system of self-government that remained in place till the 19th century. New territorial assemblies emerged after 1525 "[realizing] in a weakened form one of the demands of 1525: that the common man ought to be part of the territorial estates alongside the nobles, the clergy, and the towns." Blickle concludes that "Wherever this cause won out, we cannot say that there the lords crowned their military conquest with political victory, [as] the prince was still bound to the consent of the common man. Only later, during the formation of the absolute state, did the prince succeed in freeing himself from that consent" (*ibid*.: 181-182).

17. Referring to the growing pauperization brought about across the world by capitalist development, the French anthropologist Claude Meillassoux, in *Maidens, Meal and Money* (1981), has argued that this contradiction spells a future crisis for capitalism: "In the end imperialism — as a means of reproducing cheap labor power — is leading capitalism to a major crisis, for even if there are still millions of people in the world...not directly involved in capitalist employment... how many are still capable owing to the social disruption, famine and wars it brings about, of producing their own subsistence and feeding their children?" (1981:140).

18. The extent of the demographic catastrophe caused by "the Columbian Exchange" is still debated. Estimates of the population decline in South and Central America, in the first post-Columbian century, range widely, but contemporary scholarly opinion is almost unanimous in likening its effects to an American Holocaust. André Gunder Frank writes that: "Within little more than a century, the Indian population declined by ninety percent and even ninety-five percent in Mexico, Peru, and some other regions" (1978: 43). Similarly, Noble David Cook argues that: "Perhaps 9 million people resided within the limits delineated by Peru's contemporary boundaries. The number of inhabitants remaining a century after contact was roughly a tenth of those that were there when the Europeans invaded the Andean world" (Cook 1981: 116).

19. On the changes in the nature of war in early modern Europe see, Cunningham and Grell (2000), 95–102; Kaltner (1998). Cunningham and Grell write that: "In the 1490s a large army would have consisted of 20,000 men, by the 1550s it would have been twice that, while towards the end of the Thirty Years War the leading European states would have field armies of close to 150,000 men" (2000: 95).

20. Albrecht Dürer's engraving was not the only representation of the "Four Horsemen." We have also one by Lucas Cranach (1522) and by Mattheus Merian (1630). Representations of battlefields, portraying slaughters of soldiers and civilians, villages in flames, rows of hanging bodies, are too numerous to mention. War is possibly the main theme of 16th and 17th-century painting, leaking into every representation, even those ostensibly devoted to sacred subjects.

Mattheus Merian, FOUR HORSEMEN OF THE APOCALYPSE (1630).

21.   This outcome reveals the two souls of the Reformation: a popular one and elitist one, which very soon split along opposite lines. While the conservative side of the Reformation stressed the virtues of work and wealth accumulation, the popular side demanded a society run by "godly love" equality, and communal solidarity. On the class dimensions of the Reformation see Henry Heller (1986) and Po-Chia Hsia (1988).

22.   Hoskins (1976),121-123. In England the pre-Reformation Church had owned twenty-five to thirty per cent of the country's real property. Of this land, Henry VIII sold sixty per cent (Hoskins 1976:121-123). Those who most gained from the confiscation and more eagerly enclosed the newly acquired lands were not the old nobility, nor those who depended on the commons for their keep, but the gentry and the "new men," especially the lawyers and the merchants, who were the face of greed in the peasants' imagination (Cornwall 1977: 22-28). It was against these "new men" that the peasants were prone to vent their anger. A fine snapshot of the winners and losers in the great transfer of land produced by the English Reformation is Table 15 in Kriedte (1983: 60), showing that twenty to twenty-five per cent of the land lost to the Church became the gentry's property. Following are the most relevant columns.

121

DISTRIBUTION OF LAND BY SOCIAL GROUPS IN ENGLAND AND WALES:

	1436*	1690
Great owners	15–20	15–20
Gentry	25	45–50
Yeomen/freeholders	20	25–33
Church and Crown	25–33	5–10

[*excl. Wales]

On the consequences of the Reformation in England for land tenure, see also Christopher Hill who writes:

"We need not idealize the abbeys as lenient landlords to admit some truth in contemporary allegations that the new purchasers shortened leases, racked rents and evicted tenants.... 'Do ye not know,' said John Palmer to a group of copy-holders he was evicting, 'that the king's grace hath put down all houses of monks, friars, and nuns, therefore now is the time come that we gentlemen will pull down the houses of such poor knaves as yet be?' " (Hill 1958: 41).

23. See Midnight Notes (1990); see also *The Ecologist* (1993); and the ongoing debate on the "enclosures" and the "commons" in *The Commoner*, especially n.2, (September 2001), and n.3., (January 2002).

24. Primarily, "enclosure" meant "surrounding a piece of land with hedges, ditches, or other barriers to the free passage of men and animals, the hedge being the mark of exclusive ownership and land occupation. Hence, by enclosure, collective land use, usually accompanied by some degree of communal land ownership, would be abolished, superseded by individual ownership and separate occupation" (G. Slater 1968: 1-2). There were a variety ways to abolish collective land use in the 15th and 16th centuries. The legal paths were (a) the purchase by one person of all tenements and their appurtenant common rights;" (b) the issuing by the King of a special license to enclose, or the passage of an enclosure act by the Parliament; (c) an agreement between the landlord and tenants, embodied in a Chancery decree; (d) the making of partial enclosures of waste by the lords, under the provisions of the Statutes of Merton (1235) and Westminister (1285). Roger Manning notes, however, that these "legal methods... frequently concealed the use of force, fraud, and intimidation against the tenants" (Manning 1998: 25). E. D. Fryde, too, writes that "[p]rolonged harassment of tenants combined with threats of evictions at the slightest legal opportunity" and physical violence were used to bring about mass evictions "particularly during the disorder years 1450–85 [i.e., the War of the Roses]" (Fryde 1996: 186). Thomas More's *Utopia* (1516) expressed the anguish and desolation that these mass expulsions produced when he spoke of sheep which had become so great devourers and so wild that "they eat up and swallow the very men themselves." "Sheep"— he added — that "consume and destroy and devour whole fields, houses and cities."

25. In *The Invention of Capitalism* (2000), Michael Perelman has emphasized the importance of "customary rights" (e.g., hunting) noting how they were often of vital signifi-

cance, making the difference between survival and total destitution (pp. 38ff.).

26. Garret Hardin's essay on the "tragedy of the commons" (1968) was one of the mainstays in the ideological campaign in support of land privatization in the 1970s. The "tragedy," in Hardin's version, is the inevitability of Hobbesian egoism as a determinant of human behavior. In his view, in a hypothetical common, each herdsman wants to maximize his gain regardless of the implications of his action for the other herdsmen, so that "ruin is the destination to which all men rush, each pursuing his best interest" (In Baden and Noonan, eds., 1998: 8-9).

27. The "modernization" defense of the enclosures has a long history, but it has received new energy from neo-liberalism. Its main advocate has been the World Bank, which has often demanded that governments in Africa, Asia, Latin America and Oceania privatize communal lands as a condition for receiving loans (World Bank 1989). A classic defense of the productivity gains derived from enclosure is found in Harriett Bradley (1968, originally published in 1918). The more recent academic literature has taken a more even-handed "costs/gains" approach, exemplified by the works of G. E. Mingay (1997) and Robert S. Duplessis (1997: 65–70). The battle concerning the enclosures has now crossed the disciplinary boundaries and is being debated also among literary scholars. An example of disciplinary border-crossing is Richard Burt and John Michael Archer, eds., *Enclosure Acts. Sexuality Property and Culture in Early Modern England* (1994) — especially the essays by James R. Siemon, "Landlord Not King: Agrarian Change and Interarticulation;" and William C. Carroll, "'The Nursery of Beggary': Enclosure, Vagrancy, and Sedition in the Tudor-Stuart Period." William C. Carroll has found that there was a lively defense of enclosures and critique of the commons in the Tudor period carried out by the spokesmen of the enclosing class. According to this discourse, the enclosures encouraged private enterprise, which in turn increased agricultural productivity, while the commons were the "nurseries and receptacles of thieves, rogues and beggars" (Carroll 1994: 37-38).

28. De Vries (1976), 42–43; Hoskins (1976), 11–12.

29. The commons were the sites of popular festivals and other collective activities, like sports, games, and meetings. When they were fenced off, the sociality that had characterized the village community was severely undermined. Among the rituals that came to an end was "Rogationtide perambulation," a yearly procession among the fields meant to bless the future crops, that was prevented by the hedging of the fields (Underdown 1985: 81).

30. On the breaking down of social cohesion see (among others) David Underdown, *Revel, Riot and Rebellion: Popular Politics and Culture in England, 1603–1660* (1985), especially Chapter 3, which also describes the efforts made by the older nobility to distinguish itself from the *nouveaux riches.*

31. Kriedte (1983), 55; Briggs (1998), 289–316.

32. Cottage industry was an extension of the manorial, rural industry, reorganized by the capitalist merchants to take advantage of the large pool of labor liberated by the enclosures. With this move the merchants aimed to circumvent the high wages and power of the urban guilds. This is how the putting-out system was born — a system by which the capitalist merchants distributed among rural families wool or cotton to spin or weave, and often also the instruments of work, and then picked

up the finished product. The importance of the put-out system and cottage industry for the development of British industry can be deduced from the fact that the
entire textile industry, the most important sector in the first phase of capitalist
development, was organized in this fashion. The cottage industry had two main
advantages for employers: it prevented the danger of 'combinations'; and it cheapened the cost of labor, since its home-based organization provided the workers
with free domestic services and the cooperation of their children and wives, who
were treated as helpers and paid low "auxiliary" wages.

33.   Wage labor was so identified with slavery that the Levellers excluded waged workers from the vote, not considering them sufficiently independent from their
employers to be able to cast a vote. "Why should a free person make oneself a
slave?" asked The Fox, a character in Edmund Spenser's *Mother Hubbard's Tale*
(1591). In turn Gerrard Winstanley, the leader of the Diggers, declared that it did
not make any difference whether one lived under one's enemy or under one's
brother if one worked for a wage (Hill 1975).

34.   Herzog (1989), 45-52. The literature on vagabonds is vast. Among the most important on this topic are A. Beier (1974) and B. Geremek's *Poverty, A History* (1994).

35.   Fletcher (1973), 64-77; Cornwall (1977), 137-241; Beer (1982),82-139. At the
beginning of the 16th century many enclosure riots involved the lesser gentry who
used the popular hatred for enclosures, engrossments, and emparkments to settle
their feuds with their betters. But, after 1549, "the gentry's leadership in enclosure
disputes diminished and small-holders or artisans and cottagers were more likely
to take the initiative in heading agrarian protests" (Manning 1988: 312). Manning
describes the typical victim of an enclosure riot as "the outsider." "Merchants
attempting to buy their way into the landed gentry were particularly vulnerable
to enclosure riots, as were farmers of leases. New owners and farmers were the
victims of enclosure riots in 24 of the 75 Star Chamber cases. A closely-related
category consists of six absentee gentlemen" (Manning 1988: 50).

36.   Manning (1988), 96-97, 114-116, 281; Mendelson and Crawford (1998).

37.   The increasing presence of women in anti-enclosure riots was influenced by a
popular belief that women were "lawless" and could level hedges with impunity
(Mendelson and Crawford 1998: 386–387). But the Court of the Star Chamber
went out of its way to disabuse people of this belief. In 1605, one year after James
I's witchcraft law, it ruled that "if women offend in trespass, riot or otherwise, and
an action is brought against them and their husbands, they [the husbands] shall pay
the fines and damages, notwithstanding the trespass or the offense is committed
without the privity of the husbands" (Manning 1988: 98).

38.   On this subject see, among others, Maria Mies (1986).

39.   By 1600, real wages in Spain had lost thirty percent of their purchasing power with
respect to what they had been in 1511 (Hamilton 1965: 280). On the Price
Revolution, see in particular Earl J. Hamilton's now classic work, *American Treasure
and the Price Revolution in Spain, 1501–1650* (1965), which studies the impact of
the America bullion on it; David Hackett Fischer *The Great Wave: Price Revolutions
and the Rhythms of History* (1996), which studies price hikes from the Middle Ages

to the present — in particular Chapter 2 (pp. 66–113); and Peter Ramsey's edited volume, *The Price Revolution in Sixteenth Century England* (1971).

40.   Braudel (1966),Vol. I, 517–524.

41.   As Peter Kriedte (1983) sums up the economic developments of this period:

"The crisis sharpened the differentials in income and property. Pauperization and proletarianization were paralleled by an increased accumulation of wealth.... Work on Chippenham in Cambridgeshire has shown that the bad harvests of [the late 16th and early 17th centuries] resulted in a decisive shift. Between 1544 and 1712 the medium-sized farms all but disappeared. At the same time the proportion of properties of 90 acres or more rose from 3% to 14%; households without land increased from 32% to 63%" (Kriedte 1983: 54-55).

42.   Wallerstein (1974), 83; Le Roy Ladurie (1928–1929). The growing interest of capitalist entrepreneurs for money-lending was perhaps the motivation behind the expulsion of the Jews from most cities and countries of Europe in the 15th and 16th centuries — Parma (1488), Milan (1489), Geneva (1490), Spain (1492), and Austria (1496). Expulsions and pogroms continued for a century. Until the tide was turned by Rudolph II in 1577, it was illegal for Jews to live in most of Western Europe. As soon as money-lending became a lucrative business, this activity, previously declared unworthy of a Christian, was rehabilitated, as shown by this dialogue between a peasant and a wealthy burgher, written anonymously in Germany around 1521:

Peasant: What brings me to you? Why, I would like to see how you spend your time.

Burgher: How should I spend my time? I sit here counting my money, can't you see?

Peasant: Tell me, burgher, who gave you so much money that you spend all your time counting it?

Burgher: You want to know who gave me my money? I shall tell you. A peasant comes knocking at my door and asks me to lend him ten or twenty gulden. I inquire of him whether he owns a plot of good pasture land or a nice field for plowing. He says: 'Yes, burgher, I have a good meadow and a fine field, worth a hundred gulden the two of them.' I reply: 'Excellent! Pledge your meadow and your field as collateral, and if you will undertake to pay one gulden a year as interest, you can have your loan of twenty gulden.' Happy to hear the good news, the peasant replies: 'I gladly give you my pledge.' 'But I must tell you,' I rejoin, 'that if ever you fail to pay your interest on time, I will take possession of your land and make it my property.' And this does not worry the peasant, he proceeds to assign his pasture and field to me as his pledge. I lend him the money and he pays interest punctually for one year or two; then comes a bad harvest and soon he is behind in his payment. I confiscate his land, evict him and meadow and field are mine. And I do this not only with peasants but with artisans as well. If a tradesman owns a good house I lend him a sum of money on it, and before long the house belongs to me. In this way I acquire much property and wealth, which is why I spend all my time counting my money.

Peasant: And I thought only the Jews practiced usury! Now I hear that Christians do it, too.

Burgher: Usury? Who is talking about usury? Nobody here practices usury. What the debtor pays is interest (G. Strauss: 110–111).

43. With reference to Germany, Peter Kriedte writes that:

"Recent research has shown that a building worker in Augsburg [in Bavaria] was able adequately to maintain his wife and two children from his annual income during the first three decades of the 16th century. Thenceforth his living standard began to fall. Between 1566 and 1575 and from 1585 to the outbreak of the Thirty Years War his wages could no longer pay for the subsistence minimum of his family" (Kriedte 1983: 51–52). On the impoverishment of the Europen working class due to the enclosures and the Price Revolution see also C. Lis & H. Soly (1979), 72-79. As they write, in England "between 1500 and 1600 grain prices rose sixfold, while wages rose threefold. Not surprisingly, workers and cottars were but 'house beggars' for Francis Bacon." In the same period, in France, the purchasing power of cottars and waged workers fell by forty five percent. "In New Castile… wage labour and poverty were considered synonymous." (*ibid.*:72–4).

44. On the growth of prostitution in the 16th century see, Nickie Roberts, *Whores in History: Prostitution in Western Society* (1992).

45. Manning (1988); Fletcher (1973); Cornwall (1977); Beer (1982); Bercé (1990); Lombardini (1983).

46. Kamen (1971), Bercé (1990), 169–179; Underdown (1985). As David Underdown notes:

"The prominent role played by female [food] rioters has often been noted. At Southampton in 1608 a group of women refused to wait while the corporation debated what to do about a ship being loaded with grain for London; they boarded it and seized the cargo. Women were thought to be the likely rioters in the incident in Weymouth in 1622, while at Dorchester in 1631 a group (some of them inmates of the workhouse) stopped a cart in the mistaken belief that it contained wheat; one of them complained of a local merchant who "did send away the best fruits of the land, as butter, cheese, wheat, etc., over the seas" (1985: 117). On women's presence in food riots, see also Sara Mendelson and Patricia Crawford (1998), who write that "women played a prominent role in grain riots [in England]." For instance, "[a]t Maldon in 1629 a crowd of over a hundred women and children boarded the ships to prevent grain from being shipped away." They were led by a "Captain Ann Carter, later tried and hanged" for her leading role in the protest (*ibid.*: 385–86).

47. In a similar vein were the comments of a physician in the Italian city of Bergamo, during the famine of 1630:

"The loathing and terror engendered by a maddened crowd of half dead people who importune all comers in the streets, in piazzas, in the churches, at street doors, so that life is intolerable, and in addition the foul stench rising from them as well as the constant spectacle of the dying…this cannot be believed by anyone who has not experienced it" (quoted by Carlo M. Cipolla 1993: 129).

48. On 16th and 17th-century protest in Europe, see Henry Kamen, *The Iron Century*

(1972), in particular Chapter 10, "Popular Rebellion. 1550-1660" (pp. 331-385). As Kamen writes, "The crisis of 1595-7 was operative throughout Europe, with repercussions in England, France, Austria, Finland, Hungary, Lithuania, and Ukraine. Probably never before in European history had so many popular rebellions coincided in time" (p. 336). There were rebellions in Naples in 1595, 1620, 1647 (*ibid.*: 334-35, 350, 361-63). In Spain, rebellions erupted in 1640 in Catalonia, in Grenada in 1648, in Cordova and Seville in 1652. For riots and rebellions in 16th and 17th-century England, see Cornwall (1977); Underdown (1985), and Manning (1988). On revolt in Spain and Italy, see also Braudel (1976, Vol. II), 738-739.

49. On vagrancy in Europe, beside Beier and Geremek, see Braudel (1976), Vol. II, 739-743; Kamen (1972), 390-394.

50. On the rise of property crimes in the wake of the Price Revolution see Richard J. Evans (1996), 35; Kamen (1972), 397-403; and Lis and Soly (1984). Lis and Soly write that "[t]he available evidence suggests that the overall crime rate did indeed rise markedly in Elizabethan and early Stuart England, especially between 1590 and 1620" (p. 218).

51. In England, among the moments of sociality and collective reproduction that were terminated due to the loss of the open fields and the commons there were the processions that were held in the spring to bless the fields — which could no longer take place once the fields were fenced off — and the dances that were held around the Maypole on May First (Underdown 1985).

52. Lis and Soly (1979), 92. On the institution of Public Assistance, see Geremek's *Poverty A History* (1994), Chapter 4: "The Reform of Charity" (pp. 142-177).

53. Yann Moulier Boutang, *De L'esclavage au salariat* (1998), 291–293. I only partially agree with Moulier Boutang when he claims that Poor Relief was not so much a response to the misery produced by land expropriation and price inflation, but a measure intended to prevent the flight of workers and thereby create a local labor market (1998). As already mentioned, Moulier Boutang overemphasizes the degree of mobility available to the dispossessed proletariat as he does not consider the different situation of women. Furthermore, he underplays the degree to which assistance was the result of a struggle — a struggle that cannot be reduced to the flight of labor, but included assaults, the invasion of towns by masses of starving rural people (a constant feature, in mid-16th-century France) and other forms of attack. It is not coincidence, in this context, that Norwich, the center of the Kett Rebellion became, shortly after its defeat, the center and the model of Poor Relief reforms.

54. The Spanish humanist Juan Luis Vives, who was knowledgeable about the poor relief systems of the Flanders and Spain, was one of the main supporters of public charity. In his *De Subvention Pauperum* (1526) he argued that "secular authority rather than the Church should be responsible for the aid to the poor" (Geremek 1994: 187). He also stressed that authorities should find work for the able-bodied, insisting that "the dissolute, the crooked, the thieving and the idle should be given the hardest work, and the most badly paid, in order that their example might serve as a deterrent to others" (*ibid.*).

55. The main work on the rise of work-house and correction houses is Dario Melossi

and Massimo Pavarini, *The Prison and the Factory: Origins of the Penitantiary System* (1981).The authors point out that the main purpose of incarceration was to break the sense of identity and solidarity of the poor. See also Geremek (1994), 206-229. On the schemes concocted by English proprietors to incarcerate the poor in their parishes, see Marx, *Capital* Vol. 1 (1909: 793). For France, see Foucault, *Madness and Civilization* (1965), especially Chapter 2:"The Great Confinement" (pp. 38-64).

56.   While Hackett Fischer connects the 17th century decline of poulation in Europe to the social effects of the Price Revolution (pp. 91-92), Peter Kriedte presents a more complex picture, arguing that demographic decline was a combination of both Malthusian and socio-economic factors. The decline was, in his view, a response to both the population increase of the early 16th century, on one side, and on the other to the landlords' appropriation of the larger portion of the agricultural income (p. 63).

      An interesting observation which supports my arguments concerning the connection between demographic decline and pro-natalist state policies is offered by Robert S. Duplessis (1997) who writes that the recovery after the population crisis of the 17th century was far swifter than that after the Black Death. It took a century for the population to start growing again after the epidemic of 1348, while in the 17th century the growth process was reactivated within less than half a century (p. 143).This estimates would indicate the presence in 17th-century Europe of a far higher natality rate, possibly to be attributed to the fierce attack on any form of contraception.

57.   "Bio-power"is the concept Foucault used in his *History of Sexuality:An Introduction* (1978) to describe the shift from an authoritarian form of government to one more decentralized, centered on the "fostering of the power of life"in 19th-century Europe."Bio-power" expresses the growing concern, at the state level, for the sanitary, sexual, and penal control of individual bodies, as well as population growth and population movements and their insertion into the economic realm. According to this paradigm, the rise of bio-power went hand in hand with the rise of liberalism and marked the end of the juridical and monarchic state.

58.   I make this distinction with the Canadian sociologist Bruce Curtis' discussion of the Foucauldian concept of"population" and "bio-power" in mind. Curtis contrasts the concept of"populousness," which was current in the 16th and 17th centuries, with the notion of"population" that became the basis of the modern science of demography in the 19th century. He points out that "populousness" was an organic and hierarchical concept.When the mercantilists used it they were concerned with the part of the social body that creates wealth, i.e., actual or potential laborers.The later concept of"population"is an atomistic one."Population consists of so many undifferentiated atoms distributed through abstract space and time" — Curtis writes — "with its own laws and structures." I argue, however, that there is a continuity between these two notions, as in both the mercantilist and liberal capitalist period, the notion of population has been functional to the reproduction of labor-power.

59.   The heyday of Mercantilism was in the second half of the 17th century, its domi-

nance in economic life being associated with the names of William Petty (1623–1687) and Jean Baptiste Colbert, the finance minister of Louis XIV. However, the late 17th-century mercantilists only systematized or applied theories that had been developing since the 16th century. Jean Bodin in France and Giovanni Botero in Italy are considered proto-mercantilist economists. One of the first systematic formulations of mercantilist economic theory is found in Thomas Mun's *England's Treasure by Forraign Trade* (1622).

60. For a discussion of the new legislation against infanticide see (among others) John Riddle (1997), 163–166; Merry Wiesner (1993), 52-53; and Mendelson and Crawford (1998), who write that "[t]he crime of infanticide was one that single women were more likely to commit than any other group in society. A study of infanticide in the early seventeenth century showed that of sixty mothers, fifty three were single, six were widows"(p. 149). Statistics also show that infanticide was punished even more frequently than witchcraft. Margaret King writes that Nuremberg "executed fourteen women for that crime between 1578 and 1615, but only one witch. The Parliament of Rouen from 1580s to 1606 prosecuted about as many cases of infanticide as witchcraft, but punished infanticide more severely. Calvinist Geneva shows a much higher rate of execution for infanticide that witchcraft; from 1590 to 1630, nine women of eleven charged were executed for infanticide, compared to only one of thirty suspects for witchcraft (p.10). These estimates are confirmed by Merry Wiesner, who writes that "in Geneva, for example, 25 women out of 31 charged with infanticide during the period 1595–1712 were executed, as compared with 19 out of 122 charged with witchcraft (1993: 52). Women were executed for infanticide in Europe as late as the 18th century.

61. An interesting article on this topic is Robert Fletcher's "The Witches Pharmakopeia" (1896).

62. The reference is to an Italian feminist song from 1971 titled "Aborto di Stato" (State Abortion).

63. Margaret L. King, *Women of the Renaissance* (1991), 78. For the closing of brothels in Germany see Merry Wiesner, *Working Women in Renaissance Germany* (1986), 194-209.

64. An extensive catalogue of the places and years in which women were expelled from the crafts is found in David Herlihy, *Women, Family and Society in Medieval Europe: Historical Essays*. Providence: Berghahan, 1978–1991. See also Merry Wiesner (1986), 174–185.

65. Martha Howell (1986), Chapter 8, 174–183. Howell writes:
    "Comedies and satires of the period, for example, often portrayed market women and trades women as shrews, with characterizations that not only ridiculed or scolded them for taking on roles in market production but frequently even charged them with sexual aggression"(p.182).

66. In a thorough critique of 17th-century social contract theory, as formulated by Thomas Hobbes and John Locke, Carol Pateman (1988) argues that the "social contract" was based on a more fundamental "sexual contract," which recognized men's right to appropriate women's bodies and women's labor.

67. Ruth Mazo Karras (1996) writes that "'Common woman' meant a woman avail-

able to all men; unlike 'common man' which denoted someone of humble origins and could be used in either a derogatory or a laudatory sense, it did not convey any meaning either of non-gentile behavior or of class solidarity"(p. 138).

68. For the family in the period of the "transition," see Lawrence Stone (1977); and André Burguière and François Lebrun, "Priests, Prince, and Family,"in Burguière, et al., *A History of the Family: The Impact of Modernity* (1996). Volume Two, 95ff.

69. On the character of 17th-century patriarchalism and, in particular, the concept of patriarchal power in social contract theory, see again Pateman (1988); Zilla Eisenstein, *The Radical Future of Liberal Feminism* (1981); andMargaret R. Sommerville, *Sex and Subjection: Attitudes To Women In Early Modern Society* (1995).

   Discussing the changes contract theory brought about in England, in the legal and philosophical attitude towards women, Sommerville argues that the contractarians supported the subordination of women to men as much as the patriarchalists, but justified it on different grounds. Being at least formally committed to the principle of "natural equality," and "government by consent,"in defense of male supremacy they invoked the theory of women's "natural inferiority," according to which women would consent to their husbands' appropriation of their property and voting rights upon realizing their intrinsic weakness and necessary dependence on men.

70. See Underdown (1985a), "The Taming of the Scold: The Enforcement of Patriarchal Authority in Early Modern England," in Anthony Fletcher and John Stevenson (1985), 116–136; Mendelson and Crawford (1998), 69-71.

71. On women's loss of rights in 16th and 17th-century Europe, see (among others) Merry Wiesner (1993), who writes that:

   "The spread of Roman law had a largely negative effect on women's civil legal status in the early modern period both because of the views of women which jurists chose to adopt from it and the stricter enforcement of existing laws to which it gave rise" (p. 33).

72. Adding to the dramas and tracts also the court records of the period, Underdown concludes that "between 1560 and 1640... such records disclose an intense preoccupation with women who are a visible threat to the patriarchal system. Women scolding and brawling with their neighbors, single women refusing to enter service, wives domineering or beating their husbands: all seem to surface more frequently than in the period immediately before or afterwards. It will not go unnnoticed that this is also the period when witchcraft accusations reach a peak" (1985a: 119).

73. James Blaut (1992a)points out that within a few decades after 1492 "the rate of growth and change speeded up dramatically and Europe entered a period of rapid development." He writes:

   "Colonial enterprise in the 16th century produced capital in a number of ways. One was gold and silver mining. A second was plantation agriculture, principally in Brazil. A third was trade with Asia in spice, cloth and much more. A fourth element was the profit returned to European houses from a variety of productive and commercial enterprises in the Americas....A fifth was slaving. Accumulation from these sources was massive (p. 38).

74. Exemplary is the case of Bermuda, cited by Elaine Forman Crane (1990). Crane writes that several white women in Bermuda were owners of slaves — usually other women — thanks to whose labor they were able to maintain a certain degree of economic autonomy (pp. 231–258).

75. June Nash (1980) writes that "A significant change came in 1549 when racial origin became a factor, along with legally sanctioned marital unions, in defining rights of succession. The new law stated that no mulatto (offspring of a black man and an Indian women), mestizo, person born out of wedlock was allowed to have Indians in encomienda. … Mestizo and illegitimate became almost synonymous" (p. 140).

76. A *coyota* was a part-mestiza and part-Indian woman. Ruth Behar (1987), 45.

77. The most deadly ones were the mercury mines, like that in Huancavelica, in which thousands of workers died of slow poisoning amidst horrible sufferings. As David Noble Cook writes:

    "Laborers in the Huancavelica mine faced both immediate and long term dangers. Cave-ins, floods, and falls as a result of slipping shafts posed daily threats. Intermediate health hazards were presented by a poor diet, inadequate ventilation in the underground chambers, and a sharp temperature difference between the mine interiors and the rarefied Andean atmosphere.... Workers who remained for long periods in the mines perhaps suffered the worst fate of all. Dust and fine particles were released into the air by the striking of the tools used to break the ore loose. Indians inhaled the dust, which contained four dangerous substances: mercury vapors, arsenic, arsenic anhydride, and cinnabar. Long exposure... resulted in death. Known as *mal de la mina*, or mine sickness, it was incurable when advanced. In less severe cases the gums were ulcerated and eaten away...(pp.205-6).

78. Barbara Bush (1990) points out that, if they wanted to abort, slave women certainly knew how to, having had available to them the knowledge brought from Africa (p. 141).

Title page of Andreas Vesalius' DE HUMANI CORPORIS FABRICA (Padua, 1543). The triumph of the male, upper class, patriarchal order through the constitution of the new anatomical theatre could not be more complete. Of the woman dissected and delivered to the public gaze, the author tells us that "in fear of being hanged [she] had declared herself pregnant," but after it was discovered that she was not, she was hung. The female figure in the back (perhaps a prostitute or a midwife) lowers her eyes, possibly ashamed in front of the obscenity of the scene and its implicit violence.

The Great Caliban
The Struggle Against the Rebel Body

Life is but a motion of limbs.... For what is the heart, but a spring; and the nerves, but so many strings; and the joints but so many wheels, giving motion to the whole body.

(Hobbes, *Leviathan*, 1650)

Yet I will be a more noble creature, and at the very time when my natural necessities debase me into the condition of the Beast, my Spirit shall rise and soar and fly up towards the employment of the angels.

(Cotton Mather, *Diary, 1680–1708*)

...take some Pity on me... for my Friends is very Poor, and my Mother is very sick, and I am to die next Wednesday Morning, so I hope you will be so good as to give my Friends a small Trifill of Money to pay for a Coffin and a Sroud, for to take my body a way from the Tree in that I am to die on... and dont be faint Hearted... so I hope you will take it into Consideration of my poor Body, consedar if it was your own Cace, you would be willing to have your Body saved from the Surgeons.

(Letter of Richard Tobin, condemned to death in London in 1739)

One of the preconditions for capitalist development was the process that Michel Foucault defined as the "disciplining of the body," which in my view consisted of an attempt by state and church to transform the individual's powers into labor-power. This chapter examines how this process was conceived and mediated in the philosophical debates of the time, and the strategic interventions which it generated.

It was in the 16th century, in the areas of Western Europe most affected by the Protestant Reformation and the rise of the mercantile bourgeoisie, that we see emerging in every field — the stage, the pulpit, the political and philosophical imagination — a new concept of the person. Its most ideal embodiment is the Shakespearean Prospero of

133

15th century woodcut. "The devil's assault on the dying man is a theme that pervades all the [medieval] popular tradition." (From Alfonso M. di Nola, 1987.)

the *The Tempest* (1612), who combines the celestial spirituality of Ariel and the brutish materiality of Caliban. Yet he betrays an anxiety over the equilibrium achieved that rules out any pride for "Man's" unique position in the Great Chain of Being.[1] In defeating Caliban, Prospero must admit that "this thing of darkness is mine," thus reminding his audience that our human partaking of the angel and the beast is problematic indeed.

In the 17th century, what in Prospero remains a subliminal foreboding is formalized as the conflict between Reason and the Passions of the Body, which reconceptualizes classic Judeo-Christian themes to produce a new anthropological paradigm. The outcome is reminiscent of the medieval skirmishes between angels and devils for the possession of the departing soul. But the conflict is now staged within the person who is reconstructed as a battlefield, where opposite elements clash for domination. On the one side, there are the "forces of Reason": parsimony, prudence, sense of responsibility, self-control. On the other, the "low instincts of the Body": lewdness, idleness, systematic dissipation of one's vital energies. The battle is fought on many fronts because Reason must be vigilant against the attacks of the carnal self, and prevent "the wisdom of the flesh" (in Luther's words) from corrupting the powers of the mind. In the extreme case, the person becomes a terrain for a war of all against all:

> Let me be nothing, if within the compass of my self I do not find
> the battail of Lepanto: Passions against Reason, Reason against
> Faith, Faith against the Devil, and my Conscience against all.
> (Thomas Browne 1928: 76)

In the course of this process a change occurs in the metaphorical field, as the philosophical representation of individual psychology borrows images from the body-politics of the state, disclosing a landscape inhabited by "rulers" and "rebellious subjects," "multitudes" and "seditions," "chains" and "imperious commands" and (with Thomas Browne) even the executioner (*ibid.*: 72).[2] As we shall see, this conflict between Reason and the Body, described by the philosophers as a riotous confrontation between the "better" and the "lower sorts," cannot be ascribed only to the baroque taste for the figurative, later to be purged in favor of a "more masculine" language.[3] The battle which the 17th-century discourse on the person imagines unfolding in the microcosm of the individual has arguably a foundation in the reality of the time. It is an aspect of that broader process of social reformation, whereby, in the "Age of Reason," the rising bourgeoisie attempted to remold the subordinate classes in conformity with the needs of the developing capitalist economy.

It was in the attempt to form a new type of individual that the bourgeoisie engaged in that battle against the body that has become its historic mark. According to Max Weber, the reform of the body is at the core of the bourgeois ethic because capitalism makes acquisition "the ultimate purpose of life," instead of treating it as a means for the satisfaction of our needs; thus, it requires that we forfeit all spontaneous enjoyment of life (Weber 1958: 53). Capitalism also attempts to overcome our "natural state," by breaking the barriers of nature and by lengthening the working day beyond the limits set by the sun, the seasonal cycles, and the body itself, as constituted in pre-industrial society.

Marx, too, sees the alienation from the body as a distinguishing trait of the capitalist work-relation. By transforming labor into a commodity, capitalism causes workers to submit their activity to an external order over which they have no control and with which they cannot identify. Thus, the labor process becomes a ground of self-estrangement: the worker "only feels himself outside his work, and in his work feels outside himself. He is at home when he is not working and when he is working is not at home" (Marx 1961: 72). Furthermore, with the development of a capitalist economy, the worker becomes (though only formally) the "free owner" of "his" labor-power, which (unlike the slave) he can place at the disposal of the buyer for a limited period of time. This implies that "[h]e must constantly look upon his labour-power" (his energies, his faculties) "as his own property, his own commodity" (Marx 1906, Vol. I: 186).[4] This too leads to a sense of dissociation from the body, which becomes reified, reduced to an object with which the person ceases to be immediately identified.

The image of a worker freely alienating his labor, or confronting his body as capital to be delivered to the highest bidder, refers to a working class already molded by the capitalist work-discipline. But only in the second half of the 19th century can we glimpse that type of worker — temperate, prudent, responsible, proud to possess a watch (Thompson 1964), and capable of looking upon the imposed conditions of the capitalist mode of production as "self-evident laws of nature" (Marx 1909, Vol. I: 809) — that personifies the capitalist utopia and is the point of reference for Marx.

The situation was radically different in the period of primitive accumulation when the emerging bourgeoisie discovered that the "liberation of labor-power" — that is, the expropriation of the peasantry from the common lands — was not sufficient to force the dispossessed proletarians to accept wage-labor. Unlike Milton's Adam, who, upon being

Woman selling rags and vagabond. The expropriated peasants and artisans did not peacefully agree to work for a wage. More often they became beggars, vagabonds or criminals. Design by Louis-Léopold Boilly (1761–1845).

expelled from the Garden of Eden, set forth cheerfully for a life dedicated to work,[5] the expropriated peasants and artisans did not peacefully agree to work for a wage. More often they became beggars, vagabonds or criminals. A long process would be required to produce a disciplined work-force. In the 16th and 17th centuries, the hatred for wage-labor was so intense that many proletarians preferred to risk the gallows, rather than submit to the new conditions of work (Hill 1975: 219–39).[6]

This was the first capitalist crisis, one far more serious than all the commercial crises that threatened the foundations of the capitalist system in the first phase of its development.[7] As is well-known, the response of the bourgeoisie was the institution of a true regime of terror, implemented through the intensification of penalties (particularly those punishing the crimes against property), the introduction of "bloody laws" against vagabonds, intended to bind workers to the jobs imposed on them, as once the serfs had been bound to the land, and the multiplication of executions. In England alone, 72,000 people were hung by Henry th15e VIII during the thirty-eight years of his reign; and the massacre continued into the late 16th century. In the 1570s, 300 to 400 "rogues" were "devoured by the gallows in one place or another every year" (Hoskins 1977: 9; Holinshed, 1577). In Devon alone, seventy-four people were hanged just in 1598 (*ibid.*).

But the violence of the ruling class was not confined to the repression of transgressors. It also aimed at a radical transformation of the person, intended to eradicate in the proletariat any form of behavior not conducive to the imposition of a stricter work-discipline. The dimensions of this attack are apparent in the social legislation that, by the middle of the 16th century, was introduced in England and France. Games were forbidden, particularly games of chance that, besides being useless, undermined the individual's sense of responsibility and "work ethic." Taverns were closed, along with public baths.

Nakedness was penalized, as were many other "unproductive" forms of sexuality and sociality. It was forbidden to drink, swear, curse.[8]

It was in the course of this vast process of social engineering that a new concept of the body and a new policy toward it began to be shaped. The novelty was that the body was attacked as the source of all evils, and yet it was studied with the same passion that, in the same years, animated the investigation of celestial motion.

Why was the body so central to state politics and intellectual discourse? One is tempted to answer that this obsession with the body reflects the fear that the proletariat inspired in the ruling class.[9] It was the fear felt by the bourgeois or the nobleman alike who, wherever they went, in the streets or on their travels, were besieged by a threatening crowd, begging them or preparing to rob them. It was also the fear felt by those who presided over the administration of the state, whose consolidation was continuously undermined — but also determined — by the threat of riots and social disorders.

Yet, there was more. We must not forget that the beggarly and riotous proletariat — who forced the rich to travel by carriage to escape its assaults, or to go to bed with two pistols under the pillow — was the same social subject who increasingly appeared as the source of all wealth. It was the same of whom the mercantilists, the first economists of capitalist society, never tired of repeating (though not without second thoughts) that "the more the better," often deploring that so many bodies were wasted on the gallows.[10]

Many decades were to pass before the concept of the value of labor entered the pantheon of economic thought. But that work ("industry"), more than land or any other "natural wealth," is the primary source of accumulation was a truth well understood at a time when the low level of technological development made human beings the most important productive resource. As Thomas Mun (the son of a London merchant and spokesman for the mercantilist position) put it:

> ...we know that our own natural wares do not yield us so much
> profit as our industry.... For Iron in the Mines is of no great worth,
> when it is compared with the employment and advantage it yields
> being digged, tried, transported, bought, sold, cast into Ordnance,
> Muskets...wrought into Anchors, bolts, spikes, nails and the like, for
> the use of Ships, Houses, Carts, Coaches, Ploughs, and other instru-
> ments for Tillage.   (Abbott 1946: 2)

Even Shakespeare's Prospero insists on this crucial economic fact in a little speech on the value of labor, which he delivers to Miranda after she manifests her utter disgust with Caliban:

> But, as 'tis
> We cannot miss him. He does make our fire
> Fetch in our wood, and serves in office
> That profit us.   (*The Tempest*, Act I, Scene 2)

The body, then, came to the foreground of social policies because it appeared not only as a beast inert to the stimuli of work, but also as the container of labor-power, a means of production, the primary work-machine. This is why, in the strategies adopted by the state towards it, we find much violence, but also much interest; and the study of bodily motions and properties becomes the starting point for most of the theoretical speculation of the age — whether aiming, with Descartes, to assert the immortality of the soul, or to investigate, with Hobbes, the premises of social governability.

Indeed, one of the central concerns of the new Mechanical Philosophy was *the mechanics of the body,* whose constitutive elements — from the circulation of the blood to the dynamics of speech, from the effects of sensations to voluntary and involuntary motions — were taken apart and classified in all their components and possibilities. Descartes' *Treatise of Man* (published in 1664)[11] is a true anatomical handbook, though the anatomy it performs is as much psychological as physical. A basic task of Descartes' enterprise is to institute an ontological divide between a purely mental and a purely physical domain. Every manner, attitude, and sensation is thus defined; their limits are marked, their possibilities weighed with such a thoroughness that one has the impression that the "book of human nature" has been opened for the first time or, more likely, that a new land has been discovered and the conquistadors are setting out to chart its paths, compile the list of its natural resources, assess its advantages and disadvantages.

In this, Hobbes and Descartes were representatives of their time. The care they display in exploring the details of corporeal and psychological reality reappears in the Puritan analysis of *inclinations* and individual *talents,*[12] which was the beginning of a bourgeois psychology, explicitly studying, in this case, all human faculties from the viewpoint of their potential for work and contribution to discipline. A further sign of a new curiosity about the body and "of a change in manners and customs from former times whereby

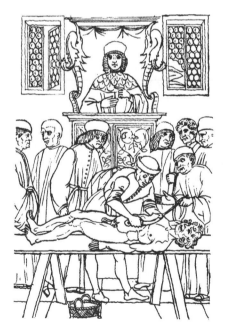

The anatomy lesson at the University of Padova.
The anatomy theatre disclosed to the public eye a disenchanted, desecrated body. In DE FASCICULO DE MEDICINA. *Venezia (1494).*

the body can be opened" (in the words of a 17th-century physician) was also the development of *anatomy* as a scientific discipline, following its long relegation to the intellectual underground in the Middle Ages (Wightman 1972: 90–92; Galzigna 1978).

But while the body emerged as the main protagonist in the philosophical and medical scenes, a striking feature of these investigations is the degraded conception they formed of it. The anatomy "theatre"[13] discloses to the public eye a disenchanted, desecrated body, which only in principle can be conceived as the site of the soul, but actually is treated as a separate reality (Galzigna 1978: 163–64).[14] To the eye of the anatomist the body is a factory, as shown by the title that Andreas Vesalius gave to his epochal work on the "dissecting industry": *De humani corporis fabrica* (1543). In Mechanical Philosophy, the body is described by analogy with the *machine*, often with emphasis on its *inertia*. The body is conceived as brute matter, wholly divorced from any rational qualities: it does not know, does not want, does not feel. The body is a pure "collection of members" Descartes claims in his 1634 *Discourse on Method* (1973, Vol. I, 152). He is echoed by Nicholas Malebranche who, in the *Dialogues on Metaphysics and on Religion* (1688), raises the crucial question "Can a body think?" to promptly answer, "No, beyond a doubt, for all the modifications of such an extension consist only in certain relations of distance; and it is obvious that such relations are not perceptions, reasonings, pleasures, desires, feelings, in a word, thoughts" (Popkin 1966: 280). For Hobbes, as well, the body is a conglomerate of mechanical motions that, lacking autonomous power, operates on the basis of an external causation, in a play of attractions and aversions where everything is regulated as in an automaton (*Leviathan* Part I, Chapter VI).

It is true, however, of Mechanical Philosophy what Michel Foucault maintains with regard to the 17th and 18th-century social disciplines (Foucault 1977: 137). Here, too, we find a different perspective from that of medieval asceticism, where the degradation of the body had a purely negative function, seeking to establish the temporal and illusory nature of earthly pleasures and consequently the need to renounce the body itself.

In Mechanical Philosophy we perceive a new bourgeois spirit that calculates, classifies, makes distinctions, and degrades the body only in order to rationalize its faculties, aiming not just at intensifying its subjection but at maximizing its social utility (*Ibid.*: 137–38). Far from renouncing the body, mechanical theorists seek to conceptualize it in ways that make its operations intelligible and controllable. Thus the sense of pride (rather than commiseration) with which Descartes insists that "this machine" (as he persistently calls the body in the *Treatise of Man*) is just an automaton, and its death is no more to be mourned than the breaking of a tool.[15]

Certainly, neither Hobbes nor Descartes spent many words on economic matters, and it would be absurd to read into their philosophies the everyday concerns of the English or Dutch merchants. Yet, we cannot fail to see the important contribution which their speculations on human nature gave to the emerging capitalist science of work. To pose the body as mechanical matter, void of any intrinsic teleology — the "occult virtues" attributed to it by both Natural Magic and the popular superstitions of the time — was to make intelligible the possibility of subordinating it to a work process that increasingly relied on uniform and predictable forms of behavior.

Once its devices were deconstructed and it was itself reduced to a tool, the body could be opened to an infinite manipulation of its powers and possibilities. One could investigate the vices and limits of imagination, the virtues of habit, the uses of fear, how certain passions can be avoided or neutralized, and how they can be more rationally utilized. In this sense, Mechanical Philosophy contributed to increasing the ruling-class control over the natural world, control over human nature being the first, most indispensable step. Just as *nature*, reduced to a "Great Machine," could be conquered and (in Bacon's words) "penetrated in all her secrets," likewise the *body*, emptied of its occult forces, could be "caught in a system of subjection," whereby its behavior could be calculated, organized, technically thought and invested of power relations" (Foucault 1977: 26).

In Descartes, body and nature are identified, for both are made of the same particles and act in obedience to uniform physical laws set in motion by God's will. Thus, not only is the Cartesian body pauperized and expropriated from any magical virtue; in the great ontological divide which Descartes institutes between the essence of humanity and its accidental conditions, the body is divorced from the person, it is literally dehumanized. "I am not this body," Descartes insists throughout his *Meditations* (1641). And, indeed, in his philosophy the body joins a continuum of clock-like matter that the unfettered will can now contemplate as the object of its domination.

As we will see, Descartes and Hobbes express two different projects with respect to corporeal reality. In Descartes, the reduction of the body to mechanical matter allows for the development of mechanisms of self-management that make the body the subject of the will. In Hobbes, by contrast, the mechanization of the body justifies the total submission of the individual to the power of the state. In both, however, the outcome is a redefinition of bodily attributes that makes the body, ideally, at least, suited for the regularity and automatism demanded by the capitalist work-discipline.[16] I emphasize "ideally" because, in the years in which Descartes and Hobbes were writing their treatises, the ruling class had to confront a corporeality that was far different from that appearing in their prefigurations.

It is difficult, in fact, to reconcile the insubordinate bodies that haunt the social literature of the "Iron Century" with the clock-like images by which the body is represented in Descartes' and Hobbes' works. Yet, though seemingly removed from the daily affairs of the class struggle, it is in the speculations of the two philosophers that we find first conceptualized the development of the body into a work-machine, one of the main tasks of primitive accumulation. When, for example, Hobbes declares that "the heart (is) but a spring... and the joints so many wheels," we perceive in his words a bourgeois spirit, whereby not only is work the *condition and motive of existence of the body,* but the need is felt to transform all bodily powers into work powers.

This project is a clue to understanding why so much of the philosophical and religious speculation of the 16th and 17th centuries consists of a true *vivisection of the human body,* whereby it was decided which of its properties could live and which, instead, had to die. It was a *social alchemy* that did not turn base metals into gold, but bodily powers into work-powers. For the same relation that capitalism introduced between land and work was also beginning to command the relation between the body and labor. While labor was beginning to appear as a dynamic force infinitely capable of development, the body was seen as inert, sterile matter that only the will could move, in a condition similar to that which Newton's physics established between mass and motion, where the mass tends to inertia unless a force is applied to it. Like the land, the body had to be cultivated

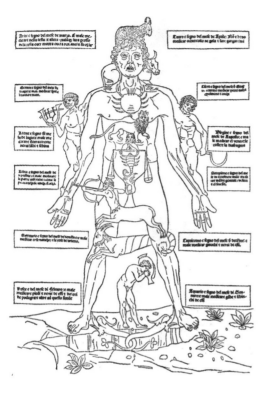

The conception of the body as a receptacle of magical powers largely derived from the belief in a correspondence between the microcosm of the individual and the macrocosm of the celestial world, as illustrated in this 16th-century image of the "zodiacal man."

and first of all broken up, so that it could relinquish its hidden treasures. For while the body is the *condition of the existence of labor-power,* it is also its limit, as the main element of resistance to its expenditure. It was not sufficient, then, to decide that *in itself* the body had no value. The body had to die so that labor-power could live.

What died was the concept of the body as a receptacle of magical powers that had prevailed in the medieval world. In reality, it was destroyed. For in the background of the new philosophy we find a vast initiative by the state, whereby what the philosophers classified as "irrational" was branded as crime. This state intervention was the necessary "subtext" of Mechanical Philosophy. "Knowledge" can only become "power" if it can enforce its prescriptions. This means that the mechanical body, the body-machine, could not have become a model of social behavior without the destruction by the state of a vast range of pre-capitalist beliefs, practices, and social subjects whose existence contradicted the regularization of corporeal behavior promised by Mechanical Philosophy. This is why, at the peak of the "Age of Reason" — the age of scepticism and methodical doubt — we have a ferocious attack on the body, well-supported by many who subscribed to the new doctrine.

This is how we must read the attack against witchcraft and against that magical view of the world which, despite the efforts of the Church, had continued to prevail on a popular level through the Middle Ages. At the basis of magic was an animistic conception of nature that did not admit to any separation between matter and spirit, and thus imagined the cosmos as a *living organism,* populated by occult forces, where every element

Frontispiece to the first edition of Christopher Marlowe's DOCTOR FAUSTUS *(1604), picturing the magician conjuring the Devil from the protected space of his magical circle.*

was in "sympathetic" relation with the rest. In this perspective, where nature was viewed as a universe of signs and signatures, marking invisible affinities that had to be deciphered (Foucault 1970: 26–27), every element — herbs, plants, metals, and most of all the human body — hid virtues and powers peculiar to it. Thus, a variety of practices were designed to appropriate the secrets of nature and bend its powers to the human will. From palmistry to divination, from the use of charms to sympathetic healing, magic opened a vast number of possibilities. There was magic designed to win card games, to play unknown instruments, to become invisible, to win somebody's love, to gain immunity in war, to make children sleep (Thomas 1971; Wilson 2000).

Eradicating these practices was a necessary condition for the capitalist rationalization of work, since magic appeared as an illicit form of power and an instrument *to obtain what one wanted without work,* that is, a refusal of work in action. "Magic kills industry," lamented Francis Bacon, admitting that nothing repelled him so much as the assumption that one could obtain results with a few idle expedients, rather than with the sweat of one's brow (Bacon 1870: 381).

Magic, moreover, rested upon a qualitative conception of space and time that precluded a regularization of the labor process. How could the new entrepreneurs impose regular work patterns on a proletariat anchored in the belief that there are lucky and unlucky days, that is, days on which one can travel and others on which one should not move from home, days on which to marry and others on which every enterprise should be cautiously avoided? Equally incompatible with the capitalist work-discipline was a conception of the cosmos that attributed special powers to the individual: the magnetic look, the power to make oneself invisible, to leave one's body, to chain the will of others by magical incantations.

It would not be fruitful to investigate whether these powers were real or imaginary. It can be said that all precapitalist societies have believed in them and, in recent times, we have witnessed a revaluation of practices that, at the time we refer to, would have been condemned as witchcraft. Let us mention the growing interest in parapsychology and biofeedback practices that are increasingly applied even by mainstream medicine. The revival of magical beliefs is possible today because it no longer represents a social threat. The mechanization of the body is so constitutive of the individual that, at least in industrialized countries, giving space to the belief in occult forces does not jeopardize the regularity of social behavior. Astrology too can be allowed to return, with the certainty that even the most devoted consumer of astral charts will automatically consult the watch before going to work.

However, this was not an option for the 17th-century ruling class which, in this initial and experimental phase of capitalist development, had not yet achieved the social control necessary to neutralize the practice of magic, nor could they functionally integrate magic into the organization of social life. From their viewpoint it hardly mattered whether the powers that people claimed to have, or aspired to have, were real or not, for the very existence of magical beliefs was a source of social insubordination.

Take, for example, the widespread belief in the possibility of finding hidden treasures by the help of magical charms (Thomas 1971: 234–37). This was certainly an impediment to the institution of a rigorous and spontaneously accepted work-discipline. Equally threatening was the use that the lower classes made of *prophecies,* which, particularly during the English Civil War (as already in the Middle Ages), served to formulate a program of struggle (Elton 1972: 142ff). Prophecies are not simply the expression of a fatalistic resignation. Historically they have been a means by which the "poor" have externalized their desires, given legitimacy to their plans, and have been spurred to action. Hobbes recognized this when he warned that "There is nothing that... so well directs men in their deliberations, as the foresight of the sequels of their actions; prophecy being many times the principal cause of the events foretold" (Hobbes, "Behemot," *Works VI:* 399).

But regardless of the dangers which magic posed, the bourgeoisie had to combat its power because it undermined the principle of individual responsibility, as magic placed the determinants of social action in the realm of the stars, out of their reach and control. Thus, in the rationalization of space and time that characterized the philosophical speculation of the 16th and 17th centuries, prophecy was replaced with the *calculation of probabilities* whose advantage, from a capitalist viewpoint, is that here the future can be anticipated only insofar as the regularity and immutability of the system is assumed; that is, only insofar as it is assumed that the future will be like the past, and no major change, no revolution, will upset the coordinates of individual decision-making. Similarly, the bourgeoisie had to combat the assumption that it is possible to be in two places at the same time, for the *fixation of the body in space and time,* that is, the *individual's spatio-temporal identification,* is an essential condition for the regularity of the work-process.[17]

The incompatibility of magic with the capitalist work-discipline and the requirement of social control is one of the reasons why a campaign of terror was launched against it by the state — a terror applauded without reservations by many who are presently considered among the founders of scientific rationalism: Jean Bodin, Mersenne, the mechanical philosopher and member of the Royal Society Richard Boyle, and Newton's teacher, Isaac Barrow.[18] Even the materialist Hobbes, while keeping his distance, gave his approval. "As for witches," he wrote, "I think not that their witchcraft is any real power; but yet that they are justly punished, for the false belief they have that they can do such mischief, joined with their purpose to do it if they can" (*Leviathan* 1963: 67). He added

The torture chamber. 1809 engraving by Manet in Joseph Lavallee,
HISTOIRES DES INQUISITIONS RELIGIEUSES D'ITALIE, D'ESPAGNE
ET DE PORTUGAL.

that if these superstitions were eliminated, "men would be much more fitted than they are for civil obedience" (*ibid.*). Hobbes was well advised. The stakes on which witches and other practitioners of magic died, and the chambers in which their tortures were executed, were a laboratory in which much social discipline was sedimented, and much knowledge about the body was gained. Here those irrationalities were eliminated that stood in the way of the transformation of the individual and social body into a set of predictable and controllable mechanisms. And it was here again that the scientific use of torture was born, for blood and torture were necessary to "breed an animal" capable of regular, homogeneous, and uniform behavior, indelibly marked with the memory of the new rules (Nietzsche 1965: 189–90).

A significant element in this context was the condemnation as *maleficium* of abortion and contraception, which consigned the female body — the *uterus* reduced to a machine for the reproduction of labor — into the hands of the state and the medical profession. I will return later to this point, in the chapter on the witch-hunt, where I argue that the persecution of the witches was the climax of the state intervention against the proletarian body in the modern era.

Here let us stress that despite the violence deployed by the state, the disciplining of the proletariat proceeded slowly throughout the 17th century and into the 18th century in the face of a strong resistance that not even the fear of execution could overcome. An emblematic example of this resistance is analyzed by Peter Linebaugh in "The Tyburn Riots Against the Surgeons." Linebaugh reports that in early 18th-century London, at the time of an execution, a battle was fought by the friends and relatives of the condemned to prevent the assistants of the surgeons from seizing the corpse for use in anatomical studies (Linebaugh 1975). This battle was fierce, because the fear of being dissected was no less than the fear of death. Dissection eliminated the possibility that the condemned might revive after a poorly executed hanging, as often occurred in 18th-century England (*ibid*.: 102-04). A magical conception of the body was spread among the people according to which the body continued to live after death, and by death was enriched with new powers. It was believed that the dead possessed the power to "come back again" and exact their last revenge upon the living. It was also believed that a corpse had healing virtues, so that crowds of sick people gathered around the gallows, expecting from the limbs of the dead effects as miraculous as those attributed to the touch of the king (*ibid*.: 109–10).

Dissection thus appeared as a further infamy, a second and greater death, and the condemned spent their last days making sure that their body should not be abandoned into the hands of surgeons. This battle, significantly occurring at the foot of the gallows, demonstrates both the violence that presided over the scientific rationalization of the world, and the clash of two opposite concepts of the body, two opposite investments in it. On one side, we have a concept of the body that sees it endowed with powers even after death; the corpse does not inspire repulsion, and is not treated as something rotten or irreducibly alien. On the other, the body is seen as dead even when still alive, insofar as it is conceived as a mechanical device, to be taken apart just like any machine. "At the gallows, standing at the conjunction of the Tyburn and Edgware roads," Peter Linebaugh writes, "we find that the history of the London poor and the history of English science intersect." This was not a coincidence; nor was it a coincidence that the progress of anatomy depended on the ability of the surgeons to snatch the bodies of the hanged at Tyburn.[19] The course of scientific rationalization was intimately connected to the attempt by the state to impose its control over an unwilling workforce.

This attempt was even more important, as a determinant of new attitudes towards the body, than the development of technology. As David Dickson argues, connecting the new scientific worldview to the increasing mechanization of production can only hold as a metaphor (Dickson 1979: 24). Certainly, the clock and the automated devices that so much intrigued Descartes and his contemporaries (e.g. hydraulically moved statues), provided models for the new science, and for the speculations of Mechanical Philosophy on the movements of the body. It is also true that starting from the 17th century, anatomical analogies were drawn from the workshops of the manufacturers: the arms were viewed as levers, the heart as a pump, the lungs as bellows, the eyes as lenses, the fist as a hammer (Mumford 1962: 32). But these mechanical metaphors reflect not the influence of technology *per se,* but the fact that the *machine was becoming the model of social behavior.*

The inspirational force of the need for social control is evident even in the field of astronomy. A classic example is that of Edmond Halley (the secretary of the Royal Society), who, in concomitance with the appearance in 1695 of the comet later named after him, organized clubs all over England in order to demonstrate the predictability of natural phenomena, and to dispel the popular belief that comets announced social disorders. That the path of scientific rationalization intersected with the disciplining of the social body is even more evident in the social sciences. We can see, in fact, that their development was premised on the homogenization of social behavior, and the construc-

A telling example of the new mechanical conception of the body is this 16th-century German engraving where the peasant is represented as nothing more than a means of production, with his body composed entirely of agricultural implements.

tion of a prototypical individual to whom all would be expected to conform. In Marx's terms, this is an "abstract individual," constructed in a uniform way, as a social average, and subject to a radical decharacterization, so that all of its faculties can be grasped only in their most standardized aspects. The construction of this new individual was the basis for the development of what William Petty would later call (using Hobbes' terminology) *Political Arithmetics* — a new science that was to study every form of social behavior in terms of *Numbers, Weights,* and *Measures.* Petty's project was realized with the development of *statistics* and *demography* (Wilson 1966; Cullen 1975) which perform on the social body the same operations that anatomy performs on the individual body, as they dissect the population and study its movements — from natality to mortality rates, from generational to occupational structures — in their most massified and regular aspects. Also from the point of view of the abstraction process that the individual underwent in the transition to capitalism, we can see that the development of the "human machine" was the main technological leap, the main step in the development of the productive forces that took place in the period of primitive accumulation. *We can see, in other words, that the human body and not the steam engine, and not even the clock, was the first machine developed by capitalism.*

J. Case, *Compendium Anatomicum* (1696).
In contrast to the "mechanical man" is this image of the "vegetable man,"
in which the blood vessels are seen as twigs growing out of the human body.

147

But if the body is a machine, one problem immediately emerges: how to make it work? Two different models of body-government derive from the theories of Mechanical Philosophy. On one side, we have the Cartesian model that, starting from the assumption of a purely mechanical body, postulates the possibility of developing in the individual mechanisms of self-discipline, self-management, and self-regulation allowing for voluntary work-relations and government based on consent. On the other side, there is the Hobbesian model that, denying the possibility of a body-free Reason, externalizes the functions of command, consigning them to the absolute authority of the state.

The development of a self-management theory, starting from the mechanization of the body, is the focus of the philosophy of Descartes, who (let us remember it) completed his intellectual formation not in the France of monarchical absolutism but in the bourgeois Holland so congenial to his spirit that he elected it as his abode. Descartes' doctrines have a double aim: to deny that human behavior can be influenced by external factors (such as the stars, or celestial intelligences), and to free the soul from any bodily conditioning, thus making it capable of exercising an unlimited sovereignty over the body.

Descartes believed that he could accomplish both tasks by demonstrating the mechanical nature of animal behavior. Nothing, he claimed in his *Le Monde* (1633), causes so many errors as the belief that animals have a soul like ours. Thus, in preparation for his *Treatise of Man,* he devoted many months to studying the anatomy of animal organs; every morning he went to the butcher to observe the quartering of the beasts.[20] He even performed many vivisections, likely comforted by his belief that, being mere brutes "destitute of Reason," the animals he dissected could not feel any pain (Rosenfield 1968: 8).[21]

To be able to demonstrate the brutality of animals was essential for Descartes, because he was convinced that here he could find the answer to his questions concerning the location, nature, and extent of the power controlling human conduct. He believed that in the dissected animal he would find proof that the body is only capable of mechanical, and involuntary actions; that, consequently, it is not constitutive of the person; and that the human essence, therefore, resides in purely immaterial faculties. The human body, too, is an automaton for Descartes, but what differentiates "man" from the beast and confers upon "him" mastery over the surrounding world is the presence of thought. Thus, the soul, which Descartes displaces from the cosmos and the sphere of corporeality, returns at the center of his philosophy endowed with infinite power under the guise of individual reason and will.

Placed in a soulless world and in a body-machine, the Cartesian man, like Prospero, could then break his magic wand, becoming not only responsible for his own actions, but seemingly the center of all powers. In being divorced from its body, the rational self certainly lost its solidarity with its corporeal reality and with nature. Its solitude, however, was to be that of a king: in the Cartesian model of the person, there is no egalitarian dualism between the thinking head and the body-machine, only a master/slave relation, since the primary task of the will is to dominate the body and the natural world. In the Cartesian model of the person, then, we see the same centralization of the functions of command that in the same period was occurring at the level of the state: as the task of the state was to govern the social body, so the mind became sovereign in the new personality.

Descartes concedes that the supremacy of the mind over the body is not easily achieved, as Reason must confront its inner contradictions. Thus, in *The Passions of the*

Soul (1650), he introduces us to the prospect of a constant battle between the lower and higher faculties of the soul which he describes in almost military terms, appealing to our need to be brave, and to gain the proper arms to resist the attacks of our passions. We must be prepared to suffer temporary defeats, for our will might not always be capable of changing or arresting its passions. It can, however, neutralize them by diverting its attention to some other thing, or it can restrain the movements to which they dispose the body. It can, in other words, prevent the *passions* from becoming *actions* (Descartes 1973, I: 354–55).

With the institution of a hierarchical relation between mind and body, Descartes developed the theoretical premises for the work-discipline required by the developing capitalist economy. For the mind's supremacy over the body implies that the will can (in principle) control the needs, reactions, reflexes of the body; it can impose a regular order on its vital functions, and force the body to work according to external specifications, independently of its desires.

Most importantly, the supremacy of the will allows for the interiorization of the mechanisms of power. Thus, the counterpart of the mechanization of the body is the development of Reason in its role as judge, inquisitor, manager, administrator. We find here the origins of bourgeois subjectivity as self-management, self-ownership, law, responsibility, with its corollaries of memory and identity. Here we also find the origin of that proliferation of "micro-powers" that Michel Foucault has described in his critique of the juridico-discursive model of Power (Foucault 1977). The Cartesian model shows, however, that Power can be decentered and diffused through the social body only to the extent that it is recentered in the person, which is thus reconstituted as a micro-state. In other words, in being diffused, Power does not lose its vector — that is, its content and its aims — but simply acquires the collaboration of the Self in their promotion.

Consider, in this context, the thesis proposed by Brian Easlea, according to which the main benefit that Cartesian dualism offered to the capitalist class was the Christian defense of the immortality of the soul, and the possibility of defeating the atheism implicit in Natural Magic, which was loaded with subversive implications (Easlea 1980: 132ff). Easlea argues, in support of this view, that the defense of religion was a central theme in Cartesianism, which, particularly in its English version, never forgot that "No Spirit, No God; No Bishop, No King" (*ibid.*: 202). Easlea's argument is attractive; yet its insistence on the "reactionary" elements in Descartes's thought makes it impossible for Easlea to answer a question that he himself raises. Why was the hold of Cartesianism in Europe so strong that, even after Newtonian physics dispelled the belief in a natural world void of occult powers, and even after the advent of religious tolerance, Cartesianism continued to shape the dominant worldview? I suggest that the popularity of Cartesianism among the middle and upper class was directly related to the program of *self-mastery* that Descartes' philosophy promoted. In its social implications, this program was as important to Descartes's elite contemporaries as the hegemonic relation between humans and nature that is legitimized by Cartesian dualism.

The development of self-management (i.e., self-government, self-development) becomes an essential requirement in a capitalist socio-economic system in which self-ownership is assumed to be the fundamental social relation, and discipline no longer relies purely on external coercion. The social significance of Cartesian philosophy lies in part in the fact that it provides an intellectual justification for it. In this way, Descartes' theory of self-management *defeats but also recuperates* the active side of Natural Magic. For it replaces the unpredictable power of the magician (built on the subtle manipulation of astral influences and correspondences) with a power far more profitable — a power for which no soul has to be forfeited — generated only through the administration and domination of one's body and, by extension, the administration and domination of the bodies of other fellow beings. We cannot say, then, as Easlea does (repeating a criticism raised by Leibniz), that Cartesianism failed to translate its tenets into a set of practical regulations, that is, that it failed to demonstrate to the philosophers — and above all to the merchants and manufacturers — how they would benefit from it in their attempt to control the matter of the world (*ibid.*: 151).

If Cartesianism failed to give a technological translation of its precepts, it nonetheless provided precious information with regard to the development of "human technology." Its insights into the dynamics of self-control would lead to the construction of a new model of the person, wherein the individual would function at once as both master and slave. It is because it interpreted so well the requirements of the capitalist work-discipline that Descartes' doctrine, by the end of the 17th century, had spread throughout Europe and survived even the advent of vitalistic biology as well as the increasing obsolescence of the mechanistic paradigm.

The reasons for Descartes' triumph are clearest when we compare his account of the person with that of his English rival, Thomas Hobbes. Hobbes' biological monism rejects the postulate of an immaterial mind or soul that is the basis of Descartes' concept of the person, and with it the Cartesian assumption that the human will can free itself from corporeal and instinctual determinism.[22] For Hobbes, human behavior is a conglomerate of reflex actions that follow precise natural laws, and compel the individual to incessantly strive for power and domination over others (*Leviathan*: 141ff). Thus the war of all against all (in a hypothetical state of nature), and the necessity for an absolute power guaranteeing, through fear and punishment, the survival of the individual in society.

> For the laws of nature, as justice, equity, modesty, mercy, and, in sum, doing to others as we would be done to, of themselves, without the terror of some power to cause them to be observed, are contrary to our natural passions, that carry us to partiality, pride, revenge and the like (*ibid.*: 173).

As is well known, Hobbes' political doctrine caused a scandal among his contemporaries, who considered it dangerous and subversive, so much so that, although he strongly desired it, Hobbes was never admitted to the Royal Society (Bowle 1952: 163).

Against Hobbes, it was the Cartesian model that prevailed, for it expressed the already active tendency to democratize the mechanisms of social discipline by attributing to the individual will that function of command which, in the Hobbesian model, is left solely in the hands of the state. As many critics of Hobbes maintained, the foundations of public discipline must be rooted in the hearts of men, for in the absence of an interior legislation men are inevitably led to revolution (quoted in Bowle 1951: 97–98). "In Hobbes," complained Henry Moore, "there is no freedom of will and consequently no remorse of conscience or reason, but only what pleases the one with the longest sword" (quoted in Easlea 1980: 159). More explicit was Alexander Ross, who observed that "it is the curb of conscience that restrains men from rebellion, there is no outward law or force more powerful... there is no judge so severe, no torturer so cruel as an accusing conscience" (quoted in Bowle 1952: 167).

The contemporaneous critique of Hobbes' atheism and materialism was clearly not motivated purely by religious concerns. His view of the individual as a machine moved only by its appetites and aversions was rejected not because it eliminated the concept of the human creature made in the image of God, but because it eliminated the possibility of a form of social control not depending wholly on the iron rule of the state. Here, I argue, is the main difference between Hobbes' philosophy and Cartesianism. This, however, cannot be seen if we insist on stressing the feudal elements in Descartes' philosophy, and in particular its defense of the existence of God with all that this entailed, as a defense of the power of the state. If we do privilege the feudal Descartes we miss the fact that the elimination of the religious element in Hobbes (i.e., the belief in the existence of incorporeal substances) was actually a response to *the democratization implicit in the Cartesian model of self-mastery* which Hobbes undoubtedly distrusted. As the activism of the Puritan sects during the English Civil War had demonstrated, self-mastery could easily turn into a subversive proposition. For the Puritans' appeal to return the management of one's behavior to the individual conscience, and to make of one's conscience the ultimate judge of truth, had become radicalized in the hands of the sectaries into an anarchic refusal of established authority.[23] The example of the Diggers and Ranters, and of the scores of mechanic preachers who, in the name of the "light of conscience," had opposed state legislation as well as private property, must have convinced Hobbes that the appeal to "Reason" was a dangerously double-edged weapon.[24]

The conflict between Cartesian "theism" and Hobbesian "materialism" was to be resolved in time in their reciprocal assimilation, in the sense that (as always in the history of capitalism) the decentralization of the mechanisms of command, through their location in the individual, was finally obtained only to the extent that a centralization occurred in the power of the state. To put this resolution in the terms in which the debate was posed in the course of the English Civil War: "neither the Diggers nor Absolutism," but a well-calculated mixture of both, whereby the democratization of command would rest on the shoulders of a state always ready, like the Newtonian God, to reimpose order on the souls who proceeded too far in the ways of self-determination. The crux of the matter was lucidly expressed by Joseph Glanvil, a Cartesian member of the Royal Society who, in a polemic against Hobbes, argued that the crucial issue was the control of the mind over the body. This, however, did not simply imply the control of the ruling class (the mind *par excellence*) over the body-proletariat, but, equally important, the development of the capacity for self-control within the person.

As Foucault has demonstrated, the mechanization of the body did not only involve the repression of desires, emotions, or forms of behavior that were to be eradicated. It also involved the development of new faculties in the individual that would appear as *other* with respect to the body itself, and become the agents of its transformation. The product of this alienation from the body, in other words, was the development of individual *identity,* conceived precisely as "otherness" from the body, and in perennial antagonism with it.

The emergence of this *alter ego,* and the determination of a historic conflict between mind and body, represent the birth of the individual in capitalist society. It would become a typical characteristic of the individual molded by the capitalist work-discipline to confront one's body as an alien reality to be assessed, developed and kept at bay, in order to obtain from it the desired results.

As we pointed out, among the "lower classes" the development of self-management as self-discipline remained, for a long time, an object of speculation. How little self-discipline was expected from the "common people" can be judged from the fact that, right into the 18th century, 160 crimes in England were punishable by death (Linebaugh 1992), and every year thousands of "common people" were transported to the colonies or condemned to the galleys. Moreover, when the populace appealed to reason, it was to voice anti-authoritarian demands, since self-mastery at the popular level meant the rejection of the established authority, rather than the interiorization of social rule.

Indeed, through the 17th century, self-management remained a bourgeois prerogative. As Easlea points out, when the philosophers spoke of "man" as a rational being they made exclusive reference to a small elite made of white, upper-class, adult males. "The great multitude of men," wrote Henry Power, an English follower of Descartes, "resembles rather Descartes' automata, as they lack any reasoning power, and only as a metaphor can be called men" (Easlea1980: 140).[25] The "better sorts" agreed that the proletariat was of a different race. In their eyes, made suspicious by fear, the proletariat appeared as a "great beast," a "many-headed monster," wild, vociferous, given to any excess (Hill 1975: 181ff; Linebaugh and Rediker 2000). On an individual level as well, a ritual vocabulary identified the masses as purely instinctual beings. Thus, in the Elizabethan literature, the beggar is always "lusty," and "sturdy," "rude," "hot-headed," "disorderly" are the ever-recurrent terms in any discussion of the lower class.

In this process, not only did the body lose all naturalistic connotations, but a *body-function* began to emerge, in the sense that the body became a purely relational term, no longer signifying any specific reality, but identifying instead any impediment to the domination of Reason. This means that while the proletariat became a "body," the body became "the proletariat," and in particular the weak, irrational female (the "woman in us," as Hamlet was to say) or the "wild" African, being purely defined through its limiting function, that is through its "otherness" from Reason, and treated as an agent of internal subversion.

Yet, the struggle against this "great beast" was not solely directed against the "lower sort of people." It was also interiorized by the dominant classes in the battle they waged against their own "natural state." As we have seen, no less than Prospero, the bourgeoisie too had to recognize that "[t]his thing of darkness is mine," that is, that Caliban was part of itself (Brown1988; Tyllard 1961:34–35). This awareness pervades the literary production of the 16th and 17th centuries. The terminology is revealing. Even those who did not follow Descartes saw the body as a beast that had to be kept incessantly under control. Its instincts were compared to "subjects" to be "governed," the senses were seen as a prison for the reasoning soul.

> O who shall, from this Dungeon, raise
> A Soul inslav'd so many wayes?

asked Andrew Marvell, in his "Dialogue Between the Soul and the Body."

> With bolts of Bones, that fetter'd stands
> In Feet; and manacled in Hands.
> Here blinded with an Eye; and there
> Deaf with the drumming of an Ear.
> A Soul hung up, as t'were, in Chain
> Of Nerves, and Arteries, and Veins
>   (quoted by Hill 1964b: 345).

The conflict between appetites and reason was a key theme in Elizabethan literature (Tillyard 1961: 75), while among the Puritans the idea began to take hold that the "Antichrist" is in every man. Meanwhile, debates on education and on the "nature of man" current among the "middle sort" centered around the body/mind conflict, posing the crucial question of whether human beings are voluntary or involuntary agents.

But the definition of a new relation with the body did not remain at a purely ideological level. Many practices began to appear in daily life to signal the deep transformations occurring in this domain: the use of cutlery, the development of shame with respect to nakedness, the advent of "manners" that attempted to regulate how one laughed, walked, sneezed, how one should behave at the table, and to what extent one could sing, joke, play (Elias 1978: 129ff). While the individual was increasingly dissociated from the body, the latter became an object of constant observation, as if it were an enemy. The body began to inspire fear and repugnance. "The body of man is full of filth," declared Jonathan Edwards, whose attitude is typical of the Puritan experience, where the subjugation of the body was a daily practice (Greven 1977: 67). Particularly repugnant were those bodily functions that directly confronted "men" with their "animality." Witness the case of Cotton Mather who, in his *Diary*, confessed how humiliated he felt one day when, urinating against a wall, he saw a dog doing the same:

> Thought I 'what vile and mean Things are the Children of Men
> in this mortal State. How much do our natural Necessities abase us,
> and place us in some regard on the same level with the very Dogs'...
> Accordingly I resolved that it should be my ordinary Practice, when-
> ever I step to answer the one or the other Necessity of Nature, to make
> it an Opportunity of shaping in my Mind some holy, noble, divine
> Thought (*ibid.*).

The great medical passion of the time, the *analysis of excrements* — from which manifold deductions were drawn on the psychological tendencies of the individual (vices, virtues) (Hunt 1970: 143–46) — is also to be traced back to this conception of the body as a receptacle of filth and hidden dangers. Clearly, this obsession with human excrements reflected in part the disgust that the middle class was beginning to feel for the non-productive aspects of the body — a disgust inevitably accentuated in an urban environment where excrements posed a logistic problem, in addition to appearing as pure waste. But in this obsession we can also read the bourgeois need to regulate and cleanse the body-machine from any element that could interrupt its activity, and create "dead time" in the expenditure of labor. Excrements were so much analyzed and debased because they were the symbol of the "ill humors" that were believed to dwell in the body, to which every perverse tendency in human beings was attributed. For the Puritans they became the visible sign of the corruption of human nature, a sort of original sin that had to be combatted, subjugated, exorcised. Hence the use of purges, emetics, and enemas that were administered to children or the "possessed" to make them expel their devilries (Thorndike 1958: 553ff).

In this obsessive attempt to conquer the body in its most intimate recesses, we see reflected the same passion with which, in these same years, the bourgeoisie tried to conquer — we could say "colonize" — that alien, dangerous, unproductive being that in its eyes was the proletariat. For the proletarian was the great Caliban of the time. The proletarian was that "material being by itself raw and undigested" that Petty recommended be consigned to the hands of the state, which, in its prudence, "must better it, manage it, and shape it to its advantage" (Furniss 1957: 17ff).

Like Caliban, the proletariat personified the "ill humors" that hid in the social body, beginning with the disgusting monsters of idleness and drunkenness. In the eyes of his masters, its life was pure inertia, but at the same time was uncontrolled passion and unbridled fantasy, ever ready to explode in riotous commotions. Above all, it was indiscipline, lack of productivity, incontinence, lust for immediate physical satisfaction; its utopia being not a life of labor, but the land of Cockaigne (Burke 1978; Graus 1987),[26] where houses were made of sugar, rivers of milk, and where not only could one obtain what one wished without effort, but one was paid to eat and drink:

> To sleep one hour
> of deep sleep
> without waking
> one earns six francs;
> and to drink well
> one earns a pistol;
> this country is jolly,
> one earns ten francs a day
> to make love (Burke: 190).

The idea of transforming this lazy being, who dreamt of life as a long Carnival, into an indefatigable worker, must have seemed a desperate enterprise. It meant literally to "turn the world upside down," but in a totally capitalist fashion, where inertia to command would be transformed into lack of desire and autonomous will, where *vis erotica* *would become vis lavorativa*, and where need would be experienced only as lack, abstinence, and eternal indigence.

Hence this battle against the body, which characterized the early phase of capitalist development, and which has continued, in different ways, to our day. Hence that mechanization of the body, which was the project of the new Natural Philosophy, and the focal point for the first experiments in the organization of the state. If we move from the witch-hunt to the speculations of Mechanical Philosophy, and the Puritans' meticulous investigations of individual talents, we see that a single thread ties the seemingly divergent paths of social legislation, religious reform, and the scientific rationalization of the universe. This was the attempt to rationalize human nature, whose powers had to be rechannelled and subordinated to the development and formation of labor-power.

As we have seen, the body was increasingly politicized in this process; it was denaturalized and redefined as the "other," the outer limit of social discipline. Thus, the birth of the body in the 17th century also marked its end, as the concept of the body would cease to define a specific organic reality, and become instead a political signifier of class relations, and of the shifting, continuously redrawn boundaries which these relations produce in the map of human exploitation.

Endnotes

1. Prospero is a "new man." Didactically, his misfortunes are attributed by Shakespeare to his excessive interest in magic books, which in the end he renounces for a more active life in his native kingdom, where he will draw his power not from magic, but from the government of his subjects. But already in the island of his exile, his activities prefigure a new world order, where power is not gained through a magic wand but through the enslavement of many Calibans in far distant colonies. Prospero's exploitative management of Caliban prefigures the role of the future plantation master, who will spare no torture nor torment to force his subjects to work.

2. "[E]very man is his own greatest enemy, and as it were, his own executioner," Thomas Browne writes. Pascal, too, in the *Pensée,* declares that: "There is internal war in man between reason and the passions. If he had only reasons without passions.... If he had only passions without reason.... But having both, he cannot be without strife... . Thus he is always divided against, and opposed to himself (*Pensee,* 412: 130). On the Passions/Reason conflict, and the "correspondences" between the human "microcosm" and the "body politic," in Elizabethan literature see Tillyard (1961: 75–79; 94–99).

3. The reformation of language — a key theme in 16th and 17th-century philosophy, from Bacon to Locke — was a major concern of Joseph Glanvil, who in his *Vanity of Dogmatizing* (1665), after proclaiming his adherence to the Cartesian world view, advocates a language fit to describe clear and distinct entities (Glanvil 1970: xxvi–xxx). As S. Medcalf sums it up in his introduction to Glanvil's work, a language fit to describe such a world will bear broad similarities to mathematics, will have words of great generality and clarity; will present a picture of the universe according to its logical structure; will distinguish sharply between mind and matter, and between subjective and objective, and "will avoid metaphor as a way of knowing and describing, for metaphor depends on the assumption that the universe does not consist of wholly distinct entities and cannot therefore be fully described in positive distinct terms..." (*ibid.*: xxx).

4. Marx does not distinguish between male and female workers in his discussion of the "liberation of labor-power." There is, however, a reason for maintaining the masculine in the description of this process. While "freed" from the commons, women

were not channeled onto the path of the wage-labor market.

5. "With labour I must earn / My bread; what harm? Idleness had been worse; / My labour will sustain me" is Adam's answer to Eve's fears at the prospect of leaving the blessed garden (*Paradise Lost*, verses 1054–56, p. 579).

6. As Christopher Hill points out, until the 15th century, wage-labor could have appeared as a conquered freedom, because people still had access to the commons and had land of their own, thus they were not solely dependent on a wage. But by the 16th century, those who worked for a wage had been expropriated; moreover, the employers claimed that wages were only complementary, and kept them at their lowest level. Thus, working for a wage meant to fall to the bottom of the social ladder, and people struggled desperately to avoid this lot (Hill, 1975: 220–22). By the 17th century wage-labor was still considered a form of slavery, so much so that the Levelers excluded wage workers from the franchise, as they did not consider them independent enough to be able to freely choose their representatives (Macpherson 1962: 107–59).

7. When in 1622 Thomas Mun was asked by James I to investigate the causes of the economic crisis that had struck the country, he concluded his report by blaming the problems of the nation on the idleness of the English workers. He referred in particular to "the general leprosy of our piping, potting, feasting, factions and misspending of our time in idleness and pleasure" which, in his view, placed England at a disadvantage in its commercial competition with the industrious Dutch (Hill, 1975: 125).

8. (Wright 1960: 80–83; Thomas 1971; Van Ussel 1971: 25–92; Riley 1973: 19ff; Underdown 1985: 7–72).

9. The fear the lower classes (the "base," "meaner sorts," in the jargon of the time) inspired in the ruling class can be measured by this tale narrated in *Social England Illustrated* (1903). In 1580, Francis Hitchcock, in a pamphlet titled "New Year's Gift to England," forwarded the proposal to draft the poor of the country into the Navy, arguing: "the poorer sort of people are... apt to assist rebellion or to join with whomsoever dare to invade this noble island... then they are meet guides to bring soldiers or men of war to the rich men's wealth. For they can point with their finger 'there it is', 'yonder it is' and 'He hath it', and so procure martyrdom with murder to many wealthy persons for their wealth...." Hitchcock's proposal, however, was defeated; it was objected that if the poor of England were drafted into the navy they would steal the ships or become pirates (*Social England Illustrated* 1903: 85–86).

10. Eli F. Heckscher writes that "In his most important theoretical work *A Treatise of Taxes and Contributions* (1662) [Sir William Petty] suggested the substitution of compulsory labour for all penalties, 'which will increase labour and public wealth'. " "Why [he inquired] should not insolvent Thieves be rather punished with slavery than death? So as being slaves they may be forced to as much labour, and as cheap fare, as nature will endure, and thereby become as two men added to the Commonwealth, and not as one taken away from it" (Heckscher 1962, II: 297). In France, Colbert exhorted the Court of Justice to condemn as many convicts as possible to the galleys in order to "maintain this corps which is necessary to the state" (*ibid.*: 298–99).

11. The *Treatise on Man* (*Traité de l'Homme*), which was published twelve years after Descartes' death as *L'Homme de René Descartes* (1664), opens Descartes' "mature

period." Here, applying Galileo's physics to an investigation of the attributes of the body, Descartes attempted to explain all physiological functions as matter in motion. "I desire you to consider" (Descartes wrote at the end of the *Treatise*) "...that all the functions that I have attributed to this machine... follow naturally... from the disposition of the organs — no more no less than do the movements of a clock or other automaton, from the arrangement of its counterweights and wheels" (*Treatise*: 113).

12. It was a Puritan tenet that God has given "man" special gifts fitting him for a particular Calling; hence the need for a meticulous self-examination to resolve the Calling for which we have been designed (Morgan1966:72–73;Weber1958: 47ff).

13. As Giovanna Ferrari has shown, one of the main innovations introduced by the study of anatomy in 16th-century Europe was the "anatomy theater," where dissection was organized as a public ceremony, subject to regulations similar to those that governed theatrical performances:

> Both in Italy and abroad, public anatomy lessons had developed in modern times into ritualized ceremonies that were held in places specially set aside for them. Their similarity to theatrical performances is immediately apparent if one bears in mind certain of their features: the division of the lessons into different phases...the institution of a paid entrance ticket and the performance of music to entertain the audience, the rules introduced to regulate the behaviour of those attending and the care taken over the "production." W.S. Heckscher even argues that many general theater techniques were originally designed with the performance of public anatomy lessons in mind (Ferrari 1987: 82–83).

14. According to Mario Galzigna, the epistemological revolution operated by anatomy in the 16th century is the birthplace of the mechanistic paradigm. It is the anatomical *coupure* that breaks the bond between microcosm and macrocosm, and posits the body both as a separate reality and as a place of production, in Vesalius' words: a factory (*fabrica*).

15. Also in *The Passions of the Soul* (Article VI), Descartes minimizes "the difference that exists between a living body and a dead body":

> ...we may judge that the body of a living man differs from that of a dead man just as does a watch or other automaton (i.e. a machine that moves of itself), when it is wound up and contains in itself the corporeal principle of those movements...from the same watch or other machine when it is broken and when the principle of its movement ceases to act (Descartes 1973,Vol. I, *ibid.*).

16. Particularly important in this context was the attack on the "imagination" (*"vis imaginativa"*) which in 16th and 17th-century Natural Magic was considered a powerful force by which the magician could affect the surrounding world and bring about "health or sickness, not only in its proper body, but also in other bodies" (Easlea 1980: 94ff). Hobbes devoted a chapter of the *Leviathan* to demonstrating that the imagination is only a "decaying sense," no different from memory, only gradually weakened by the removal of the objects of our perception (Part I, Chapter 2); a critique of imagination is also found in Sir Thomas Browne's *Religio Medici* (1642).

17. Writes Hobbes: "No man therefore can conceive any thing, but he must conceive it in some place... not that anything is all in this place and all in another place at the same time; nor that two or more things can be in one and the same place at once" (*Leviathan*: 72).

18. Among the supporters of the witch-hunt was Sir Thomas Browne, a doctor and reputedly an early defender of "scientific freedom," whose work in the eyes of his contemporaries "possessed a dangerous savour of skepticism" (Gosse 1905: 25). Thomas Browne contributed personally to the death of two women accused of being "witches" who, but for his intervention, would have been saved from the gallows, so absurd were the charges against them (Gosse 1905: 147–49). For a detailed analysis of this trial see Gilbert Geis and Ivan Bunn (1997).

19. In every country where anatomy flourished, in 16th-century Europe, statutes were passed by the authorities allowing the bodies of those executed to be used for anatomical studies. In England "the College of Physicians entered the anatomical field in 1565 when Elizabeth I granted them the right of claiming the bodies of dissected felons" (O'Malley 1964). On the collaboration between the authorities and anatomists in 16th and 17th-century Bologna, see Giovanna Ferrari (pp. 59, 60, 64, 87–8), who points out that not only those executed but also the "meanest" of those who died at the hospital were set aside for the anatomists. In one case, a sentence to life was commuted into a death sentence to satisfy the demand of the scholars.

20. According to Descartes' first biographer, Monsieur Adrien Baillet, in preparation for his *Treatise of Man,* in 1629, Descartes, while in Amsterdam, daily visited the slaughterhouses of the town, and performed dissections on various parts of animals:

    ...he set about the execution of his design by studying anatomy, to which he devoted the whole of the winter that he spent in Amsterdam. To Father Mersenne he testified that his eagerness for knowledge of this subject had made him visit, almost daily, a butcher's, to witness the slaughter; and that he had caused to be brought thence to his dwelling whichever of the animals' organs he desired to dissect at greater leisure. He often did the same thing in other places where he stayed after that, finding nothing personally shameful, or unworthy his position, in a practice that was innocent in itself and that could produce quite useful results. Thus, he made fun of certain maleficent and envious person who... had tried to make him out a criminal and had accused him of "going through the villages to see the pigs killed".... [H]e did not neglect to look at what Vesalius and the most experienced of other authors had written about anatomy. But he taught himself in a much surer way by personally dissecting animals of different species (Descartes 1972: xiii–xiv).

    In a letter to Mersenne of 1633, he writes: "J'anatomize maintenant les têtes de divers animaux pour expliquer en quoi consistent l'imagination, la memoire..." (Cousin Vol.IV: 255). Also in a letter of January 20 he refers in detail to experiments of vivisection: "Apres avoir ouverte la poitrine d'un lapin vivant... en sorte que le tron et le coeur de l'aorte se voyent facilement.... Poursuivant la dissection de cet animal vivant je lui coupe cette partie du coeur qu'on nomme sa pointe" (*ibid*. Vol VII: 350).

Finally, in June 1640, in response to Mersenne, who had asked him why animals feel pain if they have no soul, Descartes reassured him that they do not; for pain exists only with understanding, which is absent in brutes (Rosenfield 1968: 8).

This argument effectively desensitized many of Descartes' scientifically minded contemporaries to the pain inflicted on animals by vivisection. This is how Nicholas Fontaine described the atmosphere created at Port Royal by the belief in animal automatism: "There was hardly a *solitaire*, who didn't talk of automata.... They administered beatings to dogs with perfect indifference and made fun of those who pitied the creatures as if they had felt pain. They said that animals were clocks; that the cries they emitted when struck were only the noise of a little spring which had been touched, but that the whole body was without feeling. They nailed poor animals on boards by their four paws to vivisect them and see the circulation of the blood which was a great subject of conversation" (Rosenfield 1968: 54).

21. Descartes' doctrine concerning the mechanical nature of animals represented a total inversion with respect to the conception of animals that had prevailed in the Middle Ages and until the 16th century, which viewed them as intelligent, responsible beings, with a particularly developed imagination and even the ability to speak. As Edward Westermarck, and more recently Esther Cohen, have shown, in several countries of Europe, animals were tried and at times publicly executed for crimes they had committed. They were assigned a lawyer and the entire procedure — trial, sentence, execution — was conducted with all formal legalities. In 1565, the citizens of Arles, for example, asked for the expulsion of the grasshoppers from their town, and in a different case the worms that infested the parish were excommunicated. The last trial of an animal was held in France in 1845. Animals were also accepted in court as witnesses for the *compurgatio*. A man who had been condemned for murder appeared in court with his cat and his cock and in their presence swore that he was innocent and was released. (Westermarck 1924: 254ff.; Cohen 1986).

22. It has been argued that Hobbes arch-mechanistic perspective actually conceded more powers and dynamism to the body than the Cartesian account. Hobbes rejects Descartes dualistic ontology, and in particular the notion of the mind as an immaterial, incorporeal substance. Viewing body and mind as a monistic continuum, he accounts for mental operations on the basis of physical and physiological principles. However, no less than Descartes, he disempowers the human organism, as he denies self-motion to it, and reduces bodily changes to action-reaction mechanisms. Sense perception, for instance, is for Hobbes the product of an action-reaction, due to the resistance opposed by the sense organ to the atomic impulses coming from the external object; imagination is a decaying sense. Reason too is but a computing machine. No less than in Descartes, in Hobbes the operations of the body are understood in terms of a mechanical causality, and are subjected to the same universal legislation that regulates the world of inanimate matter.

23. As Hobbes lamented in *Behemoth*:

[A]fter the Bible was translated into English, every man, nay, every boy and wench, that could read English, thought they spoke with God Almighty and understood what he said when by a certain number of chapters a day they had read the Scriptures once or twice. The reverence and obedience due to the Reformed Church here, and to the bishops and pastors therein was cast off, and every man became a judge of religion and an interpreter of the Scriptures to himself." (p. 190).

He added that "numbers of men used to go forth of their own parishes and towns on working-days, leaving their calling" in order to hear mechanical preachers (p. 194).

24. Exemplary is Gerrard Winstanley's "New Law of Righteousness" (1649), in which the most notorious Digger asks:

> Did the light of Reason make the earth for some men to ingrosse up into bags and barns, that others might be opprest with poverty? Did the light of Reason make this law, that if one man did not have such an abundance of the earth as to give to others he borrowed of; that he that did lend should imprison the other, and starve his body in a close room? Did the light of Reason make this law, that some part of mankinde should kill and hang another part of mankinde, that would not walk in their steps? (Winstanley 1941: 197).

25. It is tempting to suggest that this suspicion concerning the humanity of the "lower classes" may be the reason why, among the first critics of Cartesian mechanism, few objected to Descartes' mechanical view of the human body. As L.C. Rosenfield points out: "this is one of the strange things about the whole quarrel, none of the ardent defenders of the animal soul in this first period took up the cudgel to preserve the human body from the taint of mechanism" (Rosenfield 1968: 25).

26. F. Graus (1967) states that "The name 'Cockaigne' first occurred in the 13th century (*Cucaniensis* comes presumably from *Kucken*), and seems to have been used in parody," since the first context in which it is found is a satire of an English monastery in the time of Edward II (Graus 1967: 9). Graus discusses the difference between the medieval concept of "Wonderland" and the modern concept of Utopia, arguing that:

Pieter Bruegel, LAND OF COCKAIGNE (1567).

In modern times the basic idea of the constructability of the ideal world means that Utopia must be populated with ideal beings who have rid themselves of their faults. The inhabitants of Utopia are marked by their justice and intelligence....The utopian visions of the Middle Ages on the other hand start from man as he is and seek to fulfill his present desires (*ibid*.: 6).

In Cockaigne (*Schlaraffenland*), for instance, there is food and drink in abundance, there is no desire to "nourish oneself" sensibly, but only to gluttonize, just as one had longed to do in everyday life.

In this Cockaigne...there is also the fountain of youth, which men and women step into on one side to emerge at the other side as handsome youths and girls. Then the story proceeds with its "Wishing Table" attitude, which so well reflects the simple view of an ideal life (Graus 1967: 7-8).

In other words, the ideal of Cockaigne does not embody any rational scheme or notion of "progress," but is much more "concrete," "lean[ing] heavily on the village setting," and "depicts a state of perfection which in modern times knows no further advance (Graus *ibid*.).

Lucas Cranach. THE FOUNTAIN OF YOUTH.

Jan Luyken. The execution of Anne Hendricks for witchcraft in Amsterdam in 1571.

The Great Witch-Hunt in Europe

Une bête imparfaicte, sans foy, sans crainte, sans costance.
(French 17th-century saying about women)

Down from the waiste they are Centaurs,
Though Women all above,
But to the girdle do the gods inherit,
Beneath is all the fiends;
There is hell, there is darkness,
There is the sulphurous pit,
Burning, scalding, stench, consumption.
(Shakespeare, *King Lear*)

You are the true Hyenas, that allure us with the fairness of your skins
and when folly has brought us within your reach, you leap upon us.
You are the traitors of Wisdom, the impediment to Industry… the
clogs to Virtue and the goads that drive us to all vices, impiety and
ruin. You are the Fool's Paradise, the wiseman's Plague and the Grand
Error of Nature (Walter Charleton, *Ephesian Matron,* 1659).

Introduction

The witch-hunt rarely appears in the history of the proletariat. To this day, it remains one
of the most understudied phenomena in European history[1] or, rather, world history, if
we consider that the charge of devil worshipping was carried by missionaries and conquistadors to the "New World" as a tool for the subjugation of the local populations.

That the victims, in Europe, were mostly peasant women may account for the historians' past indifference towards this genocide, an indifference that has bordered on complicity, since the elimination of the witches from the pages of history has contributed to
trivializing their physical elimination at the stake, suggesting that it was a phenomenon
of minor significance, if not a matter of folklore.

Even those who have studied the witch-hunt (in the past almost exclusively men)
were often worthy heirs of the 16th-century demonologists. While deploring the exter-

mination of the witches, many have insisted on portraying them as wretched fools, afflicted by hallucinations, so that their persecution could be explained as a process of "social therapy," serving to reinforce neighborly cohesion (Midelfort 1972: 3) or could be described in medical terms as a "panic," a "craze," an "epidemic," all characterizations that exculpate the witch hunters and depoliticize their crimes.

Examples of the misogyny that has inspired the scholarly approach to the witch-hunt abound. As Mary Daly pointed out as late as 1978, much of the literature on this topic has been written from "a woman-executing viewpoint" that discredits the victims of the persecution by portraying them as social failures (women "dishonored" or frustrated in love), or even as perverts who enjoyed teasing their male inquisitors with their sexual fantasies. Daly cites the example of F. G. Alexander's and S.T. Selesnick's *The History of Psychiatry* where we read that:

> ...accused witches oftentimes played into the hands of the persecutors. A witch relieved her guilt by confessing her sexual fantasies in open court; at the same time, she achieved some erotic gratification by dwelling on all the details before her male accusers. These severely emotionally disturbed women were particularly susceptible to the suggestion that they harbored demon and devils and would confess to cohabiting with evil spirits, much as disturbed individuals today, influenced by newspaper headlines, fantasy themselves as sought-after murderers (Daly 1978: 213).

There have been exceptions to this tendency to blame the victims, both among the first and second generation of witch-hunt scholars. Among the latter we should remember Alan Macfarlane (1970), E. W. Monter (1969, 1976, 1977), and Alfred Soman (1992). But it was only in the wake of the feminist movement that the witch-hunt emerged from the underground to which it had been confined, thanks to the feminists' identification with the witches, who were soon adopted as a symbol of female revolt (Bovenschen 1978: 83ff).[2] Feminists were quick to recognize that hundreds of thousands of women could not have been massacred and subjected to the cruelest tortures unless they posed a challenge to the power structure. They also realized that such a war against women, carried out over a period of at least two centuries, was a turning point in the history of women in Europe, the "original sin" in the process of social degradation that women suffered with the advent of capitalism, and a phenomenon, therefore, to which we must continually return if we are to understand the misogyny that still characterizes institutional practice and male-female relations.

Marxist historians, by contrast, even when studying the "transition to capitalism," with very few exceptions, have consigned the witch-hunt to oblivion, as if it were irrelevant to the history of the class struggle. Yet, the dimensions of the massacre should have raised some suspicions, as hundreds of thousands of women were burned, hanged, and tortured in less than two centuries.[3] It should also have seemed significant that the witch-hunt occurred simultaneously with the colonization and extermination of the populations of the New World, the English enclosures, the beginning of the slave trade, the enactment of "bloody laws" against vagabonds and beggars, and it climaxed in that interregnum between the end of feudalism and the capitalist "take off" when the peasantry in Europe reached the peak of its power but, in time, also consummated its historic defeat. So far, however, this aspect of primitive accumulation has truly remained a secret.[4]

Witch-burning times and the State Initiative

What has not been recognized is that the witch-hunt was one of the most important events in the development of capitalist society and the formation of the modern proletariat. For the unleashing of a campaign of terror against women, unmatched by any other persecution, weakened the resistance of the European peasantry to the assault launched against it by the gentry and the state, at a time when the peasant community was already disintegrating under the combined impact of land privatization, increased taxation, and the extension of state control over every aspect of social life. The witch-hunt deepened the divisions between women and men, teaching men to fear the power of women, and destroyed a universe of practices, beliefs, and social subjects whose existence was incompatible with the capitalist work discipline, thus redefining the main elements of social reproduction. In this sense, like the contemporary attack on "popular culture," and the "Great Confinement" of paupers and vagabonds in work-houses and correction houses, the witch-hunt was an essential aspect of primitive accumulation and the "transition" to capitalism.

Later, we will see what fears the witch-hunt dispelled for the European ruling class and what were its effects for the position of women in Europe. Here I want to stress that, contrary to the view propagated by the Enlightenment, the witch-hunt was not the last spark of a dying feudal world. It is well established that the "superstitious" Middle Ages did not persecute any witches; the very concept of "witchcraft" did not take shape until the late Middle Ages, and never, in the "Dark Ages," were there mass trials and executions, despite the fact that magic permeated daily life and, since the late Roman Empire, it had been feared by the ruling class as a tool of insubordination among the slaves.[5]

In the 7th and 8th centuries, the crime of *maleficium* was introduced in the codes of the new Teutonic kingdoms, as it had been in the Roman code. This was the time of the Arab conquest that, apparently, inflamed the hearts of the slaves in Europe with the prospect of freedom, inspiring them to take arms against their owners.[6] Thus, this legal innovation may have been a reaction to the fear generated among the elites by the advance of the "Saracens" who were, reputedly, great experts in the magical arts (Chejne 1983: 115–32). But, at this time, under the name of *maleficium*, only magical practices were punished that inflicted damage to persons and things, and the church criticized those who believed in magical deeds.[7]

The situation changed by the mid 15th century. It was in this age of popular revolts, epidemics, and incipient feudal crisis that we have the first witch trials (in Southern France, Germany, Switzerland, Italy), the first descriptions of the Sabbat,[8] and the development of the doctrine of witchcraft, by which sorcery was declared a form of heresy and the highest crime against God, Nature, and the State (Monter 1976: 11–17). Between 1435 and 1487, twenty-eight treatises on witchcraft were written (Monter 1976: 19) culminating, on the eve of Columbus' voyage, with the publication in 1486 of the infamous *Malleus Maleficarum* (*The Hammer of Witches*) that, following a new papal Bull on the subject, Innocent VIII's *Summis Desiderantes* (1484), indicated that the Church considered witchcraft a new threat. However, the intellectual climate that prevailed during the Renaissance, especially in Italy, was still characterized by skepticism towards anything relating to the supernatural. Italian intellectuals, from Ludovico Ariosto, to Giordano Bruno, and Nicoló Machiavelli looked with irony at the clerical tales concerning the deeds of the devil, stressing, by contrast (especially in the case of Bruno), the nefarious power of gold and money. *"Non incanti ma contanti"* ("not charms but coins") is the motto of a character in one of Bruno's comedies, summing up the perspective of the intellectual elite and the aristocratic circles of the time (Parinetto 1998: 29–99).

It was after the mid-16th century, in the very decades in which the Spanish conquistadors were subjugating the American populations, that the number of women tried as witches escalated, and the initiative for the persecution passed from the Inquisition to the secular courts (Monter 1976: 26). Witch-hunting reached its peak between 1580 and 1630, in a period, that is, when feudal relations were already giving way to the economic and political institutions typical of mercantile capitalism. It was in this long "Iron Century" that, almost by a tacit agreement, in countries often at war against each other, the stakes multiplied and the state started denouncing the existence of witches and taking the initiative of the persecution.

It was the Carolina — the Imperial legal code enacted by the Catholic Charles V in 1532 — that established that witchcraft be punished by death. In Protestant England, the persecution was legalized by three Acts of Parliament passed in 1542, 1563 and 1604, this last introducing the death penalty even in the absence of any damage inflicted upon persons and things. After 1550, laws and ordinances making witchcraft a capital crime and inciting the population to denounce suspected witches, were also passed in Scotland, Switzerland, France, and the Spanish Netherlands. These were re-issued in subsequent years to expand the number of those who could be executed and, again, make *witchcraft as such*, rather than the damages presumably provoked by it, the major crime.

The mechanisms of the persecution confirm that the witch-hunt was not a spontaneous process, "a movement from below to which the ruling and administrative classes were obliged to respond" (Larner 1983: 1). As Christina Larner has shown in the case of Scotland, a witch-hunt required much official organization and administration.[9] Before neighbor accused neighbor, or entire communities were seized by a "panic," a steady indoctrination took place, with the authorities publicly expressing anxiety about the spreading of witches, and travelling from village to village in order to teach people how to recognize them, in some cases carrying with them lists with the names of suspected witches and threatening to punish those who hid them or came to their assistance (Larner 1983: 2).

In Scotland, with the Synod of Aberdeen (1603), the ministers of the Presbyterian Church were ordered to ask their parishioners, under oath, if they suspected anyone of being a witch. Boxes were placed in the churches to allow the informers to remain anonymous; then, after a woman had fallen under suspicion, the minister exhorted the faithful from the pulpit to testify against her and forbid anyone to give her help (Black 1971: 13). In the other countries too, denunciations were solicited. In Germany, this was the task of the "visitors" appointed by the Lutheran Church with the consent of the German princes

WITCHES SABBATH. This was the first and most famous of a series of engravings the German artist Hans Baldung Grien produced, starting in 1510, pornographically exploiting the female body under the guise of denunciation.

(Strauss 1975: 54). In Northern Italy, it was the ministers and the authorities who fueled suspicions, and made sure that they would result in denunciations; they also made sure that the accused would be totally isolated, forcing them, among other things, to carry signs on their dresses so that people would keep away from them (Mazzali 1988: 112).

The witch-hunt was also the first persecution in Europe that made use of a multi-media propaganda to generate a mass psychosis among the population. Alerting the public to the dangers posed by the witches, through pamphlets publicizing the most famous trials and the details of their atrocious deeds, was one of the first tasks of the printing press (Mandrou 1968: 136). Artists were recruited to the task, among them the German Hans Baldung, to whom we owe the most damning portraits of witches. But it was the jurists, the magistrates, and the demonologists, often embodied by the same person, who most contributed to the persecution. They were the ones who systematized the arguments, answered the critics and perfected a legal machine that, by the end of the 16th century, gave a standardized, almost bureaucratic format to the trials, accounting for the similarities of the confessions across national boundaries. In their work, the men of the law could count on the cooperation of the most reputed intellectuals of the time, including philosophers and scientists who are still praised as the fathers of modern rationalism. Among them was the English political theorist Thomas Hobbes, who despite his skepticism concerning the reality of witchcraft, approved the persecution as a means of social control. A fierce enemy of witches — obsessive in his hatred for them and in his calls for bloodshed — was Jean Bodin, the famous French lawyer and political theorist, whom historian Trevor Roper calls the Aristotle and Montesquieu of the 16th century. Bodin, who is credited with authoring the first treatise on inflation, participated in many trials, wrote a volume of "proofs" (*Demomania,* 1580), in which he insisted that witches should be burned alive instead of being "mercifully" strangled before being thrown to the flames, that they should be cauterized so that their flesh should rot before death, and that children too be burned.

Bodin was not an isolated case. In this "century of geniuses" — Bacon, Kepler, Galileo, Shakespeare, Pascal, Descartes — a century that saw the triumph of the Copernican Revolution, the birth of modern science, and the development of philosophical and scientific rationalism, witchcraft became one of the favorite subjects of debate for the European intellectual elites. Judges, lawyers, statesmen, philosophers, scientists, theologians all became preoccupied with the "problem," wrote pamphlets and demonologies, agreed that this was the most nefarious crime, and called for its punishment.[10]

There can be no doubt, then, that the witch-hunt was a major *political* initiative. To stress this point is not to minimize the role that the Church played in the persecution. The Roman Catholic Church provided the metaphysical and ideological scaffold of the witch-hunt and instigated the persecution of witches as it had previously instigated the persecution of the heretics. Without the Inquisition, the many papal bulls urging the secular authorities to seek out and punish "witches" and, above all, without centuries of the Church's misogynous campaigns against women, the witch-hunt would not have been possible. But, contrary to the stereotype, the witch-hunt was not just a product of popish fanaticism or of the machinations of the Roman Inquisition. At its peak, the secular courts conducted most of the trials, while in the areas where the Inquisition operated (Italy and Spain) the number of executions remained comparatively low. After the Protestant

Reformation, which undermined the Catholic Church's power, the Inquisition even began to restrain the zeal of the authorities against witches, while intensifying its persecution of Jews (Milano 1963:287-9).[11] Moreover, the Inquisition always depended on the cooperation of the state to carry out the executions, as the clergy wanted to be spared the embarrassment of shedding blood. The collaboration between Church and state was even closer in the areas of the Reformation, where the State had become the Church (as in England) or the Church had become the State (as in Geneva, and, to a lesser extent, Scotland). Here one branch of power legislated and executed, and religious ideology openly revealed its political connotations.

The political nature of the witch-hunt is further demonstrated by the fact that both Catholic and Protestant nations, at war against each other in every other respect, joined arms and shared arguments to persecute witches. Thus, it is no exaggeration to claim that *the witch-hunt was the first unifying terrain in the politics of the new European nation-states, the first example, after the schism brought about by the Reformation, of a European unification*. For, crossing all boundaries, the witch-hunt spread from France and Italy to Germany, Switzerland, England, Scotland, and Sweden.

What fears instigated such concerted policy of genocide? Why was so much violence unleashed? And why were its primary targets women?

Devil Beliefs and Changes in the Mode of Production

It must be immediately stated that, to this day, there are no sure answers to these questions. A major obstacle in the way of an explanation has been the fact that the charges against the witches are so grotesque and unbelievable as to be incommensurable with any motivation or crime.[12] How to account for the fact that for more than two centuries, in several European countries, *hundreds of thousands* of women were tried, tortured, burned alive or hanged, accused of having sold body and soul to the devil and, by magical means, murdered scores of children, sucked their blood, made potions with their flesh, caused the death of their neighbors, destroyed cattle and crops, raised storms, and performed many other abominations? (However, even today, some historians ask us to believe that the witch-hunt was quite reasonable in the context of the contemporary belief structure!)

An added problem is that we do not have the viewpoint of the victims, for all that remains of their voices are the confessions styled by the inquisitors, usually obtained under torture, and no matter how well we listen — as Carlo Ginzburg (1991) has done — to what transpires of traditional folklore from between the cracks in the recorded confessions, we have no way of establishing their authenticity. Further, one cannot account for the extermination of the witches as simply a product of greed, as no reward comparable to the riches of the Americas could be obtained from the execution and the confiscation of the goods of women who in the majority were very poor.[13]

It is for these reasons that some historians, like Brian Levack, abstain from presenting any explanatory theory, contenting themselves with identifying the preconditions for the witch-hunt — for instance, the shift in legal procedure from a private to a public accusatory system that occurred in the late Middle Ages, the centralization of state-power, the impact of the Reformation and Counter-Reformation on social life (Levack 1987).

There is no need, however, for such agnosticism, nor do we have to decide whether the witch hunters truly believed in the charges which they leveled against their victims or cynically used them as instruments of social repression. If we consider the historical context in which the witch-hunt occurred, the gender and class of the accused, and the effects of the persecution, then we must conclude that witch-hunting in Europe was an attack on women's resistance to the spread of capitalist relations and the power that women had gained by virtue of their sexuality, their control over reproduction, and their ability to heal.

Witch hunting was also instrumental to the construction of a new patriarchal order where women's bodies, their labor, their sexual and reproductive powers were placed under the control of the state and transformed into economic resources. This means that the witch hunters were less interested in the punishment of any specific transgressions than in the elimination of generalized forms of female behavior which they no longer tolerated and had to be made abominable in the eyes of the population. That the charges in the trials often referred to events that had occurred decades earlier, that witchcraft was made a *crimen exceptum*, that is, a crime to be investigated by special means, torture included, and it was punishable even in the absence of any proven damage to persons and things — all these factors indicate that the target of the witch-hunt — (as it is often true with political repression in times of intense social change and conflict) — were not socially recognized crimes, but previously accepted practices and groups of individuals that had to be eradicated from the community, through terror and criminalization. In this sense, the charge of witchcraft performed a function similar to that performed by "high treason" (which, significantly, was introduced into the English legal code in the same years), and the charge of "terrorism" in our times. The very vagueness of the charge — the fact that it was impossible to prove it, while at the same time it evoked the maximum of horror — meant that it could be used to punish any form of protest and to generate suspicion even towards the most ordinary aspects of daily life.

A first insight into the meaning of the European witch-hunt can be found in the thesis proposed by Michael Taussig, in his classic work *The Devil and Commodity Fetishism in South America* (1980), where the author maintains that devil-beliefs arise in those historical periods when one mode of production is being supplanted by another. In such periods not only are the material conditions of life radically transformed, but so are the metaphysical underpinnings of the social order — for instance, the conception of how value is created, what generates life and growth, what is "natural" and what is antagonistic to the established customs and social relations (Taussig 1980: 17ff). Taussig developed his theory by studying the beliefs of Colombian agricultural laborers and Bolivian tin miners at a time when, in both countries, monetary relations were taking root that in peoples' eyes seemed deadly and even diabolical, compared with the older and still-surviving forms of subsistence-oriented production. Thus, in the cases Taussig studied, it was the poor who suspected the better-off of devil worship. Still, his association between the devil and the commodity form reminds us that also in the background of the witch-hunt there was the expansion of rural capitalism, which involved the abolition of customary rights, and the first inflationary wave in modern Europe. These phenomena not only led to the growth of poverty, hunger, and social dislocation (Le Roy Ladurie 1974: 208), they also transferred power into the hands of a new class of "modernizers" who looked with fear and repulsion at the communal forms of life that had been typical of pre-capitalist Europe. It was by the initiative of this proto-capitalist class that the witch-hunt took off, both as "a platform on which a wide range of popular beliefs and practices... could be pursued" (Normand and Roberts 2000: 65), and a weapon by which resistance to social and economic restructuring could be defeated.

It is significant that, in England, most of the witch trials occurred in Essex, where by the 16th century the bulk of the land had been enclosed,[14] while in those regions of the British Isles where land privatization had neither occurred nor was on the agenda we have no record of witch-hunting. The most outstanding examples in this context are Ireland and the Scottish Western Highlands, where no trace can be found of the persecution, likely because a collective land-tenure system and kinship ties still prevailed in both areas that precluded the communal divisions and the type of complicity with the state that made a witch-hunt possible. Thus — while in the Anglicized and privatized Scottish Lowlands, where the subsistence economy was vanishing under the impact of the Presbyterian Reformation, the witch-hunt claimed at least 4,000 victims, the equivalent of one percent of the female population — in the Highlands and in Ireland, women were safe during the witch-burning times.

That the spread of rural capitalism, with all its consequences (land expropriation, the deepening of social distances, the breakdown of collective relations) was a decisive factor in the background of the witch-hunt is also proven by the fact that the majority of those accused were poor peasant women — cottars, wage laborers — while those who accused them were wealthy and prestigious members of the community, often their employers or landlords, that is, individuals who were part of the local power structures and often had close ties with the central state. Only as the persecution progressed, and the fear of witches (as well as the fear of being accused of witchcraft, or of "subversive association") was sowed among the population, did accusations also come from neighbors. In England, the witches were usually old women on public assistance or women who survived by going from house to house begging for bits of food or a pot of wine or milk; if they were married, their husbands were day laborers, but more often they were widows and lived alone. Their poverty stands out in the confessions. It was in times of need that the Devil appeared to them, to assure them that from now on they "should never want," although the money he would give them on such occasions would soon turn to ashes, a detail perhaps related to the experience of superinflation common at the time (Larner 1983: 95; Mandrou 1968: 77). As for the diabolical crimes of the witches, they appear to us as nothing more than the class struggle played out at the village level: the 'evil eye,' the curse of the beggar to whom an alm has been refused, the default on the payment of rent, the demand for public assistance (Macfarlane 1970: 97; Thomas 1971: 565; Kittredge 1929: 163). The many ways in which the class struggle contributed to the making of an English witch are shown by the charges against Margaret Harkett, an old widow of sixty-five hanged at Tyburn in 1585:

> She had picked a basket of peas in the neighbor's field without permission. Asked to return them she flung them down in anger; since then no pears would grow in the field. Later William Goodwin's servant denied her yeast, whereupon his brewing stand dried up. She was struck

A classic image of the English witch: old, decrepit, surroundered by her animals and her cronies, and yet maintaining a defiant posture.
From THE WONDERFUL DISCOVERIES OF THE WITCHCRAFTS
OF MARGARET AND PHILLIP FLOWERS, *1619.*

by a baillif who had caught her taking wood from the master's ground; the baillif went mad. A neighbor refused her a horse; all his horses died. Another paid her less for a pair of shoes than she had asked; later he died. A gentleman told his servant to refuse her buttermilk; after which they were unable to make butter or cheese (Thomas 1971: 556).

One finds the same pattern in the case of the women who were "presented" to court at Chelmsford, Windsor and Osyth. Mother Waterhouse, hanged at Chelmsford in 1566, was a "very poor woman," described as begging for some cake or butter and "falling out" with many of her neighbors (Rosen 1969: 76–82). Elizabeth Stile, Mother Devell, Mother Margaret and Mother Dutton, executed at Windsor in 1579, were also poor widows; Mother Margaret lived in the almshouse, like their alleged leader Mother Seder, and all of them went around begging and presumably taking revenge when denied. (*ibid.*: 83–91). On being refused some old yeast, Elizabeth Francis, one of the Chelmsford witches, cursed a neighbor who later developed a great pain in her head. Mother Staunton suspiciously murmured, going away, when denied yeast by a neighbor, upon which the neighbor's child fell vehemently sick (*ibid.*: 96). Ursula Kemp, hanged at Osyth in 1582, made one Grace lame after being denied some cheese; she also caused a swelling in the bottom of Agnes Letherdale's child after the latter denied her some scouring sand. Alice Newman plagued Johnson, the Collector for the poor, to death after he refused her twelve pence; she also punished one Butler, who denied her a piece of meat (*ibid.*: 119). We find a similar pattern in Scotland, where the accused were also poor cottars, still holding on to a piece of land of their own, but barely surviving and often arousing the hostility of their neighbors on account of having pushed their cattle to graze on their land, or not having paid the rent (Larner 1983).

Witch Hunting and Class Revolt

As we can see from these cases, the witch-hunt grew in a social environment where the "better sorts" were living in constant fear of the "lower classes," who could certainly be expected to harbor evil thoughts because in this period they were losing everything they had.

That this fear expressed itself as an attack on popular magic is not surprising. The battle against magic has always accompanied the development of capitalism, to this very day. Magic is premised on the belief that the world is animated, unpredictable, and that there is a force in all things: "water, trees, substances, words…" (Wilson, 2000: xvii) so that every event is interpreted as the expression of an occult power that must be deciphered and bent to one's will. What this implied in everyday life is described, probably with some exaggeration, in the letter of a German minister sent after a pastoral visit to a village in 1594:

> The use of incantations is so widespread that there is no man or woman here who begins or does anything… without first taking recourse to some sign, incantation, magic or pagan means. For example during labor pains, when picking up or putting down the child… when taking the beasts to the field… when they have lost an object or failed to find it…closing the windows at night, when someone gets ill or a cow behaves in a strange way they run at once to the soothsayer to ask who robbed them, who's enchanted them or to get an amulet. The daily experience of these people shows there is no limit to the use of superstitions…. Everyone here takes part in superstitious practices, with words, names, rhymes, using the names of God, of the Holy Trinity, of the Virgin Mary, of the twelve Apostles…. These words are uttered both openly and in secret; they are written on pieces of paper, swallowed, carried as amulets. They also make strange signs, noises and gestures. And then they practice magic with herbs, roots, and the branches of a certain tree; they have their particular day and place for all these things (Strauss 1975: 21).

As Stephen Wilson points out in *The Magical Universe* (2000), the people who practiced these rituals were mostly poor people who struggled to survive, always trying to stave off disaster and wishing therefore "to placate, cajole, and even manipulate these controlling forces… to keep away harm and evil, and to procure the good which consisted of fertility, well-being, health, and life" (p. xviii). But in the eyes of the new capitalist class, this anarchic, molecular conception of the diffusion of power in the world was anathema. Aiming at controlling nature, the capitalist organization of work must refuse the unpredictability implicit in the practice of magic, and the possibility of establishing a privileged relation with the natural elements, as well as the belief in the existence of powers available only to particular individuals, and thus not easily generalized and exploitable. Magic was also an obstacle to the rationalizaion of the work process, and a threat to the establishment of the principle of individual responsibility. Above all, magic seemed a form of refusal of work, of insubordination, and an instrument of grassroots resistance to power. The world had to be "disenchanted" in order to be dominated.

By the 16th century, the attack against magic was well under way and women were its most likely targets. Even when they were not expert sorcerers/magicians, they were the ones who were called to mark animals when they fell sick, heal their neighbors, help them find lost or stolen objects, give them amulets or love potions, help them forecast the future. Though the witch-hunt targeted a broad variety of female practices, it was above all in this capacity — as sorcerers, healers, performers of incantations and divinations — that women were persecuted.[15] For their claim to magical power undermined the power of the authorities and the state, giving confidence to the poor in their ability to manipulate the natural and social environment and possibly subvert the constituted order.

It is doubtful, on the other hand, that the magical arts that women had practiced for generations would have been magnified into a demonic conspiracy had they not occurred against a background of an intense social crisis and stuggle. The coincidence between social-economic crisis and witch-hunting has been noted by Henry Kamen, who has observed that it was "precisely in the period when there was the main price hike (between the end of the 16th century and the first half of the 17th) [that] there were the greatest number of charges and persecutions" (Kamen 1972: 249).[16]

Even more significant is the coincidence between the intensification of the persecution and the explosion of urban and rural revolts. These were the "peasant wars" against land privatization, including the uprisings against the "enclosures" in England (in 1549, 1607, 1628, 1631), when hundreds of men, women and children, armed with pitchforks and spades, set about destroying the fences erected around the commons, proclaiming that "from now on we needn't work any more." In France, in 1593–1595, there was the revolt of the Croquants against the tithes, excessive taxation, and the rising price of bread, a phenomenon that caused mass starvation in large areas of Europe.

During these revolts, it was often women who initiated and led the action. Exemplary were the revolt that occurred at Montpellier in 1645, which was started by women who were seeking to protect their children from starvation, and the revolt at Cordoba in 1652 that likewise was initiated by women. It was women, moreover, who (after the revolts were crushed, with many men imprisoned or slaughtered) remained to carry on the resistance, although in a more subterranean manner. This is what may have happened in Southwestern Germany, where a witch-hunt followed by two decades the end of the Peasant War. Writing on the subject, Erik Midelfort has excluded the existence of a connection between these two phenomena (Midelfort 1972: 68). However, he has not asked if there were family or community relations, such as the ones Le Roy Ladurie found in the Cevennes,[17] between the thousands of peasants who, from 1476 to 1525,

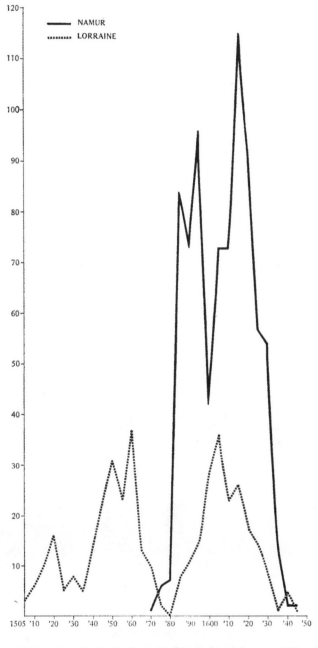

*This graph, indicating the dynamics of the witch trials between 1505 and
1650, refers specifically to the area of Namur and Lorraine in France, but it is
representative of the persecution in other European countries. Everywhere, the
key decades were those from the 1550s to the 1630s, when the price of food
escalated. (From Henry Kamen, 1972.)*

continuously rose up in arms against feudal power and were so brutally defeated, and the scores of women who, less than two decades later, in the same region and villages, were brought to the stake. Yet, we can well imagine that the ferocious work of repression which the German princes conducted, and the hundreds and thousands of peasants crucified, decapitated, burned alive, sedimented unquenchable hatreds, secret plans of revenge, above all among older women, who had seen and remembered, and were likely to make their hostility known in numerous ways to the local elites.

The persecution of witches grew on this terrain. It was class war carried out by other means. In this context, we cannot fail to see a connection between the fear of uprising and the prosecutors' insistence on the Witches Sabbat, or Synagogue,[18] the famous nocturnal reunion where thousands of people presumably congregated, travelling often from far distant places. Whether or not, by evoking the horrors of the Sabbat, the authorities targeted actual forms of organization, cannot be established. But there is no doubt that, through the judges' obsession with these devilish gatherings, besides the echo of the persecution of the Jews, we hear the echo of the secret meetings the peasants held at night, on lonesome hills and in the forests, to plot their revolts.[19] The Italian historian Luisa Muraro has written on this matter, in *La Signora del Gioco* (*The Lady of the Game*)(1977), a study of witch trials that took place in the Italian Alps at the beginning of the 16th century:

> During the trials in Val di Fiemme one of the accused spontaneously told the judges that one night, while she was in the mountains with her mother in law, she saw a great fire in the distance. "Run away, run away," her grand-mother had cried, "this is the fire of the Lady of the game." 'Game' (*gioco*) in many dialects of Northern Italy is the oldest name for the Sabbat (in the trials of Val di Fiemme there is still mention of a female figure who directed the game).... In the same region in 1525 there was a vast peasant uprising. They demanded the elimination of tithes and tributes, the freedom to hunt, less convents, hostels for the poor, the right of each village to elect its priest.... They burned castles, convents and the clergy's houses. But they were defeated, massacred, and those who survived for years were hunted by the revenge of the authorities.

Muraro concludes:

> The fire of the lady of the game fades in the distance, while in the foreground there are the fires of the revolt and the pyres of the repression.... But to us there seems to be a connection between the peasant revolt that was being prepared and the tales of mysterious nightly gatherings.... We can only assume that the peasants at night secretly met around a fire to warm up and to communicate with each other... and that those who knew guarded the secret of these forbidden meetings, by appealing to the old legend.... If the witches had secrets this may have been one (Muraro 1977: 46-47).

Class revolt, together with sexual transgression, was a central element in the descriptions of the Sabbat, which was portrayed both as a monstrous sexual orgy and as a subversive political gathering, culminating with an account of the crimes which the participants had committed, and with the devil instructing the witches to rebel against their masters. It is also significant that the pact between the witch and the Devil was called *conjuratio*, like the pacts often made by slaves and workers in struggle (Dockes 1982: 222; Tigar and Levy 1977: 136), and that in the eyes of the prosecutors, the Devil represented a promise of love, power, and riches for whose sake a person was willing to sell her (or his) soul, that is, to infringe every natural and social law.

The threat of cannibalism, a central theme in the morphology of the Sabbat, also recalls, according to Henry Kamen, the morphology of the revolts, as rebel workers at times showed their contempt for those who sold their blood by threatening to eat them.[20] Kamen mentions what happened in the town of Romans (Dauphiné, France), in the winter of 1580, when the peasants in revolt against the tithes, proclaimed that "before three days Christian flesh will be sold" and, then, during the Carnival, "the rebels' leader, dressed in a bear skin, ate delicacies which passed for Christian flesh" (Kamen 1972: 334; Le Roy Ladurie 1981: 189, 216). Again, in Naples, in 1585, during a riot against the high cost of bread, the rebels mutilated the body of the magistrate responsible for the price rise and offered pieces of his flesh for sale (Kamen 1972: 335). Kamen points out that eating human flesh symbolized a total inversion of social values, consistent with the image of the witch as the personification of moral perversion which is suggested by many of the rituals attributed to the practice of witchcraft: the mass celebrated backwards, the counter-clockwise dances. (Clark 1980; Kamen 1972). Indeed, the witch was the living symbol of "the world turned upside down," a recurrent image in the literature of the Middle Ages, tied to millenarian aspirations of subversion of the social order.

The subversive, utopian dimension of the witches' Sabbat is also stressed, from a different angle, by Luciano Parinetto who, in *Streghe e Potere* (1998), has insisted on the need to give a modern interpretation of this gathering, reading its transgressive features from the viewpoint of the developing capitalist discipline of work. Parinetto points out that the nocturnal dimension of the Sabbat was a violation of the contemporary capitalist regularization of work-time, and a challenge to private property and sexual orthodoxy, as the night shadows blurred the distinctions between the sexes and between "mine and thine." Parinetto also argues that *the flight, the travel*, an important element in the charges against the witches, should be interpreted as an attack on the mobility of immigrant and itinerant workers, a new phenomenon, reflected in the fear of vagabonds, that much preoccupied the authorities in this period. Parinetto concludes that, viewed in its historical specificity, the nocturnal Sabbat appears as a demonization of the utopia embodied in the rebellion against the masters and the break-down of sexual roles, and it also represents a use of space and time contrary to the new capitalist work-discipline.

In this sense, there is a continuity between the witch-hunt and the earlier persecution of the heretics which also punished specific forms of social subversion under the guise of imposing religious ortodoxy. Significantly, the witch-hunt developed first in the areas where the persecution of the heretics had been most intense (Southern France,

Waldensian heretics as represented in Johannes Tinctoris, TRACTATUS CONTRA SECTUM VALDENSIUM. The witch-hunt developed first in the areas where the persecution of the heretics had been most intense. In the early period in some areas of Switzerland, witches were often referred to as "waudois."

the Jura, Northern Italy). In some regions of Switzerland, in an early phase, witches were called *Herege* ("heretic") or *Waudois* ("Waldenses") (Monter 1976: 22; Russell 1972: 34ff).[21] Further, the heretics too were burned at the stake as traitors to the true religion, and they were accused of crimes that entered the decalogue of witchcraft: sodomy, infanticide, animal worship. In part, these were ritual charges that the Church had always moved against rival religions. But, as we have seen, a sexual revolution had been an essential ingredient of the heretic movement, from the Cathars to the Adamites. The Cathars, in particular, had challenged the Church's degraded view of women and advocated the rejection of marriage and even of procreation, which they considered a form of entrapment for the soul. They had also embraced a Manichean religion that, according to some historians, was responsible for the increased preoccupation of the Church in the late Middle Ages with the presence of the Devil in the world and the Inquisitorial view of witchcraft as a counter-church. Thus, the continuity between heresy and witchcraft, at least in the first phase of the witch-hunt, cannot be doubted. But the witch-hunt occurred in a different historical context, one that had been dramatically transformed, first by the traumas and dislocations produced by the Black Death — a watershed in European history — and later, in the 15th and 16th centuries, by the profound change in class relations brought about by the capitalist reorganization of economic and social life. Inevitably, then, even the apparent elements of continuity (e.g. the nocturnal promiscuous banquet) had a different meaning than their anticipations in the Church's struggle against the heretics.

Witch-Hunting, Woman-Hunting, and the Accumulation of Labor

The most important difference between heresy and witchcraft is that witchcraft was considered a female crime. This was especially true at the peak of the persecution, in the period between 1550 and 1650. In an earlier phase, men had represented up to forty percent of the accused, and a smaller number continued to be prosecuted later, mostly drawn from the ranks of the vagabonds, beggars, itinerant laborers, as well as the gypsies and lower-class priests. By the 16th century, moreover, the charge of devil worship had become a common theme in political and religious struggle; there was hardly a bishop or a politician who, in the heat of the moment, was not accused of being a witch. Protestants accused Catholics, especially the pope, of serving the devil; Luther himself was accused of magic, and so were John Knox in Scotland, Jean Bodin in France, and many others. Jews too were ritually accused of worshipping the devil, often being portrayed with horns and claws. But the outstanding fact is that more than eighty percent of those who were tried and executed in Europe in the 16th and 17th centuries for the crime of witchcraft were women. In fact, more women were persecuted for witchcraft in this period than for any other crime, except, significantly, infanticide.

That the witch was a woman was also stressed by the demonologists, who rejoiced that God had spared men from such a scourge. As Sigrid Brauner (1995) has noted, the arguments used to justify this phenomenon changed. While the authors of the *Malleus Maleficarum* explained that women were more prone to witchcraft because of their "insatiable lust," Martin Luther and humanist writers stressed women's moral and mental weakness as the origin of this perversion. But all singled out women as evil beings.

A further difference between the persecutions of the heretics and that of the witches is that in the latter the charges of sexual perversion and infanticide had a central role, being accompanied by the virtual demonization of contraceptive practices.

The association between contraception, abortion, and witchcraft first appeared in the Bull of Innocent VIII (1484) which complained that

> by their incantations, spells, conjurations and other accursed supersti-
> tions and horrid charms, enormities and offenses, (witches) destroy the
> offspring of women....They hinder men from generating and women
> from conceiving; whence neither husbands with their wives nor wives
> with their husbands can perform their sexual acts (Kors and Peters
> 1972: 107–08).

From then on, reproductive crimes featured prominently in the trials. By the 17th century witches were accused of conspiring to destroy the generative power of humans and animals, of procuring abortions, and of belonging to an infanticidal sect devoted to killing children or offering them to the devil. In the popular imagination as well, the witch came to be associated with a lecherous old woman, hostile to new life, who fed upon infant flesh or used children's bodies to make her magical potions — a stereotype later popularized by children's books.

Why such a change in the trajectory from heresy to witchcraft? Why, in other words, in the course of a century, did the heretic become a woman, and why was religious and social transgression refocused as predominantly a reproductive crime?

In the 1920s the English anthropologist Margaret Murray in *The Witch-Cult in Western Europe* (1921) proposed an explanation that has recently been revived by eco-feminists and practitioners of "Wicca." Murray argued that witchcraft was an ancient matrifocal religion to which the Inquisition turned its attention after the defeat of heresy, spurred by a new fear of doctrinal deviation. In other words, the women whom demo-nologists prosecuted as witches were (according to this theory) practitioners of ancient fertility cults aiming to propitiate birth and reproduction — cults that had existed in the Mediterranean areas for thousands of years, but which the Church opposed as pagan rites and a challenge to its power.[22] The presence of midwives among the accused, the role that women played in the Middle Ages as community healers, the fact that until the 16th century child-birth was considered a female "mystery," all of these factors have been cited in support of this view. But this hypothesis cannot explain the timing of the witch-hunt, nor tell us why these fertility cults became so abominable in the eyes of the authorities as to call for the extermination of the women practicing the old religion.

A different explanation is that the prominence of reproductive crimes in the witch-trials was a consequence of the high infant mortality rates that were typical in the 16th and 17th centuries due to the growth of poverty and malnutrition. Witches, it is argued, were blamed for the fact that so many children died, died so suddenly, died shortly after birth, or were vulnerable to a broad array of ailments. But this explanation too does not go far enough. It does not account for the fact that women labelled as

*Witches cooking children. From Francesco Maria
Guazzo's* Compendium Maleficarum, *1608.*

witches were also accused of preventing conception, and it fails to place the witch-hunt in the context of 16th-century economic and institutional policy. Thus, it misses the significant connection between the attack on witches and the development of a new concern, among European statists and economists, with the question of reproduction and population size, the rubric under which the question of the size of the workforce was discussed at the time. As we have seen earlier, the labor question became especially urgent in the 17th century, when population in Europe began again to decline, raising the spectre of a demographic collapse similar to that which had occurred in the American colonies in the decades after the Conquest. Against this background, it seems plausible that the witch-hunt was, at least in part, an attempt to criminalize birth control and place the female body, the uterus, at the service of population increase and the production and accumulation of labor-power.

This is a hypothesis; what is certain is that the witch-hunt was promoted by a political class that was preoccupied with population decline and motivated by the conviction that a large population is the wealth of the nation. The fact that the 16th and 17th centuries were the heyday of Mercantilism, and saw the beginning of demographic recording (of births, deaths and marriages), of census-taking, and the formalization of demography itself as the first "state-science" is a clear proof of the strategic importance that controlling population movements was acquiring in the political circles that instigated the witch-hunt (Cullen 1975: 6ff)[23].

We also know that many witches were midwives or "wise women," traditionally

The drama of infant mortalilty is well-captured by this image from Hans Holbein theYounger's "The Dance of Death," a series of forty-one designs first printed in France in 1538.

the depository of women's reproductive knowledge and control (Midelfort 1972:172). The *Malleus* dedicated an entire chapter to them, arguing that they were worse than any other woman, since they helped the mother destroy the fruit of her womb, a conspiracy made easier, they charged, by the exclusion of men from the rooms where women gave birth.[24] Observing that there was not a hut that did not board a midwife, the authors recommended that no woman should be allowed to practice this art, unless she first demonstrated to have been a "good Catholic." This recommendation did not go unheard. As we have seen, midwives were either recruited to police women — to check, for instance, that they did not hide their pregnancies or deliver children out of wedlock — or were marginalized. Both in France and England, starting from the end of the 16th century, few women were allowed to practice obstetrics, an activity that, until that time, had been their inviolable mystery. Then, by the beginning of the 17th century, the first male midwives began to appear and, within a century, obstetrics has come almost entirely

Witches offer children to the Devil. A woodcut from a tract on the trial of Agnes Sampson, 1591.

under state control. According to Alice Clark:

> The continuous process by which women were supplanted by men in the profession is one example of the way in which they were excluded from all branches of professional work, through being denied the opportunity of obtaining an adequate professional training (Clark 1968: 265).

But interpreting the social decline of the midwife as a case of female de-professionalization misses its significance. There is convincing evidence, in fact, that midwives were marginalized because they were not trusted, and because their exclusion from the profession undermined women's control over reproduction.[25]

Just as the Enclosures expropriated the peasantry from the communal land, so the witch-hunt expropriated women from their bodies, which were thus "liberated" from any impediment preventing them to function as machines for the production of labor. For the threat of the stake erected more formidable barriers around women's bodies than were ever erected by the fencing off of the commons.

We can, in fact, imagine what effect it had on women to see their neighbors, friends and relatives being burned at the stake, and realize that any contraceptive initiative on their side might be construed as the product of a demonic perversion.[26] Seeking to understand what the women hunted as witches and the other women in their community must have thought, felt, and concluded from this horrendous attack waged upon them — looking, in other words, at the persecution "from within," as Anne L. Barstow has done in her *Witchcraze* (1994) — also enables us to avoid speculating on the intentions of the persecutors, and concentrate instead on the effects of the witch-hunt on the social position of women. From this point of view, there can be no doubt that the witch-hunt destroyed the methods that women had used to control procreation, by indicting them as diabolical devices, and institutionalized the state's control over the female body, the precondition for its subordination to the reproduction of labor-power.

But the witch was not only the midwife, the woman who avoided maternity, or the beggar who eked out a living by stealing some wood or butter from her neighbors. She was also the loose, promiscuous woman — the prostitute or adulteress, and generally, the woman who exercised her sexuality outside the bonds of marriage and procreation. Thus, in the witchcraft trials, "ill repute" was evidence of guilt. The witch was also the rebel woman who talked back, argued, swore, and did not cry under torture. "Rebel" here refers not necessarily to any specific subversive activity in which women might be involved. Rather, it describes the *female personality* that had developed, especially among the peasantry, in the course of the struggle against feudal power, when women had been in the forefront of the heretical movements, often organizing in female associations, posing a growing challenge to male authority and the Church. Descriptions of witches remind us of women as they were represented in the medieval morality plays and the *fabliaux*: ready to take initiatives, as aggressive and lusty as men, wearing male clothes, or proudly riding on their husbands' backs, holding a whip.

Certainly, among those indicted there were women suspected of specific crimes. One was accused of poisoning her husband, another of causing the death of her employer, another again of having prostituted her daughter (Le Roy Ladurie 1974: 203–04). But

In the market of Guernsey, England, three women are burnt alive.
Anonymous engraving, 16th century.

it was not only the deviant woman, but *the woman as such, particularly the woman of the lower classes, that was put on trial*, a woman who generated so much fear that in her case the relation between education and punishment was turned upside down. "We must," Jean Bodin declared, "spread terror among some by punishing many." And indeed, in some villages few were spared.

Also the sexual sadism displayed by the tortures to which the accused were subjected reveals a misogyny that has no parallel in history, and cannot be accounted for on the basis of any specific crime. According to the standard procedure, the accused were stripped naked and completely shaved (it was argued that the devil hid among their hair); then they were pricked with long needles all over their bodies, including their vaginas, in search for the mark with which the devil presumably branded his creatures (just as the masters in England did with runaway slaves). Often they were raped; it was investigated whether or not they were virgins — a sign of innocence; and if they did not confess, they were submitted to even more atrocious ordeals: their limbs were torn, they were seated on iron chairs under which fires were lit; their bones were crushed. And when they were hung or burnt, care was taken so that the lesson to be drawn from their end would not go unheeded. The execution was an important public event, which all the members of the community had to attend, including the children of the witches, especially their daughters who, in some cases, would be whipped in front of the stake on which they could see their mother burning alive.

The witch-hunt, then, was a war against women; it was a concerted attempt to degrade them, demonize them, and destroy their social power. At the same time, it was in the torture chambers and on the stakes on which the witches perished that the bourgeois ideals of womanhood and domesticity were forged.

In this case, too, the witch-hunt amplified contemporary social trends. There is, in fact, an unmistakable continuity between the practices targeted by the witch-hunt and those banned by the new legislation that in the same years was introduced to regulate family life, gender and property relations. Across western Europe, as the witch-hunt was progressing, laws were passed that punished the adulteress with death (in England and Scotland by the stake, as in the case of High Treason). At the same time prostitution was outlawed and so was birth out of wedlock, while infanticide was made a capital crime.[27] Simultaneously, female friendships became an object of suspicion, denounced from the pulpit as subversive of the alliance between husband and wife, just as women-to-women relations were demonized by the prosecutors of the witches who forced them to denounce each other as accomplices in crime. It was also in this period that the word "gossip," which in the Middle Ages had meant "friend," changed its meaning, acquiring a derogatory connotation, a further sign of the degree to which the power of women and communal ties were undermined.

Also at the ideological level, there is a close correspondence between the degraded image of women forged by the demonologists and the image of femininity constructed by the contemporary debates on the "nature of the sexes,"[28] which canonized a stereotypical woman, weak in body and mind and biologically prone to evil, that effectively served to justify male control over women and the new patriarchal order.

Witch-Hunting and Male Supremacy: The Taming of Women

The sexual politics of the witch-hunt is revealed by the relation between the witch and the devil, which is one of the novelties introduced by the 16th and 17th-century trials. The Great Witch-Hunt marked a change in the image of the devil compared with that to be found in the medieval lives of the saints or in the books of Renaissance magicians. In the former, the devil was portrayed as an evil being, but one who had little power — a sprinkling of holy water and a few holy words were usually sufficient to defeat his schemes. His image was that of an unsuccessful illdoer who, far from inspiring horror, was credited with some virtues. The medieval devil was a logician, competent in legal matters, sometimes represented in the act of defending his case in front of a court of law (Seligman 1948: 151–58).[29] He was also a skillful worker who could be used to dig mines or build city walls, although he was routinely cheated when the time came for his recompense. Also, the Renaissance view of the relationship between the devil and the magician always portrayed the devil as subordinate being called to task, willing or not, like a servant, and made to perform according to his master's will.

The witch-hunt reversed the power relation between the devil and the witch. It

The devil carries away the soul of a woman who served him. Woodcut from Olaus Magnus, HISTORIA DE GENTIBUS SEPTENTRIONALIBUS (Rome, 1555).

was the woman now who was the servant, the slave, the *succubus* in body and soul, while the Devil functioned as her owner and master, pimp and husband at once. It was the Devil, for instance, who "approached the intended witch. She rarely conjured him up" (Larner 1983: 148). After revealing himself to her, he would ask her to become his servant, and what would follow then would be a classic example of a master/slave, husband/wife relation. He stamped her with his mark, had sexual intercourse with her and, in some instances, he even changed her name (Larner 1983: 148). Moreover, in a clear pre-figuration of women's matrimonial destiny, the witch-hunt introduced *one single Devil,* in the place of the multitude of devils to be found in the medieval and Renaissance world, and a *masculine Devil at that,* in contrast with the female figures (Diana, Hera, "*la Signora del zogo*"), whose cults were spread among women in the Middle Ages, in both the Mediterranean and Teutonic regions.

How preoccupied were the witch hunters with the affirmation of male supremacy can be seen from the fact that, even when in revolt against human and divine law, women had to be portrayed as subservient to a man, and the culmination of their rebellion — the famous pact with the devil — had to be represented as a perverted marriage contract. The marital analogy was carried so far that the witches would confess that they "did not dare to disobey the devil," or, more curiously, that they did not find any pleasure in their copulations with him — a contradiction with respect to the ideology of the witch-hunt which derived witchcraft from women's insatiable lust.

Not only did the witch-hunt sanctify male supremacy, it also instigated men to fear women, and even to look at them as the destroyers of the male sex. Women, the authors of the *Malleus Maleficarum* preached, are lovely to look at but contaminating to the touch; they attract men, but only to undermine them; they do everything to please them, but the pleasure they give is more bitter than death, for their vices cost men the loss of their souls — and perhaps their sexual organs (Kors and Peters 1972: 114-115). A witch, presumably, could castrate men or make them impotent, either by freezing their generative forces or causing their penis to come out and draw back as she wished.[30] Some stole male penises, which they hid in great numbers in bird nests or boxes, until, under duress, they were forced to return them to their owners.[31]

But who were these witches who castrated men or made them impotent? Potentially, every woman. In a village or small town of a few thousand people, where at the peak of the witch-hunt dozens of women were burned in the space of a few years or even a few weeks, no man could feel safe and be sure that he did not live with a witch.

Women fly on their brooms to the Sabbat after applying unguents to their bodies. 16th-century French print from Thomas Erastus's DIALOGUES TOUCHANT LE POUVOIR DES SORCIÈRES (1570)

Many must have been terrified upon hearing that at night some women left the marriage bed to travel to the Sabbat, fooling their sleeping husbands by putting a stick next to them; or hearing that women had the power to make their penises disappear, like the witch mentioned in the *Malleus,* who had stored dozens in a tree.

That this propaganda successfully divided women from men is suggested by the fact that, despite individual attempts by sons, husbands, or fathers to save their female relatives from the stake, with one exception, we have no record of any male organizations opposing the persecution. The exception is the case of the fishermen of the Basque region where the French Inquisitor Pierre Lancre was conducting mass trials that led to the burning of perhaps as many as six hundred women. Mark Kurlansky reports that the fishermen had been been absent, engaged in the annual cod season. But,

> [when the men] of the St.-Jean-de-Luz cod fleet, one of the largest [from Basque country] heard rumors of their wives, mothers, and daughters [being] stripped, stabbed, and many already executed, the 1609 cod campaign was ended two months early. The fishermen returned, clubs in hands, and liberated a convoy of witches being taken to the burning place. This one popular resistance was all it took to stop the trials... (Kurlansky 2001: 102)

The intervention of the Basque fishermen against the persecution of their female relatives was a unique event. No other group or organization rose up in defense of the witches. We know, instead, that some men made a business of denouncing women, appointing themselves as "witch finders," travelling from village to village threatening to expose women unless they paid up. Other men took advantage of the climate of suspicion surrounding women to free themselves from unwanted wives and lovers, or to blunt the revenge of women they had raped or seduced. Undoubtedly, men's failure to act against the atrocities to which women were subjected was often motivated by the fear of being implicated in the charges, as the majority of the men tried for this crime were relatives of suspected or convicted witches. But there is no doubt that years of propaganda and terror sowed among men the seeds of a deep psychological alienation from women, that broke class solidarity and undermined their own collective power. We can agree with Marvin Harris that,

> The witch-hunt... scattered and fragmented all the latent energies of protest. [It] has made everyone feel impotent and dependent upon the dominant social groups, and has furthermore given them a local outlet for their frustrations. By this it has prevented the poor, more than any other social group, from confronting ecclesiastical authority and the secular order, and making their claims within the redistribution of wealth and the leveling of social status (Harris 1974: 239-240).

Just as today, by repressing women, the ruling classes more effectively repressed the entire proletariat. They instigated men who had been expropriated, pauperized, and criminalized to blame their personal misfortunes on the castrating witch, and to view the power that women had won against the authorities as a power women would use against them. All the deep-seated fears that men harbored with regard to women (mostly because of the Church's misogynous propaganda) were mobilized in this context. Not only were women accused of making men impotent; even their sexuality was turned into an object of fear, a dangerous, demonic force, as men were taught that a witch could enslave them and chain them to her will (Kors and Peters 1972: 130–32).

A recurrent charge in the witch trials was that witches engaged in degenerate sexual practices, centering on copulation with the devil and participation in the orgies that presumably took place at the Sabbat. But witches were also accused of generating an excessive erotic passion in men, so that it was an easy step for men caught in an illicit affair to claim they had been bewitched, or, for a family wanting to terminate a son's relation with a woman of whom they did not approve, to accuse the latter of being a witch. Wrote the *Malleus*:

> there are…seven methods by which [witches] infect … the venereal
> act and the conception of the womb: First, by inclining the minds of

The Devil seduces a woman into making a pact with him. From Ulrich Molitor, De Lamies (1489)

men to inordinate passion; Second, by obstructing their generative force; Third, by removing the member accomodated to that act; Fourth, by changing men into beasts by their magic art; Fifth, by destroying the generative force in women; Sixth, by procuring abortion; Seventh, by offering children to the devil... (1971: 47).

That witches were accused simultaneously of rendering men impotent and arousing an excessive sexual passion in them is only apparently a contradiction. In the new patriarchal code that was developing in concomitance with the witch-hunt, physical impotence was the counterpart of moral impotence; it was the physical manifestation of the erosion of male authority over women, since "functionally" there would be no difference between a man who was castrated and one who was helplessly in love. The demonologists looked with suspicion at both states, clearly convinced that it would be impossible to realize the type of family the contemporary bourgeois wisdom demanded — modeled on the state, with the husband as the king, and the wife subordinate to his will, selflessly devoted to the management of the household (Schochet 1975) — if women with their *glamour* and love philters could exercise so much power as to make men the *succubi* of their desires.

Sexual passion undermined not only male authority over women — as Montaigne lamented, man can preserve his *decor* in everything except in the sexual act (Easlea 1980: 243) — it also undermined a man's capacity for self-government, causing him to lose that precious head wherein Cartesian philosophy was to locate the source of Reason. A sexually active woman, then, was a public danger, a threat to the social order as she subverted a man's sense of responsibility, and his capacity for work and self-control. If women were not to ruin men morally — or more important, financially — female sexuality had to be exorcised. This was accomplished by means of torture, death by fire, as well as the meticulous interrogations to which witches were subjected, which were a mixture of sexual exorcism and psychological rape.[32]

For women, then, the 16th and 17th centuries did inaugurate an age of sexual repression. Censorship and prohibition did come to define their relationship with sexuality. With Michel Foucault's critique of the "repressive hypothesis" in mind, we must also insist that it was *not* the Catholic pastoral, nor the confession, that best demonstrate how "Power," at the dawn of the modern era, made it compulsory for people to speak of sex (Foucault 1978: 116). The "discursive explosion" on sex, that Foucault detected in this time, was in no place more powerfully exhibited than in the torture chambers of the witch-hunt. But it had nothing in common with the mutual titillation that Foucault imagines flowing between the woman and her confessor. Far outstripping any village priest, the inquisitors forced the witches to reveal their sexual adventures in every detail, undeterred by the fact that they were often old women and their sexual *exploits* dated back many decades. In an almost ritual manner, they forced the alleged witches to explain how in their youth they were first taken by the devil, what they had felt upon penetration, the impure thoughts they had harbored. But the stage upon which this peculiar discourse on sex unfolded was the torture chamber, and the questions were asked between applications of the *strappado*, to women driven mad by pain, and by no stretch of imagination can we presume that the orgy of words the women thus tortured were forced to utter incited their pleasure or re-oriented, by linguistic sublimation, their desire. In the case of the witch-hunt — which Foucault surprisingly ignores in his *History of Sexuality* (Vol. 1, 1978) — the "interminable discourse on sex" was not deployed as an alternative to, but in the service of repression, censorship, denial. Certainly we can say that the language of the witch-hunt "produced" the Woman as a different species, a being *suis generis*, more carnal and perverted by nature. We can also say that the production of the "female pervert" was a step in the transformation of the female *vis erotica* into *vis lavorativa* — *that is, a first step in the transformation of female sexuality into work*. But we should appreciate the destructive character of this process, which also demonstrates the limits of a general "history of sexuality" of the type Foucault has proposed, which treats sexuality from the perspective of an undifferentiated, gender-neutral subject, and as an activity presumably carrying the same consequences for men and women.

The Witch-Hunt and the Capitalist Rationalization of Sexuality

The witch-hunt did not result in new sexual capacities or sublimated pleasures for women. Instead, it was the first step in the long march towards "clean sex between clean sheets" and the transformation of female sexual activity into work, a service to men, and procreation. Central to this process was the banning, as anti-social and virtually demonic, of all non-productive, non-procreative forms of female sexuality.

The repulsion that non-procreative sexuality was beginning to inspire is well captured by the myth of the old witch flying on her broom, which, like the animals she also rode upon (goats, mares, dogs), was the projection of an extended penis, symbol of an unbridled lust. This imagery betrays a new sexual discipline that denied the "old and ugly" woman, no longer fertile, the right to a sexual life. In the creation of this stereotype the demonologists conformed to the moral sensibility of their time, as illustrated by the words of two illustrious contemporaries of the witch-hunt:

> To see an old lecher, what more odious? What can be more absurd? And yet so common....Worse it is in women than in men....Whilst she is an old crone, a beldam, she can neither see nor hear, a mere carcass, she caterwauls and must have a stallion (Burton 1977: 56).

> Yet it is even more fun to see the old women who can scarcely carry their weight of years and look like corpses that seem to have risen from the dead. They still go around saying "life is good," still in heat, looking for a mate...they are forever smearing their faces with make up and taking tweezers to their pubic hair, exposing their sagging, withered breasts and trying to rouse failing desire with their quavery whining voices, while they drink, dance among girls and scribble their love letters (Erasmus 1941: 42).

This was a far cry from the world of Chaucer, where the Wife of Bath, after burying five husbands, could still openly declare: "Welcome the sixth....I don't mean to be chaste

A dispute between a witch and an Inquisitor. Hans Burkmair (before 1514).

Many women accused and tried for witchcraft were old and poor. Often they depended on public charity for their survival. Witchcraft — we are told — is the weapon of the powerless. But old women were also those in the community most likely to resist the destruction of communal relations caused by the spread of capitalist relations. They were the ones who embodied the community's knowledge and memory. The witch-hunt turned the image of the old woman upside down: traditionally considered a wise woman, she became a symbol of sterility and hostility to life.

at all cost. When a spouse of mine is gone, another Christian man shall take me on" (Chaucer 1977: 277). In the world of Chaucer, the sexual vitality of the old woman was an affirmation of life against death; in the iconography of the witch-hunt, old age precludes in women the possibility of a sexual life, contaminates it, turns sexual activity into a tool of death rather than a means of regeneration.

Regardless of age (but not class) in the witch trials, there is a constant identification between female sexuality and bestiality. This was suggested by copulation with the goat-god (one of the representations of the devil), the infamous kiss *sub cauda*, and the charge that the witches kept a variety of animals — "imps" or "familiars" — that helped them in their crimes and with whom they entertained a particularly intimate relation. These were cats, dogs, hares, frogs, that the witch cared for, presumably suckling them from special teats.

Other animals, too, played a role in the witch's life as instruments of the devil: goats, and (night)mares flew her to the Sabbat, toads provided her with poison for her concoctions. Such was the presence of animals in the witches' world that one must presume that they too were being put on trial.[33]

The marriage between the witch and her "familiars" was perhaps a reference to the "bestial" practices that characterized the sexual life of peasants in Europe, which remained a capital offense long after the end of the witch-hunt. In an era that was beginning to worship reason and to dissociate the human from the corporeal, animals, too, were subjected to a drastic devaluation — reduced to mere brutes, the ultimate "Other" — perennial symbol of the worst human instincts. No crime, then, would inspire more horror than copulation with a beast, a true attack on the ontological foundations of a human nature increasingly identified with its most immaterial aspects. But the surplus of animal presences in the witches' lives also suggests that women were at a (slippery) crossroad between men and animals, and that not only female sexuality, but femininity as such, was akin to animality. To seal this equation, witches were often accused of shifting their shape and morphing into animals, while the most commonly cited familiar was the toad, which as a symbol of the vagina synthesized sexuality, bestiality, femininity, and evil.

The witch-hunt condemned female sexuality as the source of every evil, but it was also the main vehicle for a broad restructuring of sexual life that, conforming with the new capitalist work-discipline, criminalized any sexual activity that threatened procreation, the transmission of property within the family, or took time and energies away from work.

The witch trials provide an instructive list of the forms of sexuality that were banned as "non-productive": homosexuality, sex between young and old,[34] sex between people of different classes, anal coitus, coitus from behind (reputedly leading to sterile relations), nudity, and dances. Also proscribed was the public, collective sexuality that had prevailed in the Middle Ages, as in the Spring festivals of pagan origins that, in the 16th-century, were still celebrated all over Europe. Compare, in this context, the way in which P. Stubbes, in *Anatomy of Abuse (1583)*, described the celebration of May Day in England, with the standard accounts of the Sabbat which charged that the witches always danced at these gatherings, jumping up and down at the sound of pipes and flutes, and indulged in much collective sex and merrymaking.

The execution of the Chelmsford witches in 1589. Joan Prentice, one of the victims, is shown with her familiars

Towards May…every parish, town and village gets together, both men, women and children, old and young…they run to the bushes and woods, hills and mountains, where they spend all the night in pleasant pastimes, and in the morning they return bringing home birch bows and branches of trees…(T)he chiefest jewel they bring home is their maypole, which they bring home with great veneration…then they fall to banquet and feast, to leap and dance about it, as heathen people did at the dedication of their idols… (Partridge: III).

An analogous comparison can be made between the descriptions of the Sabbat and the descriptions which Scottish Presbyterian authorities made of pilgrimages (to holy wells and other holy localities), which the Catholic Church had encouraged, but which the Presbyterians opposed as congregations of the devil and occasions for lewd affairs. As a general tendency, throughout this period, any potentially transgressive meeting — peasants' gatherings, rebel camps, festivals, and dances — was described by the authorities as a virtual Sabbat.[35]

It is also significant that, in some areas of Northern Italy, going to the Sabbat was called "going to the dance" or "going to the game" *(al zogo),* particularly when one considers the campaign that Church and state were conducting against such pastimes (Muraro 1977: 109ff; Hill 1964: 183ff). As Ginzburg points out, "once we remove [from the Sabbat] the myths and the fantastic trappings, we discover a gathering of people, accompanied by dances and sexual promiscuity" (Ginzburg 1966: 189), and, we must add, much eating and drinking, surely a fantasy at a time when hunger was a common experience in Europe. (How revealing concerning the nature of class relations at the time of the witch-hunt, that dreams of roasted mutton and ale could be frowned upon by a well-fed, beef-eating bourgeoisie as signs of a diabolical connivance!) Ginzburg, however, following a well-trodden path, labels the orgies associated with the Sabbat as "hallucinations of poor women, to whom they serve as a recompense for a squalid existence," *(ibid.:* 190).

Feasting is an important theme in many representations of the Sabbat — a fantasy at a time when famines were a common experience in Europe. Detail from Jan Ziarnko's plate for Pierre De Lancre's TABLEAU DE L'INCONSTANCE *(1612)*

In this way, he blames the victims for their demise; he also ignores that it was not the women accused of being witches, but Europe's elite who devoted reams of papers to discussing such "hallucinations," debating, for instance, the roles of *succubi* and *incubi,* or whether the witch could be impregnated by the Devil, a question that, apparently, was still of interest for intellectuals in the 18th century (Couliano 1987: 148–51). Today, these grotesque disquisitions are screened from the histories of "Western Civilization," or are simply forgotten, although they wove a web that condemned hundreds of thousands of women to death.

Thus, the role that the witch-hunt has played in the development of the bourgeois world, and specifically in the development of the capitalist discipline of sexuality, has been erased from our memory. Yet, we can trace back to this process some of the main taboos of our time. This is the case with homosexuality, which in several parts of Europe was still fully accepted during the Renaissance, but was weeded out in the course of the witch-hunt. So fierce was the persecution of homosexuals that its memory is still sedimented in our language. "Faggot" reminds us that homosexuals were at times the kindling for the stakes upon which witches were burned, while the Italian *finocchio* (fennel) refers to the practice of scattering these aromatic vegetables on the stakes in order to mask the stench of burning flesh.

Of particular significance is the relation the witch-hunt established between the prostitute and the witch, reflecting the process of devaluation which prostitution underwent in the capitalist reorganization of sexual work. As the saying went, "a prostitute when young, a witch when old," for both used sex only to deceive and corrupt men, faking a love that was only mercenary (Stiefelmeir 1977: 48ff.). And both *sold themselves* in order to obtain money and an illicit power, the witch (who sold her soul to the Devil) being the magnified image of the prostitute (who sold her body to men). Furthermore, both the (old) witch and the prostitute were symbols of sterility, the very personification of non-procreative sexuality. Thus, while in the Middle Ages the prostitute and the witch were considered positive figures who performed a social service for the community, with the witch-hunt both acquired the most negative connotations and were rejected as possible female identities, physically by death and socially by criminalization. For the prostitute died as a legal subject only after having died a thousand times on the stake as a witch. Or better, the prostitute would be allowed to survive (she would even become useful, although in a clandestine fashion) only as long as the witch would be killed; for the witch was the more socially dangerous subject, the one who (in the eyes of the inquisitors) was less controllable; it was she who could give pain or pleasure, heal or harm, stir up the elements and chain the will of men; she could even cause damage solely by her look, a *malocchio* ("evil eye") that presumably could kill.

It was the sexual nature of her crimes and her lower-class status that distinguished the witch from the Renaissance magician, who was largely immune from the persecution. High Magic and witchcraft shared many elements. Themes derived from the learned magical tradition were introduced by the demonologists into the definition of witchcraft. Among them was the belief, of Neoplatonic origin, that Eros is a cosmic force, binding the universe through relations of "sympathy" and attraction enabling the magician to manipulate and imitate nature in his experiments. A similar power was attributed to the witch, who reputedly could raise storms by mimetically stirring a puddle, or could exercise an "attraction" similar to the bonding of metals in the alchemic tradition. (Yates 1964: 145ff; Couliano 1987). The ideology of witchcraft also reflected the biblical tenet, common to both magic and alchemy, that stipulates a connection between *sexuality* and *knowledge*. The thesis that witches acquired their powers by copulating with the devil echoed the alchemic belief that women had appropriated the secrets of chemistry by copulating with rebel demons (Seligman 1948: 76). High Magic, however, was not persecuted, though alchemy was increasingly frowned upon, as it appeared an idle pursuit and, as such, a waste of time and resources. The magicians were an elite, who often serviced princes and other highly positioned people (Couliano 1987: 156ff), and the demonologists carefully distinguished between them and the witches, by including High Magic (particularly astrology and astronomy) in the range of the sciences.[36]

The witch-hunt and the New World

The counterparts of the typical European witch, then, were not the Renaissance magicians, but the colonized native Americans and the enslaved Africans who, in the plantations of the "New World," shared a destiny similar to that of women in Europe, providing for capital the seemingly limitless supply of labor necessary for accumulation.

So connected were the destinies of women in Europe and those of Amerindians and Africans in the colonies that their influences were reciprocal. Witch-hunting and charges of devil-worshipping were brought to the Americas to break the resistance of the local populations, justifying colonization and the slave trade in the eyes of the world. In turn, according to Luciano Parinetto, it was the American experience that persuaded the European authorities to believe in the existence of entire populations of witches, and instigated them to apply in Europe the same techniques of mass extermination developed in America (Parinetto 1998).

In Mexico, "[f]rom 1536 to 1543 the Bishop Zumarraga conducted 19 trials involving 75 Indian heretics, mainly drawn from the political and religious leaders of central Mexican communities, a number of whom ended their lives at the stake. The friar Diego de Landa led idolatry trials in the Yucatan during the 1560s, in which torture, whippings, and *auto-de fe* figured prominently" (Behar 1987: 51). Witch-hunts were conducted also in Peru, to destroy the cult of the local gods, considered demons by the Europeans. "Everywhere the Spaniards saw the face of the devil: in the foods... [in] the 'primitive vices of the indians'... in their barbaric languages" (de Leon 1985 I: 33–34). In the colonies, too, it was women who were more vulnerable to being accused of being witches, for, being held in special contempt by the Europeans as weak-minded females, they soon became the staunchest defenders of their communities (Silverblatt 1980: 173, 176–79).

The common fate of Europe's witches and Europe's colonial subjects is further demonstrated by the growing exchange, in the course of the 17th century, between the ideology of witchcraft and the racist ideology that developed on the soil of the Conquest and the slave trade. The Devil was portrayed as a black man and black people were increasingly treated like devils, so that "devil worship and diabolical interventions [became] the most widely reported aspect of the non-European societies the slave traders encountered"

16th-century representation of Caribbean Indians as devils from Tobias George Smollett [compiler], "A COMPENDIUM OF AUTHENTIC AND ENTERTAINING VOYAGES, DIGESTED IN A CHRONOLOGICAL SERIES..." (From Tobias George Smollet, 1766.)

(Barker 1978:91). "From Lapps to Samoyed, to the Hottentots and Indonesians…there was no society" — Anthony Barker writes — "which was not labeled by some Englishman as actively under diabolical influence" (1978:91). Just as in Europe, the trademark of diabolism was an abnormal lust and sexual potency.[37] The Devil was often portrayed as possessing two penises, while tales of brutish sexual practices and inordinate fondness for music and dancing became staples in the reports of missionaries and travelers to the "New World."

According to historian Brian Easlea, this systematic exaggeration of black sexual potency betrays the anxiety that white men of property felt towards their own sexuality; presumably, white upper-class males feared the competition of the people they enslaved, whom they saw as closer to nature, because they felt sexually inadequate due to excessive doses of self-control and prudential reasoning (Easlea 1980: 249–50). But the oversexualization of women and black men — the witches and the devils — must also be rooted in the position which they occupied in the international division of labor that was emerging on the basis of the colonization of America, the slave trade, and the witch-hunt. For the definition of blackness and femaleness as marks of bestiality and irrationality conformed with the exclusion of women in Europe and women and men in the colonies from the social contract implicit in the wage, and the consequent naturalization of their exploitation.

The Witch, the Healer and the Birth of Modern Science

Other motives operated behind the persecution of witches. Charges of witchcraft often served to punish the attack on property, primarily thefts, which increased dramatically in the 16th and 17th centuries, following the increasing privatization of land and agriculture. As we have seen, in England, poor women who begged for or stole milk or wine from the houses of their neighbors, or were on public assistance, were likely to be suspected of practicing evil arts. Alan Macfarlane and Keith Thomas have shown that in this period there was a marked deterioration in the condition of old women, following the loss of the commons and the reorganization of family life, which gave priority to child-raising at the expense of the care previously provided to the elderly (Macfarlane 1970:205).[38] These elders were now forced to rely on their friends or neighbors for their survival, or joined the Poor Rolls (at the very time when the new Protestant ethic was beginning to finger alms-giving as a waste and an encouragement to sloth), and as the institutions that in the past had catered to the poor were breaking down. Some poor women presumably used the fear that their reputation as witches inspired to obtain what they needed. But it was not just the "bad witch," who cursed and allegedly lamed cattle, ruined crops, or caused her employer's children to die, that was condemned. The "good witch," who made sorcery her career, was also punished, often more severely.

Historically, the witch was the village midwife, medic, soothsayer or sorceress, whose privileged area of competence (as Burckhardt wrote concerning the Italian witches) was amorous intrigue (Burckhardt 1927:319–20). An urban embodiment of this type of witch was the Celestina, in the play by Fernando de Rojas (*The Celestina* 1499). Of her it was said that:

She had six trades, to wit: launderess, perfumer, a master hand at making cosmetics and replacing damaged maidenheads, procuress, and
something of a witch.... Her first trade was a cover for the rest and
with this excuse many servant girls went to her house to do their
washing....You can't imagine the traffic she carried on. She was a baby
doctor; she picked up flax in one house and brought it to another, all
this as an excuse to get in everywhere. One would say: "Mother, come
here!" Or "Here comes the mistress!" Everyone knew her. And yet in
spite of her many duties she found time to go to Mass or Vesper" (Rojas
1959:17–18).

A more typical healer, however, was Gostanza, a woman tried as a witch in San
Miniato, a small town of Toscana in 1594. After becoming a widow Gostanza had set herself up as a professional healer, soon becoming well-known in the region for her thera-
peutic remedies and exorcisms. She lived with her niece and two other women, widows
as well. A next-door neighbor, also a widow, gave her the spices for her drugs. She received
her clients in her home, but she also traveled wherever she was needed, to "mark" an animal, visit a sick person, help people carry out a revenge or free themselves from the effects
of medical charms (Cardini 1989: 51-58). Her tools were natural oils and powders, as
well as devices apt to cure and protect by "sympathy" or "contact." It was not in her interest to inspire fear in her community, as practicing her arts was her way of making a living.
She was, in fact, very popular, everyone would go to her to be cured, to have his or her
fortune told, to find missing objects or to buy love potions. But she did not escape persecution. After the Council of Trento (1545–1563), the Counter-Reformation took a
strong position against popular healers, fearing their power and deep roots in the culture
of their communties. In England as well, the fate of the "good witches" was sealed in
1604 when a statute passed by James I established the death penalty for anyone who used
spirits and magic, even if they caused no visible harm.[39]

With the persecution of the folk healer, women were expropriated from a patri-
mony of empirical knowledge, regarding herbs and healing remedies, that they had accumulated and transmitted from generation to generation, its loss paving the way for a new
form of enclosure. This was the rise of professional medicine, which erected in front of
the "lower classes" a wall of unchallengeable scientific knowledge, unaffordable and alien,
despite its curative pretenses (Ehrenreich and English 1973; Starhawk 1997).

The displacement of the folk-healer/witch by the doctor raises the question of
the role that the development of modern science and the scientific worldview played in
the rise and fall of the witch-hunt. On this question we have two opposite viewpoints.

On one side we have the theory descending from the Enlightenment, which cred-
its the advent of scientific rationalism as the key factor in the termination of the persecution. As formulated by Joseph Klaits (1985), this theory argues that the new science
transformed intellectual life, generating a new skepticism as "it revealed the universe as
a self-regulating mechanism in which direct and constant divine intervention was unnecessary" (p.162). However, Klaits admits that the same judges who by the 1650s were put-

THE WITCH'S HERBARY, *engraving by Hans Weiditz (1532).*
As the starry globe suggests, the "virtue" of the herbs was
strengthened by the proper astral conjunction.

ting a break on witch trials never questioned the reality of witchcraft. "Neither in France nor anywhere else did the seventeenth-century judges who put an end to witch-hunting profess that there were no witches. Like Newton and other scientists of the time, judges continued to accept supernatural magic as theoretically plausible" *(ibid.*: 163).

Indeed, there is no evidence that the new science had a liberating effect. The mechanistic view of Nature that came into existence with the rise of modern science "disenchanted the world." But there is no evidence that those who promoted it ever spoke in defense of the women accused as witches. Descartes declared himself an agnostic on this matter; other mechanical philosophers (like Joseph Glanvil and Thomas Hobbes) strongly supported the witch-hunt. What ended the witch-hunt (as Brian Easlea has convincingly shown) was the annihilation of the world of the witches and the imposition of the social discipline that the victorious capitalist system required. In other words, the witch-hunt came to an end, by the late 17th century, because the ruling class by this time enjoyed a growing sense of security concerning its power, not because a more enlightened view of the world had emerged.

The question that remains is whether the rise of the modern scientific method can be considered the cause of the witch-hunt. This view has been argued most forcefully by Carolyn Merchant in *The Death of Nature* (1980) which roots the persecution of the witches in the paradigm shift the scientific revolution, and particularly the rise of Cartesian mechanistic philosophy, provoked. According to Merchant, this shift replaced an organic worldview that had looked at nature, women, and the earth as nurturing mothers, with a mechanical one that degraded them to the rank of "standing resources," removing any ethical constraints to their exploitation (Merchant 1980:127ff). The woman-as-witch, Merchant argues, was persecuted as the embodiment of the "wild side" of nature, of all that in nature seemed disorderly, uncontrollable, and thus antagonistic to the project undertaken by the new science. Merchant finds a proof of the connection between the persecution of the witches and the rise of modern science in the work of Francis Bacon, one of the reputed fathers of the new scientific method, showing that his concept of the scientific investigation of nature was modeled on the interrogation of the witches under torture, portraying nature as a woman to be conquered, unveiled, and raped (Merchant 1980: 168–72).

Merchant's account has the great merit of challenging the assumption that scientific rationalism was a vehicle of progress, and focuses our attention on the profound alienation that modern science has instituted between human beings and nature. It also links the witch-hunt to the destruction of the environment, and connects the capitalist exploitation of the natural world with the exploitation of women.

Merchant, however, overlooks the fact that the "organic worldview" which the elites embraced in pre-scientific Europe, left room for slavery and the extermination of the heretics. We also know that the aspiration to the technological domination of nature and the appropriation of women's creative powers has accommodated different cosmological frameworks. The Renaissance magicians were no less interested in these objectives,[40] while Newtonian physics owed its discovery of gravitational attraction not to a mechanistic but to a magical view of nature. Furthermore, when the vogue for philosophical mechanism had run its course, by the beginning of the 18th century, new philosophical trends emerged that stressed the value of "sympathy," "sensibility," and "passion," and yet were easily integrated in the project of the new science (Barnes and Shapin 1979).

We should also consider that the intellectual scaffold that supported the persecution of the witches was not directly taken from the pages of philosophical rationalism. Rather, it was a transitional phenomenon, a sort of ideological *bricolage* that evolved under the pressure of the task it had to accomplish. Within it, elements taken from the fantastic world of medieval Christianity, rationalistic arguments, and modern bureaucratic court procedures combined, in the same way as in the forging of Nazism the cult of science and technology combined with a scenario pretending to restore an archaic, mythical world of blood bonds and pre-monetary allegiances.

This point is suggested by Parinetto who observes that the witch-hunt was a classical instance (unfortunately, not the last) of how, in the history of capitalism, "going back" was a means of stepping forward, from the viewpoint of establishing the conditions for capital accumulation. For in conjuring the devil, the inquisitors disposed of popular animism and pantheism, redefining in a more centralized fashion the location and distribution of power in the cosmos and society. Thus, paradoxically (Parinetto writes), in the witch-hunt the devil functioned as the true servant of God; he was the operator that most contributed to paving the way to the new science. Like a bailiff, or God's secret agent, the Devil brought order into the world, emptying it from competing influences, and reasserting God as the exclusive ruler. He so well consolidated God's command over human affairs

The alchemist's "desire to appropriate the function of maternity" is well-reflected in this picture of Hermes Trismegistus (alchemy's mythical founder) holding a fetus in his womb and suggesting "the inseminating role of the male."

that, within a century, with the advent of Newtonian physics, God would be able to retire from the world, content to guard its clock-like operations from afar.

Rationalism and mechanism, then, were not the *immediate* cause of the persecutions, although they contributed to create a world committed to the exploitation of nature. More important, in instigating the witch-hunt, was the need of the European elites to eradicate an entire mode of existence which, by the late Middle Ages, was threatening their political and economic power. When this task was accomplished — when social discipline was restored and the ruling class saw its hegemony consolidated — witch trials came to an end. The belief in witchcraft could even become an object of ridicule, decried as a superstition, and soon put out of memory.

This process began throughout Europe toward the end of the 17th century, though witch trials continued in Scotland for three more decades. A factor contributing to the end of the witch-hunt was the fact that the ruling class was beginning to lose control over it, coming under the fire of its own repressive machine, with denunciations targeting even its own members. Midelfort writes that in Germany:

> as the flames licked closer to the names of people who enjoyed high rank and power, the judges lost confidence in the confessions and the panic ceased... (Midelfort 1972: 206).

In France, too, the final wave of trials brought widespread social disorder: servants accused their masters, children accused their parents, husbands accused their wives. Under these circumstances, the King decided to intervene, and Colbert extended Paris' jurisdiction to the whole of France to end the persecution. A new legal code was promulgated in which witchcraft was not even mentioned (Mandrou 1968: 443).

Just as the state had started the witch-hunt, so too, one by one, various governments took the initiative in ending it. From the mid-17th century on, efforts were made to brake judicial and inquisitorial zeal. One immediate consequence was that, in the 18th century, "common crimes" suddenly multiplied (*ibid.*: 437). In England, between 1686 and 1712, as the witch-hunt died down, arrests for damage to property (burning of granaries, houses, and hay stacks in particular) and assaults rose enormously (Kittredge 1929: 333), while new crimes entered the statute books. Blasphemy began to be treated as a punishable offense — in France, it was decreed that after the sixth conviction the blasphemers would have their tongues cut out — and so was sacrilege (the profanation of relics and the theft of hosts). New limits were also put on the sale of poisons; their private use was forbidden, their sale was made conditional upon the acquisition of a license, and the death penalty was extended to poisoners. All this suggests that the new social order was by now sufficiently consolidated for crimes to be identified and punished as such, without any recourse to the supernatural. In the words of a French parliamentarian:

> Witches and sorcerers are no longer condemned, firstly because it is difficult to establish proof of witchcraft, and secondly because such condemnations have been used to do harm. One has ceased therefore to accuse them of the uncertain in order to accuse them of the certain (Mandrou 1968: 361).

Once the subversive potential of witchcraft was destroyed, the practice of magic could even be allowed to continue. After the witch-hunt came to an end, many women continued to support themselves by foretelling the future, selling charms and practicing other forms of magic. As Pierre Bayle reported in 1704, "in many provinces of France, in Savoy, in the canton of Berne and many other places of Europe... there is no village or hamlet, no matter how small, where someone is not considered a witch" (Erhard 1963: 30). In 18th-century France, an interest for witchcraft developed also among the urban nobility who — being excluded from economic production and sensing that their privileges were coming under attack — satisfied their desire for power by recourse to the magical arts (*ibid.*: 31–32). But now the authorities were no longer interested in prosecuting these practices, being inclined, instead, to view witchcraft as a product of ignorance or a disorder of the imagination (Mandrou 1968: 519). By the 18th century the European intelligentsia even began to take pride in its acquired enlightenment, and confidently proceeded to rewrite the history of the witch-hunt, dismissing it as a product of medieval superstition.

Yet the specter of the witches continued to haunt the imagination of the ruling class. In 1871, the Parisian bourgeoisie instinctively returned to it to demonize the female *Communards,* accusing them of wanting to set Paris aflame. There can be little doubt, in fact, that the models for the lurid tales and images used by the bourgeois press to create the myth of the *petroleuses* were drawn from the repertoire of the witch-hunt. As described by Edith Thomas, the enemies of the Commune claimed that thousands of proletarian women roamed (like witches) the city, day and night, with pots full of kerosene and stickers with the notation "B.P.B." ("bon pour bruler," "good for torching"), presumably following instructions given to them, as part of a great conspiracy to reduce Paris to ashes in front of the troops advancing from Versailles. Thomas writes that "*petroleuses* were to be found everywhere. In the areas occupied by the Versailles army it was enough that a woman be poor and ill-dressed, and that she be carrying a basket, box, or milk-bottle" to be suspected" (Thomas 1966: 166–67). Hundreds of women were thus summarily executed, while the press vilified them in the papers. Like the witch, the *petroleuse* was depicted as an older woman with a wild, savage look and uncombed hair. In her hands was the container for the liquid she used to perpetrate her crimes.[41]

Endnotes

1. As Erik Midelfort has pointed out "With a few notable exceptions, the study of witch-hunts has remained impressionistic…. It is indeed striking how few decent surveys of witchcraft exist for Europe, surveys that attempt to list all the witch trials in a given town or region" (Midelfort 1972: 7).

2. An expression of this identification was the creation of WITCH (Women's International Conspiracy from Hell), a network of autonomous feminist groups that played an important role in the initial phase of the women's liberation movement in the United States. As Robin Morgan reports, in *Sisterhood is Powerful* (1970), WITCH was born on Halloween 1968 in New York, but "covens" soon were formed in several cities. What the figure of the witch meant to these activists is shown in a flyer written by the New York coven which, after recalling that witches were the first practitioners of birth control and abortion, stated:

    > Witches have always been women who dared to be courageous,
    > aggressive, intelligent, non-conformists, curious, independent,
    > sexually liberated, revolutionary… WITCH lives and laughs in
    > every woman. She is the free part of each of us… You are a
    > Witch by being female, untamed, angry, joyous and immortal.
    > (Morgan 1970: 605-6).

    Among North American feminist writers, those who have most consciously identified the history of the witches with the struggle for women's liberation are Mary

Above: "Petroleuses," color lithograph by Bertall reproduced in LES COMMUNEAUX, n. 20.

Right: "The Women of Paris." Wood engraving reproduced in THE GRAPHIC, April 29, 1871.

Daly (1978), Starhawk (1982), and Barbara Ehrenreich and Deidre English, whose *Witches, Midwives and Nurses: A History of Women Healers (1973)* was for many feminists, myself included, the first introduction to the history of the witch-hunt.

3. How many witches were burned? This has been a controversial question in the scholarship on the witch-hunt and a difficult one to answer, since many trials were not recorded or, if they were, the number of women executed was not specified. In addition, many documents in which we may find references to witchcraft trials have not yet been studied or have been destroyed. In the 1970s, E. W. Monter noted, for instance, that it was impossible to calculate the number of secular witch-trials that had taken place in Switzerland because these were often mentioned only in fiscal records and these records had not yet have not been analyzed (1976: 21). Thirty years later, accounts still widely differ.

    While some feminist scholars argue that the number of witches executed equals that of the Jews killed in Nazi Germany, according to Anne L. Barstow, on the basis of the present state of archival work, we are justified if we assume that approximately 200,000 women were accused of witchcraft over a space of three centuries and a lesser number of them were killed. Barstow admits, however, that it is very difficult to establish how many women were executed or died due to the tortures inflicted upon them.

    > Many records [she writes] do no list the verdicts of the trials ...
    > [or] do not include those who died in prison ... Others driven
    > to despair by torture killed themselves themselves in prison ...
    > Many accused witches were murdered in prison... Others died
    > in prison from the tortures inflicted on them (Barstow: 22-3)..

    Taking into account also those who were lynched, Barstow concludes that at least 100,000 women were killed, but she adds that those who escaped were "ruined for life," for once accused, "suspicion and ill will followed them to their graves" (ibid.)

    While the controvery concerning the size of the witch-hunt continues, regional estimates have been provided by Midelfort and Larner. Midelfort (1972) has found that in Southwestern Germany at least 3,200 witches were burned just between 1560 and 1670, a period when "they no longer burnt one or two witches, they burned twenties and hundreds" (Lea 1922: 549). Christina Larner (1981) places the number of women executed in Scotland between 1590 and 1650 at 4,500; but she too agrees that the number may be much higher, since the prerogative of conducting witch-hunts was granted also to local notables, who had a free hand not only with arresting "witches" but with record keeping.

4. Two feminist writers — Starhawk and Maria Mies — have placed the witch-hunt in the context of primitive accumulation, reaching conclusions very similar to those presented in this volume. In *Dreaming the Dark* (1982) Starhawk has connected the witch-hunt with the dispossession of the European peasantry from the commons, the social effects of the price inflation caused by the arrival in Europe of the American gold and silver, and the rise of professional medicine. She has also noted that:

    > The [witch] is gone now ... [but] Her fears, and the forces
    > she struggled against in her lifetime, live on.
    > We can open our newspapers, and read the same charges

against the idle poor...The expropriators move into the
Third World, destroying cultures... plundering the
resources of land and people... If we turn on the radio,
we can hear the crackle of flames... But the
struggle also lives on (Starhawk 1997: 218-9).

While Starhawk examines the witch-hunt mostly in the context of the rise of a market economy in Europe, Maria Mies' *Patriarchy and Accumulation on a World Scale* (1986) connects it to the colonization process and the increasing domination of nature which have characterized the capitalist ascendency. She argues that the witch-hunt was part of the attempt by the emerging capitalist class to establish its control over the productive capacity of women, and first and foremost over their generative powers, in the context of a new sexual and international division of labor built upon the exploitation of women, the colonies, and nature (Mies 1986: 69-70;78-88).

5. Since the late Roman Empire, magic had been held in suspicion by the ruling classes as part of the ideology of the slaves and an instrument of insubordination. Pierre Dockes quotes *De re rustica* by Columella, a Roman agronomist of the Late Republic, who himself quoted Cato, to the effect that familiarity with astrologers, soothsayers and sorcerers was to be kept in check, because it had a dangerous influence on the slaves. Columella recommended that the *villicus* "shall make no sacrifices without orders from his master. He shall receive neither soothsayers nor magicians, who take advantage of men's superstititions to lead them into crime.... He shall shun familiarity with haruspices and sorcerers, two sorts of people who infect ignorant souls with the poison of baseless superstititions" (Quoted by Dockes 1982: 213).

6. Dockes quotes the following excerpt from Jean Bodin's *Les Six Livres de la Republique* (1576):"[T]he might of the Arabs grew only in this way [by giving or promising freedom to the slaves]. For as soon as captain Homar, one of Mehemet's lieutenants, promised freedom to the slaves who followed him, he attracted so many of them that within a few years they made themselves lords of all the East. Rumors of freedom and the conquests made by the slaves inflamed the hearts of slaves in Europe, whereupon they took up arms, first in Spain in 781, and later in this kingdom in the time of Charlemagne and of Louis the Piteous, as may be seen in the edicts issued at the time against sworn conspiracies among the slaves.... All at once this blaze broke out in Germany, where slaves, having taken up arms, shook the estates of princes and cities, and even Louis, king of the Germans, was forced to assemble all his forces to rout them. Little by little this forced the Christians to relax servitude and to free the slaves, excepting only certain *corvées*..." (quoted in Dockes 1982: 237).

7. The most important text documenting the tolerance of the Church toward magical beliefs is considered to be the *Canon Episcopi* (tenth century), which labelled as "infidels" those who believed in demons and night flights, arguing that such "illusions" were products of the devil (Russell 1972: 76-7). However, in his study of the witch-hunt in Southwestern Germany, Erik Midelfort has disputed the idea that the Church in the Middle Ages was skeptical and tolerant with regard to witchcraft. He has been particularly critical of the use that has been made of the *Canon Episcopi*, arguing that it states the opposite of what it has been made to say. That is,

we should not conclude that the Church condoned magical practices because the author of the *Canon* attacked the belief in magic. According to Midelfort, the position of the *Canon* was the same that the Church held until the 18th century. The Church condemned the belief that magical deeds are possible, because it considered it a Manicheian heresy to attribute divine powers to witches and devils. Yet, it maintained that those who practiced magic were rightly punished, because they harbored an evil will and allied themselves with the devil (Midelfort 1975: 16–19).

Midelfort stresses that even in 16th-century Germany, the clergy insisted on the need not to believe in the powers of the devil. But he points out that (a) most of the trials were instigated and managed by secular authorities who were not concerned with theological disquisitions; (b) among the clergy as well, the distinction between "evil will" and "evil doing" had little practical effect, for in the final analysis many clergymen recommended that the witches should be punished with death.

8.   Monter (1976), 18. The Sabbat first appeared in Medieval literature toward the middle of the 15th century. Rossell Hope Robbins writes that:

> To the early demonologist Johannes Nieder (1435) the Sabbat
> was unknown, but the anonymous French tract *Errores Gazariarum*
> (1459) has a detailed account of the 'synagogue.' Nicholas Jaquier
> about 1458 used the actual word 'sabbat,' although his account was
> sketchy; 'sabbat' also appeared in a report of the witch persecution
> at Lyons in 1460... by the 16th century the sabbat was an established
> part of witchcraft (1959: 415).

9.   The witch trials were expensive, as they could continue for months and they became a source of employment for many people (Robbins 1959: 111). Payments for the "services" and the people involved — the judge, the surgeon, the torturer, the scribe, the guards — including their meals and wine, are shamelesssly included in the records of the trials, in addition to the cost of the executions and the cost of keeping the witches in prison. The following is the bill for a trial in the Scottish town of Kirkcaldy in 1636:

	Pounds	Shilling	Pence
For ten loads of coal, to burn them five marks or	3	6	8
For a tar barrel		14	
For hurden (hemp fabric) to be jumps (short coats) for them	3	10	
For making of them		8	
For one to go to Finmouth for the laird to sit upon their assize as judge		6	
For the executioner for his pains	8	14	
For his expenses here		16	4

(Robbins 1959: 114)

The costs for a witch-trial were paid by the victim's relatives, but "where the victim was penniless" they were born by the citizens of the town or the landlord (Robbins, *ibid.*). On this subject, see Robert Mandrou (1968: 112); and Christina Larner (1983: 115), among others.

10. H. R. Trevor-Roper writes: "[The witch-hunt] was forwarded by the cultivated Popes of the Renaissance, by the great Protestant Reformers, by the Saints of the Counter-Reformation, by the scholars, lawyers and churchmen.... If these two centuries were an age of light, we have to admit that in one respect at least the dark ages were more civilized...." (Trevor-Roper 1967: 91).

11 Cardini 1989: 13–6; Prosperi 1989: 217ff; Martin 1989: 32. As Ruth Martin writes concerning the work of the Inquisition in Venice: "A comparison by [P.F.] Grendler of the number of death sentences awarded by the Inquisition and by civilian tribunals has led him to conclude that 'Italian Inquisitions exercised great restraint compared to civil tribunals,' and that 'light punishment and commutation, rather than severity, marked the Venetian Inquisition,' a conclusion more recently confirmed by E.W. Monter in his study of the Mediterranean Inquisition.... As far as the Venetian trials were concerned, neither execution nor mutilation was given as a sentence and galley service was rare. Long prison sentences were also rare, and where these or banishments were issued, they were often commuted after a comparatively short space of time.... Pleas from those in prison that they may be allowed to transfer to house arrest on grounds of ill-health were also treated with sympathy" (Martin 1989: 32-33).

12. There is also evidence of significant shifts in the weight attributed to specific accusations, the nature of the crimes commonly associated with witchcraft, and the social composition of the accusers and accused. The most significant shift, perhaps, is that in an early phase of the persecution (during the 15th-century trials) witchcraft was seen predominantly as a collective crime, relying on mass gatherings and organization, while by the 17th century it was seen as a crime of an individual nature, an evil career in which isolated witches specialized — this being a sign of the breakdown of communal bonds brought about by the increasing privitization of land tenure and the expansion of commercial relations in this period.

13. Germany is an exception to this pattern, since the witch-hunt here affected many members of the bourgeoisie, including town councillors. Arguably, in Germany the confiscation of property was a major reason behind the persecution, accounting for the fact that it reached there proportions unmatched in any other country, except for Scotland. However, according to Midelfort the legality of confiscation was controversial; and even in the case of rich families, no more than one third of the property was taken. Midelfort adds that in Germany too "it is beyond question that most of the people executed were poor" (Midelfort 1972: 164-169).

14. A serious analysis of the relation between changes in land tenure, above all land privatization, and witch-hunting, is still missing. Alan Macfarlane, who first suggested a significant connection between the Essex enclosures and the witch-hunt in the same area, later recanted (Macfarlane 1978). But the relation between the two phenomena is unquestionable. As we have seen (in Chapter 2), land privatiza-

tion was a significant factor — directly and indirectly — in the pauperization that women suffered in the period in which the witch-hunt assumed mass proportions. As soon as land was privatized and a land market developed, women became vulnerable to a double process of expropriation: by well-to-do land-buyers and by their own male relations.

15. As the witch-hunt expanded, however, the distinctions between the professional witch and those who turned to her for help or engaged in magical practices without any special claim to expertise were blurred.

16. Midelfort, too, sees a connection between the Price Revolution and the persecution of the witches. Commenting upon the escalation of witch-trials in Southwestern Germany after 1620, he writes:

> The years 1622–23 saw the total disruption of coinage. Money became so depreciated that prices soared out of sight. Food prices, moreover, did not need monetary policy to rise. The year 1625 had a cold spring and bad harvests from Wurzburg across Wuttemberg to the whole Rhine valley. The next year found famine along the Rhine valley.... These conditions of themselves drove prices beyond what many laborers could afford (1972: 123–24).

17. Writes Le Roy Ladurie: "Between these frenzied uprisings (*sic*) [the witch-hunts] and authentic popular revolts which also reached their climax in the same mountains about 1580-1600, there existed a series of geographical, chronological, and sometimes family coincidences" (Le Roy Ladurie 1987: 208).

18. In the obsession with the Sabbat or Synagogue, as the mythical witches' gathering was called, we find a proof of the continuity between the persecution of the witches and the persecution of the Jews. As heretics and propagators of Arabic wisdom, Jews were regarded as sorcerers, poisoners and devil worshippers. To the portrait of Jews as devilish beings contributed the tales surrounding the practice of circumcision, which claimed that Jews ritually murdered children. "Time and again the Jews were described [in the miracle plays as well as in sketches] as 'devils from Hell, enemies of the human race'" (Trachtenberg 1944: 23). On the connection between the persecution of the Jews and the witch-hunt, see also Carlo Ginzburg's *Ecstasies* (1991), Chapters 1 and 2.

19. The reference here is to the conspirators of the "Bundschuh" — the German peasant union, whose symbol was the clog — which in the 1490s, in Alsace, plotted to rise against the church and the castle. Of them Friedrich Engels wrote that they were wont to hold their meetings at night on the lonesome Hunger Hill (Engels 1977: 66).

20. The Italian historian Luciano Parinetto has suggested that the theme of cannibalism may be an import from the New World, as cannibalism and devil-worship merged in the reports about the "Indians" made by the conquistadors and their clerical accomplices. In support of this thesis Parinetto cites Francesco Maria Guazzo's *Compendium Maleficarum* (1608) which, in his view, demonstrates that demonologists in Europe were influenced, in their portrayal of witches as cannibals, by the reports coming from the New World. However, witches in Europe were accused of sacrificing children to the devil long before the conquest and colonization of the Americas.

21. In the 14th and 15th centuries, the Inquisition accused women, heretics, and Jews of witchcraft. It was in the course of trials held in 1419–1420 in Lucerne and Interlaken that the word *Hexerei* ("witchcraft") was first used (Russell 1972: 202).

22. Murray's thesis has been revived in recent years, in the midst of a renewed interest among eco-feminists for the woman-nature relation in early matrifocal societies. Among those who have read the witches as the defenders of an ancient female-centered religion that worshipped women's reproductive powers is Mary Condren. In *The Serpent and the Goddess* (1989), Condren argues that the witch-hunt was part of a long process whereby Christianity displaced the priestesses of the older religion, first by asserting that they used their powers for evil purposes and later by denying they had such powers(Condren 1989: 80–86). One of the most interesting claims Condren makes in this context concerns the connection between the persecution of the witches and the attempt by the Christian priests to appropriate women's reproductive powers. Condren shows how the priests engaged in a true competition with the "wise women," performing reproductive miracles, making barren women pregnant, changing the sex of infants, performing supernatural abortions and, last but not least, fostering abandoned children (Condren 1989: 84).

23. By the middle of the 16th century most European countries began to gather regularly demographic statistics. In 1560 the Italian historian Francesco Guicciardini expressed surprise upon learning that in Antwerp and generally in the Netherlands the authorities did not gather demographic data except in case of "urgent necessity" (Helleneir 1958: 1–2). By the 17th century all the states where the witch-hunt was taking place were also promoting population growth (*ibid.*: 46).

24. Monica Green, however, has challenged the idea that in the Middle Ages there existed a rigid sexual division of medical labor, such that men were excluded from the care of women and particularly from gynecology and obstetrics. She also argues that women were present, although in smaller number, throughout the medical community, not just as midwives but as physicians, apothecaries, barber-surgeons. Green questions the common claim that midwives were especially targeted by the authorities, and that we can trace a connection between the witch-hunt and the expulsion of women from the medical profession starting in the 14th and 15th centuries. She claims that the restrictions placed on practicing resulted from many social tensions (in Spain, e.g., from the conflict between Christians and Muslims) and, while the increasing limitations placed on women's practice can be documented, the reasons behind them cannot. She admits that the prevailing concerns behind these limitations were of "moral" origin; that is, they related to considerations about the woman's character (Green 1989: 435ff).

25. J. Gelis writes that "the state and church traditionally distrusted this woman whose practice often remained secret, and steeped in magic if not witchcraft, and who could definitely count on the support of the rural community." ("*L'état et l'église se mefient traditionellement de cette femme dont la pratique reste souvent secrète, empreinte de magie, voire de sorcellerie et qui dispose au sein de la communauté rurale d'une audience certaine.*") He adds that it was above all necessary to break the complicity, true or imagined, of the *sages femmes* in such crimes as abortion, infanticide, child abandonment (Gelis 1977: 927ff). In France the first edict regulating the activity of the *sages femmes* was

promulgated in Strasbourg at the end of the 16th century. By the end of the 17th century the *sages femmes* were completely under the control of the state, and were used by the state as a reactionary force in its campaign of moral reform (Gelis 1977).

26. This may explain why contraceptives, which had been widely used in the Middle Ages, disappeared in the 17th century, surviving only in the *milieu* of prostitution, and when they reappeared on the scene they were placed in male hands, so that women were not allowed to use them except with male permission. For a long time, in fact, the only contraceptive offered by bourgeois medicine was to be the condom. The "sheath" begins to appear in England in the 18th century, one of the first mentions of it is in James Boswell's *Diary* (quoted by Helleiner 1958: 94).

27. In 1556, Henry II in France passed a law punishing as murderous any woman who hid her pregnancy and whose child was born dead. A similar law was passed in Scotland in 1563. Until the 18th century in Europe infanticide was punished with the death penalty. In England, during the Protectorate, the death penalty was introduced for adultery.

    To the attack on women's reproductive rights, and the introduction of new laws sanctioning the subordination of the wife to the husband within the family, we must add the criminalization of prostitution, starting in the mid-16th century. As we have seen (in Chapter 2), prostitutes were subjected to atrocious punishments such as that of the *acabussade*. In England, they were branded on the forehead with hot irons in a manner reminiscent of the "devil's mark," and they were whipped and shaved like witches. In Germany, the prostitute could be drowned, burned or buried alive. Here, too, she was shaved — hair was viewed as a favorite seat of the devil. At times her nose was cut off, a practice of Arab origin, used to punish "crimes of honor" and inflicted also on women charged with adultery.

    Like the witch, the prostitute was presumably recognized by her "evil eye." It was assumed that sexual transgression was diabolical and gave women magical powers. On the relation between eros and magic in the Renaissance, see Ioan P. Couliano (1987).

28. The debate on the nature of the sexes began in the late Middle Ages and then reopened in the 17th century.

29. "Tu non pensavi ch'io loico fossi!" ("You didn't think I was a logician!") chuckles the Devil in Dante's *Inferno,* while snatching the soul of Boniface the VIII, who had cunningly thought of escaping the eternal fire by repenting in the very act of perpetrating his crimes (*Divine Comedy, Inferno,* canto XXVII, verse 123).

30. The sabotage of the conjugal act was a major theme also in contemporary judicial proceedings regarding matrimony and separation, especially in France. As Robert Mandrou observes, men were so afraid of being made impotent by women, that village priests often forbade women who were suspected of being experts in the "tying of knots" (an alleged device for causing male impotence) from attending weddings (Mandrou 1968: 81–82, 391ff.; Le Roy Ladurie 1974: 204-205; Lecky 1886: 100).

31. This tale appears in several demonologies. It always ends with the man discovering the injury inflicted on him and forcing the witch to return his penis to him. She accompanies him to the top of a tree where she has many hidden in a nest; the man chooses one but the witch objects: "No, that one belongs to the Bishop."

32. Carolyn Merchant argues that the interrogations and tortures of the witches provided the model for the methodology of the New Science, as defined by Francis
Bacon:

> Much of the imagery [Bacon] used in delineating his scientific
> objectives and methods derives from the courtrooms, and
> because it treats nature as a female to be tortured through
> mechanical inventions, strongly suggests the interrogations of
> the witch-trials and the mechanical devices used to torture witches.
> In a relevant passage, Bacon stated that the method by which
> nature's secrets might be discovered consisted in investigating
> the secrets of witchcraft by inquisition...." (Merchant 1980: 168).

33. On the attack against animals, see Chapter 3 of this volume, pp. 158–59..

34. It is significant, in this context, that witches were often accused by children. Norman
Cohn has interpreted this phenomenon as a revolt of the young against the elderly,
and in particular against parental authority (N. Cohn 1975; Trevor Roper 2000). But
other factors need to be considered. First, it is plausible that the climate of fear created by the witch-hunt over the years was responsible for the large presence of children among the accusers, which began to materialize in the 17th century. It is also
important to notice that those charged as witches were mostly proletarian women,
while the children who accused them were often the children of their employers.
Thus, we can presume that children were manipulated by their parents to make
charges which they themselves were reluctant to pursue, as it was undoubtedly the
case in the Salem witch-trials. We must also consider that, in the 16th and 17th centuries, there was a growing preoccupation among the well-to-do with the physical
intimacy between their children and their servants, above all their nurses, which was
beginning to appear as a source of indiscipline. The familiarity that had existed
between masters and servants in the Middle Ages vanished with the rise of the bourgeoisie, who formally instituted more egalitarian relations between employers and
their subordinates (for instance, by levelling clothing styles), but in reality increased
the physical and psychological distance between them. In the bourgeois household,
the master would no longer undress in front of his servants, nor would he sleep in
the same room with them.

35. For a true-to-life Sabbat, in which sexual elements and themes evoking class revolt
combine, see Julian Cornwall's description of the rebel camp that peasants set up
during the Norfolk uprising of 1549. The camp caused much scandal among the
gentry, who apparently looked at it as a veritable Sabbat. Writes Cornwall:

> [T]he conduct of the rebels was misrepresented in every way. It
> was alleged that the camp became the Mecca for every dissolute per-
> son in the county.... Bands of rebels foraged for supplies and money.
> 3,000 bullocks and 20,000 sheep, to say nothing of pigs, fowl, deer,
> swans and thousands of bushels of corn, were driven in and consumed,
> it was said, in a few days. Men whose ordinary diet was too often sparse
> and monotonous revelled in the abundance of flesh, and there was
> reckless waste. It tasted all the sweeter for coming from the beasts
> which were the root of so much resentment (Cornwall 1977: 147).

The "beasts" were the much prized wool-producing sheep, which were indeed, as Thomas Moore put it in his *Utopia*, 'eating humans', as arable lands and common fields were being enclosed and turned to pasture in order to raise them.

36. Thorndike 1923–58v: 69; Ronald Holmes 1974: 85–86; Monter 1969: 57–58. Kurt Seligman writes that from the middle of the 14th century to the 16th century alchemy was universally accepted, but with the rise of capitalism the attitude of the monarchs changed. In Protestant countries, alchemy became an object of ridicule. The alchemist was depicted as a smoke-seller, who promised to change metals into gold, but failed in his performance (Seligman 1948: 126ff). He was often represented at work in his study, surrounded by strange vases and instruments, oblivious to every-thing around him, while across the street his wife and children would be knocking at the poor house. Ben Jonson's satirical portrait of the alchemist reflects this new attitude.

Astrology, too, was practiced into the 17th century. In his *Demonology* (1597), James I maintained that it was legitimate, above all when confined to the study of seasons and weather forecasts. A detailed description of the life of an English astrologer at the end of the 16th century is found in A. L. Rowse's *Sex and Society in Shakespeare's Age* (1974). Here we learn that in the same period when the witch-hunt was peaking, a male magician could continue to carry on his work, although with some difficulty and taking some risks at times.

37. With reference to the West Indies, Anthony Barker writes that no aspect of the unfa-vorable image of the Negro built by the slave owners had wider or deeper roots than the allegation of insatiable sexual appetite. Missionaries reported that the Negros refused to be monogamous, were excessively libidinous, and told stories of Negroes having intercourse with apes (pp. 121–23). The fondness of Africans for music was also held against them, as proof of their instinctual, irrational nature (*ibid.*: 115).

38. In the Middle Ages when a child took over the family property, s/he would auto-matically assume the care of the aging parents, while in the 16th century the parents began to be abandoned and priority was given to investment into one's children (Macfarlane 1970: 205).

39. The statute which James I passed in 1604, imposed the death penalty for all who "used spirits and magic" regardless of whether they had done any harm. This statute later became the basis upon which the persecution of witches was carried on in the American colonies.

40. In "Outrunning Atlanta: Feminine Destiny in Alchemic Transmutations," Allen and Hubbs write that:

> The recurrent symbolism in alchemical works suggests an obses-sion with reversing, or perhaps even arresting, the feminine hegemony over the process of biological creation.... This desired mastery is also depicted in such imageries as that of Zeus giving birth to Athena from his head...or Adam being delivered of Eve from his chest. The alchemist who exemplifies the primordial striving for control over the natural world seeks nothing less than the magic of maternity....Thus the great alchemist Paracelsus gives an affirmative answer to the ques-tion 'Whether it was possible for art and nature that a man should be

*A witch rides a goat through the sky, causing a rain of fire.
Woodcut from Francesco-Maria Guazzo, COMPENDIUM
MALEFICARUM (1610).*

born outside a woman's body and a natural mother's' (Allen and Hubbs
1980: 213).

41. On the image of the *petroleuse* see Albert Boime's *Art and the French Commune* (1995:
109–11;196–99), and Rupert Christiansen's *Paris Babylon: The Story of the Paris
Commune* (1994: 352–53).

Amerigo Vespucci landing on the South American coast in 1497. Before him,
seductively lying on a hammock, is "America." Behind her some cannibals are
roasting human remains. Design by Jan van der Straet, and engraved by
Théodore Galle (1589).

Colonization and Christianization

Caliban and Witches in the New World

"...and so they say that we have come to this earth to destroy the world. They say that the winds ruin the houses, and cut the trees, and the fire burns them, but that we devour everything, we consume the earth, we redirect the rivers, we are never quiet, never at rest, but always run here and there, seeking gold and silver, never satisfied, and then we gamble with it, make war, kill each other, rob, swear, never say the truth, and have deprived them of their means of livelihood. And finally they curse the sea which has put on the earth such evil and harsh children." (Girolamo Benzoni, *Historia del Mondo Nuovo*, 1565).

"...overcome by torture and pain, [the women] were obliged to confess that they did adore huacas.... *They lamented, 'Now in this life we women...are Christian; perhaps then the priest is to blame if we women adore the mountains, if we flee to the hills and* puna, *since there is no justice for us here."* (Felipe Guaman Poma de Ayala, *Nueva Chronica y Buen Gobierno*, 1615)

Introduction

The history of the body and the witch-hunt that I have presented is based on an assumption that is summed up by the reference to "Caliban and the Witch," the characters of *The Tempest* symbolizing the American Indians' resistance to colonization.[1] The assumption is the continuity between the subjugation of the populations of the New World and that of people in Europe, women in particular, in the transition to capitalism. In both cases we have the forcible removal of entire communities from their land, large-scale impoverishment, the launching of "Christianizing" campaigns destroying people's autonomy and communal relations. We also have a constant cross-fertilization whereby forms of repression that had been developed in the Old World were transported to the New and then re-imported into Europe.

The differences should not be underestimated. By the 18th century, due to the flow of gold, silver and other resources coming from the Americas into Europe, an international division of labor had taken shape that divided the new global proletariat by means of different class relations and systems of discipline, marking the beginning of often conflicting histories within the working class. But the similarities in the treatments to which the populations of Europe and the Americas were subjected are sufficient to demonstrate the existence of one single logic governing the development of capitalism and the structural character of the atrocities perpetrated in this process. An outstanding example is the extension of the witch-hunt to the American colonies.

The persecution of women and men through the charge of witchcraft is a phenomenon that, in the past, was largely considered by historians to be limited to Europe. The only exception admitted to this rule were the Salem witch trials, which remain the focus of the scholarship on witch-hunting in the New World. It is now recognized, however, that the charge of devil-worshipping played a key function also in the colonization of the American aboriginal population. On this subject, two texts, in particular, must be mentioned that form the basis for my discussion in this chapter. The first is Irene Silverblatt's *Moon, Sun, and Witches* (1987), a study of witch hunting and the redefinition of gender relations in Inca society and colonial Peru, which (to my knowledge) is the first in English to reconstruct the history of the Andean women persecuted as witches. The other is Luciano Parinetto's *Streghe e Potere* (1998), a series of essays that document the impact of witch-hunting in America on the witch trials in Europe, marred, however, by the author's insistence that the persecution of the witches was gender-neutral.

Both these works demonstrate that also in the New World witch-hunting was *a deliberate strategy used by the authorities to instill terror*, destroy collective resistance, silence entire communities, and turn their members against each other. *It was also a strategy of enclosure* which, depending on the context, could be enclosure of land, bodies or social relations. Above all, as in Europe, witch-hunting was a means of dehumanization and as such the paradigmatic form of repression, serving to justify enslavement and genocide.

Witch-hunting did not destroy the resistance of the colonized. Due primarily to the struggle of women, the connection of the American Indians with the land, the local religions and nature survived beyond the persecution providing, for more than five hundred years, a source of anti-colonial and anti-capitalist resistance. This is extremely important for us, at a time when a renewed assault is being made on the resources and mode of existence of indigenous populations across the planet; for we need to rethink how the conquistadors strove to subdue those whom they colonized, and what enabled the latter to subvert this plan and, against the destruction of their social and physical universe, create a new historical reality.

The Birth of the Cannibals

When Columbus sailed to "Indies" the witch-hunt in Europe was not yet a mass phenomenon. Nevertheless, the use of devil-worship as a weapon to strike at political enemies and vilify entire populations (like Muslims and Jews) was already common among the elite. More than that, as Seymour Phillips writes, a "persecuting society" had developed within medieval Europe," fed by militarism and Christian intolerance, that looked at the "Other" as mainly an object of aggression (Phillips 1994). Thus, it is not surprising if "cannibal," "infidel," "barbarian," "monstrous races," and devil worshipper were the "ethnographic models" with which the Europeans "entered the new age of expansion" (*ibid*. 62), providing the filter through which missionaries and conquistadors interpreted the cultures, religions, and sexual customs of the peoples they encountered.[2] Other cultural marks contributed to the invention of the "Indians". Most stigmatizing and perhaps projecting the Spaniards' labor needs were "nakedness" and "sodomy," that qualified the Amerindians as beings living in an animal state (thus capable of being turned into beasts of burden), though some reports also stressed, as a sign of their bestiality, their propensity to share and "give everything they have in return for things of little value" (Hulme 1994: 198).

Defining the aboriginal American populations as cannibals, devil-worshippers, and sodomites supported the fiction that the Conquest was not an unabashed quest for gold and silver but was a converting mission, a claim that, in 1508, helped the Spanish Crown gain for it the blessing of the Pope and complete authority over the Church in the Americas. It also removed, in the eyes of the world and possibly of the colonizers themselves, any sanction against the atrocities which they would commit against the "Indians," thus functioning as a license to kill regardless of what the intended victims might do. And, indeed, "The whip, gibbet, and stock, imprisonment, torture, rape, and occasional killing became standard weapons for enforcing labor discipline" in the New World (Cockroft 1990:19).

In a first phase, however, the image of the colonized as devil-worshippers could coexist with a more positive, even idyllic one, picturing the "Indians" as innocent, and generous beings, living a life "free of toil and tyranny," recalling the mythical "Golden Age" or an earthly paradise (Brandon 1986: 6–8; Sale 1991: 100–101).

This characterization may have been a literary stereotype or, as Roberto Retamar, among others, has suggested, the rhetorical counterpart of the image of the "savage," expressing the Europeans' inability to see the people they met as real human beings.[3] But this optimistic view also corresponded to a period in the conquest (from 1520 to 1540s) in which the Spaniards still believed that the aboriginal populations would be easily converted and subjugated (Cervantes 1994). This was the time of mass baptisms, when much zeal was deployed in convincing the "Indians" to change their names and abandon their gods and sexual customs, especially polygamy and homosexuality. [B]are-breasted women were forced to cover themselves, men in loincloths had to put on trousers (Cockroft: 1983: 21). But at this time, the struggle against the devil consisted mainly of bonfires of local "idols," even though many political and religious leaders from central Mexico were put on trial and burned at the stake by the Franciscan father Juan de Zumarraga, in the years between 1536 (when the Inquisition was introduced in South America) and 1543.

As the Conquest proceeded, however, no space was left for any accommodations. Imposing one's power over other people is not possible without denigrating them to the point where the possibility of identification is precluded. Thus, despite the earlier homilies about the gentle Tainos, an ideological machine was set in motion, complementing the military one, that portrayed the colonized as "filthy" and demonic beings practicing all kinds of abominations, while the same crimes that previously had been attributed to lack of religious education — sodomy, cannibalism, incest, cross dressing — were now treated as signs that the "Indians" were under the dominion of the devil and they could be justifiably deprived of their lands and their lives (Williams 1986: 136–137). In reference to this image-shift, Fernando Cervantes writes in *The Devil in The New World* (1994):

> before 1530 it would have been difficult to predict which one of these views would emerge as the dominant one. By the middle of the sixteenth century, however, [a] negative demonic view of Amerindian cultures had triumphed, and its influence was seen to descend like a thick fog on every statement officially and unofficially made on the subject (1994: 8).

It could be surmised, on the basis of the contemporary histories of the "Indies" — such as De Gomara's (1556) and Acosta's (1590) — that this change of perspective was prompted by the Europeans' encounter with imperialistic states like the Aztec and Inca, whose repressive machinery included the practice of human sacrifices (Martinez et al 1976). In the *Historia Natural Y Moral de Las Indias*, published in Sevilla, in 1590, by the Jesuit Joseph de Acosta, there are descriptions that give us a vivid sense of the repulsion generated, among the Spaniards, by the mass sacrifices carried out, particularly by the Aztecs, which involved thousands of youths (war captives or purchased children and slaves).[4] Yet, when we read Bartolemé De Las Casas' account of the destruction of the Indies or any other account of the Conquest, we wonder why should the Spaniards have been shocked by this practice when they themselves had no qualms committing unspeakable atrocities for the sake of God and gold and, according to Cortez, in 1521, they had slaughtered 100,000 people, just to conquer Tenochtitlan (Cockroft 1983: 19).

Similarly, the cannibalistic rituals they discovered in America, which figure prominently in the records of the Conquest, must not have been too different from the medical practices that were popular in Europe at the time. In the 16th, 17th and even 18th centuries, the drinking of human blood (especially the blood of those who had died of a violent death) and mummy water, obtained by soaking human flesh in various spirits, was a common cure for epilepsy and other illnesses in many European countries. Furthermore, this type of cannibalism, "involving human flesh, blood, heart, skull, bone marrow, and other body parts was not limited to fringe groups of society but was practiced in the most respectable circles" (Gordon-Grube 1988: 406–407).[5] Thus, the new horror that the Spaniards felt for the aboriginal populations, after the 1550s, cannot be easily attributed to a cultural shock, but must be seen as a response inherent to the logic of colonization that inevitably must dehumanize and fear those it wants to enslave.

How successful was this strategy can be seen from the ease with which the Spaniards rationalized the high mortality rates caused by the epidemics that swept the region in the wake of the Conquest, which they interpreted as God's punishment for the Indians beastly conduct.[6] Also the debate that took place in 1550, at Valladolid, in Spain, between Bartolomé de Las Casas and the Spanish jurist Juan Gines de Sepulveda, on whether or not the "Indians" were to be considered as human beings, would have been unthinkable without an ideological campaign representing the latter as animals and demons.[7]

Travel logs illustrated with horrific images of cannibals stuffing themselves with human remains proliferated in Europe in the aftermath of the conquest. A cannibal banquet in Bahia (Brazil), according to the description of the German J. G. Aldenburg.

The spread of illustrations portraying life in the New World, that began to circulate in Europe after the 1550s, completed this work of degradation, with their multitudes of naked bodies and cannibalistic banquets, reminiscent of witches' Sabbats, featuring human heads and limbs as the main course. A late example of this genre of literature is *Le Livre des Antipodes* (1630), compiled by Johann Ludwig Gottfried, which displays a number of horrific images: women and children stuffing themselves with human entrails, or the cannibal community gathered around a grill, feasting on legs and arms while watching the roasting of human remains. Prior contributions to the cultural production of the Amerindians as bestial beings are the illustrations in *Les Singularitéz de la France Antarctique* (Paris 1557) by the French Franciscan André Thevet, already centered on the themes of the human quartering, cooking, and banquet; and Hans Staden's *Wahrharftige Historia* (Marburg 1557), in which the author describes his captivity among the cannibal indios of Brazil (Parinetto 1998: 428).

*Cannibals in Bahia feasting on human remains. Illustrations displaying
the Amerindian community roasting and feeding on human remains
completed the degradation of the aboriginal American populations
begun by the work of the missionaries.*

Exploitation, Resistance, and Demonization

A turning point, in the anti-Indian propaganda and anti-idolatry campaign that accompanied the colonization process, was the decision by the Spanish Crown, in the 1550s, to introduce in the American colonies a far more severe system of exploitation. The decision was motivated by the crisis of the "plunder economy" that had been introduced after the Conquest whereby the accumulation of wealth continued to depend on the expropriation of the "Indians'" surplus goods more than on the direct exploitation of their labor (Spalding 1984; Steve J. Stern 1982). Until the 1550s, despite the massacres and the exploitation associated with the system of the *encomienda*, the Spaniards had not completely disrupted the subsistence economies which they had found in the areas they colonized. Instead, they had relied, for the wealth they accumulated, on the tribute systems put into place by the Aztecs and Incas, whereby designated chiefs (*caciquez* in Mexico, *kuracas* in Peru) delivered them quotas of goods and labor supposedly compatible with the survival of the local economies. The tribute which the Spaniards exacted was much higher than that the Aztecs and Incas had ever demanded of those they conquered; but it was still not sufficient to satisfy their needs. By the 1550s, they were finding it difficult to obtain enough labor for the both the *obrajes* (manufacturing workshops where goods were produced for the international market) and the exploitation of the newly discovered silver and mercury mines, like the legendary one at Potosi.[8]

The need to squeeze more work from the aboriginal populations largely derived from the situation at home where the Spanish Crown was literally floating on the American bullion, which bought food and goods no longer produced in Spain. In addition, the plundered wealth financed the Crown's European territorial expansion. This was so dependent on the continuous arrival of masses of silver and gold from the New World that, by the 1550s, the Crown was ready to undermine the power of the *encomenderos* in order to appropriate the bulk of the Indians' labor for the extraction of silver to be shipped to Spain.[9] But resistance to colonization was mounting (Spalding 1984: 134–135; Stern 1982).[10] It was in response to this challenge that, both in Mexico and Peru, a war was declared on indigenous cultures paving the way to a draconian intensification of colonial rule.

In Mexico, this turn occurred in 1562 when, by the initiative of the Provincial Diego de Landa, an anti-idolatry campaign was launched in the Yucatan peninsula, in the course of which more than 4,500 people were rounded up and brutally tortured under the charge of practicing human sacrifices. They were then subjected to a well-orchestrated public punishment which finished destroying their bodies and their morale (Clendinnen 1987: 71–92). So cruel were the penalties inflicted (floggings so severe that they made the blood flow, years of enslavement in the mines) that many people died or remained unfit for work; others fled their homes or committed suicide, so that work came to an end and the regional economy was disrupted. However, the persecution that Landa mounted was the foundation of a new colonial economy, since it signaled to the local population that the Spaniards were there to stay and that the rule of the old gods was over (*ibid.*: 190).

In Peru, as well, the first large-scale attack on diabolism occurred in the 1560s, coinciding with the rise of the Taki Onqoy movement,[11] a native millenarian movement that preached against collaboration with the Europeans and for a pan-Andean alliance of the local gods (*huacas*) putting an end to colonization. Attributing the defeat suffered and the rising mortality to the abandonment of the local gods, the Takionqos encouraged people to reject the Christian religion, and the names, food, clothing received from the Spaniards. They also urge them to refuse the tribute payments and labor drafts the Spaniards imposed on them, and to "stop wearing shirts, hats, sandals or any other clothes from Spain" (Stern 1982: 53). If this was done — they promised — the revived *huacas* would turn the world around and destroy the Spaniards by sending sickness and floods to their cities, the ocean rising to erase any memory of their existence (Stern 1982: 52–64).

The threat posed by the Taquionqos was a serious one since, by calling for a pan-Andean unification of the *huacas*, the movement marked the beginning of a new sense of identity capable of overcoming the divisions connected with the traditional organization of the *ayullus* (family unit). In Stern's words, it marked the first time that the people of the Andes began to think of themselves as one people, as "Indians" (Stern 1982: 59) and, in fact, the movement spread widely, reaching "as far north as Lima, as far east as Cuzco, and over the high puna of the South to La Paz in contemporary Bolivia (Spalding 1984: 246). The response came with the ecclesiastical Council held in Lima in 1567, which established that the priests should "extirpate the innumerable superstitions, ceremonies and diabolical rites of the Indians. They were also to stamp out drunkenness, arrest witch-doctors, and above all discover and destroy shrines and talismans" connected with the worship of the local gods (*huacas*). These recommendations were repeated at a synod in Quito, in 1570, where, again, it was denounced that "[t]here are famous witch doctors who... guard the *huacas* and converse with the devil" (Hemming 1970: 397).

The *huacas* were mountains, springs, stones, and animals embodying the spirits of the ancestor. As such, they were collectively cared for, fed, and worshipped for everyone recognized them as the main link with the land, and with the agricultural practices central to economic reproduction. Women talked to them, as they apparently still do, in some regions of South America, to ensure a healthy crop (Descola 1994: 191–214).[12] Destroying them or forbidding their worship was to attack the community, its historical roots, people's relation to the land, and their intensely spiritual relation to nature. This was understood by the Spaniards who, in the 1550s, embarked in a systematic destruction of anything resembling an object of worship. What Claude Baudez and Sydney Picasso write about the anti-idolatry drive conducted by the Franciscans against the Mayas in the Yucatan also applies to the rest of Mexico and Peru.

"Idols were destroyed, temples burned, and those who celebrated native rites and practiced sacrifices were punished by death; festivities such as banquets, songs, and dances, as well as artistic and intellectual activities (painting, sculpture, observation of stars, hieroglyphic writing) — suspected of being inspired by the devil — were forbidden and those who took part in them mercilessly hunted down" (Baudez and Picasso 1992: 21).

This process went hand in hand with the reform demanded by the Spanish Crown that increased the exploitation of indigenous labor to ensure a better flow of bullion into its coffers. Two measures were introduced for this purpose, both facilitated by the anti-idolatry campaign. First, the quota of labor that the local chiefs had to provide for the mines and the *obrajes* was vastly increased, and the enforcement of the new rule was placed under the super-

Andean woman forced to work in the obrajes, *manufacturing work-shops producing for the international market. Scenes by Felipe Guaman Poma de Ayala.*

vision of a local representative of the Crown (*corregidore*) with the power to arrest and administer other forms of punishment in case of failure to comply. Further, a resettlement program (*reducciones*) was introduced removing much of the rural population into designated villages, so as to place it under a more direct control. The destruction of the *huacas* and the persecution of the ancestor religion associated with them was instrumental to both, since the *reducciones* gained strength from the demonization of the local worshipping sites.

It was soon clear, however, that, under the cover of Christianization, people continued to worship their gods, in the same way as they continued to return to their *milpas* (fields) after being removed from their homes. Thus, instead of diminishing, the attack on the local gods intensified with time, climaxing between 1619 and 1660 when the destruction of the idols was accompanied by true witch-hunts, this time targeting women in particular. Karen Spalding has described one of these witch-hunts conducted in the *repartimiento* of Huarochiri', in 1660, by the priest-inquisitor Don Juan Sarmiento. As she reports, the investigation was conducted according to the same pattern of the witch-hunts in Europe. It began with the reading of the edict against idolatry and the preaching of a sermon against this sin. This was followed by secret denunciations supplied by anonymous informants, then came the questioning of the suspects, the use of torture to extract confessions, and then the sentencing and punishment, in this case consisting of public whipping, exile, and various other forms of humiliation:

> The people sentenced were brought into the public square.... They were placed upon mules and donkeys, with wooden crosses about six inches long around their necks. They were ordered to wear these marks

Scenes from Felipe Guaman Poma de Ayala representing the ordeal of Andean women and the followers of the ancestors' religion.

Scene 1: Public humiliation during an anti-idolatry campaign. Scene 2: Women "as spoils of conquest." Scene 3: The huacas, represented as the devil, speak through a dream. Scene 4: A member of the Taki Onqoy movement with a drunken Indian who is seized by a huaca represented as the devil. (From Steve J. Stern, 1982.)

of humiliation from that day forward. On their heads, the religious authorities put a medieval coroza, a cone shaped hood made of pasteboard, that was the European Catholic mark of infamy and disgrace. Beneath these hoods the hair was cut off — an Andean mark of humiliation. Those who were condemned to receive lashes had their backs bared. Ropes were put around their necks. They were paraded slowly through the streets of the town with a crier ahead of them reading out their crimes... After this spectacle the people were brought back, some with their backs bleeding from the 20, 40 or 100 lashes with the cat-o'-nine-tails wielded by the village executioner (Spalding 1984: 256).

Spalding concludes that:

> The idolatry campaigns were exemplary rituals, didactic theatre pieces directed to the audience as much as to the participants, much like a public hanging in medieval Europe (ibid.: 265)

Their objective was to intimidate the population, to create a "space of death"[13] where potential rebels would be so paralyzed with fear that they would accept anything rather than having to face the same ordeal of those publicly beaten and humiliated. In this, the Spaniards were in part successful. Faced with torture, anonymous denunciations and public humiliations, many alliances and friendships broke down; people's faith in the effectiveness of their gods weakened, and worship turned into a secret individual practice rather than a collective one, as it had been in pre-conquest America.

How deeply the social fabric was affected by these terror campaigns can be deduced, according to Spalding, from the changes that over time took place in the nature of the charges. While in the 1550s people could openly acknowledge theirs and their community's attachment to the traditional religion, by the 1650s the crimes of which they were accused revolved around "witchcraft," a practice now presuming a secretive behavior, and they increasingly resembled the accusations made against witches in Europe. In the campaign launched in 1660, in the Huarochiri area, for instance, "the crimes uncovered by the authorities... dealt with curing, finding lost goods, and other forms of what might be generally called village 'witchcraft'." Yet, the same campaign revealed that despite the persecution, in the eyes of the communities, "the ancestors and waks (*huacas*) continued to be essential to their survival" (Spalding 1984: 261).

Women and Witches in America

It is not a coincidence that "[m]ost of the people convicted in the investigation of 1660 in Huarochiri' were women (28 out of 32)" (Spalding 1984: 258), in the same way as women had been the main presence in the Taki Onqoy movement. It was women who most strongly defended the old mode of existence and opposed the new power structure, plausibly because they were also the ones who were most negatively affected by it.

Women had held a powerful position in pre-Columbian societies, as reflected by the existence of many important female deities in their religions. Reaching an island off the coast of the Yucatan peninsula, in 1517, Hernandez de Cordoba named it Isla Mujeres "because the temples they visited there contained numerous female idols" (Baudez and Picasso 1992: 17). Pre-conquest American women had their organizations, their socially recognized spheres of activity and, while not equal to men,[14] they were considered complementary to them in their contribution to the family and society.

In addition to being farmers, house-workers and weavers, in charge of producing the colorful cloths worn in everyday life and during the ceremonies, they were potters, herbalists, healers (*curanderas*), and priestesses (*sacerdotisas*) at the service of household gods. In Southern Mexico, in the region of Oaxaca, they were connected with the production of pulque-maguey, a sacred substance believed to have been invented by the gods and associated with Mayahuel, an earth-mother goddess that was "the focal point of peasant religion" (Taylor 1979: 31–32).

But with the Spaniards' arrival everything changed, as they brought their baggage of misogynous beliefs and restructured the economy and political power in ways that favored men. Women suffered also at the hands of the traditional chiefs who, in order to maintain their power, began to take over the communal lands and expropriate the female members of the community from land use and water rights. Thus, within the colonial economy, women were reduced to the condition of servants working as maids (for the *encomenderos, the priests,* the *corregidores*) or as weavers in the *obrajes*. Women were also forced to follow their husband when they would have to do *mita* work in the mines — a fate that people recognized to be worse than death — for, in 1528, the authorities established that spouses could not be separated, so that women and children, from then on, could be compelled to do mine labor in addition to preparing food for the male workers.

Another source of degradation for women was the new Spanish legislation which declared polygamy illegal, so that, overnight, men had to either separate from their wives or reclassify them as maids (Mayer 1981), while the children issued from these unions were labeled according to five different types of illegitimacy (Nash 1980: 143). Ironically, while polygamous unions were dissolved, with the arrival of the Spaniards, no aboriginal woman was safe from rape or appropriation, so that many men, instead of marrying, began to turn to public prostitutes (Hemming 1970). In the European fantasy, America itself was a reclining naked woman seductively inviting the approaching white stranger. At times, it was the "Indian" men themselves who delivered their female kin to the priests or *encomenderos* in exchange for some economic reward or a public post.

For all these reasons, women became the main enemies of colonial rule, refusing to go to Mass, to baptize their children or to cooperate in any way with the colonial authorities and priests. In the Andes, some committed suicide and killed their male children, presumably to prevent them from going to the mines and also out of disgust, apparently, for the mistreatment inflicted upon them by their male relatives (Silverblatt 1987). Others organized their communities and, in front of the defection of many local chiefs who were co-opted by the colonial structure, became priests, leaders, and guardians of the *huacas*, taking on functions which they had never previously exercised. This explains why women were the backbone of the Taki Onqoy movement. In Peru, they also held confessions to prepare people for when they would meet with the catholic priests, advising them as to what it should be safe to tell them and what they should not reveal. And while before the Conquest women had been in charge exclusively of the ceremonies dedicated to female deities, afterwards, they became assistants or principal officiants in cults dedicated to the male-ancestors-huacas — something that before the Conquest had been forbidden (Stern 1982). They also fought the colonial power by withdrawing to the higher planes (*punas*) where they could practice the old religion. As Irene Silverblatt writes:

> While indigenous men often fled the oppression of the *mita* and tribute by abandoning their communities and going to work as *yaconas* (quasi-serfs) in the merging haciendas, women fled to the *punas*, inaccessible and very distant from the *reducciones* of their native communities. Once in the *punas* women rejected the forces and symbols of their oppression, disobeying Spanish administrators, the clergy, as well as their own community officials. They also vigorously rejected the colonial ideology, which reinforced their oppression, refusing to go to Mass, participate in Catholic confessions, or learn catholic dogma. More important, women did not just reject Catholicism; they returned to their native religion and, to the best that they could, to the quality of social relations which their religion expressed (1987: 197).

By persecuting women as witches, then, the Spaniards targeted both the practitioners of the old religion and the instigators of anti-colonial revolt, while attempting to redefine "the spheres of activity in which indigenous women could participate" (Silverblatt 1987: 160). As Silverblatt points out, the concept of witchcraft was alien to Andean society. In Peru as well, as in every pre-industrial society, many women were "specialists in medical knowledge," being familiar with the properties of herbs and plants, and they were also diviners. But the Christian notion of the devil was unknown to them. Nevertheless, by the 17th century, under the impact of torture, intense persecution, and "forced acculturation" the Andean women arrested, mostly old and poor, were accusing themselves of the same crimes with which women were being charged in the European witch trials : pacts and copulation with the devil, prescribing herbal remedies, using ointments, flying through the air, making wax images (Silverblatt 1987: 174). They also confessed to worshipping stones, mountains, and springs, and feeding the *huacas*. Worst of all, they confessed to bewitching the authorities or other men of power and causing them to die (*ibid*. 187–88).

As it was in Europe, torture and terror were used to force the accused to deliver other names so that the circles of the persecution became wider and wider. But one of the objectives of the witch-hunt, the isolation of the witches from the rest of the community, was not achieved. The Andean witches were not turned into outcasts. On the contrary, "they were actively sought for as *comadres* and their presence was required in informal village reunions, for in the consciousness of the colonized, witchcraft, the maintenance of ancient traditions, and conscious political resistance became increasingly intertwined" (*ibid*.). Indeed, it was largely due to women's resistance that the old religion was preserved. Changes occurred in the meaning of the practices associated with it. Worship was driven underground at the expense of its collective nature in pre-conquest times. But the ties with the mountains and the other sites of the *huacas* were not destroyed.

We find a similar situation in Central and Southern Mexico where women, priestesses above all, played an important role in the defense of their communities and cultures. In this region, according to Antonio Garcia de Leon's *Resistencia y Utopia*, from the Conquest on, women "directed or counseled all the great anti-colonial revolts" (de Leon 1985, Vol. 1: 31). In Oaxaca, the presence of women in popular rebellions continued into the 18th century when, in one out of four cases, they led the attack against the authorities "and were visibly more aggressive, insulting, and rebellious" (Taylor 1979: 116). In Chiapas too, they were the key actors in the preservation of the old religion and the anti-colonization struggle. Thus, when, in 1524, the Spaniards launched a war campaign to subjugate the rebellious Chiapanecos, it was a priestess who led the troops against them. Women also participated in the underground networks of idol-worshippers and resisters that periodically were discovered by the clergy. In 1584, for instance, upon visiting Chiapas, the bishop Pedro de Feria was told that several among the local Indian chiefs were still practicing the old cults, and that they were being counseled by women, with whom they entertained filthy practices, such as (sabbat-like) ceremonies during which they mixed together and turned into gods and goddesses, the women being in charge of sending rain and giving wealth to those who asked for it" (de Leon 1985, Vol. 1: 76).

It is ironic, then, in view of this record, that Caliban and not his mother Sycorax, the witch, should be taken by Latin American revolutionaries as a symbol of the resistance to colonization. For Caliban could only fight his master by cursing him in the language he had learned from him, thus being dependent in his rebellion on his "master's tools." He could also be deceived into believing that his liberation could come through a rape and through the initiative of some opportunistic white proletarians transplanted in the New World whom he worshipped as gods. Sycorax, instead, a witch "so strong that she could control the moon, make flows and ebbs" (*The Tempest,* Act V, Scene 1) might have taught her son to appreciate the local powers — the land, the waters, the trees, "nature's treasuries" — and those communal ties that, over centuries of suffering, have continued to nourish the liberation struggle to this day, and that already haunted, as a promise, Caliban's imagination:

> Be not afeard, the isle is full of noises,
> Sounds, and sweet airs, that give delight and hurt not.
> Sometimes a thousand twangling instruments
> Will hum about mine ears; and sometimes voices,
> That if then had wak'd after long sleep.
> Will make me sleep again and then dreaming,
> The clouds methought would open, and show riches
> Ready to drop upon me, that when wak'd
> I cried to dream again (*The Tempest,* Act III).

The European Witches and the "Indios"

Did the witch-hunts in the New World have an impact on events in Europe? Or were the two persecutions simply drawing from the same pool of repressive strategies and tactics which the European ruling class had forged since the Middle Ages with the persecution of the heretics?

I ask these questions having in mind the thesis advanced by the Italian historian Luciano Parinetto, who argues that witch-hunting in the New World had a major impact on the elaboration of the witchcraft ideology in Europe, as well as the chronology of the European witch-hunt.

Briefly put, Parinetto's thesis is that it was under the impact of the American experience that the witch-hunt in Europe became a mass phenomenon in the second part of the 16th century. For in America, the authorities and the clergy found the confirmation for their views about devil-worship, coming to believe in the existence of entire populations of witches, a conviction which they then applied in their Christianization drive at home. Thus, another import from the New World, described by missionaries as "the land of the devil," was the adoption by the European state of *extermination as a political strategy* which, presumably, inspired the massacre of the Huguenots and the massification of the witch-hunt starting in the last decades of the 16th century (Parinetto 1998: 417–35).[15]

Evidence of a crucial connection between the two persecutions is, in Parinetto's view, the use made by the demonologists in Europe of the reports from the Indies. Parinetto focuses on Jean Bodin, but he also mentions Francesco Maria Guazzo and cites, as an example of the "boomerang effect" produced by the transplanting of the witch-hunt in America, the case of the inquisitor Pierre Lancre who, during a several months' persecution in the region of the Labourd (Basque Country), denounced its entire population as witches. Not last, Parinetto cites, as evidence of his thesis, a set of themes that, in the second half of the 16th century, became prominent in the repertoire of witchcraft in Europe: cannibalism, the offering of children to the devil, the reference to ointments and drugs, and the identification of homosexuality (sodomy) with diabolism — all of which, he argues, had their matrix in the New World.

What to make of this theory and where to draw the line between what is accountable and what is speculative? This is a question that future scholarship will have to settle. Here I limit myself to a few observations.

Parinetto's thesis is important since it helps us dispel the Eurocentrism that has characterized the study of the witch-hunt and can potentially answer some of the questions raised by the persecution of the European witches. But its main contribution is that it broadens our awareness of the global character of capitalist development and makes us realize that, by the 16th century, a ruling class had formed in Europe that was at all points involved — practically, politically, and ideologically — in the formation of a world proletariat, and therefore was continually operating with knowledge gathered on an international level in the elaboration of its models of domination.

As for its claims, we can observe that the history of Europe before the Conquest is sufficient proof that the Europeans did not have to cross the oceans to find the will to exterminate those standing in their way. It is also possible to account for the chronology of the witch-hunt in Europe without resorting to the New World impact hypothesis, since the decades between the 1560s and 1620s saw a widespread impoverishment and social dislocations throughout most of western Europe.

More suggestive, in provoking a rethinking of the European witch-hunt from the viewpoint of witch-hunting in America, are the thematic and the iconographic corre-

Top: Francesco Maria Guazzo, COMPENDIUM
MALEFICARUM (Milan, 1608). Guazzo was one of the
demonologists most influenced by the reports from the
Americas. This portrait of witches surrounding the remains of
bodies excavated from the ground or taken from the gallows is
reminiscent of the cannibal banquet.

Bottom: Cannibals preparing their meal. Hans Staden's
WAHRHAFTIGE HISTORIA (Marburg 1557).

Top: Preparation for the Sabbat. German engraving from the 16th century.

Bottom: Preparing a cannibal meal. Hans Staden's WAHRHAFTIGE HISTORIA *(Marburg 1557).*

spondences between the two. The theme of self-ointing is one of the most revealing, as the descriptions of the behavior of the Aztec or Incan priests on the occasion of human sacrifices evoke those found in some demonologies describing the preparations of the witches for the Sabbat. Consider the following passage found in Acosta, which reads the American practice as a perversion of the Christian habit of consecrating priests by anointing them:

> The idol-priests in Mexico oint themselves in the following way. They greased themselves from the feet to the head, including the hair... the substance with which they stained themselves was ordinary tea, because from antiquity it was always an offering to their gods and for this much worshipped... this was their ordinary greasing...except when they went to sacrifice... or went to the caves where they kept their idols when they used a different greasing to give themselves courage....This grease was made of poisonous substances... frogs, salamanders, vipers... with this greasing they could turn into magicians (*brujos*) and speak with the devil (Acosta, pp. 262–63).

The same poisonous brew was presumably spread by the European witches on their bodies (according to their accusers) in order to gain the power to fly to the Sabbat. But it cannot be assumed that this theme was generated in the New World, as references to women making ointments from the blood of toads or children's bones are found already in the 15th-century trials and demonologies.[16] What is plausible, instead, is that the reports from America did revitalize these charges, adding new details and giving more authority to them.

The same consideration may serve to explain the iconographic correspondence between the pictures of the Sabbat and the various representations of the cannibal family and clan that began to appear in Europe in the later 16th century, and it can account for many other "coincidences," such as the fact that both in Europe and America witches were accused of sacrificing children to the devil (see figures pp. 234–5).

Witch–Hunting and Globalization

Witch-hunting in America continued in waves through the end of the 17th century, when the persistence of demographic decline and increased political and economic security on the side of the colonial power-structure combined to put an end to the persecution. Thus, in the same region that had witnessed the great anti-idolatry campaigns of the 16th and 17th centuries, by the 18th, the Inquisition had renounced any attempts to influence the moral and religious beliefs of the population, apparently estimating that they could no longer pose a danger to colonial rule. In the place of the persecution a paternalistic perspective emerged that looked at idolatry and magical practices as the foibles of ignorant people not worthy of being taken into consideration by "la gente de razon" (Behar 1987). From then on, the preoccupation with devil-worshipping would migrate to the developing slave plantations of Brazil, the Caribbean, and North America where (starting with King Philip's Wars), the English settlers justified their massacres of the native American Indians by labeling them as servants of the devil (Williams and Williams Adelman 1978: 143).

The Salem trials were also explained by the local authorities on this ground, with the argument that the New Englanders had settled in the land of the devil. As Cotton Mather wrote, years later, recalling the events in Salem:

> I have met with some strange things... which have made me think that this inexplicable war [i.e., the war made by the spirits of the invisible world against the people of Salem] might have its origins among the Indians whose chief sagamores are well known unto some of our captive to have been horrid sorcerers and hellish conjurers and such as conversed with the demons (ibid. 145).

It is significant, in this context, that the Salem trials were sparked by the divinations of a West Indian slave — Tituba — who was among the first to be arrested, and that the last execution of a witch, in an English-speaking territory, was that of a black slave, Sarah Bassett, killed in Bermuda in 1730 (Daly 1978: 179). By the 18th century, in fact, the witch was becoming an African practitioner of *obeah,* a ritual that the planters feared and demonized as an incitement to rebellion.

Witch hunting did not disappear from the repertoire of the bourgeoisie with the abolition of slavery. On the contrary, the global expansion of capitalism through colonization and Christianization ensured that this persecution would be planted in the body of colonized societies, and, in time, would be carried out by the subjugated communities in their own names and against their own members.

In the 1840s, for instance, a wave of witch-burnings occurred in Western India. More women in this period were burned as witches than in the practice of *sati* (Skaria 1997: 110). These killings occurred in the context of the social crisis caused both by the colonial authorities' attack on the communities living in the forests (among whom women had a far higher degree of power than in the caste societies that dwelled in the plains) and the colonial devaluation of female power, resulting in the decline of the worship of female goddesses (*ibid.* 139–40).

Witch-hunting also took hold in Africa, where it survives today as a key instrument of division in many countries especially those once implicated in the slave trade, like Nigeria and Southern Africa. Here, too, witch-hunting has accompanied the decline in the status of women brought about by the rise of capitalism and the intensifying struggle for resources which, in recent years, has been aggravated by the imposition of the neo-liberal agenda. As a consequence of the life-and-death competition for vanishing resources, scores of women — generally old and poor — have been hunted down in the 1990s in Northern Transvaal, where seventy were burned just in the first four months of 1994. Witch-hunts have also been reported in Kenya, Nigeria, Cameroon, in the 1980s and 1990s, concomitant with the imposition by the International Monetary Fund and the World Bank of the policy of structural adjustment which has led to a new round of enclosures, and caused an unprecedented impoverishment among the population.[17]

The Africanization of the witch is reflected in this caricature of a "petroleuse." Note her unusual earrings, cap, and African features suggesting a kinship between the female communards and the "wild" African women who instilled in the slaves the courage to revolt, haunting the imagination of the French bourgeoisie as an example of political savagery.

In Nigeria, by the 1980s, innocent girls were confessing to having killed dozens of people, while in other African countries petitions were addressed to governments begging them to persecute more strongly the witches. Meanwhile, in South Africa and Brazil older women were murdered by neighbors and kin under the charge of witch-craft. At the same time, a new kind of witch-beliefs is presently developing, resembling that documented by Michael Taussig in Bolivia, whereby poor people suspect the *nouveau riches* of having gained their wealth through illicit, supernatural means, and accuse them of wanting to transform their victims into zombies in order to put them to work (Geschiere and Nyamnjoh 1998: 73–74).

The witch hunts that are presently taking place in Africa or Latin America are rarely reported in Europe and the United States, in the same way as the witch-hunts of the 16th and 17th centuries, for a long time, were of little interest to historians. Even when they are reported their significance is generally missed, so widespread is the belief that such phenomena belong to a far-gone era and have nothing to do with "us."

But if we apply to the present the lessons of the past, we realize that the reappearance of witch-hunting in so many parts of the world in the '80s and '90s is a clear sign of a process of "primitive accumulation," which means that the privatization of land and other communal resources, mass impoverishment, plunder, and the sowing of divisions in once-cohesive communities are again on the world agenda. "If things continue this way" — the elders in a Senegalese village commented to an American anthropologist, expressing their fears for the future — "our children will eat each other." And indeed this is what is accomplished by a witch-hunt, whether it is conducted from above, as a means to criminalize resistance to expropriation, or is conducted from below, as a means to appropriate diminishing resources, as seems to be the case in some parts of Africa today.

In some countries, this process still requires the mobilization of witches, spirits, and devils. But we should not delude ourselves that this is not our concern. As Arthur Miller already saw in his interpretation of the Salem trials, as soon as we strip the persecution of witches from its metaphysical trappings, we recognize in it phenomena that are very close to home.

Endnotes

1. Actually, Sycorax — the witch — has not entered the Latin American revolutionary imagination in the way Caliban has; she is still invisible, in the same way as the struggle of women against colonization has been for a long time. As for Caliban, what he has come to stand for has been well expressed in an influential essay by the Cuban writer Roberto Fernandez Retamar (1989: 5-21).

    "Our symbol is not Ariel... but rather Caliban. This is something that we, the mestizo inhabitants of these same isles where Caliban lived, see with particular clarity. Prospero invaded the islands, killed our ancestors, enslaved Caliban and taught him the language to make himself understood. What else can Caliban do but use the same language — today he has no other — to curse him...? From Tupac Amaru... Toussaint-Louverture, Simone Bolivar... Jose Marti... Fidel Castro... Che Guevara... Frantz Fanon — what is our history, what is our culture, if not the history and culture of Caliban?" (p. 14).

On this topic see also Margaret Paul Joseph who, in *Caliban in Exile* (1992), writes: "Prospero and Caliban thereby provide us with a powerful metaphor for colonialism. An offshoot of this interpretation is the abstract condition of being Caliban, the victim of history, frustrated by the knowledge of utter powerlessness. In Latin America, the name has been adopted in a more positive manner, for Caliban seems to represent the masses who are striving to rise against the oppression of the elite" (1992: 2).

2. Reporting about the island of Hispañola, in his *Historia General de Las Indias* (1551), Francisco Lopez De Gomara could declare with utter certainty that "the main god which they have in this island is the devil," and that the devil lived among women (de Gomara: 49). Similarly, Book V of Acosta's *Historia* (1590), in which Acosta discusses the religion and customs of the inhabitants of Mexico and Peru, is dedicated to the many forms they have of devil-worshipping, including human sacrifices.

3. "The carib/cannibal image," Retamar writes, "contrasts with another one, of the American man present in the writing of Columbus: that of Aruaco of the Greater Antilles — our Taino primarily — whom he describes as peaceful, meek, and even timorous, and cowardly. Both visions of the American aborigene will circulate vertiginously through Europe.... The Taino will be transformed into the paradisiacal inhabitant of a utopic world.... The Carib, on the other hand, will become a cannibal — an anthropophagus, a bestial man situated at the margin of civilization who must be opposed to the very death. But there is less contradiction than might appear at first glance between the two visions." Each image corresponds to a colonial intervention — assuming its right to control the lives of the aborigene population of the Caribbean — which Retamar sees as continuing into the present. Proof of the kinship between these two images, Retamar points out, is the fact that both the gentle Tainos and the ferocious Caribs were exterminated (*ibid*. 6-7).

4. Human sacrifices occupy a large place in Acosta's account of the religious customs of the Incas and Aztecs. He describes how, during some festivities in Peru, even three of four hundred children, from two to four-years-old, were sacrificed — "duro e inhumano spectaculo," in his words. He also describes, among others, the sacrifice of seventy Spanish soldiers captured in battle in Mexico and, like de Gomara, he states, with utter certainty, that these killings were the work of the devil (p. 250ff.).

5. In New England, medical practitioners administered remedies "made from human corpses." Among the most popular, universally recommended as a panacea for every problem, was "Mummy," a remedy prepared with the remains of a corpse dried or embalmed. As for the consumption of human blood, Gordon-Gruber writes that "it was the prerogative of executioners to sell the blood of decapitated criminals. It was given still warm, to epileptics or other customers waiting in crowds at the spot of execution 'cup in hand'." (1988: 407).

6. Walter L. Williams writes:

    [T]he Spanish did not realize why the Indians were wasting away from disease but took it as an indication that it was part of God's plan to wipe out the infidels. Oviedo concluded, "It is not without cause that God permits them to be destroyed. And I have no doubts that for their sins God's going to do away with them very soon." He further reasoned, in a letter to the king condemning the Maya for accepting homosexual behavior: "I wish to mention it in order to declare more strongly the guilt for which God punishes the Indian and the reason why they have not been granted his mercy" (Williams 1986: 138).

7. The theoretical foundation of Sepulveda's argument in favor of the enslavement of the Indians was Aristotle's doctrine of "natural slavery" (Hanke 1970: 16ff).

8. The mine was discovered in 1545, five years before the debate between Las Casas and Sepulveda took place.

9. By the 1550s, the Spanish Crown was so dependent on the American bullion for its survival — needing it to pay the mercenaries that fought its wars — that it was impounding the loads of bullion that arrived with private ships. These usually carried back the money that was set aside by those who had participated in the Conquest and now were preparing to retire in Spain. Thus, for a number of years, a conflict exploded between the expatriates and the Crown which resulted in new legislation limiting the formers' power to accumulate.

10. A powerful description of this resistance is contained in Enrique Mayer's *Tribute to the Household* (1982), which describes the famous *visitas* which the *encomenderos* used to pay to the villages to fix the tribute that each community owed to them and to the Crown. In the mountain villages of the Andes, hours before its arrival, the procession of horsemen was spotted, upon which many youths fled the village, children were rearranged in different homes, and resources were hidden.

11. The name Taki Onqoy describes the dancing trance that possessed the participants in the movement.

12. Philippe Descola writes that among the Achuar, a population living in the upper part of Amazonia, "the necessary condition for effective gardening depends on direct, harmonious, and constant commerce with Nunkui, the tutelary spirit of gardens" (p. 192). This is what every woman does by singing secret songs "from the heart" and magical incantations to the plants and herbs in her garden, urging them to grow (*ibid*. 198). So intimate is the relation between a woman and the spirit protecting her garden that when she dies "her garden follows suit, for, with the exception of her unmarried daughter, no other woman would dare step into such relationship that she had not herself initiated." As for the men, they are "therefore totally incapable of replacing their wives should the need arise.... When a man no longer has any woman (mother, wife, sister or daughter) to cultivate his garden and prepare his food, he has no choice but to kill himself" (Descola 1994: 175).

13. This is the expression used by Michael Taussig in *Shamanism, Colonialism and the Wild Man* (1991) to stress the function of terror in the establishment of colonial hegemony in the Americas:

"Whatever the conclusions we draw about how the hegemony was so speedily effected, we would be unwise to overlook the role of terror. And by this I mean us to think-through-terror, which as well as being a physiological state is also a social one whose special features allow it to serve as a mediator *par excellence* of colonial hegemony: the *space of death* where the Indian, African, and white gave birth to a New World" (p. 5) (italics mine).

Taussig adds, however, that the *space of death* is also a "space of transformation" since "through the experience of coming close to death there well may be a more vivid sense of life; through fear there can come not only growth of self-consciousness but also fragmentation, and then loss of self conforming to authority" (*ibid.*: 7).

14. On the position of women in pre-conquest Mexico and Peru, see respectively June Nash (1978, 1980), Irene Silverblatt (1987), and Maria Rostworowski (2001). Nash discusses the decline of women's power under the Aztecs in correspondence to their transformation from a "kinship based society... to a class-structured empire." She points out that, by the 15th century, as the Aztecs had evolved into a war-driven empire, a rigid sexual division of labor emerged; at the same time, women (of defeated enemies) became "the booty to be shared by the victors" (Nash 1978: 356, 358). Simultaneously, female deities were displaced by male gods — especially the bloodthirsty Huitzilopochtli — although they continued to be worshipped by the common people. Still, "[w]omen in Aztec society had many specializations as independent craft producers of pottery and textiles, and as priestesses, doctors, and merchants. Spanish development policy [instead], as carried out by priest and crown administrators, diverted home production into male-operated craft shops and mills" (*ibid.*).

15. Parinetto writes that the connection between the extermination of the Amerindian "savages" and that of the Huguenots was very clear in the consciousness and literature of the French Protestants after the Night of San Bartholomé, indirectly influencing Montaigne's essays on the cannibals and, in a completely different way, Jean Bodin's association of the European witches with the cannibalistic and sodomitic indios. Quoting French sources, Parinetto argues that this association (between the savage and the Huguenot) climaxed in the last decades of the 16th centuries when the massacres perpetrated by the Spaniards in America (including the slaughter in Florida, in 1565, of thousands of French colonists accused of being Lutherans) became "a widely used political weapon" in the struggle against Spanish dominance (Parinetto 1998: 429–30).

16. I am referring in particular to the trials that were conducted by the Inquisition in the Dauphiné in the 1440s, during which a number of poor people (peasants or shepherds) were accused of cooking children to make magic powders with their bodies (Russell 1972: 217–18); and to the work of the Swabian Dominican Joseph Naider, *Formicarius* (1435), in which we read that witches "cook their children, boil them, eat their flesh and drink the soup that is left in the pot.... From the solid matter they make a magical salve or ointment, the procurement of which is the third reason for child murder" (*ibid.*: 240). Russell points out that "this salve or ointment is one of the most important elements of witchcraft in the fifteenth century and later." (*ibid.*)

17. On "the renewed attention to witchcraft [in Africa,] conceptualized explicitly in relation to modern changes," see the December 1998 issue of the *African Studies Review*, which is dedicated to this topic. In particular, see Diane Ciekawy and Peter Geschiere's "Containing Witchcraft: Conflicting Scenarios in Postcolonial Africa" (*ibid.*: 1–14). Also see Adam Ashforth, *Witchcraft, Violence and Democracy in South Africa* (Chicago: Univ. of Chicago Press, 2005) and the video documentary "Witches in Exile" produced and directed by Allison Berg (California Newsreel, 2005).

Bibliography

Abbott, L.D. (1946). *Masterworks of Economics*. New York: Doubleday.

Accati, L. *et al.* (1980). *Parto e Maternitá: momenti della biografia femminile. Quaderni Storici*/44 Ancona-Roma/Agosto 1980.

Acosta, Joseph El P. (1590). *Historia Natural Y Moral de Las Indias*. Mexico: Fondo de Cultura Economica, 1962 (second revised edition).

Alighieri, Dante. (13xx).*Divina Commedia*. Edited by Mario Craveri. Napoli: Il Girasole, 1990.

Allen, Sally G. and Johanna Hubbs. (1980). "Outrunning Atalanta: Feminine Destiny in Alchemical Transmutation." *Signs: Journal of Women in Culture and Society*,1980,Winter, vol. 6, no. 2, 210–229.

Amariglio, Jack L. (1988). "The Body, Economic Discourse, and Power: An Economist's Introduction to Foucault." *History of Political Economy,* vol. 20, n. 4. Durham, NC: Duke University Press.

Amin, Samir. (1974). *Accumulation on a World Scale: A Critique of the Theory of Underdevelopment.* Vol. 1. New York: Monthly Review Press.

_____. (1976). *Unequal Development. An Essay on the Formation of Peripheral Capitalism*. New York: Monthly Review Press.

Amman, Jost and Hans Sachs. (1568). *The Book of Trades*. New York: Dover, 1973.

Anderson, A. and R. Gordon. (1978)."Witchcraft and the Status of Women: The Case of England." *British Journal of Sociology*. Vol. 29, n. 2, June 1987.

Anderson, Perry. (1974). *Passages From Antiquity to Feudalism*. London: Verso, 1978.

Andreas, Carol. (1985). *When Women Rebel. The Rise of Popular Feminism in Peru*. Westport (CT): Lawrence Hill & Company.

Ankarloo, Bengt and Gustav Henningsen, eds. (1993). *Early Modern European Witchcraft: Centers and Peripheries*. Oxford: Clarendon Press.

Anohesky, Stanislav. (1989). *Syphilis, Puritanism and the Witch-hunt*. New York: St. Martin's Press.

Appleby, Andrew B. (1978). *Famine in Tudor and Stuart England*. Stanford (CA): Stanford University Press.

Ariés, Philippe. (1972). "On the Origin of Contraception in France." In Orest and Patricia Ranum eds., *op.cit.* (1972), 11–20.

Ashforth, Adam. (1995)."Of Secrecy and the Commonplace: Witchcraft and Power in Soweto." Unpublished Manuscript. [APABB@CUNYVM.CUNY. EDU].

____. (1998). "Reflections on Spiritual Insecurity in Soweto." *African Studies Review*. Vol. 41, No. 3, December.

Bacon, Francis. (1870). *The Works of Francis Bacon*. London: Longman.

____.(1870). *The Advancement of Learning*. In Works,Vol.III. London: Longman.

____.(1974). *The Advancement of Learning and New Atlantis*. Oxford: Clarendon Press.

Baden, John A. and Douglas S. Noonan.(1998). *Managing the Commons*. 2nd ed. Bloomington (IN): Indiana University Press.

Badinter, Elizabeth.(1980). *L'Amour en plus. Histoire de l'amour maternel. XVII-XX siècles*. Paris: Flammarion.

_____. (1987). "Maternal Indifference." In Toril Moi, ed., *op.cit.* (1987), 150–178.

Baillet, Adrien. (1691). *La Vie de Monsieur Descartes*. Geneve: Slatkine Reprints, 1970.

Bainton, Roland H. (1965). *Here I Stand: The Life of Martin Luther*. New York: Penguin Books.

Bakhtin, Mikail. (1965). *Rabelais and His World*. (Translated from the Russian). Cambridge, MA: MIT Press.

Bales, Kevin. (1999). *Disposable People: New Slavery in the Global Economy*. Berkeley, University of California Press.

Barber, Malcolm. (1992). *The Two Cities: Medieval Europe 1050–1320*. New York: Routledge.

Barker, Anthony. (1978). *The African Link. British Attitudes to the Negro in the Era of the Atlantic Slave Trade. 1550–1807*. London: Frank Cass, Inc.

Barnes, Barry, and Steven Shapin, eds. (1979). *Natural Order: Historical Studies of Scientific Culture*. Thousand Oaks, CA: Sage.

Baroja, Julio Caro. (1961). *The World of the Witches*. Chicago: University of Chicago Press, 1973.

Barry, J., M. Hester and G. Roberts, eds. (1996). *Witchcraft in Early Modern Europe: Studies in Culture and Belief*. Cambridge: Cambridge University Press.

Bartlett, Robert. (1993). *The Making of Europe: Conquest, Colonization and Cultural Change: 950–1350*. Princeton: Princeton University Press.

Bassermann, Lujo. (1967). *Il Mestiere Piú Antico*. (Translated from the German). Milano: Edizioni Mediterranee.

Barstow, Anne Llewellyn. (1994). *Witchcraze: A New History of the European Witch Hunts, Our Legacy of Violence Against Women*. New York: Pandora HarperCollins.

Baudez, Claude and Sydney Picasso. (1987). *Lost Cities of the Mayas*. New York: Harry N. Abrams, Inc., Publishers, 1992.

Baumann, Reinhard. (1996). *I Lanzichenecchi. La loro storia e cultura dal tardo Medioevo alla Guerra dei trent'anni*. (Translated from the German). Torino: Einaudi.

Baumgartner, Frederic J. (1995). *France in the Sixteenth Century*. New York: St. Martin's Press.

Bayle, Pierre. (1697). *Dictionaire Historique et Critique*. Rotterdam: R. Leers.

_____.(1965). *Historical and Critical Dictionary: Selections*. Edited by Richard H. Popkin. Indianapolis: Bobbs–Merrill.

Beckles, Hilary McD. (1989). *Natural Rebels. A Social History of Enslaved Black Women in Barbados*. New Brunswick (NJ): Rutgers University Press.

Beckles, Hilary. (1995). "Sex and Gender in the Historiography of Caribbean Slavery." In Shepherd, Brereton, and Bailey, eds. *op. cit.*, (1995), 125–140.

Beckles, Hilary and Verene Shepherd eds. (1991). *Caribbean Slave Society and Economy: A Student Reader*. New York: The New Press.

Becker Cantarino, Barbara. (1994). "'Feminist Consciousness' and 'Wicked Witches': Recent Studies on Women in Early Modern Europe." *Signs: Journal of Women in Culture and Society*, 1994, vol. 20, no. 11 .

Beer, Barrett L. (1982). *Rebellion and Riot: Popular Disorder in England During the Reign of Edward VI*. Kent (OH): The Kent State University Press.

Beier, A. L. (1974). "Vagrants and the Social Order in Elizabethan England." *Past and Present*, no. 64, August, 3–29.

_____.(1986). *Masterless Men. The Vagrancy Problem in England, 1560–1640*. London: Methuen.

Behar, Ruth. (1987). "Sex and Sin, Witchcraft and the Devil in Late-Colonial Mexico." *American Ethnologist*. Vol. 14, no.1, February, 34–54.

Beloff, Max. (1962). *The Age of Absolutism: 1660–1815*. New York: Harper and Row.

Bennett, H. S. (1937). *Life on the English Manor. A Study of Peasant Conditions. 1150–1400*. Cambridge: Cambridge University Press, 1967.

Bennett, Judith M. (1988). "Public Power and Authority in the Medieval English Countryside." In Erler and Kowaleski, eds., *op. cit.,* (1988).

_____. *et al.*, eds. (1976). *Sisters and Workers in the Middle Ages*. Chicago: The University of Chicago Press.

Benzoni, Girolamo. (1565). *La Historia del Mondo Nuovo*. (Venezia). Milano 1965.

Bercé, Yves-Marie. (1986). *History of Peasant Revolts: The Social Origins of Rebellion in Early Modern France*. (Translated from the French). Ithaca (NY): Cornell University Press, 1990.

Birrell, Jean. (1987). "Common Rights in the Medieval Forest: Disputes and Conflicts in the Thirteenth Century." *Past and Present,* no. 117, November, 22–49.

Black, George F. (1938). *A Calendar of Cases of Witchcraft in Scotland, 1510–1727*. (1971 edition). New York: Arno Press Inc.

Blaut, J. M. (1992). *1492. The Debate on Colonialism, Eurocentrism and History*. Trenton (NJ): Africa World Press.

—. (1992a). "1492." In Blaut (1992), pp. 1–63.

Blickle, Peter. (1977). *The Revolution of 1525: The German Peasant War From a New Perspective*. (Translated from the German). Baltimore: John Hopkins University Press.

Blok, Petrus Johannes. (1898). *History of the People of the Netherlands: Part 1. From the Earliest Times to the Beginning of the Fifteenth Century*. New York: G. P. Putnam's Sons.

Bloom, Harold, ed. (1988). *William Shakespeare. The Tempest*. New York: Chelsea House Publishers.

Boas, George. (1966). *The Happy Beast*. New York: Octagon Books.

Bodin, Jean. (1577). *La République*. Paris.

___. (1992). *The Six Books of a Commonwealth*. Cambridge: Cambridge University Press.

Boguet, Henry. (1603). *An Examen of Witches.* (Translated from the French). Edited by Rev. Montague Summers. New York: Barnes and Noble, 1971.

Boime, Albert. (1995). *Art and the French Commune: Imagining Paris After War and Revolution*. Princeton: Princeton University Press.

Boissonnade, P. (1927). *Life and Work in Medieval Europe.* New York: Alfred A. Knopf.

Bolton, J. L. (1980). *The Medieval English Economy. 1150–1500*. London: J. M. Dent & Sons Ltd., 1987.

Bono, Salvatore. (1999). *Schiavi Mussulmani nell'Italia Moderna. Galeotti, Vú cumpra, domestici*. Napoli: Edizioni Scientifiche Italiane.

Bordo, Susan. (1993). *Unbearable Weight: Feminism, Western Culture and the Body*. Berkeley: University of California Press.

Bosco, Giovanna and Patrizia Castelli, eds. (1996). *Stregoneria e Streghe nell'Europa Moderna*. Convegno Internazionale di Studi, Pisa 24–26 Marzo 1994. Pisa: Biblioteca Universitari di Pisa.

Bostridge, Ian. (1997). *Witchcraft and Its Transformations, 1650–1750*. Oxford: Clarendon Press.

Boswell, John. (1980). *Christian Tolerance and Homosexuality: Gay People in Western Europe from the Beginning of the Christian Era to the Fourteenth Century*. Chicago: Chicago University Press.

Botero, Giovanni. (1588). *Delle cause della grandezza delle città*. Roma.

Bottomore, Tom, ed. (1991). *A Dictionary of Marxist Thought*. Oxford: Basil Blackwell.

Bovenschen, Silvia. (1978). "The Contemporary Witch, the Historical Witch and the Witch Myth." *New German Critique*. no.15, Fall, 83ff.

Bowle, John. (1952). *Hobbes and His Critics: A Study in Seventeenth Century Constitutionalism*. London: Oxford University Press.

Boxer, C. R. (1962). *The Golden Age of Brazil: 1965–1750*. Berkeley: University of California Press.

Bradley, Harriett. (1918). *The Enclosures in England: An Economic Reconstruction*. New York: AMS Press, 1968.

Braidotti, Rosi. (1991). *Patterns of Dissonance. A Study of Women in Contemporary Philosophy*. New York: Routledge.

Brandon, William. (1986). *New Worlds For Old: Reports from the New World and their Effect on the Development of Social Thought in Europe, 1500–1800*. Athens: Ohio University Press.

Braudel, Fernand. (1949). *The Mediterranean and the Mediterranean World in the Age of Philip the II*. Volume I and II. (Translated from the French). New York: Harper and Row, 1966.

———. (1967). *Capitalism and Material Life, 1400–1800*. (Translated from the French). New York: Harper and Row, 1973.

———. (1979). *The Wheels of Commerce: Civilization and Capitalism, 15th–18th Century*. Vol. 2. New York: Harper and Row, 1982.

Brauner, Sigrid. (1995). *Fearless Wives and Frightened Shrews: The Construction of the Witch in Early Modern Germany*. Edited with an Introduction by Robert H. Brown. Amherst: University of Massachusetts Press.

Brenner, Robert. (1982). "Agrarian Roots of European Capitalism." *Past and Present*. no.97, November, 16-113.

Brian and Pullan, eds. (1968). *Crisis and Change in the Venetian Economy in the Sixteenth and Seventeenth Century*. London: Methuen.

Bridenthal, Renate and Claudia Koonz eds. (1977). *Becoming Visible: Women in European History*. New York: Houghton Mifflin Co.

Briggs, K.M. (1962). *Pale Ecate's Team*. London: Routledge and Kegan Paul.

Briggs, Robin. (1996). *Witches and Neighbours: The Social and Cultural Context of European Witchcraft*. London: Penguin.

Brink, Jean R., et al., eds. (1989). *The Politics of Gender in Early Modern Europe*. Vol. 12 of *Sixteenth Century Essays and Studies*. Edited by Charles G. Nauert, Jr. Kirksville (MO): Sixteenth Century Journal Publishers, Inc.

Britnell, R. H. (1993). *The Commercialization of English Society, 1000–1500*. Cambridge: Cambridge University Press.

Brown, Judith and Robert C. Davis, eds. (1998). *Gender and Society in Renaissance Italy*. New York: Longman.

Brown, Paul. (1988). "'This Thing of Darkness I Acknowledge Mine': *The Tempest* and The Discourse of Colonialism." In Bloom, *op. cit.*, (1988), 131-152.

Browne, Thomas Sir. (1643). *Religio Medici*. London: J. M. Dent & Sons, 1928.

Browning, Robert. (1975). *Byzantium and Bulgaria: A Comparative Study Across the Early Medieval Frontier*. Berkeley: University of California Press.

Brundage, James. (1987). *Love, Sex and Christian Society in Medieval Europe*. Chicago: Chicago University Press.

Brunner, Otto. (1974). "Il Padre Signore." In Manoukian ed., *op. cit.*, (1974), 126–143.

Buenaventura-Posso, Elisa and Susan E. Brown. (1980). "Forced Transition from Egalitarianism to Male Dominance: The Bari of Columbia." In Etienne and Leacock, eds. *op. cit.*, (1980).

Bullough, Vern L. (1976). *Sex, Society, and History*. New York: Science History Publications.

Bullough, Vern and Bonnie Bullough. (1993). *Crossdressing, Sex and Gender*. Philadelphia: University of Pennsylvania Press.

Burguière, André, *et al.* (1996). *A History of the Family. Volume Two. The Impact of Modernity*. Cambridge (Mass): Harvard University Press.

——. and François Lebrun. (1996). "Priests, Prince and Family." In Burguière, et al. op. *cit.*, (1996), 96–160.

Burke, Peter. (1978). *Popular Culture in Early Modern Europe*. New York: New York University Press.

____. ed. (1979). *The New Cambridge Modern History Supplement*. Cambridge: Cambridge University Press.

Burkhardt, Jacob. (1927). *La Civiltá del Rinascimento in Italia*, Vol. 2. (Translated from the German). Firenze: Sansoni.

Burt, Richard and John Michael Archer, eds. (1994). *Enclosures Acts. Sexuality, Property, and Culture in Early Modern England*. Ithaca (NY): Cornell University Press.

Burton, Robert. (1621). *The Anatomy of Melancholy. What It Is, With All The Kinds, Causes, Symptomes, Prognostickes & Severall Cures Of It*. New York: Random House, 1977.

Bush, Barbara. (1990). *Slave Women in Caribbean Society: 1650–1838*. Bloomington (IN): Indiana University Press.

Butler, Judith. (1999). *Gender Trouble. Feminism and the Subversion of Identity*. New York: Routledge.

Byrne, Patrick. (1967). *Witchcraft in Ireland*. Cork: The Mercier Press.

Caffentzis, George. (1989). *Clipped Coins, Abused Words and Civil Government: John Locke's Philosophy of Money*. New York: Autonomedia.

____. (2001). "From Capitalist Crisis to Proletarian Slavery. " In Midnight Notes, eds. (2001).

Camden, Carol. (1952). *The Elizabethan Woman*. New York: Elsevier Press.

Campbell, Josie P. (1986). *Popular Culture in the Middle Ages*. Bowling Green (Ohio): Bowling Green University Popular Press.

Campbell, Mavis C. (1990). *The Maroons of Jamaica, 1655–1796*. Trenton (NJ): Africa World Press.

Capitani, Ovidio, ed. (1971). *L'eresia Medievale*. Bologna: Il Mulino.

____, ed. (1974). *La Concezione della povertá nel medioevo*. Bologna: Patron.

____, ed. (1983). *Medioevo Ereticale*. Bologna: Il Mulino.

Cardini, Franco, ed. (1989). *Gostanza, la strega di San Miniato*. Firenze: Laterza.

Carroll, William C. (1994). "The Nursery of Beggary: Enclosure; Vagrancy; and Sedition in the Tudor-Stuart Period." In Burt, Richard and John Michael Archer, eds., *op.cit.*, (1994).

Carus, Paul. (1990). *The History of the Devil and the Idea of Evil*. La Salle, Illinois: Open Court Publishing House.

Casagrande, Carla ed. (1978). *Prediche alle donne del secolo XIII*. Milano: Bompiani.

Cavallo, S. and S. Cerutti. (1980). "Onore femminile e controllo sociale della riproduzione in Piemonte tra Sei e Settecento." In L. Accati ed., *op.cit.*, (1980), 346–83.

Cervantes, Fernando. (1994). *The Devil in the New World. The Impact of Diabolism in New Spain*. New Haven: Yale University Press.

Chaucer, Geoffrey. (1386-1387). *The Canterbury Tales*. London: Penguin 1977.

Chejne, Anwar G. (1983). *Islam and the West. The Moriscos*. Albany: State University Press.

Christiansen, Rupert. (1994). *Paris Babylon: The Story of the Paris Commune*. New York: Viking.

Christie-Murray, David. (1976). *A History of Heresy.* Oxford: Oxford University Press.

Ciekawi, Diane and Peter Geschiere. (1998). "Containing Witchcraft: Conflicting Scenarios in Postcolonial Africa." In *African Studies Review.* vol. 41, Number 3, December, 1-14.

Cipolla, Carlo M. (1968). "The Economic Decline in Italy." In Brian and Pullan, eds., *op. cit.,* (1968).

————. (1994). *Before the Industrial Revolution: European Society and Economy 1000–1700.* (Third edition). New York: W.W. Norton.

Clark, Alice. (1919). *The Working Life of Women in 17th Century England.* London: Frank Cass and Co., 1968.

Clark, Stuart. (1980). "Inversion, Misrule and the Meaning of Witchcraft." *Past and Present.* no. 87, May, 98-127.

Clendinnen, Inga. (1987). *Ambivalent Conquest: Maya and Spaniards in Yucatan, 1517–1570.* Cambridge: Cambridge University Press.

Cockcroft, James D. (1990). *Mexico: Class Formation, Capital Accumulation, and the State.* New York: Monthly Review Press.

Cohen, Esther. (1986). "Law, Folklore and Animal Lore." *Past and Present.* no.110, February, 6-37.

Cohen, Mitchel. (1998). "Fredy Perlman: Out in Front of a Dozen Dead Oceans." (Unpublished Manuscript).

Cohn, Norman. (1970). *The Pursuit of the Millennium.* New York: Oxford University Press.

————. (1975). *Europe's Inner Demons.* New York: Basic Books.

Cohn, Samuel K., Jr. (1981). "Donne in Piazza e donne in tribunal a Firenze nel Rinascimento." *Studi Storici,* July–September 1981, 3, Anno 22, 515–33.

Colburn, Forrest D., ed. (1989). *Everyday Forms of Peasant Resistance.* New York: M. E. Sharpe, Inc.

The Commoner. A Web Journal For Other Values. www.commoner.org.uk

Condé, Maryse. (1992). *I, Tituba, Black Witch of Salem.* (Translated from the the French.) New York: Ballantine Books.

Condren, Mary. (1989). *The Serpent and the Goddess: Women, Religion, and Power in Celtic Ireland.* San Francisco: Harper & Row Publishers.

Cook, Noble David. (1981). *Demographic Collapse. Indian Peru, 1520–1620.* Cambridge: Cambridge University Press.

Cooper, J. P., ed. (1970). *The New Cambridge Modern History. Vol. IV. The Decline of Spain and Thirty Years' War, 1609–1649.* Cambridge: Cambridge University Press.

Cornwall, Julian. (1977). *Revolt of the Peasantry, 1549.* London: Routledge & Kegan Paul

Cornej, Peter. (1993). *Les Fondements de l'Histoire Tcheque.* Prague: PBtisk.

Coudert, Allison P. (1989). "The Myth of the Improved Status of Protestant Women." In Brink *et al.* eds., *op. cit.,* (1989).

Couliano, Ioan P. (1987). *Eros and Magic in the Renaissance.* Chicago: University of Chicago Press.

Coulton, G. G. (1955). *Medieval Panorama: The English Scene from Conquest to Reformation.* New York: The Noonday Press.

Cousin, Victor. (1824-26). *Ouvres de Descartes.* Paris: F. G. Levrault

Crosby, Alfred W., Jr. (1972). *The Columbian Exchange. Biological and Cultural Consequences of 1492.* Westport (CT): Greenwood Press. Inc.

Crown, William. (1983). *Changes in the Land. Indians, Colonists, and the Ecology of New England.* New York: Hill and Wang.

Cullen, Michael J. (1975). *The Statistical Movement in Early Victorian Britain. The Foundations of*

Empirical Social Research. New York: Barnes and Noble.

Cunningham, Andrew and Ole Peter Grell. (2000). *The Four Horsemen of the Apocalypse. Religion, War, Famine and Death in Reformation Europe.* Cambridge: Cambridge University Press.

Curtis, Bruce. (2002). "Foucault on Governmentality and Population: The Impossible Discovery." *Canadian Journal of Sociology* 27, 4 (Fall), 505–533.

Dale, Marian K. (1933). "The London Silkwomen of the Fifteenth Century." *Signs, Journal of Women in Culture and Society,* vol. 14, no. 21, Winter 1989, 489–501.

Dalla Costa, Giovanna Franca. (1978). *The Work of Love. Unpaid Housework, Poverty and Sexual Violence at the Dawn of the 21st Century.* (Translated from the Italian). New York: Autonomedia, 2004.

Dalla Costa, Mariarosa. (1972). *Potere Femminile e Sovversione Sociale.* Venezia: Marsilio Editori.

_____. (1995). "Capitalismo e Riproduzione." In *Capitalismo, Natura, Socialismo,* N. 1, 124-135.

_____. (1998). "The Native in Us. The Earth We Belong To." *Common Sense,* 23, 14-52.

Dalla Costa, M. and James, S. (1975). *The Power of Women and the Subversion of the Community.* Bristol: Falling Wall Press.

Daly, Mary. (1978). *Gyn/Ecology: The MetaEthics of Radical Feminism.* Boston: Beacon.

Davis, Robert. (1998). "The Geography of Gender in the Renaissance." In Judith C. Brown & Robert C. Davis, eds., *op. cit.,* (1998).

De Angelis, Massimo. (2001). "Marx and Primitive Accumulation: The Continuous Character of Capital's Enclosures." In *The Commoner.* no.2, September, www.thecommoner.org.uk

de Givry, Grillot. (1971). *Witchcraft, Magic and Alchemy.* (Translated from the French. New York: Dover Publications, Inc.

De Gomara, Francisco Lopez. (1556). *Historia General de Las Indias.* Barcelona: Editorial Iberia, 1954.

De Las Casas, Bartolomé. (1552). *A Short Account of the Destruction of the Indies.* New York: Penguin Books, 1992.

De Leon, Antonio Garcia. (1985). *Resistencia y Utopia.* Vols. 1 and 2. Mexico D.F.: Ediciones Era.

Demetz, Peter. (1997). *Prague in Black and Gold: Scenes from the Life of a European City.* New York: Hill and Wang.

Descartes, René. (1824-1826). *Ouvres de Descartes.* Volume 7. Correspondence. Published by Victor Cousin. Paris: F.G. Levrault.

_____. (1637). "Discourse on Method." In *Philosophical Works,* Vol. I.

_____. (1641). "Meditations." In *Philosophical Works,* Vol. I

_____. (1650). "Passions of the Soul." In *Philosophical Works,* Vol. I

_____. (1664). "Le Monde"

_____. (1640). *Treatise of Man* (Translated from the French and commented by Thomas Steele Hall. Cambridge (Mass): Harvard University Press, 1972

_____. (1973). *Philosophical Works of Descartes.* Vols. I & II. (Translated from the French by E.S. Haldane and G.R.T. Ross). Cambridge: Cambridge University Press.

Descola, Philippe. (1994). *In the Society of Nature: A Native Ecology in Amazonia.* (Translated from the French). Cambridge: Cambridge University Press.

De Vries, Jean. (1976). *The Economy of Europe in an Age of Crisis, 1660–1750.* Cambridge: Cambridge University Press.

Dickson, David. (1979). "Science and Political Hegemony in the 17th Century." *Radical Science Journal.* No. 8, 7–39.

Dingwall, E. G. (1931). *The Girdle of Chastity.* London: Routledge and Sons.

De Stefano, Antonino. (1950). "Le Eresie Popolari nel Medioevo." In Ettore Rota ed., *op. cit.*, (1950).

Di Nola, Alfonso. (1999). *Il Diavolo: La Forma, la storia, le vicende di Satana e la sua universale e malefica...* Roma: Newton and Compton Editore.

Dobb, Maurice. (1947). *Studies in the Development of Capitalism.* New York: International Publishers.

Dobson, R. B. (1983). *The Peasant Revolt of 1381.* London. Macmillan.

Dockes, Pierre. (1982). *Medieval Slavery and Liberation* (Translated from the French). London: Methuen.

Dodgshon, Robert A. (1998). *From Chiefs to Landlords: Social Economic Change in the Western Highlands and Islands, c.1493–1820.* Edinburgh: Edinburgh University Press.

Douglass, C. North and Robert Paul Thomas. (1973). *The Rise of the Western World: A New Economic History.* Cambridge: Cambridge University Press.

Duby, Georges and Jacques Le Goff. (1981). *Famiglia e parentela nell'Italia medievale.* Bologna: Il Mulino.

Duby, Georges. (1988). *Love and Marriage in the Middle Ages.* Chicago: University of Chicago Press.

Duerr, Hans Peter. (1988). *Nuditá e Vergogna. Il Mito del Processo di Civilizazzione.* (Translated from the German). Venezia: Marsilio Editori, 1991.

Dunn, Richard S. (1970). *The Age of Religious Wars. 1559–1715.* New York: W.W. Norton & Company, Inc.

Dupaquier, Jacques. (1979). "Population." In Burke ed., *op.cit.*, (1979).

Duplessis, Robert S. (1997). *Transitions to Capitalism in Early Modern Europe.* Cambridge: Cambridge University Press.

Dyer, Christopher. (1968). "A Redistribution of Income in XVth Century England." *Past and Present,* no. 39, April, 11–33.

————. (1989). *Standards of Living in the Later Middle Ages: Social Change in England. 1200–1320.* Cambridge University Press.

[The] Ecologist. (1993). *Whose Common Future? Reclaiming the Commons.* Philadelphia (PA): New Society Publishers in cooperation with Earth-scan Publications Ltd.

Easlea, Brian. (1980). *Witch-Hunting, Magic and the New Philosophy. An Introduction to the Debates of the Scientific Revolution.* Brighton (Sussex): The Harvester Press.

Ehrenreich, Barbara and Deirdre English. (1973). *Witches, Midwives and Nurses. A History of Women Healers.* Old Westbury, NY: The Feminist Press.

Elias, Norbert. (1939). *The Civilizing Process. The History of Manners.* (Translated from the German). New York: Urizen Books, 1978.

Elton, G. R. (1972). *Policy and Police.* Cambridge: Cambridge University Press.

Engels, Frederich. (1870). *The Peasant War in Germany.* Moscow: Progress Publishers, 1977.

————. (1884). *The Origin of the Family, Private Property, and the State.* New York: International Publishers, 1942.

Ennen, Edith. (1986). *Le donne nel Medioevo.* (Translated from the German). Bari: Laterza.

Erasmus, Desiderius. (1511). *The Praise of Folly.* (Translated from the Latin) New York: Modern Library, 1941.

Erbstosser, Martin. (1984). *Heretics in the Middle Ages* (Translated from the German). Edition Leipzig.

Erhard, Jean. (1963). *L'Idée de Nature en France dans la première moitiée de XVIII siècle.* Paris: Ecole

Pratique de Haute Etudes.

Erler, Mary and Maryanne Kowaleski, eds. (1988). *Women and Power in the Middles Ages.* Athens, Georgia: University of Georgia Press.

Etienne, Mona and Eleanor Leacock, eds. (1980). *Women and Colonization: Anthropological Perspectives.* New York: Praeger.

Evans, Richard J. (1996). *Rituals of Retribution: Capital Punishment in Germany, 1600–1987.* Oxford: Oxford University Press.

Farge, Arlette. (1987). "Women's History: An Overview." In Toril Moi, ed., *op. cit.,* (1987), 133-149.

Fauré, Christine. (1981). "Absent from History." (Translated from the French). *Signs: Journal of Women in Culture and Society,* vol. 7, no.1, 71-80.

Federici, Silvia and Leopoldina Fortunati. (1984). *Il Grande Calibano. Storia del corpo sociale ribelle nella prima fase del capitale.* Milano: FrancoAngeli Editore.

Federici, Silvia. (1975). "Wages Against Housework." In Malos ed., *op.cit.,* (1980), 187-194.

_____. (1988). "The Great Witch-Hunt." In *Maine Scholar,* Vol. 1, no.1, Autumn, 31-52.

_____. ed. (1995). *Enduring Western Civilization. The Construction of the Concept of the West and its 'Others'.* Westport(CT): Praeger.

Ferrari, Giovanna. (1987). "Public Anatomy Lessons and the Carnival: The Anatomy Theatre of Bologna." *Past and Present.* no.117, November, 50–106.

Firpo, Luigi, ed. (1972). *Medicina Medievale.* Torino: UTET.

Fischer, David Hackett. (1996). *The Great Wave: Price Revolutions and the Rhythm of History.* Oxford: Oxford University Press.

Fisher, F. J., ed. (1961). *Essays in the Economic and Social History of Tudor and Stuart England, in Honor of R.H. Tawney.* Cambridge: Cambridge University Press.

Flandrin, Jean Louis. (1976). *Families in Former Times. Kinship, Household and Sexuality.* (Translated from the French). Cambridge: Cambridge University Press, 1979.

Fletcher, Anthony. (1973). *Tudor Rebellions* (2nd edition). London: Longman.

Fletcher, Anthony & John Stevenson, eds. (1985). *Order and Disorder in Early Modern England.* Cambridge: Cambridge University Press.

Fletcher, Robert. (1896). "The Witches' Pharmakopeia." In *Bulletin of the Johns Hopkins Hospital,* Baltimore, August 1896, Vol. VII, No. 65, 147–56.

Foner, Philip S. (1947). *History of the Labor Movement in the United States.* Vol. 1. *From Colonial Times to the Founding of the American Federation of Labor.* New York: International Publishers.

Fontaine, Nicholas. (1738). *Mèmoires pour servir á l'histoire de Port-Royal.*

Ford, John. (1633). "Tis a Pity She's a Whore." In *Webster and Ford: Selected Plays.* London: Everyman's Library, 1964.

Forman Crane, Elaine. (1990). "The Socioeconomics of a Female Majority in Eighteenth-Century Bermuda." *Signs, Journal of Women in Culture and Society,* vol. 15, no. 2, Winter, 231–258.

Fortunati, Leopoldina. (1981). *L'Arcano della Riproduzione. Casalinghe, Prostitute, Operai e Capitale.* Venezia: Marsilio Editori.

——. (1995). *The Arcane of Reproduction: Housework, Prostitution, Labor and Capital.* Brooklyn: Autonomedia.

_____. (1984). "La ridefinizione della donna." In Federici and Fortunati, *op. cit.,* (1984).

Foucault, Michel. (1961). *Madness and Civilization. A History of Insanity in the Age of Reason.*

(Translated from the French). New York: Random House, 1973.

____. (1966). *The Order of Things: An Archeology of the Human Sciences.* (Translated from the French). New York: Vintage Books, 1970.

____. (1969). *The Archeology of Knowledge & The Discourse On Language.* (Translated from the French). New York: Routledge, 1972.

____. (1975). *Discipline and Punish: The Birth of the Prison.* (Translated from the French). New York: Vintage Books, 1977).

____. (1976). *The History of Sexuality.* Vol. 1: *An Introduction.* (Translated from the French). New York: Random House, 1978.

____. (1997). *The Politics of Truth.* ed. by Sylvère Lotringer. New York: Semiotext(e).

Fox, Sally. (1985). *Medieval Women: An Illuminated Book of Days.* New York: Little, Brown and Co.

Fraser, Antonia. (1984). *The Weaker Vessel.* New York: Alfred Knopf.

Fryde, E. D. (1996). *Peasants and Landlords in Later Medieval England.* New York: St. Martin's Press.

Furniss, Edgar. (1957). *The Position of the Laborer in a System of Nationalism.* New York: Kelly and Millan.

Galzigna, Mario. (1978). "La Fabbrica del Corpo." *Aut-Aut* (Milano), No. 167–68, September–December, 153–74.

Garrett, Clarke. (1977). "Women and Witches: Patterns of Analysis." *Signs, Journal of Women in Culture and Society.* (Winter), 1977.

Gatrell, V. A. C. *et al.* eds. (1980). *Crime and the Law: The Social History of Crime in Western Europe Since 1500.* London: Europe Publications.

Geis, Gilbert and Ivan Bunn. (1997). *A Trial of Witches. A Seventeenth-century Witchcraft Prosecution.* New York: Routledge.

Gelis, Jacques. (1977). "Sages femmes et accoucheurs, l'obstetrique populaire au XVIIème et XVIIIème siècles." *Annales,* no. 32, July–December.

Gerbi, Antonello. (1985). *Nature in the New World: From Christopher Colombus to Gonzalo Fernandez de Oviedo.* (Translated from the Italian). Pittsburgh: University of Pittsburgh Press.

Geremek, Bronislaw. (1985). *Mendicanti e Miserabili Nell'Europa Moderna. (1350–1600).* Roma: Istituto dell' Enciclopedia Italiana Treccani.

____. (1987). *The Margins of Medieval Society.* Cambridge: Cambridge University Press.

____. (1988). *La Stirpe di Caino. L'immagine dei vagabondi e dei poveri nelle letterature europee dal XV al XVII secolo.* Milano: Il Saggiatore.

____. (1994). *Poverty. A History.* Oxford: Basil Blackwell. (Translated from the Polish).

Gert, Bernard, ed. (1978). *Man and Citizen —Thomas Hobbes.* Gloucester, MA.

Geschiere, Peter and Francis Nyamnjoh. (1998). "Witchcraft as an Issue in the 'Politics of Belonging': Democratization and Urban Migrants' Involvement with the Home Village." *African Studies Review,* Vol. 49, N. 3, December 1998, 69–91.

Gilboy, Elizabeth. (1934). *Wages in Eighteenth-Century England.* Cambridge (MA): Harvard University Press.

Ginzburg, Carlo. (1966). *I Benandanti.* Torino: Einaudi.

____. (1991). *Ecstasies. Deciphering the Witches' Sabbath.* (Translated from the Italian). New York: Pantheon.

Glanvil, Joseph. (1661). *The Vanity of Dogmatizing: The Three "Versions."* Introduction by Stephen Medcalf. Hove (Sussex): Harvester Press, 1970.

Glass, D. V. and Everseley, D. E. C., eds. (1965). *Population in History.* Chicago: University of

Chicago Press.

Goetz, Hans-Werner. (1986). *Life in the Middle Ages.* London: University of Notre Dame Press.

Goldberge, Jonathan. (1992). *Sodometries. Renaissance Texts, Modern Sexualities.* Stanford (CA): Stanford University Press.

Goodare, Julian, ed. (2002). *The Scottish Witch-hunt in Context.* Manchester: Manchester University Press.

Gordon-Grube, Karen. (1988). "Anthropophagy in Post-Renaissance Europe: The Tradition of Medical Cannibalism." *American Anthropologist Research Reports.* [90], 405–08.

Gosse, Edmund. (1905). *Sir Thomas Browne.* London: The Macmillan Company.

Gottfried, Johann Ludwig. (1630). *Le Livre des Antipodes.* Paris: Maspero, 1981.

Gottliebe, Beatrice. (1993). *Family in the Western World: From the Black Death to the Industrial Age.* Oxford: Oxford University Press.

Goubert, Jean. (1977). "L'Art de Guerir: medicine savante et medicine populaire dans la France de 1790." *Annales,* no.32, July–December.

Goubert, Pierre. (1982). *The French Peasantry in the Seventeenth Century.* (Translated from the French). London: Cambridge University Press.

Graus, Frantisek. (1967). "Social Utopia in the Middle Ages." *Past and Present.* no. 38, December, 3–19.

Greaves, Richard L., *et al.* (1992). *Civilizations of the West. Vol. I: From Antiquity to 1715.* New York: HarperCollins.

___. (1992). *Civilizations of the West. Vol. 2. From 1660 to the Present.* New York: HarperCollins.

Green, Monica. (1989). "Women's Medical Practice and Healthcare in Medieval Europe." *Signs: Journal of Women in Culture and Society,* vol.14, no.2, Winter, 434-473.

Gregory, Annabel. (1991). "Witchcraft, Politics and 'Good Neighborhood' in Early Seventeenth-Century Rye." *Past and Present,* no.133, November, 31-66.

Greven, Philip. (1977). *The Protestant Temperament. Patterns of Child-Raising, Religious Experience, and the Self in Early America.* New York: Alfred Knopf.

Griffin, Susan. (1978). *Women and Nature. The Roaring Inside Her.* San Francisco: Sierra Club.

Guillaumin, Colette. (1995). *Racism, Sexism, Power and Ideology.* New York: Routledge.

Guaman Poma de Ayala, Felipe. (1615). *Nueva Chrónica y Buen Gobierno.* Paris: Institut d'Ethnologie, 1936.

Guazzo, Francesco-Maria. (1608). *Compendium Maleficarum.* Edited by Montague Summers. New York: Barnes and Nobles, 1970. (First edition 1929).

Gunder Frank, André (1978). *World Accumulation, 1492–1789.* New York: Monthly Review Press.

Hacker, Barton C. (1981). "Women and Military Institutions in Early Modern Europe: A Reconnaissance." *Signs, Journal of Women in Culture and Society,* vol. 6, no. 41, Summer, 643–71.

Hamilton, Earl J. (1965). *American Treasure and the Price Revolution in Spain, 1501–1650.* New York: Octagon Books.

Hanawalt, Barbara A. (1986a). "Peasants Resistance to Royal and Seignorial Impositions." In F. Newman, ed., *op. cit.,* (1986), 23–49.

___. (1986b). *The Ties That Bound: Peasant Families in Medieval England.* Oxford: Oxford University Press.

___. (1986c). "Peasant Women's Contribution to the Home Economy in Late Medieval

England." In Barbara Hanawalt (1986d).

___.(1986d). *Women and Work in Pre-industrial Europe.* Bloomington (Indiana): Indiana University Press.

Hanke, Lewis. (1970). *Aristotle and the American Indians: A Study in Race Prejudice in the Modern World.* Bloomington: Indiana University Press. (First edition 1959).

Hardin, Garrett. (1968). "The Tragedy of the Commons." *Science* 162, 1243-48.

Harris, Marvin. (1974). *Cows, Pigs and Witches.* New York: Random House.

Hart, Roger. (1971). *Witchcraft.* New York: G. Putnam's Sons.

Harvey, P. D. A. (1973). "The English Inflation: 1180–1220." *Past and Present*, no 61, November.

Harvey, William. (1961). *Lectures on the Whole of Anatomy.* Berkeley: University of California Press.

Hatcher, John. (1977). *Plague, Population and the English Economy, 1348–1530.* New York: Macmillan.

___. (1994). "England in the Aftermath of the Black Death." *Past and Present.* no.144, August, 3–36.

Hay, Douglas. (1975). "Property, Authority and the Criminal Law." In Hay *et al., op. cit.,* (1975),17–63.

___, et al. (1975). *Albion's Fatal Tree: Crime and Society in 18th Century England.* New York: Pantheon Books.

Heckscher, Eli J. (1965). *Mercantilism,*Vol. 1 and 2. (Translated from the Swedish). London: George Allen & Unwin Ltd.

Helleiner, K.F. (1958). "New Light on the History of Urban Populations." *Journal of Economic History*, XVIII.

Heller, Henry. (1986). *The Conquest of Poverty: The Calvinist Revolt in Sixteenth Century France.* Leiden (Netherlands): E.J. Brill.

Hemming, John. (1970). *The Conquest of the Incas.* New York: Harcourt Brace and Company.

Henderson, Katherine Usher and McManus, Barbara F. (1985). *Half Humankind: Contexts and Texts of the Controversy about Women in England, 1540–1640.* Urbana and Chicago (IL): University of Illinois Press.

Henriques, Fernando. (1966). *Storia Generale Della Prostituzione.*Vol. 2. *Il Medioevo e l'eta' moderna.* (Translated from the English). Milano: Sugar Editore.

Herlihy, David. (1995). *Women, Family and Society in Medieval Europe: Historical Essays.* 1978-91. Providence (RI): Berghahn Books.

___. (1985). *Medieval Households.* Cambridge, Mass.: Harvard University Press.

___. (1997). *The Black Death and the Transformation of the West.* Cambridge (Mass.): Harvard University Press.

Herzog, Don. (1989). *Happy Slaves. A Critique of Consent Theory.* Chicago: University of Chicago.

Hill, Christopher. (1952). "Puritans and the Poor." *Past and Present* no. 2. (November).

___. (1958). *Puritanism and Revolution: The English Revolution of the 17th Century.* New York: Schocken Books. Hill, Christopher. (1958).

___. (1961). *The Century of Revolution, 1603–1714.* New York: W.W. Norton & Company, 1980.

___. (1964). *Society and Puritanism in Pre-Revolutionary England.* New York: Schocken Books.

___. (1965). *Intellectual Origins of the English Revolution.* Oxford University Press.

___. (1971). *Antichrist in Seventeenth-Century England.* Oxford University Press.

___. (1975). *Change and Continuity in 17th-Century England.* Cambridge (MA): Harvard University Press.

_____. (1975a). *The World Upside Down*. London: Penguin.

Hilton, Rodney. (1953). "The Transition from Feudalism to Capitalism." *Science and Society,* XVII, 4, Fall, 341–51.

_____. (1966). *A Medieval Society: The West Midlands at the End of the Thirteenth Century.* Cambridge: Cambridge University Press, 1983.

_____. (1973). *Bond Men Made Free. Medieval Peasant Movements and the English Rising of 1381.* New York: Viking Press, Inc.

_____. (1985). *Class Conflict and the Crisis of Feudalism: Essays in Medieval Social History.* London: The Hambledon Press.

Hilton, Rodney, Maurice Dobb, Paul Sweezy, H. Takahashi and Christopher Hill (1976). *The Transition from Feudalism to Capitalism.* London: New Left Books.

Himes, Norman. (1963). *Medical History of Contraception.* New York: Gamut Press.

Himmelman, P. Kenneth. (1997). "The Medicinal Body: An Analysis of Medicinal Cannibalism in Europe, 1300–1700." *Dialectical Anthropology*, 22, 180–203.

Hobbes, Thomas. (1962). *Behemoth: The History of the Causes of the Civil War of England and the Counsels and Artifices by wich they were Carried on from the Year 1640 to the Year 1660. English Works.* Vol. VI. Germany: Scientia Aalen.

_____. (1963). *Leviathan.* New York: World Publishing Company.

_____. (1966). *English Works.* Vol. IV. Germany: Scientia Verlag Aalen.

Hobsbawm, E. J. (1954). "The General Crisis of the European Economy in the 17th Century." *Past and Present*, no. 5, (May 1954) 33–53.

Hodges, Richard and Whitehouse, David. (1983). *Mohammed, Charlemagne and the Origins of Europe.* Ithaca: Cornell University Press.

Holbein, Hans the Younger. (1538). *The Dance of Death.* Published by Melchior and Gaspar Trechsel, Lyons, France.

Holinshed, Raphael. (1577). *Holinshed's Chronicles of England, Scotland, and Ireland.* Ed. Vernon F. Snow. New York: AMS, 1965.

Holmes, Clive. (1993). "Women, Witnesses and Witches." *Past and Present*, no. 140 (1993) 45–78.

Holmes, George Arthur. (1975). *Europe: Hierarchy and Revolt. 1320–1450.* New York: Harper & Row.

Holmes, Ronald. (1974). *Witchcraft In British History*. London: Frederick Muller Ltd.

Holt, Richard. (1987). "Whose Were the Profits of Corn Milling? An Aspect of the Changing Relationship Between the Abbots of Glastonbury and Their Tenants. 1086–1350." *Past and Present*, no. 116, (August 1987) 3–23.

Homans, G. C. (1960). *English Villagers of the Thirteen Century.* New York: Russell and Russell.

Hone, Nathaniel J. (1906). *The Manor and Manorial Records.* London: Methuen & Co.

Hoskins, W. G. (1976). *The Age of Plunder: The England of Henry VIII, 1500–1547.* London: Longman.

Howell, Martha. (1986). *Women, Production and Patriarchy in Late Medieval Cities.* Chicago: Chicago University Press.

Hsia, R. Po-Chia (1988a). "Munster and the Anabaptists." In R. P. Hsia ed., *op.cit.*, (1988b).

_____. ed. (1988b). *The German People and the Reformation.* Ithaca (NY): Cornell University Press.

Hufton, Olwen. (1993). "Women, Work, and the Family." In Davis and Farge eds., *op. cit.,* (1993).

Hughes, Diane Owen. (1975). "Urban Growth and Family Structure in Medieval Genoa." In

Past and Present, no. 66, February, 3–28.

Hughes, William. (1991). *Western Civilization, Vol. II. Early Modern Through the 20th Century.* Guilford (CT): The Duskin Publishing Group.

Hull, Gloria T., Patricia Bell Scott, and Barbara Smith. (1982). *All Women Are White, All Blacks Are Men. But Some of Us Are Brave. Black Women's Studies.* New York: The Feminist Press.

Hulme, Peter. (1994). "Tales of Distinction: European Ethnography and the Caribbean." In Schwartz, Stuart B., ed., *op. cit.,* (1944), 157–200.

Hunt, David. (1970). *Parents and Children in History: The Psychology of Family Life in Early Modern France.* New York: Basic Books.

Hutchinson, E. P. (1967). *The Population Debate.* New York: Houghton Mifflin.

Hybel, Nils. (1989). *Crisis or Change: The Concept of Crisis in the Light of Agrarian Structural Reorganization in Late Medieval England.* Aarhus: Aarhus University Press.

Innes, Brian. (1998). *The History of Torture.* New York: St. Martin's Press.

James, Margaret. (1966). *Social Problems and Policy During the Puritan Revolution, 1640–1660.* New York: Barnes & Noble.

James, Selma. (1975). "Sex, Race and Class." Bristol: Falling Wall Press.

Jonson, Ben. (1610). *The Alchemist.* ed. by Gerald E. Bentley Wheeling (IL): Harlan Davidson Inc., 1947.

Jordan, W. C. (1996). *The Great Famine. Northern Europe in the Early Fourteenth Century.* Princeton: Princeton University Press.

Joseph, Margaret Paul. (1992). *Caliban in Exile: The Outsider in Caribbean Fiction.* Westport (CT): Greenwood).

Kaltner, Karl Hartwig. (1998). "Sulle guerre contadine in Austria." (Translated from the German). In Thea (1998).

Kamen, Henry. (1972). *The Iron Century: Social Change in Europe, 1550–1660.* New York: Praeger Publishers.

Karras, Ruth Mazo. (1989). "The Regulations of Brothels in Later Medieval England." *Signs, Journal of Women in Culture and Society,* vol. 14, no. 21, Winter, 399–433.

———. (1996). *Common Women: Prostitution and Sexuality in Medieval England.* Oxford: Oxford University Press.

Kay, Marguerite. (1969). *Bruegel.* London: The Hamlyn Publishing Group.

Kaye, Harvey J. (1984). *The British Marxist Historians.* New York: St. Martin's Press, 1995.

Kaye, Joel. (1998). *Economy and Nature in the Fourteenth Century.* Cambridge: Cambridge University Press.

Kelly, Joan. (1977). "Did Women Have a Renaissance?" In Bridenthal and Koonz eds., *op. cit.,* (1977).

———. (1982). "Early Feminist Theory and the *Querelle des Femmes,* 1400–1789." *Signs: Journal of Women in Culture and Society.* 1982, vol. 8, no. 1, Autumn, 4–28.

———. (1984). *Women, History and Theory. The Essays of Joan Kelly.* Chicago: The University of Chicago Press.

Kieckhafer, R. (1976). *European Witch-trials: Their Foundations in Popular Culture, 1300–1500.* Berkeley: University of California Press.

King, Margaret L. (1991). *Women of the Renaissance.* (Translated from the Italian). Chicago: University of Chicago Press.

Kingston, Jeremy. (1976). *Witches and Witchcraft.* Garden City, NY: Doubleday.

Kittredge, G.L. (1929). *Witchcraft in Old and New England.* Cambridge. MA: Harvard University Press.

Klaits, Joseph. (1985). *Servants of Satan: The Age of the Witch-Hunts.* Bloomington (IN): Indiana University Press.

Klapitsch-Zuber, Christiane ed. (1996). *Storia delle Donne in Occidente. Il Medioevo.* Bari: Laterza.

Koch, Gottfried. (1983). "La Donna nel Catarismo e nel Valdismo Medievali." In Capitani ed., *op. cit.,* (1983).

Koning, Hans. (1991). *Columbus: His Enterprise: Exploding the Myth.* New York: Monthly Review Press.

_____. (1993). *The Conquest of America: How the Indian Nations Lost Their Continent.* New York: Monthly Review Press.

Kors, Alan C., and Edward Peters. (1972). *Witchcraft in Europe 1100–1700: A Documentary History.* Philadelphia: University of Pennsylvania Press.

Kowaleski, Maryanne and Judith M. Bennett. (1989). "Crafts, Guilds, and Women in the Middle Ages; Fifty Years After Marian K. Dale." *Signs, Journal of Women in Culture and Society,* vol. 14, no 2, Winter, 474–88.

Kramer, Heinrich, and James Sprenger. (1486). *Malleus Maleficarum.* (Translated from the German, with an Introduction by Rev. Montague Summers). New York: Dover Publications, Inc., 1971.

Kriedte, Peter. (1983). *Peasants, Landlords, and Merchant Capitalists. Europe and the World Economy, 1500–1800.* Cambridge: Cambridge University Press.

Kuen, Thomas. (1998). "Person and Gender in the Laws." In Judith C. Brown and Robert C. Davis, eds., *op. cit.,* (1998), 87–106.

Kurlansky, Mark. (1999). *The Basque History of the World.* London: Penguin.

Lambert, Malcolm. (1977). *Medieval Heresy.* Oxford: Basil Blackwell, 1992.

Langland, William. (1362-1370). *The Vision of William Concerning Piers the Plowman.* Clarendon: Oxford University Press, 1965.

Larner, Christina. (1980). "Crimen Exceptum? The Crime of Witchcraft in Europe." In Gatrell, V.A.C. *et al.,* eds., *op. cit.,* (1980).

_____. (1981). *Enemies of God. The Witch-Hunt in Scotland.* Baltimore: The John Hopkins University Press.

_____ (1984). *Witchcraft and Religion: The Politics of Popular Belief.* Edited and with a Foreword by Alan Macfarlane. Oxford: Basil Blackwell.

La Rocca, Tommaso, ed. (1990). *Thomas Müntzer e la rivoluzione dell'uomo comune.* Torino: Claudiana.

Laslett, Peter. (1971). *The World We Have Lost.* New York: Scribner's.

Lavallee, Joseph. (1809). *Histoires des Inquisitions Religieuses d'Italie, d'Espagne et de Portugal.* Paris.

Lawson, George (Rev.). (1657). *Examination of Leviathan.*

Lea, Henry Charles. (1888). *A History of the Inquisition of the Middle Ages.* Vol. 2. New York: Harper & Brothers.

_____. (1922). *A History of the Inquisition of the Middle Ages.* London: MacMillan.

_____. (1957). *Materials Towards a History of Witchcraft.* Edited by Arthur C. Howland, with an Introduction by George Lincoln Burr, 3rd vol. New York: Thomas Yoseloff.

_____. (1961). *The Inquisition of the Middle Ages.* New York: Macmillan Company.

Leacock, Eleanor. (1980)."Montagnais Women and the Jesuit Program For Colonization." In Etienne and Leacock, eds., *op.cit.*,(1980), 25–4.

Leacock, Eleanor Burke. (1981). *Myths of Male Dominance: Collected Articles on Women Cross-Culturally*. New York: Monthly Review Press.

Lecky, W. E.H. (1886). *History of the Rise of Influence of the Spirit of Rationalism in Europe*. New York: Appleton & Co.

Le Goff, Jacques. (1956). *Tempo della Chiesa e tempo del Mercante*. (Translated from the French).Torino: Einaudi,1977.

___, ed. (1980). *La Nuova Storia.*(Translated from the French). Milano: Mondadori.

___. (1988). *Medieval Civilization*. Oxford: Basil Blackwell.

Lenoble, Robert. (1943). *Mersenne ou la Naissance du Mechanisme*. Paris:Vrin.

Lerner, Robert E. (1972). *The Heresy of the Free Spirit in the Later Middle Ages*. Berkeley: University of California Press.

LeRoy Ladurie, Emmanuel. (1966). *Les Paysans de Languedoc*. Paris, Gallimard.

___.(1974). *Peasants of Languedoc*. (Translated from the French). Carbondale (IL): University of Illinois Press.

___ (1979). *Il Carnevale di Romans*. (Translated from the French). Milano: Rizzoli, 1981.

___. (1981). *The Mind and Method of the Historian*. Chicago: University of Chicago Press.

___, et al. (1987). *Jasmin's Witch*. New York: George Braziller.

Levack, Brian P. (1987). *The Witch-Hunt in Early Modern Europe*. London: Longmans.

___, ed. (1992). *Witchcraft, Magic and Demonology*. In thirteen volumes. New York: Garland Publishing.

Levine, David ed. (1984). *Proletarianization and Family History*. New York: Academic Press.

Linebaugh, Peter. (1975)."The Tyburn Riots Against the Surgeons." In Hay *et al., op. cit.*

___. (1992). *The London Hanged. Crime and Civil Society in the Eighteenth Century*. Cambridge University Press.

Linebaugh, Peter and Marcus Rediker. (2001). *The Many-Headed Hydra: Sailors, Slaves, Commoners, and the Hidden History of the Revolutionary Atlantic*. Boston: Beacon Press.

Lis, C. & H. Soly. (1979). *Poverty and Capitalism in Pre-Industrial Europe.* Atlantic Highlands (NJ): Humanities Press.

___. (1984). "Policing the Early Modern Proletariat, 1450–1850." In Levine ed., *op. cit.*, (1984),163-228.

Little, Lester K. (1978). *Religious Poverty and the Profit Economy in Medieval Europe*. Ithaca (NY): Cornell University Press.

Lombardini, Sandro.(1983). *Rivolte Contadine in Europa* (Secoli XVI–XVIII).Torino: Loescher Editore.

Luzzati, Michele. (1981). "Famiglie nobili e famiglie mercantili a Pisa e in Toscana nel basso medioevo." In Georges Duby and Jacques Le Goff eds., *op. cit.,* (1981), 185–206.

Macfarlane, Alan. (1970). *Witchcraft in Tudor and Stuart England: A Regional and Comparative Study*. New York: Harper & Row, Publishers.

___. (1978). *Origins of English Individualism: The Family, Property and Social Transition*. Oxford: Basil Blackwell.

Macpherson, C. B. (1962). *The Political Theory of Possessive Individualism. Hobbes to Locke*. Oxford: Oxford University Press.

Malebranche, Nicolas. (1688). *Entretiens sur la metaphysique et sur la religion*. "Dialogues on

Metaphysics and Religion." In Popkin, ed., *op. cit.,* (1966).

Malos, Ellen ed. (1980). *The Politics of Housework.* New York: The New Clarion Press.

Manning, Roger B. (1988). *Village Revolts: Social Protest and Popular Disturbances in England, 1509–1640.* Oxford: Clarendon Press.

Mandrou, Robert. (1968). *Magistrates et Sorcieres en France au XVII Siècle.* Paris: Librairies Plon.

Manoukian, Agopic ed. (1974). *Famiglia e Matrimonio nel Capitalismo Europeo.* Bologna: Il Mulino.

Marks, Elaine and Isabelle Courtivron eds. (1981). *New French Feminisms. An Anthology.* New York: Schocken Books.

Marlowe, Christopher. (1604). *Doctor Faustus.* London.

Marshall, Dorothy. (1926). *The English Poor in the Eighteenth Century.* London: George Routledge & Sons.

Marshall, Rosalynd. (1983). *Virgins and Viragos: A History of Women in Scotland, 1080–1980.* Chicago: Academy Chicago Ltd.

Martin, Emily. (1987). *The Woman in the Body. A Cultural Analysis of Reproduction.* Boston: Beacon Press.

Martin, Ruth. (1989). *Witchcraft and the Inquisition in Venice, 1550–1650.* London: Basil Blackwell Inc.

Martinez, Bernardo Garcia *et al.* (1976). *Historia General De Mexico,* Tomo 1. Mexico D. F.: El Colegio de Mexico.

Marvell, Andrew. (1681). *Miscellaneous Poems.* Ed. by Mary Marvell. Scolar Press, 1969.

Marx, Karl. (1857–58). *Grundrisse.* (Translated from the German). London: Penguin, 1973.

___. (1867). *Capital. A Critique of Political Economy.* Vol. I and Vol. III. Chicago: Charles H. Kerr & Company, 1909.

___. (1932). *Economic and Philosophical Manuscripts of 1844.* Moscow: Foreign Languages Publishing House (1961).

Mather, Cotton. (1681–1708). *Diary of Cotton Mather.* 2 vols. Massachusetts Historical Society Collection, (1911–12). Quoted by Philip Greven in *The Protestant Temperament.*

Maxwell-Stuart, P.G. (2001) *Satan's Conspiracy: Magic and Witchcraft in Sixteenth-Century Scotland.* Edinburgh: Tuckwell Press.

Mayer, Enrique. (1981). *A Tribute to the Household Domestic Economy and the Encomienda in Colonial Peru.* Austin (Texas): Institute of Latin American Studies.

Mazzali, Tiziana. (1988). *Il Martirio delle streghe: Una drammatica testimonianza dell' Inquisizione laica del seicento.* Milano: Xenia.

Mazzi, Maria Serena. (1991). *Prostitute e Lenoni nella Firenze del Quattrocento.* Milano: Il Saggiatore.

McDonnell, Ernest W. (1954). *The Beguines and Beghards in Medieval Culture, with Special Emphasis on the Belgian Scene.* New Brunswick (NJ): Rutgers University Press.

McManners, J. (1981). *Death and the Enlightenment.* Oxford: Oxford University Press.

McNamara, Jo Ann and Suzanne Wemple. (1988). "The Power of Women Through the Family in Medieval Europe, 500–1100. In Erler and Kowaleski, eds., *op. cit.,* (1988).

Meillassoux, Claude. (1981). *Maidens, Meal and Money: Capitalism and the Domestic Community.* Cambridge: Cambridge University Press. (First French edition 1975.)

___. (1986). *The Anthropology of Slavery: The Womb of Iron and Gold.* (Translated from the French). Chicago: Chicago University Press, 1991.

Melossi, Dario and Massimo Pavarini. (1977). *The Prison and the Factory: Origins of the Penitentiary System*. (Translated from the Italian). Totowa (NJ): Barnes and Noble.

Mendelson, Sara and Patricia Crawford. (1998). *Women in Early Modern England, 1550–1720*. Oxford: Clarendon Press.

Merchant, Carolyn. (1980). *The Death of Nature: Women, Ecology and the Scientific Revolution*. New York: Harper and Row.

____. (1987). "Mining the Earth's Womb." In Rothschild ed., *op. cit.*, (1987), 99–117.

Mereu, Italo. (1979). *Storia dell'Intolleranza in Europa*. Milano: Mondadori.

Mergivern, James J. (1997). *The Death Penalty: An Historical and Theological Survey*. New York: Paulist Press.

Midelfort, Erik H. C. (1972). *Witch Hunting in Southwestern Germany, 1562–1684: The Social and Intellectual Foundations*. Stanford: Stanford University Press.

Midnight Notes Collective. (1990). "The New Enclosures," *Midnight Notes* no. 10, Fall.

———. (2001). *Auroras of the Zapatistas: Local and Global Struggles of the Fourth World War*. New York: Autonomedia.

Mies, Maria. (1986). *Patriarchy and Accumulation on a World Scale*. London: Zed Books.

Milano, Attilio. (1963). *Storia defli Ebrei in Italia*. Torino: Einaudi.

Milton, John. (1667). "Paradise Lost." In S. Orgel and J. Goldberg, eds., *John Milton*. Oxford: Oxford University Press, (1992).

Mingay, G. E. (1997). *Parliamentary Enclosures in England: An Introduction to Its Causes, Incidence and Impact, 1750–1850*. London: Longman.

Moi, Toril, ed. (1987). *French Feminist Thought: A Reader*. Oxford: Basil Blackwell.

Molitor, Ulrich. (1489). *De Lamiis et Pythonicis Mulieribus*.

Moller, Herbert ed. (1964). *Population Movements in Modern European History*. New York: The Macmillan Company.

____. (1964a). "Population and Society During the Old Regime, c.1640-1770." In Moller ed., *op.cit.*, (1964), 19-42.

Momsen, Janet H., ed. (1993). *Women and Change in the Caribbean: A Pan-Caribbean Perspective*. London: James Currey.

Montaigne, Michel Eyquem de. (1580). *The Essays*. London: Oxford University Press, 1942.

Montanari, Massimo. (1993). *La fame e L'abbondanza. Storia dell'alimentazione in Europa*. Roma-Bari: Laterza.

Monter, William E. Monter, E.W. (1969). *European Witchcraft*. New York: John Wiley and Sons.

____. (1969). "Law, Medicine and the Acceptance of Women." In Monter, ed., *op cit.*, (1969).

____. (1976). *Witchcraft in France and Switzerland: The Borderlands During the Reformation*. Ithaca: Cornell University Press.

____. (1977). "The Pedestal and the Stake: Courtly Love and Witchcraft." In Bridental and Koonz eds., *op. cit.*, (1977).

____. (1980). "Women in Calvinist Geneva." *Signs, Journal of Women in Culture and Society*, vol. 6, no. 2, Winter, 189-209.

Moore, Henry. (1659). *On The Immortality of the Soul*. A. Jacob ed., International Archives of the History of Ideas, no.122.

Moore, R.I. (1975). *The Birth of Popular Heresy*. New York: St. Martin's Press.

____. (1977). *The Origins of European Dissent*. New York: St. Martin's Press.

Moore, Thomas. (1518). *Utopia*. New York: W. W. Norton & Company, 1992.

Morato, Turri. (1975). "Aborto di Stato." In *Canti di Donne in Lotta*. Gruppo Musicale del Comitato per il Salario al Lavoro Domestico di Padova.

Morgan, Edmund. (1966). *The Puritan Family. Religion and Domestic Relations in Seventeenth Century England*. New York: Harper and Row.

Morgan, Robin ed. (1970). *Sisterhood is Powerful*. New York: Vintage.

Mornese, Corrado and Gustavo Buratti. (2000). *Fra Dolcino e gli Apostolici fra eresie, rivolte, e roghi*. Centro Studi Dolciniani. Novara: Derive/ Approdi.

Morrissey, Marietta.(1989).*Slave Women in the New World: Gender Stratification in the Caribbean*. Lawrence (Kansas): University Press of Kansas.

Morse Earle, Alice. (1993). *Home Life in Colonial Days*. Stockbridge (MA): Berkshire Publishers.

Mosher Stuard, Susan ed. (1987). *Women in Medieval History and Historiography*. Philadelphia: University of Pennsylvania Press.

Moulier Boutang, Yann. (1998). *De l'esclavage au salariat. Economie historique du salariat bridé*. Paris: Presses Universitaires de France.

Mumford, Lewis.(1962). *Technics and Civilization*. New York: Harcourt Brace and World Inc.

Mun, Thomas. (1622). *England's Treasure by Forraigne Trade*. London.

Müntzer, Thomas. (1524). *Open Denial of the False Belief of the Godless World*.

Muraro, Luisa. (1976). *La Signora del Gioco: Episodi di caccia alle streghe*. Milano: Feltrinelli Editore, 1977.

Murray, Margaret. (1921). *The Witch-Cult in Western Europe*. Oxford: Oxford University Press, 1971.

Murstein, B. I. (1974). *Love, Sex, and Marriage Through the Ages*. New York: Springer Publishing Company.

Nash, June. (1978). "The Aztecs and the Ideology of Male Dominance." *Signs, Journal of Women in Culture and Society*. vol. 4, no. 21, 349–62.

___. (1980). "Aztec Women: The Transition from Status to Class in Empire and Colony." In Etienne and Leacock, eds., *op.cit.*, (1980), 134–48.

Neel, Carol. (1989). "The Origins of the Beguines." *Signs, Journal of Women in Culture and Society*. vol. 14, no. 2, Winter, 321–41.

Neeson, J. M. (1993). *Commoners: common right, enclosure and social change in England, 1700-1820*. Cambridge: Cambridge University Press.

Newman, Francis X., ed. (1986). *Social Unrest in the Late Middle Ages*. Binghamton (NY): Center for Medieval and Early Renaissance Texts and Studies.

Niccoli, Ottavia ed. (1998). *Rinascimento al femminile*. Bari: Laterza.

Nicholas, David. (1992). *Medieval Flanders*. London: Longman.

Nider, Johannes. (1435-37). *Formicarius*.

Nietzsche, F. (1887). *The Birth of the Tragedy and The Genealogy of Morals*. New York: Doubleday (1965).

Noonan, John T. (1965). *Contraception: A History of Its Treatment by the Catholic Theologians and Canonists*. Cambridge: Harvard University Press.

Norberg, Kathryn. (1993). "Prostitutes." In Davis and Farge eds., *op. cit.*, (1993).

Normand, Lawrence and Gareth Roberts, eds.(2000). *Witchcraft in Early Modern Scotland: James VI's Demonology and the North Berwick Witches*. Exeter: University of Exeter Press.

North, Douglas C. and Robert Paul Thomas. (1943). *The Rise of the Western World: A New Economic History*. New York: Cambridge University Press.

Notestein,Wallace. (1911). *A History of Witchcraft in England from 1558 to 1718.* New York: Russell and Russell, 1965.

O'Brien, Mary. (1981). *The Politics of Reproduction.* Boston: Routledge & Kegan Paul.

O'Brien, Patrick and Roland Quinault, eds. (1993). *The Industrial Revolution and British Society.* Cambridge: Cambridge University Press.

O'Malley C. D., Poynter F. N. L., Russell K. F. (1961). *William Harvey. Lectures on the Whole of Anatomy.* Berkeley: University of California Press.

O'Malley, C.D. (1964). *Andreas Vesalius of Brussels.1514–1564.* Berkeley: University of California Press.

Omolade, Barbara (1983). "Heart of Darkness." In Ann Snitow, Christine Stansell, and Sharon Thompson, eds., *op.cit.,* (1983).

Opitz, Claudia. (1996). "La vita quotidiana delle donne nel tardo Medioevo. (1200-1500)." In Klapitsch-Zuber ed., *op. cit.,* (1996).

Orioli, Raniero. (1984). *Fra Dolcino. Nascita, vita e morte di un'eresia medievale.* Novara: Europia. (1993).

Orlandi,Arianna. (1989). "I Viaggi di Gostanza." In Cardini ed., *op. cit., (*1989).

Ortalli, Gherardo. (1981). "La famiglia tra la realtá dei gruppi inferiori e la mentalitá dei gruppi dominanti a Bologna nel XIII secolo." In Georges Duby and Jacques Le Goff eds., *op. cit.,* (1981),125–43.

Oten, Charlotte F., ed. (1986). *A Lycanthropy Reader:Werewolves in Western Culture.* Syracuse, NY: Syracuse University Press.

Otis, Leah Lydia. (1985). *Prostitution in Medieval Society: The History of an Urban Institution in Languedoc.* Chicago:The University of Chicago Press.

Overbeek, J. (1964). *History of Population Theories.* Rotterdam: Rotterdam University Press.

Ozment, Steven. (1983). *When Father Ruled: Family Life in Reformation Europe.* Cambridge (MA): Harvard University Press.

Parinetto, Luciano. (1983). *Streghe e Politica. Dal Rinascimento Italiano a Montaigne. Da Bodin a Naude.* Milano: Istituto Propaganda Libraria.

____. (1996). "La Traversata delle streghe nei nomi e nei luoghi." In Bosco e Castelli, eds., *op. cit.,*(1996).

____. (1998). *Streghe e Potere: Il Capitale e la Persecuzione dei Diversi.* Milano: Rusconi.

Partridge, Burgo.(1960). *A History of Orgies.* New York: Bonanza Books.

Pascal, Blaise. (1656). "Lettre escrite à un provincial," posthumously published as *Pensées de M. Pascal sur la religion et sur quelques autres subjets* (1670).

_____. *Pensées and The Provincial Letters.* New York: Modern Library, 1941.

Pateman, Carol. (1988). *The Sexual Contract.* Stanford: Stanford University Press.

Pearson, Lu Emily. (1957). *Elizabethans at Home.* Stanford (CA): Stanford University Press.

Perelman, Michael.(2000). *The Invention of Capitalism: Classical Political Economy and the Secret History of Primitive Accumulation.* Durham: Duke University Press.

Perlman, Fredy. (1985). *The Continuing Appeal of Nationalism.* Detroit: Black and Red.

Peters, Edward. (1978). *The Magician, The Witch, and the Law.* Philadelphia: University of Pennsylvania Press.

Peters, Edward, ed. (1980). *Heresy and Authority in Medieval Europe. Documents in Translation.* Philadelphia: University of Pennsylvania Press.

Petty, Sir William. (1690). *Discourse on Political Arithmetick.* London.

Pezzuoli, Giovanna. (1978). *Prigioniera in Utopia. La Condizione Della Donna Nel Pensiero Degli Utopisti*. Milano: Edizioni Il Formichiere.

Phelps Brown, E. H. and Sheila Hopkins. (1971). "Seven Centuries of the Prices of Consumables, Compared with Builders' Wage Rates." In Ramsey ed., *op. cit.*, (1971), 18-41.

___. (1981). *A Perspective of Wages and Prices*. London.

Phillips, Seymour. (1994). "The Outer World of the European Middle Ages." In Stuart B. Schwartz, ed., *op.cit.*, (1994).

Picchio, Antonella. (1992). *Social reproduction: the political economy of the labour market*. Cambridge: Cambridge University Press.

Piers, Maria W. (1978). *Infanticide*. New York: W.W. Norton and Company

Pirenne, Henri. (1937). *Economic and Social History of Medieval Europe*. New York: Harcourt Brace Jovanovich, Publishers.

___. (1952). *Medieval Cities*. Princeton: Princeton University Press.

___. (1956). *Storia d'Europa dalle invasioni al XVI secolo*. Firenze: Sansoni.

___. (1958). *A History of Europe*, Vol.1. Garden City (NY): Doubleday & Company Inc.

Po-Chia Hsia, R., ed. (1988). *The German People and the Reformation*. Ithaca (NY): Cornell University Press.

___. (1988a). "Munster and the Anabaptists." In Po-Chia Hsia ed., *op. cit.*, (1988), 51-70.

Polanyi, Karl. (1944). *The Great Transformation*. New York: Rinehart & Company, Inc.

Popkin, Richard H. (1966). *The Philosophy of the 16th and 17th Centuries*. New York: The Free Press.

Powell, Chilton Latham. (1917). *English Domestic Relations 1487–1653*. New York: Columbia University.

Preto, Paolo. (1988). *Epidemia, Paura e Politica Nell'Italia Moderna*. Roma-Bari: Laterza.

Prosperi, Adriano. (1989). "Inquisitori e Streghe nel Seicento Fiorentino." In Cardini, *op. cit.*, 1989.

Quetel, Claude. (1986). *History of Syphilis*. (Translated from the French). Baltimore: Johns Hopkins University Press, 1990.

Rabelais, François. (1552). *Gargantua and Pantagruel*. Edited by Samuel Putnam. New York: Viking Press, 1946.

Raftis, J. A. (1996). *Peasant Economic Development within the English Manorial System*. Montreal: McGill-Queen's University Press.

Ramazanoglu, Caroline. (1993). *Up Against Foucault. Exploration of Some Tensions Between Foucault and Feminism*. New York: Routledge.

Ramsey, Peter H. ed. (1971). *The Price Revolution in Sixteenth-Century England*. London: Methuen.

Randers-Pehrson, J. D. (1983). *Barbarians and Romans. The Birth of the Struggle of Europe. A.D. 400–700*. London: University of Oklahoma Press.

Ranum, Orest and Patricia Ranum, eds., (1972). *Popular Attitudes toward Birth Control in Pre-Industrial France and England*. New York: Harper and Row.

Read, Donna et al. (1990). *The Burning Times*. (Video-recording). Los Angeles: Direct Cinema Ltd.

Remy, Nicolas. (1597). *Demonolatry*. Rev. Montague Summers, ed. New York: Barnes and Noble, 1970.

Retamar, Roberto Fernandez. (1989). *Caliban and Other Essays*. Minneapolis: University of Minnesota Press.

Riddle, John M. (1997). *Eve's Herbs: A History of Contraception and Abortion in the West*. Cambridge: Cambridge University Press.

Riley, Phillip. "Louis XIV: Watchdog of Parisian Morality." *The Historian,* Volume 36, Issue 1, November ,1973, pp. 19–33.

Riquet, Michel. (1972). "Christian Population." In Orest and Patricia Ranum eds., *op. cit.,* (1972), 37ff.

Robbins, Rossell Hope. (1959). *The Encyclopedia of Witchcraft and Demonology.* New York: Crown Publishers.

Roberts, Nickie. (1992). *Whores in History. Prostitution in Western Society*. New York: HarperCollins Publishers.

Robertson, George Croom. (1971). *Hobbes.* Edinburgh: AMS Press.

Rocke, Michael. (1997). *Forbidden Friendships. Homosexuality and Male Culture in Renaissance Florence*. Oxford: Oxford University Press.

Rodolico, Niccoló. (1971). *I Ciompi. Una Pagina di storia del proletariato operaio.* Firenze: Sansoni.

Rogers, James E. Thorold. (1894). *Six Centuries of Work and Wages: The History of English Labour.* London.

Rojas, Fernando de. (1499). *The Celestina.* (Translated from the Spanish.) Berkeley: University of California Press, 1959.

Roper, Lyndal. (2000). "'Evil Imaginings and Fantasies': Child-Witches and the End of the Witch Craze." In *Past and Present,* no. 167, May.

Rosen, Barbara, ed. (1969). *Witchcraft in England, 1558–1618.* Amherst: Univ. of Massachusetts Press, 1991).

Rosenberg, Charles E., ed. (1975). *The Family in History.* Philadelphia: University of Pennsylvania Press.

Rosenfield, Leonora Cohen. (1968). *From Beast-Machine to Man-Machine. Animal Soul in French Letters. From Descartes to La Mettrie.* New York: Octagon Books Inc.

Rossiaud, Jacques. (1988). *Medieval Prostitution.* (Translated from the Italian). Oxford: Basil Blackwell.

Rostworowski, Maria. (2001). *La Mujer en El Peru Prehispanico.* Documento de Trabajo no. 72. Lima: IEP (Instituto de Estudios Peruanos).

Rota, Ettore ed. (1950). *Questioni di Storia Medievale. Secoli XI-XIV.* Milano: Marzorati.

Rotberg, R.I. and Rabb, T. K., eds. (1971). *The Family in History: Interdisciplinary Essays.* New York: Harper and Row.

Rothschild, Joaned. (1983). *Machina Ex Dea. Feminist Perspectives on Technology.* New York: Pergamon Press, 1987.

Rousseau, Jean Jacques. (1775). *Discourse on the Origin of Inequality.* Indianapolis: Hackett Publishing Company, 1992.

Rowland, Alison. (2001). "Witchcraft and Old Women in Early Modern Germany." *Past and Present,* no. 173, November.

Rowling, Nick. (1987). *Commodities: How the World Was Taken to Market.* London: Free Association Books.

Rowse, A. L. (1974). *Sex and Society in Shakespeare's Age. Simon Foreman the Astrologer.* New York: Charles Scribner's Sons.

Rublack, Ulinka. (1996)."Pregnancy, Childbirth and the Female Body in Early Modern Germany." *Past and Present.* no.150, February, 84–110.

Ruggiero, Guido. (1989). *The Boundaries of Eros: Sex, Crime and Sexuality in Renaissance Venice.* Oxford: Oxford University Press.

____. (1993). *Binding Passions. Tales of Magic, Marriage, and Power at the End of the Renaissance.* Oxford: Oxford University Press.

Russell, Jeffrey B. (1972a). *Witchcraft in the Middle Ages.* Ithaca: Cornell University Press.

____. (1972b).*Dissent and Order in the Middle Ages: The Search for Legitimate Authority.* New York: Twayne Publishers, 1992.

____. (1980). *A History of Witchcraft, Sorcerers, Heretics and Pagans.* London: Thames and Hudson Ltd.

____. (1984). *Lucifer: The Devil in the Middle Ages.* Ithaca (NY): Cornell University Press.

Sale, Kirkpatrick. (1991). *The Conquest of Paradise: Christopher Columbus and the Columbian Legacy.* New York: Penguin Books.

Sallmann, Jean-Michel. (1987). *Le Streghe. Amanti di Satana.*(Translated from the French). Paris: Electa/Gallimard.

Salleh, Ariel. (1997). *Ecofeminism as Politics: Nature, Marx and the Postmodern.* London: Zed Books.

Schephered, Verene A., ed. (1999). *Women in Caribbean History.* Princeton (N.J.): Markus Wiener Publishers.

Schochet, Gordon J. (1975). *Patriarchalism in Political Thought: The Authoritarian Family and Political Speculation and Attitudes Especially in Seventeenth-Century England.* New York: Basic Books.

Schwartz, Stuart B., ed. (1944). *Implicit Understandings. Observing, Reporting, and Reflecting on the Encounters Between Europeans and Other Peoples in the Early Modern Era.* Cambridge: Cambridge University Press.

Scot, Reginald. (1584). *The Discoverie of Witchcraft.* Introduction by Rev. Montague Summers. New York: Dover Publications, 1972.

Scott, James C. (1985). *Weapons of the Weak. Everyday Forms of Peasant Resistance.* New Haven: Yale University Press.

____. (1989). "Everyday Forms of Resistance." In F. D. Colburn, ed., *op. cit.*, (1989).

Scott, Joan Wallach ed.(1996). *Feminism and History.* Oxford: Oxford University Press.

____. (1996a). "Gender: A Useful category of Historical Analysis." In Joan Wallach Scott, ed., *op. cit.*, (1996).

Seccombe, Wally. (1992). *A Millennium of Family Change: Feudalism to Capitalism in Northwestern Europe.* London: Verso.

____. (1993). *Weathering the Storm: Working-Class Families From the Industrial Revolution To The Fertility Decline.* London: Verso.

Seligman, Kurt. (1948). *Magic, Supernaturalism and Religion.* New York: Random House.

Sennett, Richard. (1994). *Flesh and Stone. The Body and the City in Western Civilization.* New York: W.W. Norton & Company.

Shahar, Shulamith. (1983). *The Fourth Estate: A History of Women in the Middle Ages.* London: Methuen.

Shakespeare, William. (1593–1594). *The Taming of the Shrew.* New York: Washington Square Press, 1962.

____. (1600–1601). *Hamlet.* New York: New American Library, 1963.

____. (1605). *King Lear.* New York: New Folger Library, 2000

_____. (1612). *The Tempest*. New York: Bantam Books, 1964

Sharpe, J.A. (1987). *Early Modern England: A Social History, 1550–1760.* Bungay (Suffolk): Edward Arnold.

Shepherd, Verene A., ed. (1999). *Women in Caribbean History: The British-Colonised Territories.* Princeton (NJ): Markus Wiener Publishers.

Shepherd, Verene, Bridget Brereton and Barbara Bailey, eds. (1995). *Engendering History. Caribbean Women in Historical Perspective.* New York: St. Martin's Press.

Shiva, Vandana. (1989). *Staying Alive: Women, Ecology and Survival in India.* London: Zed Books.

Siemon, Richard. (1993). "Landlord Not King: Agrarian Change and Interarticulation." In Richard Burt and John Michael Archer, *op. cit.,* (1993).

Silverblatt, Irene. (1980). " 'The Universe Has Turned Inside Out...There Is No Justice For Us Here': Andean Women Under Spanish Rule." In Etienne and Leacock, eds., *op.cit.,* 149–85.

_____. (1987). *Moon, Sun and Witches: Gender Ideologies and Class in Inca and Colonial Peru.* Princeton: Princeton University Press.

Sim, Alison. (1996). *The Tudor Housewife.* Montreal: McGill-Queen's University Press.

Simmel, Georg. (1900). *The Philosophy of Money.* (Translated from the German). Boston: Routledge & Kegan Paul, 1978.

Skaria, Ajay. (1997). "Women, Witchcraft, and Gratuitous Violence in Colonial Western India." *Past and Present,* no. 155, May, 109–41.

Slater, Gilbert (1907). *The English Peasantry and the Enclosure of the Common Fields.* New York: Augustus M. Kelly, 1968.

Slicher Van Bath, B. H. (1963). *The Agrarian History of Western Europe, A.D. 500–1850.* (Translated from the German). New York: St. Martin's Press.

Smollett, Tobias George, [compiler]. (1766). *A compendium of authentic and entertaining voyages, digested in a chronological series. The whole exhibiting a clear view of the customs, manners, religion, government, commerce, and natural history of most nations in the known world....* 2nd edition. 7 vols., vol. 1, p. 96.

Smout, T.C. (1972). *A History of the Scottish People, 1560–1830.* London: Fontana.

Snitow, Ann, Christine Stansell, and Sharon Thompson, eds. (1983). *Powers of Desire: The Politics of Sexuality.* New York: Monthly Review Press.

Social England Illustrated: A Collection of XVIIth Century Tracts. (1903). Westminster: Archibald Constable and Co.

Soman, Alfred. (1977). "Les Procés de Sorcellèrie au Parlament du Paris, 1565–1640." *Annales,* no. 32, July, 790ff.

_____. (1978). "The Parlement of Paris and the Great Witch-Trials, 1565–1640." *Sixteenth Century Review,* 9, 30–44.

_____. (1992). *Sorcellerie et justice criminelle: Le Parlement de Paris, 16–18 siècles.* Brookfield/Variorum.

Sommerville, Margaret R. (1995). *Sex and Subjection: Attitudes to Women in Early Modern Society.* London: Arnold.

Spalding, Karen. (1984). *Hurochirí: An Andean Society Under Inca and Spanish Rule.* Stanford: Stanford University Press.

Spence, Louis. (1920). *The Encyclopedia of Occultism.* New York: Citadel Press.

Spencer, Colin. (1995a). *Homosexuality in History.* New York: Harcourt Brace.

_____. (1995b). *The Heretics' Feast. A History of Vegetarianism.* Hanover and London: University Press of New England.

Spengler, Joseph J. (1965). *French Predecessors of Malthus: A Study in Eighteenth Century Wage*

Spooner, F. C. (1970). "The European Economy,1609–50." In Cooper ed., *op. cit.*, (1970).

Staden, Hans. (1557). *Warhaftige Historia.* Marburg, Germany.

___. *True History of His Captivity.* Translated and edited by Malcolm Letts. London: George Routledge and Sons, 1928.

Stangeland,C. E. (1904). *Pre-malthusian Doctrines of Population.* New York.

Stannard, David E. (1992). *American Holocaust: Columbus and the Conquest of the New World.* New York: Oxford University Press.

Starhawk. (1982). *Dreaming the Dark: Magic Sex and Politics.* Boston: Beacon Press,1997.

Steifelmeier, Dora. (1977). "Sacro e Profano: Note Sulla Prostituzione Nella Germania Medievale." *Donna, Woman, Femme* n. 3.

Stern, Steven J. (1982). *Peru's Indian Peoples and the Challenge of Spanish Conquest: Huamanga to 1640.* Madison (Wisconsin): University of Wisconsin Press.

Stone, Lawrence. (1977). *The Family, Sex and Marriage in England, 1500–1800.* New York: Harper and Row.

Strauss, Gerald, ed.(1971). *Manifestations of Discontent on the Eve of the Reformation.* Bloomington: Indiana University Press.

___. (1975). "Success and Failure in the German Reformation." *Past and Present,* n. 67, May.

Stuart, Susan Mosher. (1995). "Ancillary Evidence For The Decline of Medieval Slavery." *Past and Present.* N.149, November, (3–28).

Taussig, Michael T. (1980). *The Devil and Commodity Fetishism in South America.* (Fourth edition.) University of North Carolina Press.

___. (1987). *Shamanism, Colonialism, and the Wild Man: A Study in Terror and Healing.* Chicago: Chicago University Press.

Taylor, G. R. (1954). *Sex in History.* New York: The Vanguard Press.

Taylor, William B. (1979). *Drinking, Homicide and Rebellion in Colonial Mexican Villages.* Stanford: Standford Univerity Press.

Tawney, R. H. (1967). *The Agrarian Problem in the Sixteenth Century.* New York: Harcourt Brace.

___. (1926). *Religion and the Rise of Capitalism.* New York: Harcourt Brace.

Teall, J. L. (1962). "Witchcraft and Calvinism in Elizabethean England: Divine Power and Human Agency." *Journal of the History of Ideas.* n. 23.

Terborg Penn, Rosalyn. (1995). "Through African Feminist Theoretical Lens: Viewing Caribbean Women's History Cross-Culturally." In Shepherd, Verene, Bridget Brereton and Barbara Bailey, eds., *op. cit.*

Thea, Paolo. (1998). *Gli artisti e Gli 'Spregevoli.' 1525: la creazione artistica e la guerra dei contadini in Germania.* Milano: Mimesi.

Thevet, André. (1557). *Les Singularitez del la France antaretique, autrement nomme Amerique, et de plusieurs de terres et isles decouvertes de notre temps.* Paris.

Thirsk, J. (1964). "The Common Fields." *Past and Present,* no. 29, 3–25.

Thomas, Edith. (1966). *The Women Incendiaries.* (Translated from the French). New York: George Braziller.

Thomas, Hugh. (1997). *The Slave Trade: The Story of the Atlantic Slave Trade, 1400–1870.* New York: Simon and Schuster.

Thomas, Keith. (1971). *Religion and the Decline of Magic.* New York: Charles Scribner's Sons.

Thompson, E. P. (1964). *The Making of the English Working Class.* New York: Pantheon.

___. (1991). *Customs in Common. Studies in Traditional Popular Culture.* New York:The New Press.

___. (1991a). "Time, Work-Discipline and Industrial Capitalism." In Thompson (1991), 352–403.

Thorndike, Lynn. (1958). *History of Magic and Experimental Science.* 8 vols. (1923–58).Vol.VIII. New York: Columbia University Press.

Tigar, Michael E., and Medeleine R. Levy. (1977). *Law and the Rise of Capitalism.* New York: Monthly Review Press.

Tillyard, E. M.W. (1961). *The Elizabethan World Picture.* New York:Vintage Books.

Titow, J. Z. (1969). *English Rural Society. 1200–1350.* London: George Allen and Unwin Ltd.

Trachtenberg, Joshua. (1944). *The Devil and the Jews: The Medieval Conception of the Jew and its Relation to Modern Anti-Semitism.* New Haven:Yale University Press.

Trevor-Roper, Hugh R. (1956). T*he European Witch-Craze of the Sixteenth and Seventeenth Centuries and Other Essays.* New York: Harper & Row, Publishers, 1967.

___, ed. (1968).The Age of Expansion. Europe and the World: 1559-1660.London:Thames and Hudson.

Trexler, Richard C. (1993). *The Women of Renaissance Florence. Power and Dependence in Renaissance Florence.* Vol. 2. Binghamton, NY: Medieval and Renaissance Texts and Studies.

Turner, Bryan S. (1992).*Regulating Bodies: Essays in Medical Sociology.*New York: Routledge.

Underdown, David E. (1985). *Revel, Riot and Rebellion: Popular Politics and Culture in England, 1603–1660.* Oxford: Clarendon Press.

___. (1985a). "The Taming of the Scold: The Enforcement of Patriarchal Authority in Early Modern England." In Fletcher & Stevenson, eds., *op.cit.*, (1985), 116-36.

Vallejo, Eduardo Aznar. (1994). "The Conquest of the Canary Islands." In Schwartz, ed., *op.cit.*, (1994).

Vaneigem, Raoul. (1986). *The Movement of the Free Spirit.* (Translated from the French). New York: Zone Books.

Van Ussel, Jos. (1970). *La repressione sessuale. Storia e cause del condizionamento borghese.* (Translated from the German). Milano: Bompiani.

Vauchez, André. (1990). *Ordini mendicanti e societa' italiana XIII–XV secolo.* Milano: Mondadori.

Vesalius, Andrea. (1543). *De Humani Corporis Fabrica.* Edited by O'Malley, *op. cit.*

Vigil, Mariló. (1986). *La vida de la mujeres en los siglos XVI y XVII.* Madrid: Siglo veintiuno de España Editores.

Vives, Juan Luis. (1526). *De Subvention Pauperum sive De Humanis Necessitatibus.* Bruges.

Volpe, Gioacchino. (1922).*Movimenti Religiosi e Sette Radicali Nella Societá Medievale Italiana. Secoli XI–XIV.* Firenze: Sansoni, 1971.

_____. (1926). *Il Medioevo.* Firenze: Sansoni, 1975.

Wakefield, Walter L. and Austin P. Evans. (1969). *Heresies of the High Middle Ages.* New York: Columbia University Press, 1991.

Wallach Scott, Joan.(1988).*Gender and the Politics of History.* New York: Columbia University Press.

Wallerstein, Immanuel. (1974). *The Modern World System: Capitalist Agriculture and the Origins of the European World Economy in the Sixteenth Century.* New York:Academic Press.

Watson, R. (1966). *The Downfall of Cartesianism, 1673–1712.* The Hague: Martinus Nijhoff.

Weber, Max. (1920).*The Protestant Ethics and the Spirit of Capitalism.* (Translated from German). New York: Charles Scribners Sons (1958).

Werner, E. (1974). "Poverta' e ricchezza nella concezione degli eretici della chiesa orientale e occidentale dei secoli X–XII." In O. Capitani, ed., *op. cit.,* (1974).

Westermarck, Edward. (1906–08). *The Origin and Development of Moral Ideas* Vol.1 London: Macmillan Company (1924).

Wiesner, Merry E. (1986). *Working Women in Renaissance Germany.* New Brunswick (NJ): Rutgers University Press.

_____. (1993). *Women and Gender in Early Modern Europe.* Cambridge: Cambridge University Press.

Wightman, W. P. (1972). *Science and Renaissance Society.* London: Huitchinson University Library.

Williams, Eric. (1944). *Capitalism and Slavery.* New York: Capricorn Books.

Williams, Marty and Anne Echols.(2000). *Between Pit and Pedestal. Women in the Middle Ages.* Princeton:Marcus Wiener Publications.

Williams, Selma R. and Pamela Williams Adelman. (1992). *Riding the Nightmare: Women and Witchcraft from the Old World to Colonial Salem.* New York: HarperCollins.

Williams, Walter L. (1986). *The Spirit and the Flesh: Sexual Diversity in American Indian Culture.* Boston: Beacon Press.

Wilson, Charles. (1965a). *England's Apprenticeship, 1603–1763.* New York: St. Martin's Press.

___. (1965b). "Political Arithmetic and Social Change." In Charles Wilson, *op. cit.,* (1965a), 226ff.

Wilson, Stephen. (2000). *The Magical Universe: Everyday Ritual and Magic in Pre-Modern Europe.* London and New York: Hambledon.

Winstanley, Gerrard. (1649). *The New Law of Righteousness.* In Gerrard Winstanley,*op. cit.,* (1941)

___. *Works.* Ithaca: Cornell University Press,1941.

Woolf,Virginia. (1929). *A Room of One's Own.* New York: Harcourt Brace Jovanovich Publishers, 1989.

Wright, Lawrence. (1960). *Clean and Decent.* New York:Viking Press.

Wright, Louis B. (1935). *Middle-Class Culture in Elizabethan England.* Ithaca (NY): Cornell University Press, 1965

Yates, Francis. (1964). *Giordano Bruno and the Hermetic Tradition.* Chicago: The University of Chicago Press.

Zemon Davis, Natalie. (1968). "Poor Relief, Humanism and Heresy: The Case of Lyon." *Studies in Medieval and Renaissance History,* vol. 5, no. 27, 246-269.

Ziegler, Philip. (1969). *The Black Death.* New York: Harper and Row, Publishers.

Zilborg, Gregory. (1935). *The Medical Man and the Witch During the Renaissance.* Baltimore: Johns Hopkins Press.

Zolkran, Durkon. (1996). *The Tarot of the Orishas.* St. Paul (MN): Llewellyn Publications.

Image Sources

Autonomedia is an all-volunteer, 501(c)(3) not-for-profit corporation publishing in the public interest. We acknowledge these sources for fair use of illustrations in the public domain: p. 6: From Jean-Michel Sallaman, 1995. • p. 20: In TACUINUM SANITATIS, MS Vienna. Osterreichische Nationalbibliothek. From Sally Fox 1985. • p. 23: London: British Museum. • p. 30: Detail, COLLECTED WORKS OF CHRISTINE DE PISAN. MS Harley 4431. British Library, London. From Sally Fox, 1985. • p. 32: Lauros-Giraudon/Art Resource, New York. From Richard L. Greaves et al., eds., 1992. • p. 35: From Hans Peter Duerr, 1991. • p. 37: From Hans Peter Duerr, 1991. • p. 39: From Paul Carus, 1990. • p. 44: Bibliotheque Nationale de Paris. From Marvin Perry et al., eds., 1981. • p. 55: From Peter Cornej, 1993. • p. 66: From Tommaso La Rocca, ed., 1990. • p. 67: From Paolo Thea, 1998. p. 69: From Henry Kamen, 1972. p. 71: From Hans Peter Duerr, 1991. • p. 74: From Cunningham and Grell, 2000. • p. 81: Staatliche Museen Prussischer Kulturbesitz. Berlin. From Richard L. Greaves et al. eds, 1992 • p. 83 From Holinshed Chronicles 1577. In Henry Kamen, 1972. • p. 90: From Mendelson and Crawford, 1998. • p. 93, top: From Lujo Basserman, 1967. bottom: From Lujo Basserman, 1967. • p. 95: From B. I. Murstein, 1974. • p. 96: From Olwen Hufton, 1993. • p. 101: From Mendelson and Crawford, 1998. • p. 102: From David Underdown, 1985a. • p. 109: From Verene Shepherd, 1999. • p. 114: From Barbara Bush, 1990. • p 119: From Hugh Trevor-Roper, 1968. • p. 121: From Andrew Cunningham and Ole Peter Grell, 2000. • p. 132: From C. D. O'Malley, 1964. • p. 136: Paris National Library. • p. 138: From Luigi Firpo, 1972. • p. 141: From Luigi Firpo, 1972. • p. 142: From J. B. Russell, 1980. • p. 144: Paris, Biblioteque Nationale. From J.B. Russell, 1980. • p. 146: From Henry Kamen, 1972. • p. 147: From Richard Sennett, 1994. • p. 160: From Marguerite Kay, 1969. • p. 161: From Hans Peter Duerr, 1991. • p. 162: From Jean-Michel Sallaman, 1995. • p. 172: From Barbara Rosen, 1969. • p. 178: From J.B. Russell, 1980. • p. 183: From Kors and Peters, 1972. • p. 185: From Alfonso Di Nola, 1987. • p. 187: From Richard L. Greaves ed., 1992. • p. 188: From Alfonso Di Nola, 1987. • p. 190: From J.B. Russell, 1980. • p. 193: From Jean-Michel Sallmann, 1995. • p. 195: From J. B. Russell, 1980. • p. 196: From Jeremy Kingston, 1976. • p. 202: From Louis Spence, 1920. • p. 204: From Allen and Hubbs, 1980. • p. 207: From Albert Boime, 1995. • p. 217: From Kors and Peters, 1972. • p. 223 and 224: From Johann Ludwig Gottfried, 1630. • p. 227 and 228: From Steven J. Stern, 1982. • p. 238: From Rupert Christiansen, 1994.

Subject and Author Index

272

About the Author

SILVIA FEDERICI is a long-time feminist activist and teacher. She has taught at the University of Port Harcourt (Nigeria), among others, and is now Professor Emeritus of International Studies and Political Philosophy at New College of Hofstra University. She is the author of many essays on culture, education, and women's struggles. Her published work includes: *Il Grande Calibano: Storia del corpo sociale ribelle nella prima fase del capitale* (co-author); *Enduring Western Civilization: The Construction of the Concept of Western Civilization and Its "Others"* (editor); *A Thousand Flowers: Social Struggles Against Structural Adjustment in Africa Universities* (co-editor); and *African Visions: Literary Images, Political Change, and Social Struggle in Contemporary Africa* (co-editor).

More Books from Autonomedia

Between Dog and Wolf: Essays on Art & Politics
David Levi Strauss

T.A.Z.: The Temporary Autonomous Zone
Millennium
Hakim Bey

This World We Must Leave, and Other Essays
Jacques Camatte

Pirate Utopias:
Moorish Corsairs & European Renegadoes
Peter Lamborn Wilson

Marching Plague: Germ Warfare
and Global Public Health
Molecular Invasion
Flesh Machine: Cyborgs, Designer Babies
and the New Eugenic Consciousness
Digital Resistance
Electronic Civil Disobedience
The Electronic Disturbance
Critical Art Ensemble

Whore Carnival
Shannon Bell, ed.

Film and Video: Alternative Views
Crimes of Culture
Political Essays
Richard Kostelanetz

Cracking the Movement:
Squatting Beyond the Media
Media Archive
ADILKNO

Social Overload
Henri-Pierre Jeudy

Avant Gardening
Peter Lamborn Wilson & Bill Weinberg, eds.

Marx Beyond Marx: Lessons on the Gründrisse
Antonio Negri

Scandal: Essays in Islamic Heresy
Escape from the 19th Century
Peter Lamborn Wilson

On Anarchy & Schizoanalysis
Rolando Perez

Horsexe: Essay on Transsexuality
Catherine Millot

Film and Politics in the Third World
John Downing, ed.

Enragés & Situationists in Paris, May '68
René Viénet

Midnight Oil: Work, Energy, War, 1973–1992
Midnight Notes Collective

Gone to Croatan:
Origins of North American Dropout Culture
James Koehnline & Ron Sakolsky, eds.

About Face: Race in Postmodern America
Maliqalim Simone

The Arcane of Reproduction:
Housework, Prostitution, Labor & Capital
Leopoldina Fortunati

Dreamer of the Day: Francis Parker Yockey
& the Postwar Fascist Underground
Kevin Coogan

The Rotting Goddess:
The Origin of the Witch in Classical Antiquity
Jacob Rabinowitz

Read Me! ASCII Culture and
the Revenge of Knowledge
Nettime

Against the Megamachine:
Essays on Empire and its Enemies
David Watson

Auroras of the Zapatistas
Midnight Notes Collective

Surrealist Subversions
Ron Sakolsky, ed.

Work of Love
Giovanna Franca Dalla Costa

Revolutionary Writing:
Essays in Autonomous Marxism
Werner Bonefeld, ed.

Communists Like Us
Félix Guattari and Antonio Negri

Unleashing the Collective Phantoms
Brian Holmes

Cyberfeminism. Next Protocols
Claudia Reiche & Verena Kuni, eds.

Domain Errors! Cyberfeminist Practices
a subRosa project

Orgies of the Hemp Eaters
Hakim Bey & Abel Zug, eds.

Conversations with Don Durito
Subcomandante Marcos

The Devil's Anarchy
Stephen Snelders

Visit www.autonomedia.org for online ordering, topical discussion,
events listings, book specials, and more.
Autonomedia • PO Box 568, Williamsburgh Station • Brooklyn, NY 11211-0568